Seeking Conflict
in Mesoamerica

Seeking Conflict
in Mesoamerica

**Operational, Cognitive, and
Experiential Approaches**

EDITED BY
**Shawn G. Morton
Meaghan M. Peuramaki-Brown**

UNIVERSITY PRESS OF COLORADO

Louisville

© 2019 by University Press of Colorado

Published by University Press of Colorado
245 Century Circle, Suite 202
Louisville, Colorado 80027

 ASSOCIATION of UNIVERSITY PRESSES   The University Press of Colorado is a proud member of
the Association of University Presses.

The University Press of Colorado is a cooperative publishing enterprise supported, in part, by Adams State University, Colorado State University, Fort Lewis College, Metropolitan State University of Denver, University of Colorado, University of Northern Colorado, University of Wyoming, Utah State University, and Western Colorado University.

∞ This paper meets the requirements of the ANSI/NISO Z39.48-1992 (Permanence of Paper).

ISBN: 978-1-60732-886-5 (cloth)
ISBN: 978-1-60732-887-2 (ebook)
DOI: https://doi.org/10.5876/9781607328872

Library of Congress Cataloging-in-Publication Data

Names: Morton, Shawn, editor. | Peuramaki-Brown, Meaghan, editor.
Title: Seeking conflict in Mesoamerica : operational, cognitive, and experiential approaches / Shawn G. Morton, Meaghan M. Peuramaki-Brown.
Description: Louisville : University Press of Colorado, 2019. | Includes bibliographical references and index.
Identifiers: LCCN 2019025989 (print) | LCCN 2019025990 (ebook) | ISBN 9781607328865 (cloth) | ISBN 9781607328872 (ebook)
Subjects: LCSH: Mayas—Wars. | Mayas—Antiquities. | Indians of Central America—Wars. | Indians of Central America—Antiquities.
Classification: LCC F1435.3.W2 S44 2019 (print) | LCC F1435.3.W2 (ebook) | DDC 972.81—dc23
LC record available at https://lccn.loc.gov/2019025989
LC ebook record available at https://lccn.loc.gov/2019025990

Cover illustration: Conquest of the Tz'utujils at the Battle of Tecpan Atitlán. *Lienzo de Tlaxcala* (1581–1585). Copy by Alfredo Chavero, 1979.

Dedicated to our siblings, Caitlin Peuramaki-Brown and Andrew Morton, for a childhood of practice in the art of light combat and other forms of conflict.

Contents

Figures

Tables

Foreword

M. KATHRYN BROWN

While warfare is now widely recognized to have played an important role in ancient Mesoamerican societies, it remains both understudied and insufficiently understood. In the case of the Maya, for example, views of warfare and, more broadly, conflict have shifted dramatically since the early decades of the twentieth century CE, when scholarly consensus held that the Maya were a peaceful civilization, in contrast to the warlike Aztec. This idealistic notion of the peaceful Maya gradually gave way in the face of increasing evidence of Maya warfare, beginning with the discovery of the Bonampak murals in 1948. Notably, David Webster's 1976 publication put to rest any lingering notions of a peaceful Maya civilization, and since this time, scholars have generally accepted that warfare played an important role in the history of Maya civilization. This recognition has led to research projects that focused on Maya warfare, such as Arthur Demarest's (e.g., Demarest 2004a; Demarest et al. 1997) research in the Petexbatun region and Andrew Scherer and Charles Golden's (2014) research in the Usumacinta region.

As always, more data bring more fine-grained understandings of past practices. Our evolving knowledge of warfare and conflict in ancient Mesoamerica

DOI: 10.5876/9781607328872.c000

is demonstrated by the growing number of publications dedicated to this topic, including the predecessor to this edited volume, *Ancient Mesoamerican Warfare* (Brown and Stanton 2003). Yet even with a more sustained interest in warfare, our understanding of conflict in ancient Mesoamerica remains incomplete. For example, scholars still debate the nature and frequency of Maya warfare, whether conquest warfare was practiced, the degree to which warfare shaped Teotihuacan's role in the Maya region, and similar issues. Mesoamerican scholars cannot agree as to whether conflict was driven by ritual, religious, economic, or political motives or all of the above.

As the editors discuss in chapter 1, conflict and warfare appear to be universals, despite their violent and disruptive nature. This begs the question of how ancient Mesoamerican warfare was normalized through practice and ideological beliefs. Taking an innovative approach that includes cognitive and experiential dimensions of past cultures, the editors of this volume charged the contributors with the task of trying to understand ancient conflict and warfare from an internal "emic" perspective as opposed to the "etic" outsider's point of view. Epigraphic and iconographic data are often touted as important sources of "emic" understandings of the past; however, as the editors aptly point out, scholars examining ancient Mesoamerican warfare have mostly viewed conflict through an "etic" lens, focusing on "operational" considerations. For example, although several of the chapters in the 2003 *Ancient Mesoamerican Warfare* volume flirted with emic themes, this was not the central focus of the volume.

There are several historical reasons for this perceived bias against "emic" interpretations. Most notably, scholars have been tackling some basic problems of determining what lines of empirical data constitute evidence of conflict in the archaeological record and corpus of art and texts. Furthermore, although the distinction between emic and etic perspectives is a useful heuristic—particularly because it challenges us to understand the worldviews of past peoples—it can be difficult to draw the line between the two approaches. Nonetheless, for us to gain a better understanding of conflict in the past, we need to move beyond solely etic perspectives that focus mainly on operational aspects of warfare. And although we have made great strides in gathering empirical data, we have much to learn.

As our empirical knowledge expands, we can ask new and different questions that go beyond the nature and frequency of conflict, how martial events were conducted, and how conflict was manifested in the archaeological and textual records. A more holistic approach using ethnohistoric, iconographic, epigraphic, and archaeological data that takes into consideration operational, experiential, and cognitive aspects of warfare will no doubt serve us well. With scholarly contributions that examine warfare through multiple lenses, such as those gathered together in this volume, we gain greater insight into how conflict might have been perceived in the ancient societies we study. The strength of this edited volume is that the participants focused on just this—how conflict was perceived in the past. In doing so, this volume represents an important step forward in warfare and conflict studies in Mesoamerica and beyond.

Seeking Conflict
in Mesoamerica

1

Disentangling Conflict in Maya and Mesoamerican Studies

MEAGHAN M. PEURAMAKI-BROWN,
SHAWN G. MORTON, AND HARRI KETTUNEN

It may help to understand human affairs to be clear that most of the great triumphs and tragedies of history are caused, not by people being fundamentally good or fundamentally bad, but by people being fundamentally people.

(PRATCHETT AND GAIMAN 1990, 39)

For decades prior to the 1980s, when our ability to read ancient texts became more fully developed, the narrative of the ancient Maya as peaceful stargazers dominated and even directed early studies based in ethnography, ethnohistory, art history, and archaeology (best exemplified in Morley 1946; see discussions in Sullivan 2014; Webster 2000; Wilk 1985). Alongside more general narratives surrounding the "noble savages" of the Americas (Deloria 1969; Otterbein 2000a), these biases served to limit earlier considerations of conflict in the ancient past. Since the 1980s, significant contributions to the study of ancient Maya—and, more generally, Mesoamerican—conflict have appeared in peer-reviewed articles, books and book chapters, and popular media. Although this volume is intended as a follow-up to previous scholarly contributions, such as Brown and

DOI: 10.5876/9781607328872.c001

Stanton's (2003) *Ancient Mesoamerican Warfare* and Orr and Koontz's (2009) *Blood and Beauty*, it is also unique. We present a conscious effort to consider a range of human conflict processes—from interpersonal violence and crime, to intergroup aggression and political instability, to institutional breakdown and the collapse of civilizations—and to include contributions for which archaeological materials, ancient and not-so-ancient text, and preserved images all serve as complementary touchstones.

While this volume presents new sources, new translations, and new interpretations, it also attempts to explore Maya—and comparative Mesoamerican—conflict through an *emic* (insider, subjective) approach alongside the more traditional *etic* (outsider, objective) perspective, both of which are critical to developing more social and holistic understandings of the complex, often multigenerational processes that make up conflicts (Gilchrist 2003). By including studies that intentionally adopt cognitive and experiential approaches alongside more operational considerations, this volume acts as a valuable counterpoint to its more etic predecessors. Thus while many treatments of conflict, including that of this volume, focus on the degree to which its prevalence, nature, and conduct varied across time and space, we explicitly attempt to understand how the Maya themselves—along with their Mesoamerican neighbors—understood and explained conflict, what they recognized as conflict, how conflict was experienced by various parties, and the circumstances surrounding conflict.

We are, as always, limited in our ability to fully achieve emic understandings of the past. This is the result of the physical limitations presented to us through the various disciplines encompassed in this volume, alongside the ever-present lack of a working time machine. Issues such as the psychology of conflict, including what it was like to live through periods of conflict or the beliefs that propel conflict (e.g., superiority, injustice, vulnerability, distrust, helplessness; see Eidelson and Eidelson 2003), are often within the untouchable realm for most scholars of history and prehistory, unless chance should have it that individuals recorded these thoughts and experiences for us to discover. To a degree, we might be able to take more modern experiences of conflict and project them onto the past; however, this is an extremely difficult and tentative task.

The aims of this introductory chapter are twofold. In the first half, we consider a brief history of conflict research in Maya and Mesoamerican studies and discuss the notion of conflict itself as a dynamic of emic and etic perspectives critical to understanding the concept as a process and total social fact—a common thread throughout the volume. We also elaborate on the three aforementioned categories of approaches (operational, cognitive, experiential) and consider how multiple theoretical frameworks demonstrate that conflict can, and in fact should, be viewed from a variety of angles. In the second half of the chapter, we introduce the structure of the volume and how individual contributions move forward our stated goals.

WHY STUDY CONFLICT?

> We live in an age that is said to be ahistorical. It is difficult to remember the
> past—or even acknowledge it—living as we do, focused on an "eternal present,"
> driven by busy schedules and information overload, and wrapped up in anxieties
> about careers, family, health, the environment, terrorism, the future of the world.
> It can be both comforting and discouraging to know that many of the issues we
> confront today have been with us in different forms for a long time.
>
> (LUCHT 2007, xv–xvi)

Conflict. The term is pervasive across news headlines around the globe. "The Middle East Conflict." "The Syrian Conflict." "The Columbian Armed Conflict." "The Conflict in South Sudan." "The Israeli-Palestinian Conflict." Beyond the most recent headlines, terms such as *class conflict, inner conflict, conflict resolution, conflict of interest, conflict diamond,* and *conflict tourism* surround us throughout our daily lives—at home, at work, and at play.

Since 1980, the number of studies of conflict among the ancient Maya and their Mesoamerican neighbors has risen dramatically (a small sample of such studies includes Brown and Stanton 2003; Chase and Chase 1989; Demarest et al. 1997; Dillon 1982; Freidel 1986; Hamblin and Pitcher 1980; Inomata 1997, 2014; Johnston 2001; Marcus 1992b; Miller 1986; Nahm 1994; Pohl and Pohl 1994; Redmond and Spencer 2006; Vázquez López, Valencia Rivera, and Gutierrez González 2014; Webster 1993, 1998, 1999, 2000), although the Aztec have long drawn such fascination primarily as a result of significant ethnohistoric accounts from the Conquest period (see Hassig 1995). Why has conflict become such a focus in Mesoamerican studies, particularly of the Maya, when prior to the end of the twentieth century CE it was largely avoided? The most obvious reasons are disciplinary-based, internal to modern Western approaches to the material past (e.g., archaeology, epigraphy, iconography). Conflicts, in particular violent events of interference, are "real" processes that can leave telltale signs within the physical record of the past, including dramatic shifts in human behavior (Saunders 2004). We tend to believe that we can easily define conflict as disruption or discord within the white noise that is peace. When this disruption takes the form of violence, involving physical force intended to hurt, damage, or kill, it becomes more visible in the archaeological record (Vencl 1984).

Other explanations are more broadly and historically contingent. As Wilk (1985, 307) noted in the mid-1980s, "archaeological discourse has a dual nature: at the same time that it pursues objective, verifiable knowledge about the past, it also conducts an informal and often hidden political and philosophical debate about the major issues of contemporary life." Post–World War II archaeology focused heavily on the peaceful nature of the Maya, perhaps as a direct reaction against and escape from the reality that many soldier-scholars had recently faced. A noticeable increase in the number of American scholars dealing with the topics of collapse and warfare in the 1960s to 1970s is suggested by Wilk (1985) to be a reflection of US involvement in Vietnam. By the late 1980s and early 1990s, with the eventual dissolution of the British Empire and the Soviet Union—both a series of large-scale, long-term events serving as a culmination of multigenerational conflicts (Gluckman 1955, 1963)—increased interest in conflict and even collapse among scholars the world over focused on Mesoamerica and the Maya. Perhaps even the origin of archaeology as a discipline, within the realms of military and nationalistic pursuits, foreshadowed our inevitable interest in past conflict (Evans 2014; Trigger 2006).

Finally, we must consider that this fascination is not entirely our own but is shared with the peoples of ancient Mesoamerica. The textual corpus of the Maya region and its neighbors, at least that portion recorded on (semi-) public stone monuments, shows a similar concern with conflict. In general, this typically includes events that embroil rulers against their neighbors, such as inter-site or inter-dynastic conflict involving armed engagements (militarism, conquest, and coercion) (Kettunen 2012). While the database associated with Kettunen's Corpus Epigraphy project is continually developing, we are currently able to note at least 117 different Maya monuments that specifically discuss warfare. Of these, there are 166 individual references to acts of physical domination or violence, representing 98 "events of interference" (see below), either part of the same or diverse conflict processes. References[1] to warfare in the hieroglyphic corpus include verbs such as *chuk-* "to capture" or "to tie up," *jub-* "to overthrow," *ch'ak-* "to chop, destroy," *pul-* "to burn," *nak-* "to fight," as well as the so-called star-war glyph that appears to refer to large-scale warfare. The most common of these references in the corpus of Maya inscriptions is the verb *chuk-* and its passive form *chuhkaj* "was captured." However, we must be careful when interpreting these records, as they are in many cases abundant in one geographic area and all but absent in another. This is especially the case with the *pul-* verb, which is a characteristic feature in the rhetoric of the Eastern Lowlands around Naranjo but practically nonexistent elsewhere, except for a few rare references beyond that region (Kettunen 2015).

In addition to these verbs, there are indirect references to aggression in Maya texts. One of these is *och ch'e'n* "cave entering," which may be a reference to entering a city with armed forces. Another phrase is *nahbaj uk'ik'el witzaj ujolil*, or the "pooling" of blood and "mountaining" (i.e., piling up) the skulls of enemies (?), as well as *na'waj*, or the "presentation" of captives. Besides verbs, we have nouns and compound nouns that are associated with warfare, including *baak* "captive," *to'k' pakal* "flint-shield," or "army"—appearing frequently in the phrase *jubuy uto'k' upakal*, or "defeating the army"—and titles such as the guardian (captor) of so-and-so (*ucha'n . . .*) and "he of so-and-so many captives" (*aj . . . baak*). In addition to these references, we have military titles and military offices in the corpus, including *baah te', baah to'k', baah pakal, ch'ahom ajaw, lakam, sajal, yajaw k'ahk',* and *yajaw te'*. The precise meaning and function of these titles is still under debate, and in the end, some of them may not have direct military associations. Other nouns include *to'k'* "flint," *pakal* "shield," and *ko'haw* "helmet." Kettunen (2014) has expanded this list by attempting to identify more subtle terminology and imagery related to warriors, weaponry, armor, strategies, tactics, and military geography, along with political motivations as presented in both the ancient corpus and colonial documents.

The subjective differences between various terms describing conflict are important. Languages can and do reflect the changes societies undergo; they naturally evolve over time under "normal" circumstances, and when change is rapid or traumatic, as is often the case with conflict, new words and phrases or secondary meanings of existing words and phrases often tell their own story of impact and change. In Ch'olti, *lacael* may indicate either a war or plague, the outcomes of each presumably thought of as broadly similar (Boot 2004, 8). Likewise, to "take in war" may be likened to the hunting of animals by the term *colom* (Boot 2004, 41). In K'iche', *ch'o'j* and its related terms may be used to indicate variations on an impassioned or angry dispute, while *labal* and its related terms clearly link the concept of "war" with the qualities of "badness" and "barbarism" (Christenson n.d., 24, 68). In Ch'ol, modern speakers borrow from the Spanish *guerra* to describe inter/intra-state conflicts or warfare (Hopkins, Josserand, and Cruz Guzmán 2011, 60). In Mopan, speakers distinguish between "warfare" (in the modern Western sense) and other conflicts by using the term *guerra*, while *p'isb'aj* and its related terms are used to indicate general conflicts or fights, and *lox* refers to small skirmishes or fistfights (residents of Maya Mopan, Stann Creek District, Belize, personal communication to M. Peuramaki-Brown and S. Morton, 2015; Hofling 2011, 662). Interestingly, *guerra* is a loanword from Germanic (Vandal/Visigoth) *warra*, as are some other war-related words in Spanish—in a similar way as the word was borrowed from Spanish to Mayan languages—perhaps reflecting the difference of native warfare as opposed to a "foreign" type/style of warfare. It would be foolish to expect any less variability in the ancient past. Thus the language of conflict is a critical focus in this volume.

Returning to considerations of conflict as process and total social fact, peace and negotiation are equally part of the equation, as are periods of coexistence (liminal events, discussed below), and they should be expressly included in our examinations whenever possible. While less frequent to be sure, the ancient Maya also felt compelled to record events and interactions that likely served to ameliorate or suppress the threat of conflict and maintain the peace. On Altar 21 from Caracol, the inauguration of Yajaw Te' K'inich is supervised and sponsored by the Tikal king Wak Chan K'awiil (Martin and Grube 2008, 89). On Altar 5 from Tikal, the Tikal lord Jasaw Chan K'awiil and a lord from Maasal cooperated in a joint exhumation ritual despite a long history of conflict between these two centers (Martin and Grube 2008, 37, 47). The affirmation of political domination and cooperation, while perhaps preserving the peace, could similarly be seen to foment discord. In 556 CE, three years after witnessing the inauguration of Yajaw Te' K'inich, Tikal "axed" Caracol (Martin and Grube 2008, 89)—an event that foreshadows a series of attacks and counterattacks so significant that we have taken to using the eventual fall of Tikal at the hands of its longtime rival Calakmul and its allies (Caracol included) as the marker for the end of the Early Classic period in the late sixth century CE. Such an example highlights the importance of perspective and the reality that lines between conflict and peace are not so easily drawn, as is often believed. In pointing to these issues, it is not our intention to undermine existing contributions to the study of conflict among the ancient Maya but rather to emphasize that the study of conflict, both cross-culturally and through time, may benefit from more nuanced approaches than are typically employed, an issue this volume explicitly attempts to address.

Ancient Mesoamerican Warfare (Brown and Stanton 2003) was the first comprehensive edited volume on warfare in Mesoamerica and acted as a watershed to previous studies by putting them in comparative context. What the volume may have lacked in specificity (being regionally broad), it more than made up for by showcasing the diverse ways Mesoamerican researchers, Mayanists included, were identifying and interpreting the material remains of warfare. As Brown and Stanton (2003, 2) point out, terms used to denote forms of violent aggression, along with other conflict-related concepts, are notoriously ill-defined. Confounded by arguments over motivation, scale, and even basic human nature, the task of succinctly defining such terms is daunting (Simons 1999). The editors unified the various chapters through use of the shared terms *aggression* and *conflict*, leaving particular examples to the discretion of the individual authors. This use of the broad term *conflict* belies the fact that the associated volume discussions were much narrower. As noted above, existing literature on the topic reveals that, despite significant and detailed treatments of acts and concepts that might be subsumed under the category of conflict in ancient Mesoamerica, a narrow semantic field dominates this discourse, specifically, discussions of "warfare" and related aspects of physical "violence" (Hassig 1992; Webster 2000). While both terms are frequently treated in the literature, there has historically been little attempt to define these concepts in a meaningful way, with the result being the discouragement of more nuanced, culturally relevant, or emically derived discussions of these subjects and overall processes of conflict.

DISENTANGLING CONFLICT

Man is a competitive creature, and the seeds of conflict are built deep into our genes. We fought each other on the savannah and only survived against great odds by organising ourselves into groups, which would have had a common purpose, giving morale and fortitude. Our aggression is a deep instinct, which survives in all kinds of manifestations in modern man.

(WINSTON 2005)

Conflict is a complex concept, taking myriad forms: personal and interpersonal, public and private, identified and anonymous, aggressive and passive (and passive aggressive), intimate and distant, local and global. Conflicts rarely consist of singular events; rather, they are often multi-event processes that can evolve over many days, years, or even generations. An example from recent history would be the conflict between the US government / military and the various indigenous groups of the Great Plains. In his book *The Day the World Ended at Little Bighorn*, Marshall (2007, 227–228) wisely notes:

> The Lakota world did end at the Little Bighorn because of the government's intent to end it, not because we won a great victory. But that day was the culmination of any number of days that might have been the beginning of the end over the course of several generations. It might have been the day the French explorers . . . laid coveting eyes on the northern plains, or the day someone took to heart . . . [the] angry suggestion to force the Lakota into a dependence on the government's will. Or perhaps it was the day a white man discovered gold in the Black Hills. Or any of the days a peace talker drafted a treaty that was more favorable to his side. Or the day ethnocentric arrogance declared the West to have land free for the taking.

In light of such understandings, we believe Schmidt and Kochan's (1972) definition of conflict lends itself to broad comparisons on an etic, functional level, alongside more emic, subjective pursuits of understanding and in consideration of the long time scales often required. Conflict is any overt behavior arising out of a *process* in which one or more decision-making units (individuals or collectives, each with their own motivational forces and goals) seeks the advancement of its own interests in its relationship with other units (figure 1.1). This advancement must result from determined action as opposed to fortuitous circumstance and includes coercive and hegemonic actions alongside exercised force, couched within preexisting political, social, economic, and ideological power networks (Mann 1986, 22–27). Conflict, including its various forms of disputes and negotiations, is therefore the struggle between groups or individuals over incompatible goals, scarce resources, or the sources of power needed to acquire them (Avruch 1998; Hsiang, Burke, and Miguel 2013).

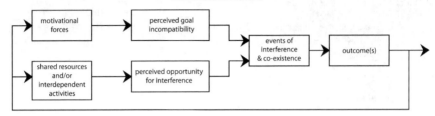

FIGURE 1.1. *The process of conflict (modified from Schmidt and Kochan 1972, figure 2)*

The struggle that is conflict is determined by perceptions of goals, resources, and power, which may differ greatly between individuals and collectives. Today, the United Nations recognizes that any discussion of conflict and its associated events, activities, and perspectives must consider a minimum of three parties: the performer, the victim, and the witness (Galtung 2000). Therefore, critical to any attempt at understanding etic as well as emic aspects of conflict in the past is a consideration of various perspectives represented on all sides of a given process. The importance of the perception factor is best portrayed in Service's (1966, 58) use of an "old Arab proverb" to discuss differing instances of conflict, quoted as "I against my brother; I and my brother against my cousin; I, my brothers, and my cousins against the next village; all of us against the foreigner." Overall, culture remains an important determinant of perceptions, and conflict that occurs across cultural boundaries also occurs across cognitive and perceptual boundaries—as it is between individuals and groups—and is especially susceptible to problems of intercultural miscommunication and misunderstanding (consider Graham's discussion of "rules of engagement," this volume). Such problems can exacerbate conflict, no matter what the root causes may be. Culture, therefore, is an important factor in many conflicts that at first glance, particularly to the archaeologist, may appear to be solely about material resources or tangible interests.

As part of this overall definition, which serves to outline an entire process, conflict is disentangled from general notions of competition, contrary to the works of many scholars that are strongly based in the sociological writings of Georg Simmel and Karl Marx (Helle 2008; Turner 1975; Wolff 1950). Competition as compared to conflict occurs where, given incompatible goals, there is no interference with each unit's goal attainment. In the case of ancient Maya and Mesoamerican states, each can compete for resources but not engage in a process of conflict until the activity of one disrupts the success of another (e.g., warfare, trade route blockades).

Key to the process of conflict is an understanding of "perceived" goals and accepted forms of interference (passive or active, violent or non-violent) from the perspective of each unit involved, as opposed to simply focusing on the events of conflict as categories of analysis (Chagnon 1988, 2009; Fry and Björkqvist 2009). It is within this context that Maya and Mesoamerican studies continue to lag; we remain uncertain of the perceived goals and accepted forms of interference within conflict processes, as many of the chapters in this volume address. This expands our considerations of conflict to include not only a sociological focus on people and practice but also the entanglement of places and things, which broadens the narrative of conflict cross-culturally and cross-temporally (Leverentz 2010). This is critical, as the causes of conflict and the experiences behind it are often understood and represented differently by the various positions of instigators, accomplices, rivals, observers, winners, losers, and other parties (Yoffee 2005). Conflict is both imagined and performed—a duality that is critical when examining its nature in diverse cultural contexts (Arkush and Stanish 2005; Schröder and Schmidt 2001). This is exemplified in a consideration of the ongoing conflicts in the Near and Middle East, where an individual's or a group's perceived goals surrounding the various engagements, whether they be economic, political, religious, or some other, will directly relate to their experience with given situations and impact what they conceive of as acceptable forms of interference (e.g., blockades, diplomacy, warfare). In addition, coexistence is presented as liminal events within the conflict process and can occur over short periods in multiple forms, including ritually regulated truces, war payments, cycles of fighting and feasting, norms allowing trade between enemies in certain places or contexts, and "neutral" groups or specialized traders.

Each dimension of the conflict process is accessible to comparative analysis; however, this assessment of the distant past has proven elusive. To date, most archaeologists have focused on developing etic classifications of conflict events, often noting the outcomes and possible motivations typically linked to resource arguments but rarely considering emic, phenomenological understandings of perceived goals and opportunities for interference. By focusing solely on events, typically in the form of etic categorizations of outcomes, we fail to achieve the more emic approaches currently on trend in archaeological theory and practices (Hegmon 2003; Oland, Hart, and Frink 2012; Schmidt 2001).

APPROACHES TO CONFLICT

Schröder and Schmidt (2001) identify three primary approaches to understanding and identifying conflict in anthropology—(1) operational, (2) cognitive, and (3) experiential approaches—which we recognize as also employed in Maya and Mesoamerican studies today. The former category typically espouses more cross-cultural, etic considerations of conflict, while the latter two categories attempt to address individual-, group-, and culture-specific, emic understandings. The majority of chapters in this volume strive to engage one or both of the latter two approaches to conflict in some manner, alongside the former.

Operational approaches have a long history in archaeology and focus on etic links between conflict and general properties of human nature and rationality (Thorpe 2003). Such studies attempt to link general concepts of social adaptation to measurable material conditions (the aforementioned etic categorizations of conflict and associated events/outcomes) and aim to explain conflict by comparing structural and innate conditions as causes affecting specific historical conditions (Fried 1967; Gat 2006; Service 1962). These are employed to create generalized "big history" and cross-cultural narratives (e.g., Bowles 2009; Flannery and Marcus 2012; Fry and Söderberg 2013; Pinker 2011; Trigger 2003, 240–263). Within these approaches, conflict is considered never so specific and culturally bounded that it cannot be cross-compared. There is a long tradition in archaeology and anthropology of linking, for better or worse, types of collective conflict to types of society and arranging them on an evolutionary scale (e.g., Otterbein 1994; Reyna and Downs 1994). This practice is controversial, but comparative approaches remain one of the primary goals of ancient studies. In many respects, such discussions can be boiled down to the essence of "what it means to be human." Is the state of nature a state of conflict—of war, dominance, and strife in the Hobbesian sense? Or are all those living in a state of nature at peace, as in a Rousseauian sense? Is civilization our road to utopia or the source of our corruption? (For a timeless example in the world of fiction, one needs only to turn to Mary Shelley's *Frankenstein*.)

By contrast, cognitive and experiential approaches focus on the emics of the cultural construction, negotiation, and agency of conflict in a given society, primarily through the "framing" of mental orientations that organize perception and interpretation (Goffman 1974). They consider narratives of individual engagement and cultural templates of appropriate behavior and decision-making (Shiv and Fedorikhin 1999). Cognitive approaches, which include affective behavior, attempt to understand conflicts as culturally constructed and representative of cultural values and are seen as contingent on cultural meaning and its form of representation. This is approached with careful attention to the socio-cultural specificity of a given historical context. Experiential approaches are often difficult to distinguish from cognitive studies, as they consider conflict to be related to individual subjectivity and narrative—something that structures people's everyday lives, even in its absence (Johnston 1995). The true nature and impact of conflict can therefore only be grasped through a consideration of individual experience and discourse, its meaning unfolding primarily through the individual's perception of a given situation (Briggs 1996). It is within these approaches that we tend to observe more holistic considerations of the people, places, and things involved in conflict processes and more complementary considerations of archaeological, textual, and visual materials of the past.

CHAPTER CONTRIBUTIONS

The inspiration for this volume derived from an invited session at the 2012 Chacmool Archaeological Conference in Calgary, Alberta, Canada. A number of the presentations sought to specifically address conflict through an emic lens. Inspired by such attempts, we solicited additional contributions (both original chapters and discussant chapters) that fit the theme to produce a unique, timely, and valuable collection of integrated papers. Through reference to art, text, and archaeology, the contributors to this volume consider how the ancient Maya and their neighbors defined, sought, and engaged in processes of conflict. Although the volume is weighted toward a Maya focus, additional chapters provide an essential contextual scope by dealing with neighboring culture areas of Mesoamerica (figure 1.2). The volume is also temporally expansive, including chapters that discuss a number of different periods in the archaeological, epigraphic, and iconographic past.

Each of the chapters is authored or coauthored by leaders in the field of Maya and Mesoamerican studies. In part I, as is typical of much archaeological research, we will move through time, starting with the most recent periods of the Maya world—in particular the Conquest (chapter 2)—and moving through to the Postclassic and Classic periods (chapters 3, 4, 5, 6, 7). We then jump to the western side of Mesoamerica in part II and visit some of the neighboring cultures of Central Mexico (chapters 8 and 9) and the Gulf Coast (chapter 10). Part III concludes the volume and features two chapters (chapters 11 and 12) that discuss the various themes presented in the previous sections. In addition, the authors present their own unique insights into the nature of conflict among the Maya and their neighbors and our attempts to pursue such understandings through both emic and etic lenses.

In part I of the volume, the authors focus on two key aspects of Maya conflict. The first is the entangled roles and agencies of people, places, and things within the processes and embodiments of conflict and the natural and supernatural forces believed and observed to be at play throughout. Each author emphasizes the role of both material and immaterial factors that are central to the causes, development, and outcomes of conflict, including the importance of embracing an entangled understanding of conflict, ritual landscapes, power, and divine protection.

Christenson (chapter 2) adopts a Tz'utujil Maya perspective to understanding the Spanish Conquest, perceived not as a catastrophic event that ended Maya culture but as a kind of death followed by rebirth, similar to other periodic world renewals. The conflict involved magic rather than force of arms, with the symbol of the Virgin Mary borne on the Spanish banner playing a decisive role in the defeat of the K'iche' warriors. This serves to remind us of the multiple perspectives that might exist regarding the causes and outcomes of a given conflict.

FIGURE 1.2. *Map of Mesoamerica, denoting prominent sites/locations discussed in this volume.*

Hernandez and Palka (chapter 3) contemplate how the protection and destruction (desecration) of material manifestations of supernatural forces, such as human remains, and the practice of Maya warfare were inextricably linked to the ritual landscapes of Chiapas and Petén. Through their discussion, they demonstrate the temporal continuity of many aspects of Maya conflict, from the Pre-Columbian into Post-Columbian periods.

Covering similar themes but with particular emphasis on iconography and ethnohistory, Bassie-Sweet (chapter 4) considers the detailed information presented in the colonial document the *Popol Vuh*, in particular the information concerning the war gods of the Postclassic K'iche' and similar deities found in Classic Maya art and writing. A common attribute of these gods is their relationship to thunderbolts and meteors and the important role these atmospheric phenomena and their material representations on earth—chert and obsidian—played in both Maya and Mesoamerican conflict. In her considerations, Bassie-Sweet highlights instances of conflict that bridge cultural, cognitive, and perceptual boundaries and the resulting implications.

Finally, Tokovinine (chapter 5) adopts an emic approach to understanding Classic Maya ways of writing about conflict—its causes and outcomes—confronting head-on the complexity of Mayan language and terminology. Of particular interest is the tying of conflict events to place names and deities. Tokovinine has identified a series of shifts in how these are referenced by the Maya over time, suggesting change in written discourse dealing with landscapes and conflict, including a move away from a focus on raiding toward political, territorial, and hegemonic warfare (later reversed). This is an interesting observation toward our understandings of perceived and accepted forms of interference among the Maya over time.

The second key aspect addressed in part I involves the process of conflict itself, its defined forms (goals, interferences/coexistence, outcomes), and roles played in the development, denouement, and collapse of complex Maya organizations.

Haines and Sagebiel (chapter 6) consider shifting political power structures and associated conflict processes in Northern Belize during the Classic period, carefully knitting together disparate lines of evidence. In particular, Stela 9 at Lamanai is considered, less in terms of context of the text but rather on its treatment and disposition as related to processes of conflict between Lamanai and Ka'kabish. A consideration of titles of rulership and overlordship is central to their discussion.

Bey and Gallareta Negrón (chapter 7) argue that warfare in the tenth century CE was the final form of interference following an almost 2,000-year process of conflict among the Puuc Maya of the Yucatan Peninsula. Traditionally, the development of social complexity in this region has been considered relatively free of conflict when compared to the southern Maya lowlands. New archaeological and iconographic information considered in this chapter focuses on the fact that the rise of social complexity in the Puuc began much earlier than has been traditionally argued, dramatically changing our view of both the nature and structure of conflict in this region. The authors propose a model for the Puuc consisting of highly institutionalized militarism that incorporated wider Mesoamerican influences in its perceived goals, forms of interference, and successful outcomes.

In part II of the volume, we turn to comparative examples of conflict from outside the Maya world; specifically, we look to the regions of Central Mexico and the Gulf Coast.

Nielsen (chapter 8) discusses how archaeologists, epigraphers, and art historians have just begun to map and understand the extent of the influence of Teotihuacan conflict during the fourth and fifth centuries CE. He considers the iconographic and architectural symbol sets of a Teotihuacan imperial expansion and subsequent local emulations in Querétaro and Michoacan, perhaps commissioned by imperial representatives.

Abtosway and McCafferty (chapter 9) continue the discussion of the people, place, and thing embodiment of conflict through reference to Mixtec codices and archaeology of the Mixteca Alta. Mixtec pictorial manuscripts contain the longest historical accounts from ancient Mesoamerica, spanning the period about 900–1600 CE. Included in these "mythstories" are genealogical registers, ritual events, political interaction, and military action within broader narratives of natural and supernatural conflict. Through their cataloging of a wide variety of weapons used in Mixtec warfare, the authors provide a cross-cultural perspective for a region and topic that is typically dominated by discussions of the Aztec and the Maya.

Finally, Koontz (chapter 10) interprets multiple levels of representation and contexts of banner stones associated with military procession as possible evidence of hierarchy within military ranks and social mobility at El Tajín, Veracruz. This discussion brings the main body of the volume full circle to Christiansen's initial discussion of the role of things, namely, the banners of saints, in the interferences and outcomes of conflict.

Part III features retrospective and discussion in the form of two chapters that conclude the volume. Both Stanton (chapter 11) and Graham (chapter 12) take pains to further define and engage the various processes of conflict addressed in the volume. Stanton emphasizes the messy, disorganized, and widespread impacts of "organized violence," ultimately asking more questions than providing answers and thus charting a path forward. Graham's deconstruction of but one of the terms addressed in many of the chapters of this volume, *war*, serves to ably highlight the aforementioned variability of the concepts, processes, and practices of conflict in the ancient past. She further considers what might have been the perceived goals and accepted forms of interference within conflict among various groups. Were rulers engaging in warfare for the purpose of captives, tribute, land, or other resources (economic and social)? What were the underlying causes that led individuals and groups to select some goals rather than others as premises for their interference decisions?

The expressed goal of this volume is to explore the topic of conflict in its various guises across the Maya area and broader Mesoamerica, with a particular attempt to develop emic understandings alongside the etic. By including ethnohistoric, art historical, epigraphic, and archaeological studies that intentionally adopt cognitive and experiential approaches alongside more operational considerations, we aim to present a volume that acts as a valuable counterpoint to its more etic predecessors.

Acknowledgments. We wish to extend our gratitude to the anonymous reviewers solicited by the University Press of Colorado and to Jessica d'Arbonne in particular for her effort, aid, and consideration. Thank you, also, to Laurie Milne for her insight. The chapter, and indeed the volume, are all the better for your contributions. Any errors remain the responsibility of the authors. We also extend our gratitude to Karen Bassie-Sweet and the organizers of the 2012 Chacmool Archaeological Conference at the University of Calgary, through which the idea for this volume was inspired and several of the contributions initially derived.

NOTE

1. We realize the limitations such lists present, as they are dependent on our subjective linking of terms to existing concepts in English, Spanish, and other languages.

PART I

Conflict in the Maya World

2

The Lady of the Lake

The Virgin Mary and the Spanish Conquest of the Maya

ALLEN J. CHRISTENSON

The Spanish Conquest was a devastating blow to the sovereignty and culture of the Maya people of highland Guatemala. The ancient K'iche' kingdom suffered perhaps the greatest losses, their capital city of Q'umarkaj having been burned to the ground and their kings executed in 1524 CE during the first wave of the Spanish invasion. Contemporary K'iche' accounts of the destruction, written by surviving members of the old K'iche' court, were fatalistic about their suffering, acknowledging the superiority of the Spanish gods and describing their own defeat as inevitable. In contrast, the neighboring Tz'utujils of Santiago Atitlan claim that European saints and deities actually sided with their ancestors, helping them defeat the foreign invaders. In these accounts, the Virgin Mary frequently appears as the daughter of the deified king of the Tz'utujils. Her tears are said to have caused the waters of Lake Atitlan to rise and drown the Spanish forces and their Kaqchikel allies. In this view, Christian divinities were not imposed on the Tz'utujils by the Spanish Conquest but actually sided with their ancestors, protecting them from the destruction that visited neighboring highland Maya kingdoms. Today, she is said to live at the bottom of nearby Lake

DOI: 10.5876/9781607328872.c002

FIGURE 2.1. *Don Pedro de Alvarado*

Atitlan, where she reigns over those who drown and protects the community from threats by outsiders.

In 1524 CE, the Maya highlands were invaded by a small force of Spaniards under the command of Pedro de Alvarado, one of the principal captains who served with Hernán Cortés, who had recently conquered the Aztec Empire in Central Mexico. Alvarado had blondish hair, which indigenous people had never seen before (figure 2.1). They nicknamed him Donadiu, the Aztec Sun God, because of the brightness of his fair skin and hair. At the time of this invasion, the three main highland Maya kingdoms were the K'iche's, the Kaqchikels, and the Tz'utujils. The Kaqchikels, having seen the superior armament of the Spaniards and knowing that they had already defeated the mighty Aztec Empire, quickly allied themselves with Alvarado and took the opportunity to help him against the K'iche's. At the time, the K'iche's and Kaqchikels had been engaged in a protracted war of their own, and, undoubtedly, the latter wished to turn the arrival of the Spaniards to their own advantage. In the long run, this turned out to be a disastrous decision on their part.

According to the K'iche' chronicle *Títulos de la Casa Ixquin-Nehaib*, the initial conflict between the K'iche's and Spaniards involved magic rather than force of arms: "At midnight, the Indians went to fight with the Spaniards along with their captain who had transformed himself into an eagle. They came to kill Governor Donadiu, but they could not because a very white young girl defended him; although they desired greatly to enter the camp, when they saw this girl they fell to the ground and could not get up. Then they saw many birds without legs, and these birds surrounded the girl, and although the Indians wished to kill her, these birds defended her and blinded them" (Recinos 1957, 87–88, translation by the author).

Victoria Bricker (1981, 39–40) suggests that the young girl defending the Spaniards was the Virgin Mary and that the footless birds were doves representing the Holy Spirit. In the sixteenth century CE, it was common for Spaniards to carry banners with Christian symbols into battle as a sign of God's favor and protection. The K'iche's may well have seen such banners or even sculpted images of the Virgin in the Spanish encampment. Regardless of the historical source of the legend, the K'iche' account interprets the battle not as a human conflict but one of supernaturals in which the divinities brought by the Spaniards triumphed over those of their own military leaders (see chapter by Tokovinine, this volume).

Following a brief battle at El Pinal in the Quetzaltenango Valley, Alvarado marched on the K'iche' capital of Q'umarkaj sometime in March or April 1524 CE, during Easter season. He was invited to enter the city but, fearing a trap, Alvarado chose to encamp on the outskirts of the city where his cavalry could better maneuver if attacked. Soon after his arrival, Alvarado invited the two rulers of the city, Oxib' Kej and Belejeb' Tz'i', to visit him at his camp. Suspecting treachery, he seized them and held them as captives. A force of K'iche' warriors attempted to liberate their kings, killing one of the Spanish soldiers and a number of their indigenous allies. In response, Alvarado executed the K'iche' kings and burned the city to the ground:

> And seeing that by fire and sword I might bring these people to the service of His Majesty, I determined to burn the chiefs who, at the time that I wanted to burn them, told me, as it will appear in their confessions, that they were the ones who had ordered the war against me and were the ones also who made it. They told me about the way they were to do so, to burn me in the city, and that with this thought (in their minds) they had brought me there, and that they had ordered their vassals not to come and give obedience to our Lord the Emperor, nor help us, nor do anything else that was right. And as I knew them to have such a bad disposition towards the service of His Majesty, and to insure the good and peace of this land, I burnt them, and sent to burn the town and to destroy it, for it is a very strong and dangerous place. (Alvarado 1924, 62–63).

FIGURE 2.2. *Conquest of the Tz'utujils at the Battle of Tecpan Atitlán.* Lienzo de Tlaxcala *(1581–1585). Copy by Alfredo Chavero, 1979.*

The two unfortunate K'iche' kings were hauled up with ropes by their necks and then burned alive, a standard punishment for rebellious lords. Alvarado then moved on to the Kaqchikel capital where he established a temporary governing court. There he inquired of his Kaqchikel allies if there were any other hostile forces that would hinder the establishment of Spanish power in Guatemala. The Kaqchikels informed him that the Tz'utujils on the southern and western shores of Lake Atitlan had been their traditional enemies for centuries and could pose a powerful threat, particularly considering their reputation as fierce warriors. Three embassies of messengers sent to the Tz'utujil capital at Chiya' to negotiate a peaceful surrender were killed outright, prompting Alvarado to invade in force with 60 cavalry, 150 Spanish infantry, and several thousand Kaqchikel and Tlaxcalan allies (Alvarado 1924, 65–70; Carlsen 1996, 142; Orellana 1984, 113). The Tz'utujils formed a defensive line against the attack northeast of present-day Santiago Atitlan, which was quickly broken up by Spanish crossbowmen. The battle is commemorated in the *Lienzo of Tlaxcala* painted soon after the Conquest (figure 2.2). Some of the defenders were able to escape by

FIGURE 2.3. *Chiya', located atop the small hill at the base of Volcán San Pedro*

jumping into Lake Atitlan and swimming to a nearby island, while others were slaughtered by the late arrival of 300 Kaqchikel war canoes (Alvarado 1924, 71). Nearly 500 years after the Kaqchikels' alliance with the Spanish invaders, there remains a lingering animosity between the Kaqchikels who occupy the northern and eastern shores of Lake Atitlan and the Tz'utujils on the southern and western shores.

That evening, Alvarado and his troops spent the night in a maize field and prepared for a morning siege of the capital city, Chiya'. The city was protected on three sides by the waters of Lake Atitlan and on the west where it abutted the slopes of a volcano, making it easily defensible from hostile attack (figure 2.3). But the ruling lords had apparently seen enough to know that defeat was inevitable and abandoned the city without a fight (Anonymous 1935 [ca. 1700], 364).

Alvarado sent several captured Tz'utujils into the mountains to invite the fleeing inhabitants to return to their homes under the promise that they would not be harmed; however, if they did not return he threatened to continue hostilities, burn their towns, and destroy their maize and cacao fields. Within three days the ruler of Chiya', Joo No'j K'iq'ab', declared fealty to the Spanish king, commending Alvarado for his skill in war and noting that until that day, "their land had never been broken into nor entered by force of arms" (Alvarado 1924, 72). The Tz'utujil king presented the victor with abundant gifts of tribute and promised that he would never again resume hostilities. Alvarado reported the Tz'utujil's submission in a letter to Cortés:

I gave them to understand the greatness and power of our lord the Emperor, and that they should appreciate that for all that had passed, I, in his Royal name, would pardon them, and that from now on they should behave themselves and not make war against anybody in the neighborhood, as all were now vassals of His Majesty; so I dismissed them, leaving them safe and peaceful, and returned to this city. At the end of three days after my arrival there, all the chiefs, principal people and captains of the said lake came to me with presents and told me that now they were our friends and considered themselves fortunate to be vassals of His Majesty and relieved of hardships, wars and differences that they had amongst themselves. And I received them very well and gave them some of my jewels and sent them back to their country with much affection, and they are the most pacific that are in this land. (Alvarado 1924, 72–73).

Despite the Tz'utujils' reputation as aggressive warriors with a penchant for shifting alliances, the rulers of Chiya' never openly rebelled against the Spaniards, and the Lake Atitlan region remained one of the most peaceful provinces in the country. This lack of aggression is unusual considering the succeeding decades of forced labor and exorbitant tribute demands that drove other Spanish "allies" to take up arms (Anonymous 1935 [ca. 1700], 436). The Kaqchikels chafed under this oppression and eventually rebelled openly against their former Spanish allies. As a result, Alvarado hanged the last Kaqchikel king on May 26, 1540 CE. Soon afterward, in the same year, the last remaining member of the K'iche' royal family, a man named Tepepul, was also hanged after a long period of imprisonment (Maxwell and Hill 2006, 287–289; Recinos and Goetz 1953, 132–133).

In gratitude for his peaceful submission to Spanish authority, Alvarado allowed the Tz'utujil king to remain *cacique* at his capital city of Chiya'. *Caciques*, the Spanish title for indigenous rulers, were exempt from tribute and labor obligations. Spanish law considered them the direct vassals of the king of Spain, not subject to the orders of local governors or military administrators, not even Alvarado. *Caciques* who proved their loyalty to the king were allowed to use the Spanish title *don*, own and ride horses, display a coat of arms, and possess weapons.

At some point soon after the Conquest, the Tz'utujil king adopted the name don Pedro, likely in honor of Pedro de Alvarado who had defeated him in battle (Carlsen 1997, 84). Rather than a hated enemy, the Tz'utujil king saw Alvarado as a warrior lord whose power he wished to emulate. The early Maya nobility adopted the names of Christian saints upon baptism as a token of their conversion. By adopting this name, don Pedro would also have adopted San Pedro as his personal patron saint. Before the arrival of the Spaniards, highland Maya kings often adopted the names of gods or the patron divinities of calendric days to assert their own power as supernatural beings (see chapter by Tokovinine, this volume). The Tz'utujils likely also chose for their city's titular saint Santiago, the patron saint of the Spanish army and the founding saint of Alvarado's first capital at Ciudad del Señor Santiago de los Caballeros ("City of Lord Santiago of the Knights"). Santiago was a warrior saint whose banner was carried into battle by the Spaniards in their interminable war against the Moors for centuries, earning him the nickname Santiago the Moor Killer. The Tz'utujils undoubtedly adopted the saint as the patron of their capital city in an effort to assimilate his warlike power that had proven so successful against them in the past (see chapters by Koontz and Nielsen, this volume, for use of banners in Pre-Columbian Mesoamerican warfare; see chapters by Bassie-Sweet and Tokovinine, this volume, for acquisition of/competition between deities in Pre-Columbian Mesoamerican warfare).

As a result of the violence and ruthlessness of the Spanish Conquest under Pedro de Alvarado, few highland Maya rulers survived to administer their lands as *caciques*. By the time Alonso López de Cerrato came to power as the governor of Guatemala in 1548 CE and instituted reforms aimed at establishing legitimate Spanish law, he lamented that "when the Spaniards entered this land, they killed some *caciques* and removed others from their thrones to such an extent that in all this province there is almost no natural nor legitimate *cacique*" (*Relación Cerrato*, in Carmack and Mondloch 1983, 379). The continuation of an unbroken sequence of Tz'utujil lords in orderly succession after the Spanish Conquest is thus exceptional among the highland Maya.

The first Tz'utujil *cacique*, don Pedro, remained in power at Chiya' until his death and the accession of his son, don Juan. Don Juan was succeeded by his son, don Bernabé, demonstrating that there was a regular order of succession within the Tz'utujil royal family. In 1630 CE a Jesuit missionary and naturalist, Father Bernabé Cobo, visited the Tz'utujil ruler. Father Cobo noted in a letter to a friend in Peru that the Tz'utujil *cacique* had in his possession a painted cloth showing his grandfather greeting the first Spaniards: "Adjacent to the Guest House was the house of the *cacique*, where I saw a painted *lienzo* showing the arrival of the Spaniards in this land and the *cacique* who received him in peace offering gifts. And the *cacique* who showed me this history was the grandson of he who was depicted in the painting" (Vásquez de Espinosa 1944, 195–196, translation by the author).

The office of *cacique* thus remained in the old ruling family in Santiago Atitlan well into the seventeenth century CE, likely preserving much of the old power structure without serious disruption. Thus immediate authority in the secular and likely religious affairs of the community remained in the hands of local Maya lords.

The Maya of Santiago Atitlan are remarkably traditional, maintaining core elements of ancient Maya theology and ceremonialism to this day. The surprising degree of conservatism in Tz'utujil compared to many other highland Maya communities may stem in part from this early colonial political arrangement. While the kings who ruled the major K'iche' and Kaqchikel lineages were tortured and executed at the hands of the Spaniards and their capital cities burned, Alvarado left the Tz'utujil ruling dynasty intact to administer its affairs much as they had done prior to the Conquest. It is likely that the Tz'utujils considered this a sign of divine favor and were thus less susceptible to radical shifts in their own traditional worldview.

Maya rulers represented the embodiment of divine power to act in earthly affairs, a belief noted by Spanish authorities. López de Cerrato wrote a warning in 1552 CE that native *caciques* like don Pedro in Santiago Atitlan wielded tremendous religious as well as political power over their subjects and could prove dangerous if they were to rebel "because anciently they revered [the *caciques*] as gods, and if this persists, the lords could raise the land easily" (Carmack 1973, 379). The survival of the Tz'utujil king and his continued dominance at Chiya' where the old temples still stood must have seemed a confirmation to the local populace that the old order continued to hold relevance in Post-Conquest society.

In contrast to the fatalistic acceptance of defeat found in K'iche' and Kaqchikel accounts of the Conquest as well as contemporary myths, most legends told by Tz'utujils about the arrival of the Spaniards emphasize the supernatural power of their ancient kings and gods in escaping the destruction that befell other highland Maya kingdoms. This version is from a personal communication from Nicolás Chávez, a traditionalist Tz'utujil Maya from Santiago Atitlan:

> In a great battle near Chukumuk [a small settlement near the lake, northeast of town], Rey Tz'utujil threw down a great stone before the invaders, which broke into 2,000 pieces, each becoming a crab, which pinched the Spaniards and halted their advance. He then blew in their direction, causing a wind, which killed many of the invaders and drove them into the lake. Rey Tepepul then hurled a long staff at them, which became a serpent that killed many more.
>
> In those days the lake was lower and you could walk on dry land to the old capital city across the bay. But when the Spaniards came[,] the daughter of Rey Tepepul, a girl named María, stood on the peninsula and wept making the water rise and drowning the Spaniards who wished to cross. That is why the Virgin María owns the lake and has her home there.

From Nicolás's account and many other similar legends about the Conquest, you would hardly know that the Tz'utujils had lost the war against the Spaniards. The Virgin Mary is already assimilated into the Maya pantheon as the daughter of the deified king of Chiya', as well as the patron goddess of Lake Atitlan. Christian gods and saints actually sided with their ancestors to protect them from the destruction that visited neighboring highland Maya kingdoms. In the

FIGURE 2.4. *Virgin Mary, Cofradía of San Gregorio, Santiago Atitlan*

Cofradía of San Gregorio is an image of the Virgin Mary dressed in traditional Tz'utujil costume and surrounded by aquatic shells (figure 2.4). This image is said to be the same Virgin Mary who saved their ancestors from the Spaniards and is now the patron goddess of Lake Atitlan. She is said to live in a house at the bottom of the lake surrounded by those who died by drowning, and a huge serpent guards her throne. Nearly everyone has stories about people falling asleep in their canoes while fishing and awaking to see eerie lights far below the surface. These lights are said to be from Mary's palace, and frequently the dead rise up to try to drag the living fishermen down below. For this reason, very few venture out on the lake after dark.

For many Tz'utujils, the Spanish Conquest was not a catastrophic event that ended Maya culture but a kind of death followed by rebirth that is not different in kind from other periodic world renewals that took place prior to the Conquest and continue to some degree today. Although Tz'utujil gods and saints

FIGURE 2.5. *Santiago, central altarpiece, Santiago Atitlan church*

commonly bear European names, they often represent fusions with ancient Maya gods who retain their Pre-Columbian roles in society, particularly as guardians of the community. Soon after the Spanish Conquest, Christian saints were adopted by the Maya as a means of integrating their power into their own indigenous theological system. Maya ceremonialism thus evolved over time by accumulation, adding newer elements to older traditions rather than replacing them by substitution. Tz'utujil gods are not omnipotent; nor do they live forever. They age, die, and are reborn parallel with the endless cycles of the world such as the change of seasons, the movements of the sun, and the orderly unfolding of the calendar. When the images of the old gods were gathered up and burned by the early Christian missionaries, they essentially died. But this was death of a certain kind, consistent with the Maya view that death is followed by rebirth, just as sunrises always follow sunsets. In this case, the old gods were reborn as Christian saints and deities, although they maintained in fundamental ways their essentially Maya character. Santiago, the adopted patron saint of the people of Santiago Atitlan, may appear to all the world to be a Christian saint, but he speaks only Tz'utujil and fiercely guards the community against its enemies, including those of Spanish descent (figure 2.5).

Recently, a traditionalist Maya priest asked me why North Americans are so fascinated by the end of the ancient Maya calendar in 2012 CE. I told him that they mistakenly believe the Maya claimed the world would end when the calendar completed its cycle. He replied that of course the world would die. When I looked surprised by his answer, he laughed and said the world dies all the time—every evening when the sun sets, at the end of the rainy season, at Easter, at harvest time, on New Year's Eve, and on and on. He told me not to worry since he and the other Maya priests were always able to get it going again with their prayers and ceremonies.

For the Maya of Santiago Atitlan, the world is under constant threat of disaster. If the proper rituals are not carried out at the proper time, the world will sink back into the primordial world of darkness and endless death. In the meantime, the Maya rely not only on their own traditional gods but also on former Christian saints like the Virgin Mary and Santiago to protect them. Rather than imposed deities, they function in Tz'utujil communities as benevolent protectors who once saved their ancestors from destruction during the Spanish Conquest and continue to watch over them today. I once asked a traditionalist Maya confraternity why it is that the Virgin Mary would help the Tz'utujils when she herself originally came from far away. He replied, "It's true that Santiago and Mary were once foreigners, but now they are Tz'utujils and only speak Tz'utujil. I don't know how it happened. It just did." The fact that they have such powerful allies is comforting in the face of a world that is often violent and cruel.

3

Maya Warfare, Symbols, and Ritual Landscapes

CHRISTOPHER L. HERNANDEZ AND JOEL W. PALKA

On April 9, 2003 CE in Firdos Square, Baghdad, Iraq, US marines along with an Iraqi crowd toppled a massive statue of Saddam Hussein. Although some reports suggest that the destruction of the statue was staged (Maass 2011; Zucchino 2004), in the United States this event was primarily disseminated by broadcast media as representing the triumph of US armed forces in Iraq. Saddam Hussein's regime was crumbling because Baghdad was entering US control. The actions in Firdos Square on April 9, 2003 CE were not of logistical importance in the Iraq War, yet the images from that day are perhaps the most enduring of the war.

Although the actions in Firdos Square and the Maya case studies examined in this chapter occur in different contexts (political, economic, cultural), the toppling of the Saddam Hussein statue provides a comparative example for the central argument: the practice of warfare and conflict in general involves material and immaterial factors that are central to associated outcomes (e.g., Ferguson 2001; Harris 1979). The destruction of the statue in Firdos Square was a symbolic act of warfare and dominance. This event symbolized triumph, not because it involved a resource or material the US armed forces were trying to

DOI: 10.5876/9781607328872.c003

FIGURE 3.1. *Aztec symbol of conquest (redrawn from Marcus 1992a, 369).*

acquire or destroy in terms of logistics but because the statue stood for Saddam Hussein and his regime. In war, appropriating symbols can be just as important as the control of material resources (e.g., Davis 1999).

The destruction of monuments and their associated landscapes is a common warfare practice for modern nation-states (Chapman 1994, 120; Davis 2000, 89; Rashid 2001). Such practice highlights the fact that objects and landscapes have meaning for people, and their destruction is central to the conduct of war. As a consequence, culture is central to understanding the practice of warfare (Nielsen and Walker 2009, 1–2). Scholars have analyzed symbols associated with Maya warfare, but few have focused on contextualizing symbols as part of combat or the theater of war. In the Maya case, we are not arguing that war was ritual-ized in the sense that it was politically and economically inconsequential and game-like because of cultural/ritual constraints (cf. Arkush and Stanish 2005; Roscoe 2011, 57). We demonstrate that war, culture, and their mutual entangle-ments are vital to understanding how war is waged, won, and lost. For the Maya, the maintenance and destruction of meaningful objects and landscapes could and did have political and economic consequences. In this chapter, we further establish and expand on the above points, in addition to those introduced in the previous chapter by Christenson (this volume), by arguing that the protection and destruction of the material manifestations of supernatural forces and the practice of Maya warfare were inextricably linked.

While Mesoamerican warfare was related to group and personal concerns (e.g., politics, economics, survival), the manner in which war was conducted and how its outcomes were determined also had religious underpinnings (Brown and Stanton 2003; Early 2006, 105–117; Gutiérrez 2014; Hassig 1992, 168–169). Victory frequently involved the destruction of the enemy's sacred places, capture of reli-gious images of the vanquished, and the severing of ties between a defeated community and its patron spiritual forces (see also chapter by Tokovinine, this

FIGURE 3.2. *Mixtec conquest of a pillar that holds the sky, or sacred mountain island. Note the* atlatl *dart embedded in the right edge of the mountain above a symbol for a cave from* Codex Nuttall.

volume). The Aztecs and Mixtecs represented conquest in their codices with images of burning temples and darts embedded in mountains (figures 3.1 and 3.2), in part because of their links to lineages, territories, and spiritual forces. For matters of the state, including warfare, Mesoamerican elites sought divine guidance and protection by consulting oracles in temples, mountains, and caves. In addition, archaeologists have discovered fortifications protecting Maya and Mesoamerican sites, their temples, and ritual areas (Armillas 1951; Demarest et al. 1997; Lothrop 1924; Rice et al. 2009, 132–135). Moreover, the Venus/star hieroglyph has been interpreted as an attack on a specific place, weeping at an attacked place, or describing the place as entering the underworld (Chinchilla Mazariegos 2006). These insights help explain why the Classic Maya portrayed conquest in hieroglyphic texts with a shell or star symbol with water or rain over the place name or sacred cave glyph of the defeated city (figure 3.3). It is possible that the shell-rain-place hieroglyph represented the war metaphor of "scorch/ fire-rain/water" or the destruction from two opposing elements from Aztec culture (Gutiérrez 2014, 146). Success in war was also related to the preservation of a community's sacred places (Brady and Colas 2005, 160–163) and religious images (Martin 1996, 228–229); in other words, the practice of Mesoamerican warfare involved attacking what was sacred for your enemies and protecting what you and your community considered sacred.

FIGURE 3.3. *Venus/star hieroglyph (redrawn from Famsi.org)*

We argue that the practices concerning the protection and destruction of sacred places in Mesoamerica were related to the covenants or agreements between people and the resident spiritual forces in ritual landscapes (e.g., Monaghan 1995). This practice was for mutual benefit and the maintenance of cosmic balance. People's lives depended on the safety of and sustained communication with these spiritual forces (Astor-Aguilera 2010; Palka 2014). This communication took place through images of the spiritual forces that were attached to sacred places, such as temples, hills, caves, and islands. These places and deity images had to be protected during times of conflict because the future of the community and the communication with its tutelary deities rested on their preservation.

Warfare was one source of power for Maya elites and according to current research could lead to the formation of polities that were regionally dominant during the Classic (250–900 CE), Postclassic (900/1000–1525 CE),[1] and early Spanish Colonial (1525–1697 CE) periods (Carmack 1981; A. Chase and D. Chase 1998, 21, 23; Chase, Chase, and Smith 2009, 175–177; Fox 1978; Hassig 1992, 123–134, 161–162; Martin and Grube 2008, 17–21). War was also a source of captives who were central to ancient Maya religion, which required the sacrifice of human blood to spiritual forces. Consequently, ancient Maya warfare was inextricably linked with the practice of human sacrifice and thus notions of the sacred and rituals of sacrifice (Boone 1984; Inomata and Triadan 2009, 71, 78; Schele and Miller 1986, 209–240; Vos 1980, 79, 109; Workinger and Joyce 2009, 8). Most commoners and elites likely shared these notions of the sacred because the presentation of captives and their sacrifice would on occasion become a mass spectacle in the plazas and temples of ancient Maya sites (Inomata 2006, 197–200; Tozzer 1941, 119). To make our points on war, religion, and their connection to sacred places, we turn to ethnohistoric evidence from the Maya region.

ETHNOHISTORY

We present the following case studies in chronological order to highlight the fact that religion, symbols, and ritual landscapes played important roles in Pre-Columbian (prior to 1525 CE), Colonial (1525–1821 CE), and Modern (1821–present CE) Maya warfare. Before we delve into the case studies, we would like to present some background on our sources to provide context for the narratives we employ—all accounts of events are culturally framed, and Spanish historical documents are no different. The Spanish Conquest of the Americas was primarily concerned with the acquisition of wealth, prestige, and the souls of the indigenous people. These concerns were not mutually exclusive. The Spanish documents reflect these concerns, and many were written as moral tales that, at the very least, support Spanish ideologies of superiority and conquest (Carrasco 2008, xv–xvi; Jones 1998, xxi). This ideological purpose frames much of the discussion in Spanish accounts of the Americas. In addition, the Spanish colonial empire's concern with conversion meant that colonial authorities, especially priests and missionaries, were greatly concerned with the religious practices of the indigenous peoples of the Americas (Chuchiak 2009). Consequently, they paid careful attention and documented Mesoamerican religious practices, often with the goal of increasing the effectiveness and quantity of indigenous conversions to Christianity; thus the inherent bias of these sources is readily acknowledged. Yet in the following sections we demonstrate how these more recent sources do contain valuable insights into indigenous modes of conflict and warfare by examining the presence of a continuity in Maya war that stretches from the Pre-Columbian to modern eras.

Sources

We begin with the *Report and Census of the Indians of Cozumel, 1570*, published by ethnohistorians Roys, Scholes, and Adams (1940), along with their analysis of ethnohistoric data from Cozumel, Yucatan, Mexico. Our analysis focuses on Roys and colleagues' investigation of the *Historia de Yucatán* by Diego Lopez de Cogolludo that was originally published in 1688 CE. For his *Historia*, the Franciscan historian Diego Lopez de Cogolludo drew from many primary sources, such as Diego de Landa's *Relación de las Cosas de Yucatán* (Jones 1973, 1807). Although Lopez de Cogolludo hailed the Spanish Conquest from a religious standpoint and despised Maya "idolatry," his *Historia* provides vivid descriptions of Cozumel and Maya practices on the island that are supported archaeologically (Patel 2005).

Juan de Villagutierre Soto-Mayor was a lawyer and the official chronicler of the Council of the Indies in Madrid (Jones 1998, xxii), and we draw from his *Historia de la conquista de la provincia de el Itza* (1983 [1701]) for our discussion of Maya warfare at Noh Peten, Petén, Guatemala. Villagutierre Soto-Mayor wrote this document in defense of Martín de Ursúa y Arizmendi, the commander of the conquistadors of Noh Peten. Ursúa's contemporary Spanish colonial authorities critiqued his conquest of the Itza of the Petén lakes region as a huge mistake, inhumane, and a waste of colonial funds (Jones 1998, xxii). Although Villagutierre Soto-Mayor's *Historia* is certainly problematic because of the circumstances under which the document was written, we employ his work because the evidence we muster lends plausibility to Villagutierre Soto-Mayor's discussion of warfare at Noh Peten. We also supplement the writings of Villagutierre Soto-Mayor with the analyses of anthropologists Thompson (1951) and Caso Barrera and Aliphat F. (2002), who synthesize the ethnohistoric data on the Petén-Itza.

In the sections that follow we also draw on historian Kevin Gosner's work on the 1712 Maya revolt in Highland Chiapas, Mexico. Gosner was trained in history and anthropology at the University of Pennsylvania, with a focus on Guatemalan and Mexican colonial history. He draws mainly from Fray Francisco Ximénez's *Historia de la Provincia de San Vicente de Chiapas y Guatemala* (1929) and numerous *testimonios* from the Archivo de las Indias, Seville (see Gosner 1992, 190–196).

We draw from Nelson Reed's (an independent scholar) analysis of the Caste War of Yucatan and *The Proclamation of Juan de la Cruz* that is dated to 1850 CE (Bricker 1981, 187–207). The proclamation was written in Yucatec Mayan, but it is unclear who wrote the document. While the exact date when the document was written is disputed, it is accepted that it dates to the mid- to late 1800s CE (Bricker 1981, 107–108). Juan de la Cruz was a Maya leader during the Caste War who claimed to be able to hear and speak for the voice of God that spoke through a cross. We cross-checked Reed's analysis with the English translated version of *The Proclamation* and with the original Mayan (both published in the appendix of *The Indian Christ, the Indian King*; Bricker 1981, 187–207).

Finally, we employ the work of Victor Montejo, a Jakaltek Maya. He was trained in anthropology at the University of Connecticut and is currently a professor of Native American studies at the University of California–Davis. In *El Q'anil: Man of Lightning* (2001), Montejo presents his critical interpretation of Jakaltek oral narratives that he compiled on the legend of El Q'anil. Monetjo's emic Jakaltek Maya perspective provides a unique departure from the mainly Spanish accounts we employ to discuss Maya warfare.

Case Studies

Communicating with oracles in temples and ritual landscapes for determining the outcomes of events was a major component of consulting spiritual forces in

Maya beliefs. For example, Maya pilgrims would arrive at the island of Cozumel off the east coast of Yucatán to consult oracles "for help in their needs and troubles" and acquire information on everything they desired (Roys, Scholes, and Adams 1940, 5–6). In Late Postclassic (1200–1525 CE) Yucatán and nearby regions, Maya needs and troubles likely included conflict and knowing outcomes of wars that were prevalent during this period (Hassig 1992, 155–161). One of the oracles consulted in temple shrines at Cozumel, which were typically located near caves and *cenotes* (Shankari 2005, 101–102), was named Ah Hulneb or Ah Hulane. Both names translate as "archer," which was derived from the Yucatec Mayan *aj*, "he of," and *hul*, "arrow/dart" (Roys, Scholes, and Adams 1940, 6). The representation of this divine being, who was perhaps consulted in matters of war, had an arrow painted on it and may have been of Aztec influence (Roys, Scholes, and Adams 1940).

The island of Noh Peten in northern Guatemala, occupied by the Itzaj Maya during the Postclassic (900–1525 CE) to early Spanish Colonial (1525–1697 CE) periods, may have also been an important place for communicating with spiritual forces during times of conflict. Itzaj Maya conceived of Noh Peten as the center of their quadripartite cosmos, and the island contained important temples that were homes for oracles (Caso Barrera and Aliphat F. 2002, 726). The island was also important for defense; however, since large numbers of Maya lived on the lakeshore and away from the lake (Villagutierre Soto-Mayor 1983 [1701], 297), it could not have immediately protected them all from attack. The walls and fortifications built on Noh Peten at the time of the conquistadors' attack were probably constructed to protect the island's inhabitants, temples, and the images of the supernatural forces housed within. Itzaj Maya effectively sought protection from their resident spiritual forces in the temples and within the walls of the island. In fact, one oracular image warned the Itzaj Maya on Noh Peten that "the following day the Spanish will come, and they should get ready and build up their morale in order to defeat them, and for this purpose the idol would offer his assistance so they [Spanish invaders] could be sacrificed and their flesh eaten" (Villagutierre Soto-Mayor 1983 [1701], 315). When the Spanish attacked, the Itzaj Maya begged the image to help them and then shot arrows at the image when it appeared that defeat was imminent (Villagutierre Soto-Mayor 1983 [1701], 315–316).

One Itzaj oracle in a main temple on Noh Peten was called Hobol ("hollow [belly]") and was used to contain sacrificial victims (Villagutierre Soto-Mayor 1983 [1701], 302) and perhaps Maya oracular priests (as was the case on Cozumel). Thompson (1951, 392) included this deity as one of the Itzaj Maya gods of battle. Perhaps this divine entity was the god of battle that was located in the main temple at Noh Peten. The conquistadors described the temple as built like a fortress (Villagutierre Soto-Mayor 1983 [1701], 313–314). Two other important images related to battle and kept in temples by the Itzaj for communication with divine forces were called Pakoc (Pecoc?) and Kexchunchan (Hunchuchan?). Both images may have been deified ancestors (Villagutierre Soto-Mayor 1983 [1701], 302–303; Thompson 1951, 392). Itzaj Maya warriors carried these images with them when they went into battle (a familiar convention; see chapters by Christenson and Tokovinine, this volume). On these occasions they would burn copal incense for the images, perform valiant actions for them, and provide them with prayers, music, dance, and offerings (Villagutierre Soto-Mayor 1983 [1701], 303). During armed campaigns, the images communicated (it is unclear exactly how) with the Itzaj Maya, who consulted them on matters of war.

The regional Maya revolt of 1712, centered on the indigenous town of Cancuc in Highland Chiapas, provides another example of the protection of Maya sacred space and spiritual forces during war. The revolt began when a Tzeltal Maya woman and town officials claimed to have communicated with the Virgin Mary, who gave them the power to preside over local religious and political matters. They constructed a shrine dedicated to the Virgin on a forested hill near Cancuc that subsequently became a major pilgrimage sanctuary for the Maya of Chiapas (Gosner 1992, 122–123, 144). After local Spanish priests threatened to dismantle and burn the shrine, the devout Maya rebelled to protect it. The Maya then fortified the high ground of the town and shrine with trenches, palisades, and walls of woven sticks and cloth to keep Spanish forces at bay (Gosner 1992, 136, 146–147). From messages spoken by the images of the Virgin Mary, the Maya understood that the Virgin would empower them against their enemies and that all Maya killed in the conflict would come back to life (Gosner 1992, 131, 145–147). The rebellion came to an end when the Spaniards breached the Maya defenses and captured the town and shrine. The Spanish then dispersed the rebel command and army. The Spaniards later forced the Maya to abandon the town and the shrine so they would not continue to rebel.

In the nineteenth century CE, before battles, Maya rebel leaders who participated in the *Guerra de Castas* (Caste War of Yucatán) would consult a small speaking cross carved in a tree near a hidden sacred *cenote* in the remote forests in the southern part of the peninsula (Reed 1964, 135). These Maya later constructed a platform on a hill just east of the *cenote*, where they erected a large wooden cross (Reed 1964, 136). On this hill, the Maya prayed to the cross, its associated divine forces, and the sacred place where the cross was located to release the Maya from oppression. The oracular cross responded to the rebels through a Maya ventriloquist. The cross told the rebels to resist their non-religious Ladino enemies, to have no fear since they would be protected from bullets, and to attack the village of Kampocolche. These statements indicate that the rebel Maya believed they were supported and protected in combat by divine forces. When a Ladino force attacked the cross shrine to destroy it and render it ineffective for rallying rebel Maya, they found that a village of more than a thousand

Maya had been quickly created around the hill. Maya from other settlements had also recently clustered nearby, seeking the protection and advice of the talking cross (Reed 1964, 136).

The contemporary and historical beliefs of Jakaltek Maya are very explicit with regard to war, ritual landscapes, power, and divine protection, as these passages by Montejo (2001, xv–xxv) indicate:

> Jakaltek elders still climb to the peak of Mount Q'anil [mountain flanking the town of Jacaltenango that contains ruins] to burn copal and black tallow candles, praying to Komam Yahaw SatKanh [*mam* and *yahaw* are common Mayan terms for mountain gods][,] the lord of the sky, for Q'anils protection of the children of Jacaltenango. This ceremony occurs especially when young men are conscripted for [modern] military service and when there are reports of imminent war . . . because the ancestors believed that in wartime a Q'anil (Man of Lightning) lives in each and every Jakaltek. Many declared that when there was war, the k'uh (lightning bolt) would thunder on the mountain and a red flag would appear on the peak of Q'anil Mountain as a sign of danger and of the presence of the town's protector. The legend tells that our protector, the Man of Lightning, always walks before the sons of Jacaltenango and protects them, destroying all dangers and obstacles in their path. Q'anil is a more humanitarian patron of war, chosen by our ancestors over the bloodthirsty Tojil of other peoples who, according to the Popol Wuj, came from the East. They [historic highland Maya] undergo magical trials, then perform an act which transforms them into spirit-beings of great power. They totally destroy the people of the faraway place, using magical weapons . . . Other ethnohistorical documents give accounts of the transformation of some indigenous captains into lightning bolts [like Tlaloc, a Mesoamerican war deity] in order to defeat Pedro de Alvarado. [bracketed comments are additions by Hernandez and Palka]

This Jakaltek Maya history underscores the importance of communicating with protective forces on mountains during times of conflict in indigenous societies. The fortified Maya ruins on mountains contained temples and altars for the purpose of this communication. Stone stelae from Maya sites across the border from the Jakaltec in Chiapas most likely depict elite warriors with "lightning spears" standing atop local ritual mountains (Palacios 1928, 121) (figure 3.4). In other Maya images, warriors with spears and spearthrowers wear Tlaloc or goggle-eyed storm god masks, which identify them as lightning bolt hurlers (Schele and Miller 1986, figs. V.3, V.4, plate 78; see chapter by Bassie-Sweet, this volume) (figure 3.5). Consequently, there is a case for a long-held belief among the Maya that protective spirits in mountains could provide supernatural abilities for warriors. The ethnohistoric case studies presented above reveal that notions of the sacred and their material manifestations were important for

FIGURE 3.5. *Maya vessel from Balankanché Cave, Yucatán, depicting a Tlaloc warrior (redrawn from Andrews 1970, 33). Image by Paulina Makuch.*

FIGURE 3.4. *Maya stela from the Chiapas highlands showing a noble warrior brandishing a spear (lightning bolt?) and shield on a ritual mountain (wits) (Palacios 1928, 121).*

not only influencing Maya warfare but also determining its outcome(s). These insights into the centrality of the assistance and protection of deities found in sacred places during times of conflict in the Maya past and present can help scholars interpret the archaeological record. Next, we turn to archaeological evidence for an attack on a Maya ritual landscape and resident spiritual forces from the Petén-Itzá region of Guatemala.

ZACPETEN MASS BURIAL, DESECRATORY TERMINATION RITUAL DEPOSITS, AND WAR

The ancient Maya practiced a variety of termination rituals that were meant to remove or kill the spiritual/animating forces of objects. A termination ritual could be part of a cycle of life and death in which an object was terminated

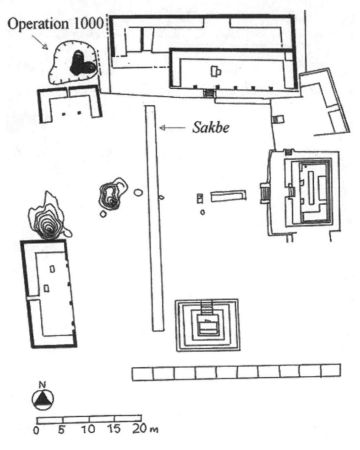

FIGURE 3.6. *Group A at Zacpeten with the mass burial (Operation 1000) in the upper left (redrawn from Pugh 2003, 421). Image by Paulina Makuch.*

to give life to or animate another object(s), such as a dedicatory cache in a plaza (Freidel, Schele, and Parker 1993, 234, 244; Mock 1998). Termination rituals could also simply serve to kill an object, ending or removing its spiritual/animating forces (Duncan 2009, 363). A mass burial recovered from Zacpeten, Petén, Guatemala likely provides archaeological evidence for a desecratory termination ritual deposit: the "result of purposeful destruction and manipulation of material culture for the furtherance of goals aimed at destroying the supernatural power of a defeated community or faction" (Pagliaro, Garber, and Stanton 2003, 77). Such deposits "exhibit purposeful destruction of material culture and symbols of power, including elite architecture and burials," and therefore are acts linked to warfare and dominance (Pagliaro, Garber, and Stanton 2003, 75, 77).

The Kowoj site of Zacpeten is located on a peninsula on the northeastern edge of Lake Salpetén and was most heavily populated during the period 1400–1697 CE (Pugh and Rice 2009b, 85). The site consists of ceremonial and residential structures that were defended by a series of ditches and walls (Rice et al. 2009, 132–135). In the northwest corner of Group A, Duncan (2009) and colleagues excavated a mass burial that they designated as Operation 1000 (figure 3.6). The burial consisted of the disarticulated human skeletal remains of at least thirty-seven individuals that were deposited in one episode (Duncan 2009, 341, 344). Once the mass burial was interred and covered with a layer of stones, the depression in the northwest corner of Group A was not used again. The bones, which in Mesoamerica were generally considered ritually potent objects that could be used to communicate with ancestral spirits (Astor-Aguilera 2010; Houston, Stuart, and Taube 2006), were interred in a secondary context with no grave goods (Duncan 2009, 362). The long bones exhibited cut marks consistent with de-fleshing that does not appear to be associated with an act of cannibalism and likely resulted from non-cannibalistic ritual removal of tissue. The unordered piling of the bones in Operation 1000 does not indicate that the mass burial was designed to honor an interred group or individual because there was no individual(s) in a central position or any that stood out from the rest of the skeletal remains (Robin 1989, 128–130).

Duncan (2009, 361) argued that it was unlikely that the creation of the mass burial resulted from the interment of war dead or "individuals killed or captured in a raid . . . the single most parsimonious scenario for the creation of Operation 1000 is the exhumation of previously interred enemy ancestors" that were then deposited in the mass burial. Duncan concedes that his argument is problematic because the source(s) of the skeletal remains is unknown; therefore, it is impossible to know if the interred individuals were enemy ancestors. Even accepting Duncan's argument that the individuals in the mass burial were enemy ancestors, we argue that Operation 1000 was still the result of war dead and captured individuals. Regardless of who the individuals in the mass burial were, we argue that Group A may be interpreted more successfully as a desecratory termination ritual deposit that was an act of warfare involving a ritual landscape. Our argument is not mutually exclusive with Duncan's thesis. Instead, we argue that Duncan too narrowly defines the concepts of war, life, and the individual in the ancient Maya context. The creation of Operation 1000 demonstrates that the interred bones had animating forces and were important objects and possibly individuals to be captured in war, especially if Duncan is correct that the skeletal remains in the mass burial were those of enemy ancestors. The positioning of the Group A mass burial is crucial to our interpretation.

The ancient Maya commonly associated West with death (Ashmore 1991, 212; Duncan 2009, 365; Miller 1974). Group A at Zacpeten is divided into eastern and western portions by a small *sakbe*, or raised path that runs north to south through the plaza (Pugh 2003, 422) (see figure 3.6). Pugh (2003, 423) argues that the east and west sides of Group A that are separated by the *sakbe* were meant to express Maya cosmology. The structures on the east side of Group A were built on top of high platforms, and two of the buildings were houses for deity effigy censers, otherwise known as god houses. In contrast, the structures on the west side were not built on platforms and contained no remains of deity effigy censers. Also, several cave formations known as speleothems, which are not local to Zacpeten, were found on the west side of the plaza. Overall, the east-west divide consists of a west side associated with the underworld, lowness, and most likely death, while the east side conversely emphasizes height that is linked to the heavens and rebirth (Ashmore 1991; Mathews and Garber 2004; Miller 1974). The placement of the mass burial in a depression in the northwest corner of the sacred landscape of Group A seems to be part of an overall scheme that represented dual oppositions of life/death and heavens/underworld that were basic components of Maya cosmologies (Bassie-Sweet 2008, 3; Schele and Miller 1986).

In the larger political context, the Group A mass burial was created during the period of political disintegration at Mayapan (Duncan 2009, 342). This political transformation is important because Kowoj elites stressed ties to Mayapan (Jones 2009, 60–62). During the late fourteenth and/or early fifteenth century CE, Group A at Zacpeten was converted into a temple assemblage that closely matches the Chen Mul group from Mayapan (Pugh and Rice 2009a, 163).

The chronologies based on ceramics, stratigraphy, and ^{14}C dating do not provide the necessary precision to determine the exact timing of when the following events took place. Archaeological data paired with ethnohistoric data on Mayapan allow us to suggest the occurrence of the following events during the mid-1300s to mid-1400s CE: (1) Mayapan politically disintegrated and was abandoned, (2) Group A was restructured to resemble architecture from Mayapan, and (3) Operation 1000 was created in a ritual space and was isolated for the remainder of Zacpeten's occupational history (Duncan 2009, 366; Pugh and Rice 2009b, 100, 103; Rice 2009, 34–35). Also, the isolation and unordered interment of bones (MNI = 37) without grave goods occurred in a location associated with death. Together, these factors suggest that Operation 1000 was an act of ritual violation and isolation that was performed by the Kowoj or people who expressed links to Mayapan. Therefore, the mass burial likely provides archaeological evidence for an attack on spiritual forces and the disruption of communication with the deceased. This was also a powerful political act because religion and ritual were important components of Maya politics (Bricker 1981; Caso Barrera and Aliphat F. 2002; Inomata 2006; Roys, Scholes, and Burnham Adams 1940; Schele and Miller 1986; Tedlock 1996; Thompson 1951; Tozzer 1941; Vos 1980).

Returning to the discussion of desecratory termination ritual deposits, Pagliaro and colleagues (2003, 79–80) provide seven lines of evidence that they argue help archaeologists distinguish desecratory termination ritual deposits. We acknowledge that context is more important than a strict adherence to their list of evidence. The case study from Zacpeten matches two of their lines of evidence: "intentional structural damage" and "rapid deposition of material" (Pagliaro, Garber, and Stanton 2003, 79–80). More important, when the Zacpeten mass burial is considered in its cultural and political economic context, it becomes clear that Operation 1000 was intended to be an act of war and ritual violation aimed at breaking the covenants among Zacpeten's inhabitants, supernatural forces, and the Group A ritual landscape. Operation 1000 also likely signaled the defeat of an old regime at Zacpeten and was an important expression of political power at the site. This power struggle materialized itself with the desecration of the bones / individuals interred in the Group A mass burial. In other words, people who expressed links to Mayapan used a ritual landscape and bones to convey a message of dominance to the inhabitants of Zacpeten.

Based on the previous findings, the skeletal materials in Operation 1000 could have been viewed as war captives. The bones had animating forces that were terminated; if they were the remains of enemy ancestors, then they may have been desecrated because of the identity(ies) associated with the skeletal remains. This practice would mirror Classic Maya art in which captives are maltreated after their capture (figure 3.7). Duncan thus seems to define ancient Maya war, life, and the individual as domains of biologically living bodies. However, for the Maya, the individual and life could continue after present-day biomedical professionals would consider a person/people to be dead (Schele and Miller 1986, 265–277; Tedlock 1996, 128–132). Consequently, there may have been little distinction between the capture of human skeletal remains and living (in biomedical terms) captives.

Another group of disarticulated bones has been uncovered at Topoxte, which is also a Kowoj site on an island in the Petén lakes region (Bullard 1970, 267; Duncan 2009, 340). The possible mass burial was found within the fill of Structure L in the northwest corner of a Mayapan-style temple assemblage at the site (Bullard 1970, 254, 267, 273–276; Duncan 2009, 341) (figure 3.8). Thus there seems to be a connection between the Kowoj and the placement of disarticulated skeletal remains within burials in the northwest corners of Mayapan-style temple assemblages. Unfortunately, a detailed analysis of the skeletal remains interred in the fill of Structure L will have to wait for future research because the osteological remains have not been fully excavated. However, based on analogy with Zacpeten, the skeletal remains from Topoxte could be another example of ritual violence executed by the Kowoj or people who expressed links to Mayapan.

FIGURE 3.7. *Image of the presentation and torture of captives from the Murals of Bonampak, Room 2. Note the bleeding fingers of the Maya seated on the stairs. Image from nashua.edu.*

SUMMARY AND CONCLUSIONS

From the evidence we present, it becomes clear that material and immaterial factors were/are central to the successful conduct of Maya warfare. The images of deities and the landscapes they inhabited required protection and were targets in times of war. This practice was a result of the covenants the Maya and other Mesoamerican people had with supernatural forces. These practices help explain archaeological findings, including fortifications around temples, the destruction of elite monuments and burials, the sacking of temples, the building of defensive works surrounding temples and plazas on hilltops, and the hiding of sacred caves. The fortified sites with temples on ritual landscapes, such as Aguateca (Inomata and Triadan 2010), Zaculeu (Fox 1978), Guengola, Monte Alban, and Mitla (Paddock 1966), exemplify the importance of divine protection during times of conflict in Mesoamerica. In these places, native combatants used collective effort to protect their deities. The communication with spiritual forces for protection and divine abilities during warfare may help explain iconography related to war on objects in caves, such as warriors with shields and spears on a carved bone in Oaxaca (Rincón Mautner 2005, 140) and spearthrower-wielding fighters dressed as Tlaloc storm gods on ceramic vessels in Yucatán (Andrews 1970, 33) (see figure 3.5).

The findings also highlight the fact that the practice of Maya and Mesoamerican warfare not only had economic and political causes and consequences but also religious motivations and impacts. Acts of warfare that involve ritual/cultural

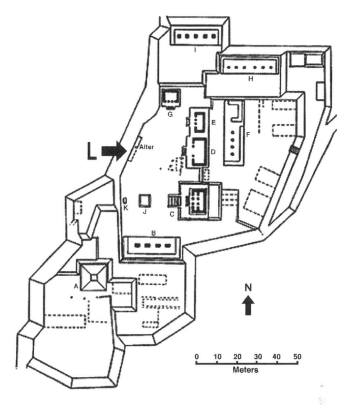

FIGURE 3.8. *Main Group at the Island of Topoxte (Bullard 1970, 254).*

constraint are not examples of fake war and are not politically insignificant, as some scholars have suggested (Alach 2011, vii–viii; Hanson 2000, xxv; Turney-High 1949, 254), but are vital to the practice of warfare. In fact, we challenge any person to find a case in which war was not practiced under cultural constraint/restraint. War is not a-cultural, and neither are the people who practice it. In the Maya examples, just as in the toppling of the Saddam Hussein statue, people found it important to draw on shared cultural understandings as they practiced war. We hope that the parallels between the events in Firdos Square and our Maya case studies have now become apparent. In Iraq, a public space and statue were used to convey a message of dominance. The Iraq War example and Maya case studies we presented also involved materially destructive conflicts between social groups in which symbols had strategic value (e.g., Clausewitz 1976 [1832]). The destruction of symbols can be more important for achieving victory than the physical destruction of life and objects. We are not excluding the possibility that the Maya associated multiple meanings and spatial patterns (triads, quadripartites) with symbols and ritual landscapes. Part of our point in discussing the Iraq case study has been to highlight the complexity of sending messages through performance and the flaw in assigning singular meanings to places and objects. We merely highlight that within the Late Postclassic Maya context, the creators of Operation 1000 drew from preexisting, culturally shared ideas of duality and cosmology to send a message of dominance. How that message was received and interpreted is a question for another paper. The Iraq case study has subsequently demonstrated that people do not interpret the destruction of meaningful objects and places in the same manner. Nonetheless, meaning and symbols are central in war.

NOTE

1. The end of the Postclassic and the onset of Contact/Colonial period varies in the Maya area because the change in culture-historical periods is marked by the arrival of the Spanish, the beginning of the Spanish Conquest in a particular region, or both. We chose to mark the end of the Postclassic with the start of Hernán Cortés and his group of con-quistadors' march across the Maya lowlands after his conquest of the Aztec Empire.

4

Classic Maya Gods of Flint and Obsidian

KAREN BASSIE-SWEET

The identification of deities with flora, fauna, materials, and objects is a well-known characteristic of Mesoamerican culture. The topic of this chapter is the deities specifically equated with flint (a sedimentary cryptocrystalline form of quartz) and obsidian (volcanic glass) by the Maya.[1] The thunderbolt deities known as Chahks are among the earliest gods documented in the Maya region, and many different types appear in Maya art and are named in the hieroglyphic texts (Bassie-Sweet 2008, 102–124; Lacadena 2004; Spero 1987; Stuart 1995; Taube 1992a, 17–27, 69–79; Thompson 1970, 251–269). It has long been established that the Maya believed thunderbolts were the flint axes of the Chahk deities. There is also a Classic-period Teotihuacan rain and thunderbolt deity who has been identified as the precursor of the Postclassic Aztec deity named Tlaloc (Pasztory 1974); it is unknown what name the Teotihuacanos used for this storm deity, so I will continue to refer to him as Tlaloc for lack of a better alternative. The Teotihuacan Tlaloc cult spread throughout the Maya lowlands during the late fourth century CE, along with Teotihuacan-style architecture, ceramic vessels, and war imagery (see Braswell 2003c for a

DOI: 10.5876/9781607328872.c004

general overview). While he appears frequently in Classic Maya art, Tlaloc did not replace the traditional Chahk deities who remained just as prominent. In Classic Maya art, Tlaloc and his avatars are consistently depicted in association with obsidian blood letters and weapons. There is significant evidence that meteors were envisioned to be obsidian weapons thrown by the gods and that the Maya categorized meteors as a type of thunderbolt (Taube 2000b, 325). It is my contention that the Teotihuacan Tlaloc was assimilated into Maya culture as an obsidian and meteor god. I will further argue that the Maya rulers and their wives who carry the title of Kaloomte' and who are often illustrated in the guise of Tlaloc performing blood sacrifices with obsidian implements were high priests and priestesses of the Tlaloc cult. Obsidian, which had to be acquired from highland locations, was also associated with the Maya patron god of long-distance traders known by the nickname God L.

SOURCES AND USES OF FLINT AND OBSIDIAN

The Maya lowland region consists predominately of a karst platform dominated by limestone bedrock. Limestone was the primary material used in ancient building construction and was also burned to produce the lime used in plaster. Flint is found in limestone formations throughout much of the lowlands, although certain areas consist of higher-quality deposits, such as the flint-bearing zone of northern Belize. In contrast to the wide distribution of flint, obsidian is only found in certain volcanic locations in the highlands of Guatemala and Mexico and had to be imported by the lowland Maya. During the Classic period (250–900 CE), the three primary Guatemalan sources in descending order of importance were El Chayal, Ixtepeque, and San Martín Jilotepeque (Golitko et al. 2012). Although not plentiful, Central Mexican obsidian, particularly the superior green obsidian from the Pachuca sources that were controlled by Teotihuacan, was also present in the Maya lowlands and even appeared at highland Guatemalan sites that had easy access to local sources.

Across Mesoamerica, flint (proto-Mayan *tyooq'*) and obsidian (proto-Mayan *tyaah*) (Kaufman 2003, 442) were used to create utilitarian and ritual tools as well as weapons such as axes, hammers, darts, spears, and arrows. In addition, both flint and obsidian were knapped into exotic shapes nicknamed "eccentrics." The superior sharpness of obsidian makes it a better cutting and slicing tool, although not as durable as flint. The Lacandon Maya, who were still using flint and obsidian arrowheads for hunting well into the twentieth century CE, observed that a flint arrowhead might kill a bird, but an obsidian one would certainly do so (Nations and Clark 1983). The durability and strength of flint is seen in the Classic-period production of jade objects that employed flint hammer stones, drills, and triangular blades (Kovacevich 2011, 155, 158; Rochette 2009).

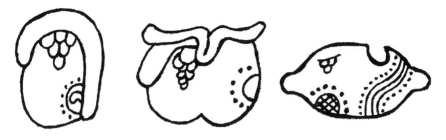

FIGURE 4.1. a, tuun *"stone" glyph;* b, witz *"mountain" glyph; and* c, tok *"flint" glyph.*

REPRESENTATIONS OF STONE AND FLINT

The words for stone and flint are represented in hieroglyphic writing by both phonetic renderings and logographic signs. The T528 sign is a logograph representing the word *tuun* "stone" (Western Mayan *toonh*) (Kaufman 2003, 436; Stuart 1996). It is a profile view of a limestone cave mouth with stylized stalactites hanging from the ceiling (Bassie-Sweet 1991, 108–109) (figure 4.1a). Caves containing such speleothems (cave deposits) are a common feature of karst topography. The stylized stalactites of the T528 sign look like a cluster of grapes, which, not surprisingly, is one of the modern nicknames for this type of formation. Given that limestone was the primary stone of the Maya region, it is predictable that the Maya would use a feature of that stone to represent the word *stone*. A second element composed of a circle surrounded by dots appears on the cave wall of the *tuun* sign. Its meaning is uncertain, although it may refer to a pool of water beneath the stalactite or to a cache of corn seeds the Maya believed was hidden in a primordial sacred mountain cave and used to create the flesh of the first humans.

The logograph for the word *witz* "mountain" incorporates these *tuun* "stone" elements, as does the zoomorphic motif that represents a mountain in Maya art (Stuart 1987) (figure 4.1b). These mountain symbols also feature a split element in reference to the myth that a thunderbolt god had to split open the primordial corn mountain to obtain the corn seeds used to create the first humans. In Maya art, illustrations of limestone objects such as altars and stelae are often marked with the *tuun* elements; for example, a scene on a carved peccary skull from Copan shows two lords flanking a stela and an altar, which are both marked with *tuun* elements (Fash 2001, figure 24). A *tuun* marked eccentric (T297) is also used to represent the word *b'ax* "quartz, to hammer" and appears in the Xultun place name B'ax Witz "Quartz Mountain" (Prager et al. 2010). A hammer stone marked with *tuun* elements represents the word *baj* "to hammer" (Zender 2010). Ritual combat scenes illustrate Chahk deities and lords using round, hand-sized stones as striking weapons, and the verb *jatz'* "to strike" is represented by a logograph of a hand holding such a stone marked with *tuun* elements (Taube and Zender 2009; Zender 2004a).

As mentioned above, flint is found in limestone formations. The logographs that represent the word *tok'* "flint" (T112, T245, T257, T354, T786) are images of axes, bifacial knives, or eccentrics that are frequently marked with wavy lines representing the texture of knapped flint, the limestone *tuun* elements, or both (Houston 1983; Schele and Miller 1986, 46; Stone and Zender 2011, figure 27) (figure 4.1c). Some illustrations of flint objects also include dotted wavy lines that refer to the banded lines often seen in flint. *Tuun* marked eccentric flints are common in Maya art, and some scenes illustrate flint axes being used to decapitate victims. The logograph of a flint axe (T190, T333) is used to represent the verb *ch'ak* "to cut or to chop" (Orejel 1990).

The Maya believed that humans who dressed in the costume of a deity became the embodiment of that deity, and many scenes show lords dressed in the mask and costume of a Chahk deity (Houston and Stuart 1996, 1998; see chapter by Christenson, this volume). An example of an axe made of flint is found on the Dumbarton Oaks Tablet that illustrates the young lord K'inich K'an Joy Chitam dressed as a Chahk (Bassie-Sweet 1991, 220–223) (figure 4.2). He is in the process of swinging the axe over his head. The flint head of the axe is marked with both flint and *tuun* elements, while the handle takes the shape of a serpent. The Maya believed not only that thunderbolts were the flint axes thrown by the Chahk gods but that such thunderbolts could also take the form of serpents. K'inich K'an Joy Chitam's lightning serpent also has a lock of tied hair that is associated with Chahk deities.

On three Palenque monuments, the lords K'inich Kan Bahlam, K'inich K'an Joy Chitam, and K'inich Ahkal Mo' Nahb are illustrated receiving an object composed of a personified eccentric flint and a shield (figure 4.3.). In these scenes, Kan Bahlam and K'an Joy Chitam received this flint-shield icon during preaccession ceremonies when they were ages 6 and 9, respectively, while the ruler Ahkal Mo' Nahb received it on the day of his accession at age 44 (Bassie-Sweet 1991, 207, 1996, 228; Bassie-Sweet, Hopkins, and Josserand 2012). In hieroglyphic inscriptions, this icon is literally named *tok'-pakal* "flint-shield" (Houston 1983). As noted by Hopkins (1996), the metonym *tok'-pakal* pairs an offensive weapon with a defensive weapon, and it is a metaphor for all weapons, including those composed of obsidian and stone.

CHAHK GODS

The word *chahk* "thunderbolt" is represented in the hieroglyphic texts by a portrait of a zoomorphic deity wearing a shell earring and a knot of hair (figure 4.4). These Chahk deities are commonly depicted in Classic-period pottery scenes wielding their thunderbolt axes as well as other stone weapons (Taube 1992a;

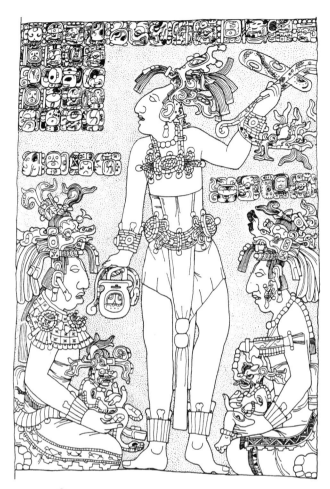

FIGURE 4.2.
Dumbarton Oaks Tablet. Drawing by Linda Schele.

FIGURE 4.3. tok'-pakal *icon*

Taube and Zender 2009). In addition to these types of Chahk deities, there are references to the births and mythological activities of a triad of thunderbolt brothers in the inscriptions of Palenque. These deities have been nicknamed GI, GII, and GIII for the order in which they appear when named together. It has been proposed that this thunderbolt triad was parallel to the three Heart of Sky thunderbolt gods of the *Popol Vuh* (Thunderbolt Huracán, Youngest Thunderbolt, and Sudden Thunderbolt) and that the three hearthstones that mark the center fire of the creator deities were manifestations of these deities (Bassie-Sweet 2008, 107–121). Stuart (2005b; Stuart and Stuart 2008) has argued that GI, GII, and GIII were patron gods of Palenque. While they certainly do function at Palenque as patron deities, all three deities also appear across the Maya region with the same features and attributes, indicating their universal recognition as primary deities (Hellmuth 1987).

The deity GI is depicted as an aquiline-nosed anthropomorphic deity and is prominently featured on Early Classic *incensarios* wearing a distinctive head-dress, nicknamed the Quadripartite Monster motif (figure 4.5). In hieroglyphic texts, GI's personal name is composed of his portrait glyph and the name Chahk. Although his portrait glyph has not been deciphered, the Chahk portion of his personal name indicates beyond a doubt that he was a thunderbolt deity. He has attributes that suggest he was specifically a storm god identified with the Milky Way (Bassie-Sweet 2008, 109–113).[2]

The deity GII is also known by the Schellhas designation of God K (Taube 1992a). In contrast to GI, GII is a zoomorphic Chahk deity who is frequently illustrated with childlike proportions. His portrait glyph has been deciphered based on phonetic substitutions as K'awiil (Stuart 1987). In GII's nominal phrase, the word K'awiil is preceded by the name Unen "child" (Martin 2002). GII is the youngest born of the triad, despite the fact that he is always named in the second position when the triad is named together. GII–Unen K'awiil also carries the *ch'ok* "youth" title, further indicating that he is the junior member of the triad. This parallels the three Heart of Sky thunderbolt gods, where Youngest Thunderbolt is always named in the second position when the triad is listed together. In his full-figure depictions, GII takes the form of a thunderbolt axe, with the blade of the axe protruding from his forehead while one of his legs takes the form of a lightning serpent (figure 4.6). Many illustrations of K'awiil show smoke and fire emanating from the axe blade in reference to the fire caused by a lightning strike. A number of flint eccentrics recovered from caches take the form of K'awiil (Fash 2001, 102, 147; Miller and Martin 2004, 150–151).

Some examples of K'awiil illustrate a burning torch in his forehead rather than an axe head. Thunderbolts are a natural source of fire. The role of fire in Maya mythology is beyond the scope of this chapter; however, as one of the

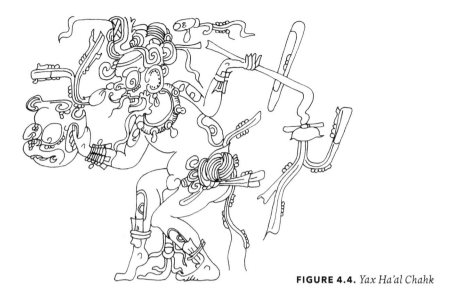

FIGURE 4.4. *Yax Ha'al Chahk*

FIGURE 4.5. *The deity GI*

FIGURE 4.6. *K'awiil*

hearthstone deities, GII was intimately connected to fire and its transformational nature. The nominal phrases of some Classic-period kings reflect Chahk's association with fire, such as the Naranjo rulers K'ahk' Tiliw Chan Chahk ("Chahk who burns the sky with fire") and K'ak' Yipiyaj Chan Chahk ("Chahk who fills the sky with fire") (Martin and Grube 2008).

The name phrase of the deity GIII is not a portrait glyph and has yet to be deciphered; however, it is prefixed with the title *k'inich* "sun-like" and carries the *k'inich ajaw* title most frequently seen in the name phrase of the Sun God but also used by the creator grandfather Itzamnaaj. GIII is also named as a *Yajawk'ahk'* (Stuart 2005b, 18, 123–125; Zender 2004b, 195–209). Zender noted that the term *ajaw* "lord" actually means "vassal" when it is stated in a possessed form such as *y-ajaw-k'ahk'*, and thus this phrase means "the fire's vassal." This title, which is also carried by secondary lords with both clerical and warrior functions, implies that GIII and the *Yajawk'ahk'* lords were vassals of the fire god. Such a role fits with GIII's function as one of the hearthstone gods.

Despite the fact that his nominal phrase is not a portrait glyph, depictions of GIII are abundant in Maya art, and hundreds of *incensarios* bearing his likeness have been found cached in the Palenque Cross Group and across the Maya realm (figure 4.7). Like his brother GI, GIII is an aquiline-nosed anthropomorphic deity, but his most important diagnostic traits are jaguar features (ears and paws) and

FIGURE 4.7. *The deity GIII*

a looped cord over his nose that represents the cord used to drill fire (Taube 2000b). Given this placement of the fire cord, a logical inference is that his body was thought to represent the stick used to create friction when drilling fire. He occasionally has an *ak'ab* "night, darkness" sign on his cheek or a *k'in* sign that is likely a *pars pro toto* reference to his *k'inich* title. On one of the *incensarios* recovered from Palenque Group B, GIII wears the headdress of the *Yajawk'ahk'* office (Lopez Bravo 2000, 40). The Palenque Temple of the Sun is dedicated to GIII, and the central motif of its interior wall panel features two crossed flint spears and a war shield emblazoned with his portrait (figure 4.8).

Given that both of his brothers are thunderbolt deities, it would be expected that GIII also had this function. In his Tablet of the Sun depiction, GIII does have the tied hair associated with Chahk gods; however, establishing his identity is complex and controversial. GIII is most often referred to as the Jaguar God of the Underworld because Thompson (1950) asserted that the jaguar was a god of the underworld. In Thompson's speculation, the Sun God was transformed into a jaguar after sunset and journeyed through the underworld in this form before being transformed back into his diurnal form at dawn. Thompson's identification of GIII as the "night sun" has been widely accepted. Taube and Houston (2015, 213) suggest that GIII may specifically represent the night sun "at his midnight nadir in the underworld." While such a role for a jaguar deity with sun attributes does sound reasonable, there is no evidence from other sources to support it. In fact, jaguars are ubiquitous in Maya writing and art, and they are not specifically associated with the underworld. When day and night are contrasted in hieroglyphic writing, the contrast is always between the Sun God and the *ak'ab* god, not between the Sun God and GIII.[3]

FIGURE 4.8. *Palenque Tablet of the Sun. Drawing by Linda Schele.*

Whether one identifies GIII as the night sun or as a Chahk deity associated with fire, what is important in the context of this discussion is that GIII had an intimate relationship with weapons of war. Across the Maya region, there are numerous depictions of lords carrying a war shield decorated with GIII's portrait. As noted above, the central icon on the Tablet of the Sun features a GIII shield. The scene illustrates two events from the life of K'inich Kan Bahlam. The right side shows him holding the *tok'-pakal* icon when he was a young boy, while the left side depicts his later accession as king where he is pictured holding a GII effigy (Bassie-Sweet 1991). The pairing of flint spears and a shield on the central icon echoes the *tok'-pakal* motif and highlights GIII's association with weapons.

Another Chahk deity with a direct relationship to flint and thunderbolts is named in a number of scenes as Yax Ha'al Chahk "first rain Chahk," who was likely identified with the first rains of the planting season and the dramatic thunderstorms at that time of year (Coe 1973, 98, 1978, 34; Lacadena 2004, 93; Martin 2002; Robicsek and Hales 1981, 1988; Spero 1991, 191–192; Taube 1992a, 19) (see figure 4.4). The anthropomorphic body of Yax Ha'al Chahk is often marked with the T24 sign and serpent scales that emphasize his identification with lightning. Yax Ha'al Chahk most frequently carries an axe with a T24 celt head and a stone *manoplas* (Taube 2004b; Taube and Zender 2009). The T24 sign is a celt-shaped stone with parallel lines drawn on the surface. Although T24 has not been definitively deciphered, it has been interpreted to be a reference to reflectiveness, shininess, or brightness when employed as an infix on objects and deities (Stone and Zender 2011, 71; Stuart 2010). The *Popol Vuh* narrative provides key information regarding the reflective nature of T24 and what it represents. The story begins with a description of the place of duality before the earth and human beings were created (Christenson 2007). It is described as a great pool of tranquil water existing in darkness. Within this water resided the creator grandparents Xpiyacoc and Xmucane who were great sages, possessors of knowledge, and the embodiment of complementary opposition (duality). The creator grandparents were joined by the three Heart of Sky thunderbolt gods, and together they envisioned a world inhabited by human beings who would honor them with offerings. Following this collaborative consultation, these creator deities formed the earth and made the first human beings. The creator grandparents are described within the waters of the place of duality as luminous beings wrapped in iridescent quetzal and cotinga bird feathers. The adjective used to describe their luminous quality is *zaktetoh*, which is defined as "the brightest that enters through cracks" (Christenson 2007, 68). In the K'iche' region, diviners are thought to have a soul that allows them to interpret messages from the gods (Tedlock 1992, 53). This soul takes the form of sheet lightning in their blood. Sheet lighting refers to lightning reflected in clouds that appears as a silent sheet of luminosity rather than a thunderous bolt. It is this luminous quality of sheeting lightning that the creator grandparents possessed. I suggest that the reflectiveness of the T24/T1017 sign represents not just the luminous quality of lightning but also its generative power and that of the creator deities.[4]

While the blade of Yax Ha'al Chahk's axe is most often marked with the T24 sign, it is also depicted as flint from which fire scrolls emanate. In images of Yax Ha'al Chahk, his arm is depicted either drawn back behind his body ready to throw the axe or to strike something or over his head in the forward motion of the throw or strike. The *manoplas* is held in his other hand and is always positioned in front of him. In Mesoamerica, *manoplas* were stone objects often used to deflect blows and were referred to as shields (Taube and Zender 2009, 180; see also chapter by Abtosway and McCafferty, this volume). Yax Ha'al Chahk's axe and *manoplas* represent offensive and defensive weapons, respectively. In some examples, Yax Ha'al Chahk's *manoplas* is marked with the T1017 sign, the personified form of T24. The implication is that both his axe and *manoplas* have luminous quality. On vessel K2208 and K2772, the head of his axe takes the form of a burning torch. This substitution between torches and stone axe heads indicates that the Maya thought thunderbolts could take the form of either object. As noted above, the use of a torch in the context of Chahk's axe emphasizes his association with the fire of the thunderbolt.

FIGURE 4.9. u ch'ab u
ak'ab *phrases*

In summary, flint was intimately identified with the Chahk deities and their thunderbolt weapons. A lord acquired the attributes of the Chahk deities, including the power of the thunderbolt, when he took on the guise of such a deity. Many Maya kings incorporate Chahk names in their regnal nominal phrases.

REPRESENTATIONS OF OBSIDIAN

Obsidian is represented in Maya hieroglyphic writing and art in a form quite distinct from flint and appears in contexts directly related to blood sacrifice. A prime example of obsidian imagery is found in the T712 *ch'ab* "creation" sign that is represented by a hook-shaped obsidian blood-letter (figure 4.9a). In Central Mexican depictions of obsidian, the hooked distal end of a prismatic blade is emphasized (Nielsen and Helmke 2008; Taube 1991, figure 2). Joralemon (1974) identified a personified obsidian blood-letter used for penis perforation that also has the curved shape of a prismatic blade. Bowls containing the T712 obsidian blood-letter as well as prismatic blades, stingray spines, and thorny cords used in bloodletting are illustrated on a number of Yaxchilan lintels (Lintels 13, 14, 15, 17, 24, and 25).

In hieroglyphic writing, two signs could be depicted in separate glyph blocks or combined into one glyph block. The scribe occasionally chose to reduce the second glyph in size and place it over top of the first glyph. This superimposing of one glyph in front of another is traditionally called infixing. There are also examples of infixes that are not intended to represent a separate word but rather that function like a visual adjective. Such is the case with the T24 sign, which is often infixed on the T712 *ch'ab* sign. The T24 sign does not affect the pronunciation of the T712 sign as *ch'ab*; instead, it acts like a visual adjective providing additional information about the luminous nature of the obsidian blood-letter.

The T712 sign appears in the couplet phrase *u ch'ab* (T712) *u ak'ab* (T504) "his creation, his darkness" that is associated with acts of devotion and creation involving bloodletting (Knowlton 2012; MacLeod and Houston cited in Stuart 1995, 231) (figure 4.9b). In some examples of the *ch'ab-ak'ab* couplet, the T712 and T504 signs are conflated into one glyph block, with the T504 sign infixed in front of the T712 sign (figure 4.9c). In such cases, the T504 sign covers up the T24 sign. The reader of such a text would understand that this single glyph block represented the couplet phrase *u ch'ab u ak'ab*. In Maya art, many examples of obsidian eccentrics, axes, spearheads, sacrificial blades, and scepters are infixed with the T504 *ak'ab* "night, darkness" sign. It has been suggested that the T504 sign functions like a visual adjective in these contexts, indicating the dark color of obsidian (Stone and Zender 2011, 145); however, it is far more likely to be a direct reference to the *ch'ab-ak'ab* couplet and the role of obsidian blood-letters in acts of devotion and creation. The conflation of the T712 sign and the T504 sign is a very clear example of how text is incorporated into Maya imagery (Bassie-Sweet and Hopkins 2018).

Another aspect of obsidian imagery is seen on Piedras Negras Stelae 7 and 8, which show a ruler holding a personified obsidian spear marked with the T504 *ak'ab* sign (figures 4.10 and 4.11). The distal point of the spear is tipped with a Teotihuacan-style symbol for a bleeding heart. The bloody heart symbol indicates the lethal nature of these obsidian objects and their association with human sacrifice (see chapter by Nielsen, this volume). Many illustrations of hook-shaped obsidian eccentrics are tipped with the bleeding-heart motif such as those found on Dos Pilas Stela 2 and Aguateca Stela 2 (figures 4.12 and 4.13). These monuments depict Dos Pilas Ruler 3 with obsidian eccentrics decorating his costume elements. The center of his loincloth and hipcloth displays Tlaloc's face with obsidian blood-letters curling out from the mouth and tipped with the bleeding-heart symbol. This is in contrast to the flint axes of the Chahk deities that have fire and smoke emitting from them. The intimate association between Tlaloc and obsidian will be further discussed below.

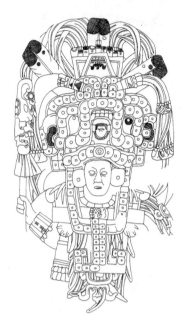

FIGURE 4.10. *Piedras Negras Stela 7. Drawing by David Stuart.*

FIGURE 4.11. *Piedras Negras Stela 8. Drawing by David Stuart.*

FIGURE 4.12. *Dos Pilas Stela 2. Drawing by Ian Graham.*

FIGURE 4.13. *Aguateca Stela 2. Drawing by Ian Graham*

FIGURE 4.14. *Tlaloc*

TLALOC GODS

The Maya depicted Tlaloc in skeletal form with round goggle-like eyes, an E-shaped nose element, *k'an* cross earrings, and a headdress that includes a so-called Central Mexican year sign (figure 4.14). The E-shaped nose element of the Tlaloc mask is an obsidian eccentric (Bassie-Sweet 2011, 2012), and such examples have been found in excavations (Chase and Chase 2007). Goggle-shaped shells representing the eyes of Tlaloc have also been recovered from archaeological excavations, and some monumental portraits of Tlaloc such as those at Copan have obsidian pupils (Fash 2001, 130). *Atlatls* frequently have two holes through which the fingers of the warrior are inserted to hold the weapon, and many illustrated examples show the finger holes as the goggle eyes of Tlaloc (Nuttall 1891). The notion that the *atlatl* and its obsidian dart were manifestations of Tlaloc is analogous to the flint thunderbolt axe being the manifestation of the Chahks.

Classic Maya rulers and their wives are often illustrated dressed in the costume of Tlaloc; for example, Dos Pilas Ruler 3 is shown wearing a stylized Tlaloc mask on Dos Pilas Stela 2 and Aguateca Stela 2 (see figures 4.12 and 4.13). In the Maya region, the weapons of choice for the Tlaloc deity were obsidian spears, *atlatls*, and darts, as is seen on Piedras Negras Stelae 7 and 8 where the ruler (dressed as Tlaloc) carries an obsidian spear and on the Dos Pilas and Aguateca monuments where the ruler carries an *atlatl* with darts as well as a spear. Although Teotihuacan was not a major supplier of obsidian to the Maya area, the association of obsidian with the Teotihuacan Tlaloc deity is not unexpected, given that Teotihuacan controlled or directed a substantial part of the Central Mexican obsidian trade.

Evidence that Tlaloc was categorized by the Maya as a type of Chahk deity is seen on Yaxchilan Lintel 25 (figure 4.15). This monument illustrates the conjuring of a Tlaloc and a female dressed as Tlaloc from the mouths of a double-headed

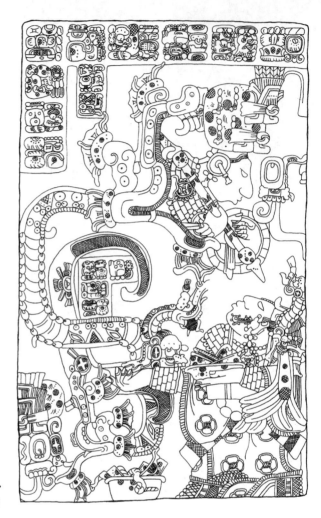

FIGURE 4.15.

Yaxchilan Lintel 25

18 Ub'aah Kan serpent (Bassie-Sweet 2008, 208–210, 2012). The main text of the lintel indicates that the conjured being is a deity called Aj K'ahk' O' Chahk "he of fire, owl, Chahk," signifying Tlaloc's identification with the Maya thunderbolt gods and the fire they produced. The Tlaloc owl avatar will be discussed below, as will the association of the 18 Ub'aah Kan serpent with Tlaloc.

In Copan Structure 10L-26, there is a hieroglyphic text that provides further evidence that the Maya categorized this foreign god as a K'awiil deity: a Chahk thunderbolt god. The text has standard Maya script paired with Teotihuacan-inspired hieroglyphs (Houston and Stuart 1998, 91; Stuart 2000, 495–497, 2005a, 388). In the Maya-style text, the word *k'awiil* in the name of the Copan ruler 18 Ub'aah K'awiil is represented by a typical K'awiil portrait glyph with fire

FIGURE 4.16. *K'awiil glyph, Copan Structure 10L-26. Drawing after David Stuart.*

(*k'ak'*) emanating from a torch in his forehead (figure 4.16). The parallel word in the Teotihuacan-style text is represented by the Tlaloc god with a torch in his forehead.

A central question to address is, what kind of Chahk did the Maya consider the obsidian deity Tlaloc to be? Across Mesoamerica, meteors and meteorites were thought to be the obsidian darts, spears, or arrows of certain deities, and they were viewed as omens of impending death and destruction (Köhler 1989; Laughlin 1975, 99, 513; Taube 2000b, 2004b, 292; Tedlock 1992, 180–181; Tozzer 1907, 157). While the Lacandon Maya and Tzotzil refer to meteors as arrows, the K'iche' specifically call them flaming arrows, and they believe the ancient obsidian points and blades they encounter in their fields are the remnants of a meteor. The Tzotzil also believe that meteors dropped obsidian. It is thought that when meteors hit the ground, they can take the form of caterpillars, worms, or maggots. Many obsidian eccentrics resemble such creatures. These beings are also referred to as the excrement of stars, as is obsidian. It is highly likely that the Maya categorized meteors as a type of thunderbolt (Taube 2000b, 325). This classification was based on the natural observation that both phenomena flash across the sky and can create fire and a booming sound. The equivalence of meteors and thunderbolts is found in the Tojolabal word *sansewal*, which is described as meteors or lightning that take the form of little worms of fire or small black snakes (Lenkersdorf 1979, 13, 312, 325, 370). The terms used for meteors in the Tzotzil, Tzeltal, and Tojolabal areas (*sanselaw, chamtzelaw, k'antzelaw, k'antzewal, sansewal, tzantzewal*) are also used to describe lightning flashes and sheet lightning, as well as lights that appear in the mountains at night (Lenkersdorf 1979; Pitarch 2010, 44; Slocum and Gerdel 1965, 193). In summary, it is highly like that the Maya incorporated Teotihuacan Tlaloc into their pantheon of Chahk deities

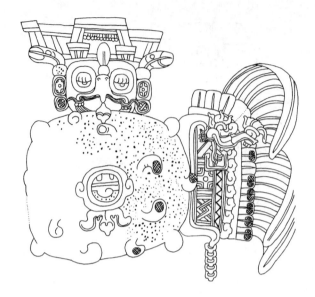

FIGURE 4.17. *Piedras Negras Stela 9. Drawing by David Stuart.*

as a meteor deity specifically identified with obsidian. The following review of Tlaloc avatars further demonstrates this deity's strong association with obsidian and meteors.

TLALOC AVATARS AND OBSIDIAN

Tlaloc was envisioned by the Maya as having a number of animal manifestations, much like the other major deities (Bassie-Sweet 2011, 2012, 2013; Bassie-Sweet et al. 2015, 129–142). These manifestations included a jaguar, an owl, a moth, and a caterpillar serpent specifically named 18 Ub'aah Kan that were all associated with obsidian. Examples include a jaguar wearing Tlaloc's goggle eyes at the waist of Dos Pilas Ruler 3, which has obsidian blood-letters and heart symbols in its mouth (see figure 4.12), and the headdress on Piedras Negras Stela 8 that incorporates a Jaguar Tlaloc with the same symbols in its mouth (see figure 4.11). A prime example of an Owl Tlaloc occurs on Piedras Negras Stela 9, where the ruler wears an owl bundle as a headdress (figure 4.17). The head of the owl has Tlaloc's goggle eyes and wears his *k'an* cross earrings. Three black-tipped feathers protrude from the head of the Owl Tlaloc. In Maya art and Mesoamerican art in general, predatory bird feathers were often equated with lithic blades, and the black-tipped owl feathers of the Owl Tlaloc were specifically identified with obsidian (Bassie-Sweet 2011, 2012, 2013; Taube et al. 2010). A rather graphic example of an owl wing decorated with obsidian blades is found on a headdress in the Teotihuacan Tetitla Portico 11, Mural 3 (Miller 1973, figure 301). The wings of this owl are composed of an open human chest with exposed heart and intestines.

FIGURE 4.18. *Tlaloc butterfly. Drawing after Donald Hales.*

An obsidian blade covered with blood extrudes from the cavity. The close association of owls with heart sacrifice is also seen in the *Popol Vuh*, where the duties of the four war councilors of the underworld included conducting heart sacrifices (Christenson 2007, 119, 132). These lords took the form of owls.

Lepidoptera is the order of insects that includes moths and butterflies. The identification of a Tlaloc god with Lepidopteran features has long been recognized (Taube 1992b) (figure 4.18). Such a creature is illustrated with Tlaloc eyes, but with the hooked proboscis and scalloped wings of a Lepidoptera. Although it was first identified as a butterfly, there is ample evidence that this Tlaloc avatar was actually based on the Black Witch Moth (*Ascalapha odorata*) (Bassie-Sweet 2011, 2012, 2013; Bassie-Sweet et al. 2015, 136–139). This impressive moth has a wing span that can reach an astonishing 17 cm. Its wings have scalloped edges like those of the Moth Tlaloc and zigzag patterns similar to those used at Teotihuacan and in the Maya region to represent obsidian (figure 4.19). The tip of a Black Witch Moth's hind wing is decorated with E-shaped motifs that are similar to Tlaloc's E-shaped obsidian nose element, while its upper wing has a motif similar to the T712 obsidian blood-letter. Furthermore, the caterpillar stage of the Black Witch Moth has distinctive round circles on its body that are reminiscent of Tlaloc eyes.

A ubiquitous belief found across all of Mesoamerica is that the appearance of a Black Witch moth inside a house is an omen that a member of the household will become ill or die (Bassie-Sweet et al. 2015, 139; Beutelspacher 1994; Hoffmann 1918; Hogue 1993). This fear of the Black Witch Moth is reflected in its Aztec name *micpapalotl* or *miquipapalotl* "death moth" (Beutelspacher 1994, 22, 29, 83–84) and its Ch'ol name *pejpem xib'aj* "moth demon" (Joljá Project field notes, 2004; Juán Jesus Vásquez, personal communication, 2004). Another widespread

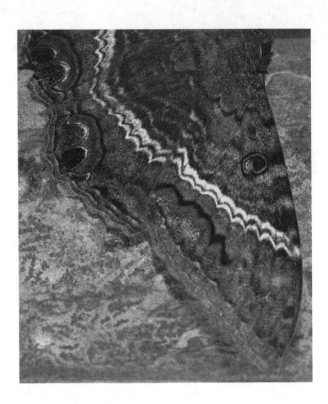

FIGURE 4.19. *Black Witch Moth*

belief in Mesoamerica is that nocturnal owls are omens of illness, death, and war (Christenson 2007, 119; Tozzer 1941, 202; Tozzer and Allen 1910; Villa Rojas 1945, 157–158). A warrior king dressed in the costume of an Owl Tlaloc or Moth Tlaloc would certainly have sent a powerful death message to his opponents. Such an image brings all new meaning to the phrase "dressed to kill."

A Teotihuacan-style serpent that is named 18 Ub'aah Kan in Maya hieroglyphic texts appears frequently in Maya art (Houston and Stuart 1996, 299; Schele and Freidel 1990; Stuart 2000, 493; Taube 1992b, 63–64, 2000b, 294–330). The 18 Ub'aah Kan has caterpillar, rattlesnake, and jaguar characteristics. The skin of the 18 Ub'aah Kan is often formed from what appears to be mosaic platelets of shell. Its body is decorated with stylized Moth Tlaloc wings with scalloped edges, and some examples include antennae. Taube (1992b, 2000b) has noted that the 18 Ub'aah Kan was the precursor for the Postclassic meteor serpent Xiuhcoatl of Central Mexico that also has similar Lepidoptera wings and often takes the form of a serpent or a caterpillar. Núñez de la Vega (1988, 133) described the Postclassic belief in Highland Chiapas that ritual specialists could transform into balls of fire (meteors). He stated that one of the co-essences of ritual specialists could take the form of *tzihuizin*, which he identified as cognate with the Aztec Xiuhcoatl (Brinton 1894, 20). Many Classic-period Maya lords are illustrated in the guise of the 18 Ub'aah Kan meteor serpent (for examples see Piedras Negras Stelae 7, 8, and 26; Naranjo Stela 2 and 19; the Palenque Temple XVII panel; and Bonampak Stela 3).

The 18 Ub'aah Kan's association with Tlaloc is well demonstrated on the facade of the Teotihuacan Temple of the Feathered Serpent, where this meteor serpent is featured wearing a Tlaloc headdress. In many Classic-period Maya scenes, Tlaloc is seen emerging from the mouth of the 18 Ub'aah Kan, further demonstrating its intimate relationship with this deity (see Yaxchilan Lintel 25, Yaxchilan Stela 35, and Copan Stela 6) (see figure 4.15). In the Copan Structure 10L-26 example of Tlaloc discussed above, the leg and foot of Tlaloc takes the form of an 18 Ub'aah Kan (see figure 4.16). Many portraits of the deity K'awiil illustrate him with a serpent leg and foot that represents his fiery thunderbolt. Given that the lightning serpent emitting from K'awiil's limb is a manifestation of that thunderbolt deity, it must be concluded that the 18 Ub'aah Kan meteor emitting from the limb of Tlaloc was a manifestation of Tlaloc. The inference is that the Maya viewed Tlaloc specifically as a meteor god.

The identification of the 18 Ub'aah Kan as a meteor serpent adds to our under-standing of the Owl Tlaloc bundle illustrated on Piedras Negras Stela 9 (see figure 4.17). The bundle is decorated with black-tipped feathers and the bleeding-heart symbol. The head of the Owl Tlaloc is positioned on top of the bundle while its wings extend out the sides. Supernatural bird wings in Maya headdresses are typically composed of a serpent's head with short secondary feathers and long primary feathers extending out from the serpent's mouth (Bardawil 1976). In the case of the Stela 9 owl wing, the serpent has been replaced with an 18 Ub'aah Kan complete with a rattlesnake tail. This means that the wings of this owl are marked with a symbol for meteors and, by extension, obsidian. Furthermore, the zigzag pattern indicating obsidian is found at the base of the owl wing.

Obsidian-related owls are illustrated in the Teotihuacan Atetelco murals and are juxtaposed with a symbol for a mountain and function as place names. The mountain is decorated with protruding obsidian blades. Nielsen and Helmke (2008) have demonstrated that the Atetelco owl represents an *atlatl* (spearthrower).

The Yaxchilan ruler Bird Jaguar IV is illustrated on Lintel 8 in the midst of a battle, while Lintel 41 shows him either preparing for or returning from that battle (Tate 1992, figsures 44, 148). In both scenes, he wears the headdress of the Moth Tlaloc and carries a long spear. In Central Mexican art, the caterpillar body of the Xiuhcoatl, which represents an obsidian dart, takes the form of trap-ezoid segments (Taube 2000b, 2004b, 292) (figure 4.20). Below the spearhead on Lintel 41, two such trapezoid segments flare out from the spear shaft. Below this pair of stylized caterpillar bodies is a series of obsidian chips embedded in the staff. The chips form the zigzag pattern that represents obsidian. Long spears as

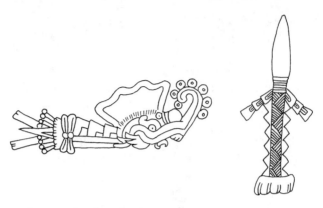

FIGURE 4.20. *Xiuhcoatl and spear*

opposed to darts and spearthrowers were the preferred weapons in the Classic period for close-contact warfare. On Copan Stela 6 and Naranjo Stela 2, the leg ornaments of the ruler are decorated with the obsidian zigzag pattern and the trapezoid segments. Similar segments appear on the leg ornaments of the rulers illustrated on Naranjo Stela 19 and Copan Structure 26 (Fash 2001, figure 91).[5] The implication of this imagery is that the legs of the ruler were thought to be like obsidian spears. The ruler did not just throw Tlaloc's meteor spear, he was equated with it.

In addition to the obsidian imagery discussed above, the costumes of rulers who are dressed as Tlaloc contain many other references to obsidian; for example, on Piedras Negras Stela 8, a personified obsidian dart is found below the Jaguar Tlaloc of the headdress (see figure 4.11), composed of a centipede serpent with an obsidian blood-letter for a tongue and a black-tipped owl feather in the tail region. As noted above, owl feathers are equated with obsidian blades. On Stela 7, the ruler's headdress includes three such owl feathers stuck in the top (see figure 4.10). The 18 Ub'aah Kan headdress on this monument has two darts protruding from it, which have small owl feathers at their base. In addition to his Tlaloc mask, Dos Pilas Ruler 3's costume contains many obsidian elements as well (see figures 4.12 and 4.13). The hipcloth and loincloth of the ruler are trimmed with a design representing the scalloped wings of the Moth Tlaloc and with the zigzag pattern used to represent obsidian. As noted above, the loincloth and hipcloth displays Tlaloc's face with obsidian blood-letters curling out from the mouth, and the Jaguar Tlaloc appears at the waist of the ruler with the same obsidian blood-letters tipped with bleeding hearts in its mouth. The ruler wears two jaguar paws hanging from a rope around his neck, which have cuffs decorated with the moth wing and zigzag pattern. On Dos Pilas Stela 2, an Owl Tlaloc perches above the Jaguar Tlaloc. These various examples show the close correlation between Tlaloc and obsidian.

TLALOC PRIESTS AND PRIESTESSES

Both the military and religious roles of Classic-period kings have been well documented (Zender 2004b). A primary clerical responsibility of Maya rulers and their consorts was to petition and appease the deities through sacrificial offerings and the burning of incense. A prevalent motif in Maya monumental art is the display of war captives kneeling in submission before a ruler. The manner in which these individuals were dispatched likely involved the common Mesoamerica tradition of decapitation or heart extraction using a knife of flint or obsidian. In addition to personal bloodletting, it is possible that the clerical duties of the king included the role of executioner of sacrificial victims.

The priestly roles of secondary lords under the authority of the king have also been noted (Coe in Coe and Kerr 1998, 91–94; Zender 2004b). The inference of this hierarchal relationship is that kings and their consorts were high priests-priestesses. An incense bag is the hallmark of a Mesoamerican priest-priestess, and many of the Maya nobility carry such items; for example, on Piedras Negras Stela 11, Ruler 4 is illustrated performing a Period Ending event while carrying an incense bag marked with the *tzolk'in* date of the event (Bassie-Sweet 1991, 50, 1996, 106–109, 2008, 101–102). In a similar fashion, the secondary lord Aj Chak Wayib' K'utiim is featured on El Cayo Altar 4 performing a Period Ending event. He is pictured casting incense before an *incensario* while holding a Tlaloc incense bag (Zender 2002, 169). The rulers dressed as Tlaloc on Dos Pilas Stela 2, Aguateca Stela 2, Bonampak Stela 3, and Piedras Negras Stelae 7 and 9 also carry incense bags decorated with Tlaloc imagery. The implication is that these lords made incense offerings to Tlaloc.

There is a general title (Ch'ajoom) found across most of the Maya region that refers to the priestly function of burning incense offerings. Some kings and consorts are specifically called Wi'te'naah Ch'ajooms. The term *Wi'te'naah* refers to a type of building (Stuart 2000, 491–495; Taube 2004b, 271–273). The narratives on Copan Altar Q and Quirigua Zoomorph P relate a series of events concerning a ruler called K'inich Yax K'uk' Mo' who founded a new Copan lineage in the Early Classic period (Stuart 2000, 2004a, 2005a). Although these narratives do not indicate where his journey began, the Altar Q text states that K'uk' Mo' Ajaw (the pre-accession name for K'inich Yax K'uk' Mo') went to a Wi'te'naah building and received a K'awiil in 426 CE. Three days later, he left the Wi'te'naah as the newly named king K'inich Yax K'uk' Mo' and journeyed for 152 days before arriving at Copan. Portraits of K'inich Yax K'uk' Mo on the side of Altar Q show him wearing a Tlaloc mask, indicating his close identification with this deity (Fash 2001, 106–107). In addition to being named *ajaw* "king," K'inich Yax K'uk' Mo' is named as a Kaloomte', a Wi'te'naah lord, and a Wi'te'naah Ch'ajoom in various texts (see below for a discussion of the Kaloomte' title). The Late Classic Copan ruler Yax Pasaj Chan Yopaat, who was also a Kaloomte', was the sixteenth king in the Copan succession. On the Temple II Reviewing Stand narrative, he is called the sixteenth successor of the Wi'te'naah Ch'ajoom. In the same regard, the thirteenth Copan ruler Waxaklajuun Ub'aah K'awiil is called the thirteenth successor of the Wi'te'nab Ch'ajoom on Stela B. The implication of these designations is that K'inich Yax K'uk' Mo's successors were not just kings of Copan but were also Wi'te'naah Ch'ajooms.

The Wi'te'naah name has three components: T600 (crossed fire sticks), *te* "tree/wood," and *naah* "house/structure" (Stuart 2000, 493; Taube 2004b, 273). In some examples, the T600 sign is replaced by a phonetic *wi'* sign, and on Yaxchilan Lintel 25, T600 includes a phonetic *wi'* sign. *Wi'* means root; hence, this name has been translated by Stuart as the tree root building. Although this interpretation is by no means certain, both Stuart and Taube noted the Wi'te'naah's close identification with Teotihuacan imagery. What is pertinent to this discussion of Tlaloc is that some examples of the Wi'te'naah place name incorporate Tlaloc's face or goggle eyes, and I have suggested elsewhere that Wi'te'naah structures were specifically Tlaloc temples (Bassie-Sweet 2011, 2012). Confirmation of the identification of Tlaloc with the Wi'te'naah is found at the site of Río Amarillo, where a building that is labeled as a Wi'te'naah is decorated with Tlaloc images (Saturno 2000; Stuart 2000, 493; Taube 2004b, 273). I deduce from this evidence that the Wi'te'naah Ch'ajoom title refers to the priestly function of offering incense to Tlaloc within a Wi'te'naah structure.

In addition to petitioning Tlaloc and taking on the guise of this god, kings and their consorts in their roles as Tlaloc priests-priestesses were likely also in charge of maintaining and caring for Tlaloc effigies and Tlaloc paraphernalia, or at the very least they oversaw subordinates with those duties. Such a supervisory role suggests that rulers and their consorts were the high priests-priestesses for Tlaloc. There is some evidence that the office of Kaloomte', which was held by both Maya kings and their queens, refers to such a function.

The first appearance of Kaloomte' lords is found in a series of Early Classic–period texts that mention three men named Sihyaj K'ahk', Spearthrower Owl, and Yax Nuun Ahiin who were closely identified with Teotihuacan-style imagery (for an overview and summary of these texts, see Estrada-Belli et al. 2009; Martin 2003; Martin and Grube 2008, 31; Stuart 2000). In chronological order, the events concerning these individuals began in 374 CE when Spearthrower Owl, who is said to be from a place called Jo' Noh Witz, was seated in rulership. He was the fourth ruler of Jo' Noh Witz and a Kaloomte'. On January 8, 378 CE, Sihyaj K'ahk', who was also a Kaloomte', performed an unnamed event at El Perú (80 km west of Tikal) and arrived at Tikal eight days later. On the same date as Sihyaj K'ahk's arrival, Chak Tok Ich'aak, who was the ruling Tikal king, was said to have "entered the water" and "entered the mountain." These death-related phrases have been interpreted to mean that Chak Tok Ich'aak died on this day, and many epigraphers have concluded that Sihyaj K'ahk's arrival in Tikal was a military incursion that resulted in the death of the Tikal king at his hand.

The next noted events occurred later in 378 CE when Yax Nuun Ahiin, the young son of Spearthrower Owl, was said to have entered and then left a Wi'te'naah structure. While the meaning of Yax Nuun Ahiin's action is unknown, nine months after descending from the Wi'te'naah, he returned to this structure for his accession ceremony as the king of Tikal (September 13, 379 CE). One assumes that this event occurred at Tikal. The accession of Yax Nuun Ahiin was overseen by Sihyaj K'ahk', and it is stated that Yax Nuun Ahiin was his vassal. Lords at La Sufricaya (35 km east of Tikal) and Bejucal (20 km west of Tikal) are also referred to as vassals of Sihyaj K'ahk' on monuments dated 379 CE and 381 CE, respectively. In 396 CE, Yax Nuun Ahiin celebrated the 8.19.0.0.0 Period Ending at Tikal while Sihyaj K'ahk' and the local ruler of Uaxactun performed this ritual at Uaxactun. This activity suggests that Sihyaj K'ahk' remained active in the region. There is no death date recorded for Sihyaj K'ahk', but the Tikal Marcador text indicates that Spearthrower Owl, who also had vassal lords under his authority, lived well into the reign of his grandson Sihyaj Chan K'awiil II, dying in 434 CE.

There has been much speculation about the identity and ethnicity of Spear-thrower Owl, Sihyaj K'ahk', and Yax Nuun Ahiin. It has been proposed that Spearthrower Owl might have been a Teotihuacan ruler who sent Sihyaj K'ahk' to Tikal and subsequently had his own son Yax Nuun Ahiin installed there as king (Stuart 2000). In such a scenario, Jo' Noh Witz would be the name of Teotihuacan. There are many problems with this interpretation, not the least of which is that the analysis of Yax Nuun Ahiin's remains indicates that he spent his childhood years in the Petén region (Wright 2005). While a further discussion of this topic is beyond the scope of this chapter, what is germane is that all three of these men had close affiliations with Tlaloc. Yax Nuun Ahiin is illustrated twice on the sides of Tikal Stela 31, decked out in Tlaloc regalia. While there are no known illustrations of Spearthrower Owl or Sihyaj K'ahk', the former's name is the pairing of Tlaloc's *atlatl* and his owl manifestation. In one example of his name, the *atlatl* is positioned over the owl's wing much like the 18 Ub'aah Kan is juxtaposed with the Owl Tlaloc wing on Piedras Negras Stela 9 (figure 4.21). Taube (2000b, 2004b) has detailed the fire associations of Tlaloc imagery and noted that fire is closely associated with meteors. The name Sihyaj K'ahk' "born from fire" suggests a connection to Tlaloc's meteor fire. The Tikal Marcador text states that Sihyaj K'ahk' brought a number of deities with him to Tikal, including an 18 Ub'aah Kan meteor serpent, which strongly suggests that he was a Tlaloc priest.

It has been concluded from the vassal statements referring to Sihyaj K'ahk' that the Kaloomte' was an overlord of conquered territories who had supreme

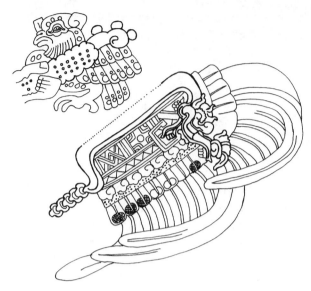

FIGURE 4.21.

*Spearthrower Owl
Name. Drawing after
David Stuart.*

status within a political hierarchy, and the office of Kaloomte' has been trans-lated as "high king" or "emperor" of a region (Martin and Grube 2008; Stuart 2000, 2004a). Various queens are also known to have carried the Kaloomte' title, and these women have been characterized by some as warrior queens. Given the close association of Kaloomte' lords and ladies with Tlaloc imagery, it is my belief that the Kaloomte' title designates a high priest or priestess whose patron god was the meteor and obsidian deity Tlaloc (Bassie-Sweet 2011, 2012, 2013; Bassie-Sweet et al. 2015, 142). This interpretation, of course, does not negate the fact that the office of Kaloomte' had a political component based on mili-tary conquest. The issue here is that Maya rulers (and their consorts) aligned themselves with a deity identified with obsidian and the supernatural powers associated with obsidian.

In many illustrations, the deity GIII is juxtaposed with Tlaloc imagery; for example, Ruler 3 on Aguateca Stela 2 who is dressed as Tlaloc carries a rectangular GIII shield. In a similar vein, the Naranjo ruler who is dressed in Tlaloc accou-terments on Naranjo Stela 19 also carries such a shield. The implication of this imagery is that Maya lords went into battle with the power and protection of both of these gods. Tlaloc did not replace Maya thunderbolt and meteor deities; rather, he was incorporated into the Maya worldview as yet another type of Chahk.

PATRON WAR GODS

In Mesoamerica, there was a long tradition of rulers receiving validation and prestige in the form of insignia and patron deities from a foreign city known as "the place of reeds" (Tollan in Nahuatl). The *Popol Vuh* provides important information about the integration of foreign gods into a local pantheon during the Epiclassic period. The first K'iche' tribes were said to have journeyed to a city named Tulan ("place of reeds") to obtain a tutelary deity (Christenson 2007, 208–227). The precise location of this Postclassic Tulan is widely debated, and suggestions have included such diverse sites as Tula, Cholula, and Chichen Itza. Although the various tribes received an assortment of patron gods at Tulan, it was the deity Tohil who became the dominant patron for the K'iche', Tamub, and Ilocab.

Tohil provided fire to the K'iche' after their initial fire was extinguished by hail and rain. He created this essential element by twisting his foot inside his shoe like a fire drill (Christenson 2007, 213–214). In this regard, Tohil was like both GIII who produced fire through drilling and Tlaloc who produced fire from his foot in the form of the meteor deity 18 Ub'aah Kan. Like GIII and Tlaloc, Tohil was also a war god who enabled the K'iche' to overcome their enemies. The K'iche' built a temple within their citadel to house their effigy of Tohil, and all the other nations defeated by the K'iche' came to Tohil's temple to burn offerings to this god before giving their tribute to the K'iche' lords (Christenson 2007, 286). The *Popol Vuh* narrative makes a crucial point when it states that the patron deity Tohil was the *k'exwach* "replacement" and *natab'al* "remembrance" for the deities Framer and Shaper (the creator grandparents Xpiyacoc and Xmucane, respectively) (Christenson 2007, 215). In other words, these foreign deities were not thought to be separate gods but alternative manifestations of the creator deities.

Stuart (2000, 2004a, 2005b) presented convincing evidence that the Early Classic Maya viewed the city of Teotihuacan as the quintessential "place of reeds." Given the history of patron god acquisition in Mesoamerica, a logical conclusion to draw from Stuart's evidence is that certain Early Classic lineages acquired Tlaloc effigies from this city as patron war gods and that the Wi'te'naah structures in the Maya area that were so closely associated with Tlaloc imagery were temples dedicated to this god and his various avatars.

GOD L, THE PATRON GOD OF LONG-DISTANCE TRADERS

The obsidian imagery of the Owl Tlaloc provides insight into the nature of the Maya underworld deity known as God L. God L was the maternal grandfather of the hero twins, and his *Popol Vuh* parallel was the underworld lord Gathered Blood (Bassie-Sweet 2008, 226–238). In addition to his role as the maternal grandfather, God L has been identified as a god of tobacco, cacao, and trade and a patron god for merchants, especially long-distance traders (Martin 2006; Taube 1992a, 79–88). While God L is frequently shown smoking a cigar, carrying a merchant backpack and walking stick, and at times carrying a spear, his primary diagnostic trait is a

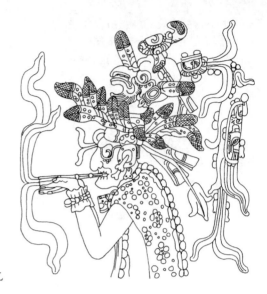

FIGURE 4.22. *God L*

wide-brimmed hat adorned with black-tipped owl feathers (figure 4.22). Given the evidence that such feathers were equated with blades of obsidian, it is apparent that God L's feather hat was a metaphor for obsidian blades. Obsidian is one of the most important highland commodities imported into the lowlands, and I have suggested elsewhere that God L was first and foremost the patron god for long-distance obsidian merchants (Bassie-Sweet 2011, 2012, 2013).

The lords of the underworld were gods of death who were intimately associated with human sacrifice and warfare and, by extension, obsidian and flint weapons. As mentioned above, the lords of the underworld in charge of heart sacrifice took an owl form. In some cases, God L's headdress includes an owl with black-tipped feathers that is named in the hieroglyphic text as 13 Sky Owl "Oxlahuun Kan Kuy" (Grube and Schele 1994). The owl has been interpreted to be his avatar. On a looted panel from the Palenque region, a secondary lord is portrayed handing a ruler his Tlaloc headdress (Schaffer 1987). The secondary lord wears a God L headdress, and the 13 Sky Owl in his headdress has Tlaloc's goggle eyes. On vessel K8740,[6] another lord wears God L's headdress, and the upper portion has Tlaloc eyes. On Dresden Codex page 74, God L is shown as a warrior wielding a spear and darts. His owl feather headdress has been replaced with a stylized *atlatl*, but his 13 Sky Owl avatar perches on top. God L's wrists and ankles are decorated with Tlaloc's moth wings, and he is painted black, the color of obsidian. This overlap between Tlaloc and God L is obviously based on their roles as an obsidian war deity and an obsidian merchant deity, respectively. Long-distance merchants faced the dangerous challenge of traveling through foreign and often sparsely inhabited territory where attack and robbery were likely common occurrences. It is not surprising that such individuals would seek powerful supernatural help.

SUMMARY AND CONCLUSIONS

In Mesoamerica, humans were thought to have co-essences who shared their souls and their fate. These co-essences could take the form of animals or natural phenomena like thunderbolts, meteors, and whirlwinds. During the Postclassic period in Highland Chiapas, it was believed that community leaders transformed into thunderbolts and meteors or that their co-essences took the form of these phenomena (Calnek 1988, 46; Núñez de la Vega 1988, 133). This identification of leaders with thunderbolts and meteors continues today (Bassie-Sweet et al. 2015; Guiteras Holmes 1961; Hermitte 1964; Laughlin 1977; Nash 1970; Spero 1987; Vogt 1969). The ancestral and current leaders are thought to use their thunderbolt and meteor co-essences to protect the community. The identification of thunderbolts and meteors with leaders has considerable longevity, and a large percentage of Maya kings use Chahk or K'awiil in their regnal names (Martin and Grube 2008). One of the most frequent actions found on public monumental sculpture is that of a king or lord holding a K'awiil scepter, which indicates that these lords were identified with thunderbolt gods and their supernatural power. In contrast to the flint association of the thunderbolt deities, the imagery associated with Tlaloc and his avatars is laden with obsidian and meteor references, and there are ample examples of rulers dressing in the costume of Tlaloc and wielding his obsidian weapons.

Flint and obsidian were not viewed by the Maya as inert rocks but ones imbued with the supernatural power of the thunderbolt and meteor gods. Anyone could use a flint or obsidian weapon or tool, but only the spiritually strong could command its supernatural powers. The ability of the lord to harness and direct that power gave him enormous spiritual strength, particularly in battle. Many accounts of the Spanish Conquest indicate that the indigenous population believed the warrior's spiritual strength dictated his success in battle (see chapter by Christenson, this volume). In the same regard, the ritual fighting scenes documented by Taube and Zender (2009) were ultimately contests of supernatural strength. In downing the tok'-pakal, the winning forces were symbolically defeating the supernatural power of their opponents. One can well imagine a Maya ruler (and his consort) petitioning the thunderbolt and meteor deities before entering battle and giving thanks afterward.

NOTES

1. I use the word *flint* rather than the more technically accurate term *chert* because it is the established name for this stone in Mayan ethnographic and iconographic studies.

2. Stuart (2005b, 170) and Taube and Houston (2015) have speculated that GI was an aquatic form of the sun as it rises from the Caribbean Sea at dawn. They make this identification because GI shares the same aquiline-nosed anthropomorphic face as the Sun God and because they identify GI's brazier headdress as a pyre used in mythological times to transform a god into the sun. While GI's headdress may indicate that he played a role in the transformation of the sun (as a hearthstone god the role would be a natural one), the bench from Copan Structure 10K-4 illustrates the rising sun not as GI but as the standard Sun God, which greatly weakens their argument.

3. The full-figure deity portraits on the Copan Structure 8N-11 bench contrast the concept of day and night using the Sun God and the *ak'ab* god. The *ak'ab* god appears in a number of other contexts such as the patron god for the month Mol, which indicates that he is a distinct deity from GIII, who was the patron for the month Wo. The *ak'ab* god has been identified as the "night sun" (Stone and Zender 2011, 145; Stuart 2005b, 62). However, the contrast between the Sun God and the *ak'ab* god is not between different aspects of the sun; rather, it is a contrast between day and night. The *ak'ab* god represents exactly what his name states, the night.

4. In Maya art, T24 celts are frequently illustrated hanging in units of three from the belts of rulers. This triadic grouping is an ancient motif that also appears in the Formative-period San Bartolo murals (Taube et al. 2010, figure 19d). Given that belts frequently have sky signs on them, Stuart (2010, 293) has suggested that these ceremonial celts "may have been likened in some way to lightning flashes descending from the heavens." In Maya household practice, the hearth fire was demarcated by three stones. I believe the T24 triadic motif may refer to the triad of thunderbolt gods (GI, GII, and GIII) who also represented the three hearthstones.

5. Illustrations of the Naranjo monument can be found at the Corpus of Maya Hieroglyphic Inscriptions website (https://www.peabody.harvard.edu/cmhi/).

6. http://research.mayavase.com/kerrmaya_hires.php?vase=8740.

5

Fire in the Land

Landscapes of War in Classic Maya Narratives

ALEXANDRE TOKOVININE

The present chapter explores the connections between two recurrent topics in Classic Maya inscriptions: places and warfare. In so doing, it follows on my previous project of investigating notions of place, individual, and group identity in the Classic-period written records of the Southern Maya Lowlands (Tokovinine 2008, 2013b). As discussed below, some of the project's findings with respect to the indigenous concepts of place and related spatial categories are of direct relevance to understanding the Classic Maya ways of writing about war, its causes, and its aftermath.

While the goal of the study presented in this chapter is much more modest in scope, it deals with a similar set of uncertainties and challenges brought about by the nature of the available sources of information (Tokovinine 2007). The database of Classic Maya place names constitutes the primary data source for both projects. Each database entry corresponds to a single occurrence of a place name, which is accompanied by a full transcription of the clause in which the toponym is mentioned and by additional descriptive fields that serve to classify the context of a place name in terms of its syntax and general meaning. A sentence

DOI: 10.5876/9781607328872.c005

FIGURE 5.1. *Detail of the Hieroglyphic Stairway, House C, Palenque*

such as *ch'ahkaj lakam ha' ukabjiiy oox kula'* chi-T316 *yajawte' . . . chan kanu'l ajaw* ("Lakam Ha' is chopped; *Kanu'l* lord 'Sky Witness,' the *yajawte'* of 'Maguey Altar,' *oox kula'*, had tended to it") from the inscription on the Palenque Hieroglyphic Stairway (figure 5.1) belongs to three database entries: a direct reference to the place of Lakam Ha' that suffered an attack from "Sky Witness," whose name phrase includes indirect references to the toponyms of Kanu'l and "Maguey Altar." The distinction between the direct and indirect references is important because the former correspond to actions that affect or happen at a certain locale, while the latter only attest to a particular relationship between an individual or a group and a place. In this case, "Sky Witness" derives his lordly rank from *Kanu'l*, but his military title of *yajawte'* ("lord of spear[s]") evokes "Maguey Altar." These connections could have been key to "Sky Witness's" identity as a lord and a warrior in general, but they could also have been intentionally highlighted by the anonymous author of the narrative at the expense of other places "Sky Witness" was associated with in the context of his attack on Lakam Ha'.

The key shortcomings of the dataset are a relatively small sample size (just under 2,400 entries) and its uneven distribution in time and space. The picture is heavily skewed toward archaeological sites with large corpora of well-preserved inscriptions, such as Yaxchilan, Naranjo, Tonina, Palenque, Tikal, and Dos Pilas. The quantity of texts on eighth-century CE monuments dwarfs everything else simply because those were the monuments left standing at the time of the collapse of Classic Maya royal courts in the early ninth century CE. In contrast, the sample from the fourth and fifth centuries CE is tiny because of the practice of termination and burial of early structures and monuments as well as possible desecration and destruction during times of war (Martin 2000a; see chapter by

Hernandez and Palka, this volume), which makes the discovery of such early narratives much less likely. To make things even worse, a vast set of inscriptions comes from unprovenanced objects in private and institutional collections, so the spatial and chronological attribution of some place name references is difficult or even impossible to ascertain. Nevertheless, the sample is large and varied enough to look for broader patterns in the written discourse.

It is worth emphasizing that the present discussion and the data collection project behind it are not centered on warfare as such. The object of the research is place names and landscape categories in various contexts, and this chapter deals with one subset of contexts. So, for example, when frequencies of specific war-related references are discussed, these are frequencies of place names in the context of warfare. The same war event may contain multiple landscape references, as we have seen above, but war events with no place names mentioned have not been considered in this particular study.

IDENTIFYING PLACES

Nearly all place names found in Classic Maya inscriptions are unknown from ethnohistoric or ethnographic accounts; therefore, they are identified on the basis of their meaning and morphology or because of specific semantic contexts. The morphological attributes include place name suffixes -*VVl* or -*V'l* ("place where X abounds") and a specialized derivational morpheme -*nal* ("corn place") (Tokovinine 2013b, 8–10). The diagnostic contexts comprise occurrences of place names with certain kinds of words and expressions: verbs of motion, positional verbs, locatives, expressions such as "it happened (at)," agentive constructions, and landscape categories (recurrent terms that accompany known place names but do not equate with them; see Stuart and Houston 1994, 7–18). Several hundred toponyms have been identified so far, and some may even be linked to specific physical locales corresponding to sections of archaeological sites, while the identification of many rare place names with no diagnostic morphological attributes remains problematic at best.

The name phrase of "Sky Witness," cited in the introduction to this chapter (see figure 5.1), illustrates common difficulties with recognizing toponyms. Kanu'l and "Maguey Altar" are certainly place names because they appear in direct contexts. *Oox kula'* may be analyzed as "*oox-kul*-person," where *oox-kul* could well be a place name; however, it lacks the morphological attributes of a toponym and does not appear in any context other than this title of Kanu'l lords. The possible translations of glosses *oox* as "paw" (Barrera Vásquez et al. 1995, 611) and *kul* as "tree trunk" (Barrera Vásquez et al. 1995, 348) cannot be verified by other contexts (although the iconography of the OOX logogram supports the "paw" translation and "paw trunk" would be a more-or-less accurate description of trees in Classic Maya iconography); therefore, *oox-kul* may not be identified as a place name.

The two most frequent landscape categories are *kab* ("land") and *ch'een* ("cave"). As I have previously argued, the latter refers not so much to natural landscape features (hence its near total absence in toponyms) as to holy grounds at the heart of Classic Maya royal courts: natural or artificial mountains with the burials of ancestors and dwellings of the divine patrons of rulers and wider political communities. An example would be the *ch'een* of Naranjo rulers, also known as *Sa'aal*, which was at the triadic acropolis on a hill in the eastern area of the archaeological site (Tokovinine 2011; Tokovinine and Fialko 2007). As discussed below, these holy grounds and their supernatural and human owners were at the very core of Classic Maya written discourse on warfare. The term *kab* refers to territories/people under the sway of a particular ruler and *ch'een*, which may also be mentioned in the context of war narratives. Only a subset of place names is classified as *ch'een*, presumably as an indicator of their political and ritual centrality in a given landscape. Places are not usually classified as *kab*, but *kab* may belong to places the way social and political entities belong to or are associated with places. In addition, the couplet *chan ch'een* ("sky-cave") refers to the divine realm associated with a locale, whereas the *kab ch'een* couplet ("land-cave") designates the sacred core and the territory/population of a city or polity.

IDENTIFYING WARFARE

Although nearly every publication on Classic Maya political history addresses the theme of warfare in one way or another, there has been no attempt at a comprehensive critical overview of the textual record and problems with identifying acts of war in the inscriptions. Miller and Martin's (2004, 163–172) introduction to the topic of courtly warfare, as well as Martin's (1996, 2000b, 2004, 2009) and Mathews's (2000) discussions of some key war-related narratives, remain the only available summaries of some of the problems involved; therefore, a brief review of these issues is in order.

There is no overarching term for war in Classic-period inscriptions. It is not even clear if the concept of war as a continuous state is applicable at all to the available textual record. The word of choice in the Colonial-period narratives is *k'atun*. It may refer to military units, fighting, and a state of war besides being the name of a twenty-year period (Barrera Vásquez et al. 1995, 385–386). The following examples from the Acalan Chontal Maldonado Paxbolon Papers illustrate the uses of *k'atun* as "war":

cahi utalel hobon cab ukatuninob (Smailus 1975, 29)
"Many communities started coming [and] they waged war"

cahi ukatuncelob tamal abi chankal kin (Smailus 1975, 32)
"They started being waged war upon for, they say, eighty days"

ma xach katunon coco xach col numicon (Smailus 1975, 52)
"I do not wage war now; I only want to pass now."

There are no comparable references to war so-defined in the pre-Contact inscriptions. Instead, several terms denote acts of aggression, which may be interpreted as acts of war. Other expressions refer to acts of war in certain contexts but not in all cases. There are also glosses that may be contextually linked to warfare, but their actual significance is unclear (see also chapter by Peuramaki-Brown, Morton, and Kettunen, this volume).

References to "chopped" (ch'ahkaj, usually spelled CH'AK-(ka)-ja; see figures 5.1 and 5.2a) places are perhaps the most obvious descriptions of war that emphasize its destructive nature, regardless of the political or economic outcomes. The targets are either place names or ch'een of a ruler or a deity/ancestor. The only mention of kab occurs in the context of a sweeping statement in the narrative on the Sabana Piletas Hieroglyphic Stairway (Grube, Pallán Gayol, and Benavides Castillo 2011, 255–256; Tokovinine 2013b, 92–93) that does not seem to be concerned with specific locations: "the land was chopped where the southern lords are, where the eastern lords are, where the northern lords are, where the western lords are." This statement of total and indiscriminate destruction nevertheless remains unique. A reference to a ch'ahkaj event may also be a casus belli statement, as on Caracol Altar 21 (Martin 2005a), when such attacks are followed by a justified retribution. People are almost never "chopped." The accounts of the only known historic "head chopping" (ch'ak-baah), when Copan ruler Waxaklajuun Ubaah K'awiil was decapitated by his Quirigua adversary, take decisively mythical overtones (Looper 2003, 76–87; Martin and Grube 2008, 205, 218–219). Perhaps that special fate was reserved for ancient heroes and deities (see below).

In contrast, "downfall" references are more metaphorical and highlight the outcome of attacks or battles. The Hieroglyphic Mayan term is jubuuy "it fell down," spelled syllabically as ju-bu-yi (figure 5.2b) or with the "star war" or "STAR.OVER.EARTH" logogram (figure 5.2c). Individuals, their weapons, and places (toponyms, ch'een, and kab) may experience the "downfall." The range of meanings seems to be from a lost battle to a failure of a political community, its holy places, and its lands. Some of the most significant military defeats in Classic Maya history, such as the outcome of a conflict between Tikal and Calakmul in 695 CE (Martin and Grube 2008, 44–45), are described as the "downfall." These statements are also curiously agent-less, as if some kind of predetermination were implied.

"Entering the ch'een" (figure 5.2d) is a potentially ambiguous expression, as it may evoke one's visits to temples or other holy places, but at least some of these "entering" events are acts of war (Martin 2004, 106–109; Tokovinine 2013b,

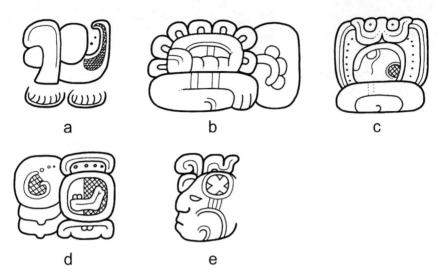

FIGURE 5.2. *War references in Classic Maya inscriptions:* a, *CH'AK-ka-ja* ch'ahkaj *"it was chopped" (Tortuguero Monument 8, 40);* b, **ju-bu-yi** jubuuy *"it fell" (Dos Pilas Hieroglyphic Stairway 4, Step 4, F1);* c, *STAR.OVER.EARTH-*yi jubuuy (?) *"it fell" (Tortuguero Monument 6, C4);* d, *OCH-u-CH'EEN-na* ochi uch'een *"it entered the cave/city of" (Palenque Temple XVII Panel, I2);* e, **PUL-yi** puluuy *"it burned" (Naranjo Stela 22, E16)*

33). Naranjo's Stela 21 (Graham 1975, 53) clearly belongs to the latter category, as it depicts its ruler standing on a bound captive from Yootz while the caption for the king states that "it is his image in the entering of the *ch'een* of Yootz" (*ubaah ti och-ch'een yootz*). Codex-style pottery scenes of Chak Xib Chaahk warriors confronting a wind or maize deity as they "enter the *ch'een*" also imply an act of aggression (Garcia Barrios 2006; Martin 2004, 107; Taube 2004a, 74–75). "Entering the *ch'een*" in the narratives on the Palenque Temple XVII panel and the blocks of the Dzibanche Hieroglyphic Stairway results in the taking of captives (Martin 2004, 105–108; Velásquez García 2004).

A special kind of fiery *ch'een* entering is cited on monuments at the archaeological sites of Naranjo and Yaxchilan (Tokovinine and Fialko 2007, 7–8, figure 10). The translation of the expression remains somewhat obscure, but its context in the text on Yaxchilan Stela 18, Hieroglyphic Stairway 3, and the scene on Naranjo Stela 24 involves taking captives. On Naranjo Stela 45 (Tokovinine and Fialko 2007, figure 4), the expression is emblazoned on a shield with flint blades on its corners. The victorious ruler on Yaxchilan Stela 18 (Tate 1992, figure 145) holds an incense burner marked with "*OCH-K'AHK'*" ("fire-entering"), whereas the expression on Naranjo Stela 24 (Graham 1975, 63) is inscribed into a plate with a blood offering held by the queen as she treads on a captive. The designs of the queen's headdress on Naranjo Stela 24 and of the king's incense burner and headdress on Yaxchilan Stela 18 constitute a clear reference to Teotihuacan iconography. The final example of the expression occurs on a stucco frieze in Yaxchilan Structure 21 (Tokovinine 2013a, 33) that depicts the king and the queens seated on the body of a Teotihuacan "War Serpent" emerging from a Storm God–shaped incense burner. This insistence on a Teotihuacan connection implies that there is more to the fire reference than a mere description of war-related destruction or even more than an allusion to the burning of holy grounds or temples—a metaphor that is well attested elsewhere in Mesoamerica, including the Cacaxtla murals (Helmke and Nielsen 2011; see chapter by Bassie-Sweet, this volume) and later Aztec pictorial manuscripts. As addressed by Nielsen (2006a, this volume), as well as by Fash and colleagues (2009), there appears to be a specific connection between fire making and establishing a new political order in Classic Maya imagination related to Teotihuacan. Such statements imply political control rather than destruction or perhaps evoke a distinct Teotihuacan way of waging ritually sanctioned wars (see Headrick 2007, 124–145).

The potential polyvalence of war-related, fire-making statements is key to understanding another category of references that deal with the "burning," *puluuy* (figure 5.2e), of enemy places, including *ch'een* locations. It is tempting to interpret such references as military raids or as violent attacks on holy grounds or, as some have suggested, specific acts of cave desecration (Brady and Colas 2005). Such interpretations lack an emphasis on order and control that allusions to Teotihuacan fire rituals imply; for example, the accession of K'ahk' Tiliw Chan Chaahk in the narrative on Naranjo Stela 22 (Graham 1975, 56) is followed by the "downfall" of K'inchil Kab and the "burning" of Bital and Tuubal. The text is concluded with a statement "it is my shield, flint, land" or perhaps, "it is my adding up / gathering of land" (Tokovinine 2013b, 44–45). Therefore, the military campaign is presented as an act of establishing order upon one's accession to kingship. That said, other references to fire making in the context of warfare may just refer to attacks with no implications of consequences or broader significance. "Drilling fire in Ik'a'" (Motul de San Jose) results in capturing a local noble in the military campaign detailed on Itzan Stela 17 (Tokovinine and Zender 2012, 54). An initial attack that preludes a retribution by the Sak Tz'i' ruler on the Denver Museum panel is described as the "scattering of fire" by the transgressor (Tokovinine 2013b, 34–35).

Capturing someone in warfare is described with two expressions, one of which is a relatively straightforward *chuhkaj* "she / he was seized." The second reference is still poorly understood despite an extensive discussion of its known occurrences and spellings by Martin (2004) and Velásquez García (2005). It is often spelled with a single character (T78, 514 in Thompson's catalog [1976]), which may be preceded by *ya-* and followed by *-he*, the latter likely a phonetic

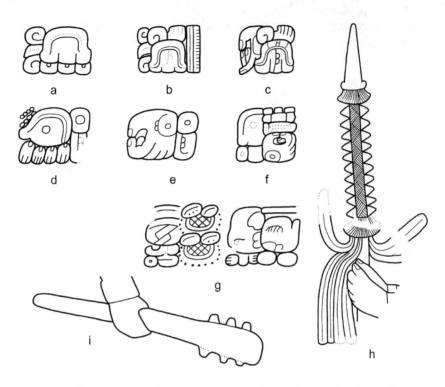

FIGURE 5.3. *Possible reading of T78, 514: a, ya-T78, 514-he (Dzibanche Hieroglyphic Stairway, Block 5, B2); b, **ya**-T78, 514-AJ (Dzibanche Hieroglyphic Stairway, Block 13, A3); c, ye-T78, 514 (Yaxchilan Lintel 35, C1); d, ye-he-TE' (Yaxchilan Hieroglyphic Stairway 5, 82); e, ye-TE' (Tonina Monument 153, A3); f, ye-TE' K'IN-ni-chi (Motul de San Jose Stela 1, C4); g, detail of Naranjo Stela 32; h, detail of Yaxchilan Stela 19; i, detail of Uaxactun Stela 5.*

complement (figure 5.3a). The -AJ character may also be added (figure 5.3b), perhaps as a spelling of the agentive -*aj* suffix meaning "person" (Houston, Robertson, and Stuart 2001, 6–7). Yet the same T78, 514 character may also be preceded by *ye-* (figure 5.3c), and the whole expression may be written as *ye-he-TE'* (figure 5.3d) and *ye-TE'* (figure 5.3e), which somehow substitute for T78, 514. As pointed out by Martin (2004, 110), in a single example T78, 514 substitutes for the usual *TE'* logogram in a different lexical context, but the uniqueness of the example implies that T78, 514 and *TE'* were seen as having different values, even though -*te'* was part of the phonetic value of T78, 514.

The substantial variation in the spelling of this possible term for captives is consistent with the way diphrastic kennings (*difrasismos*) appear in the Classic Maya script. The most relevant cases would be *saak sak ik'il*, "seed, white breath" (Kettunen 2005), and *saak mijjin*, "seed, child of father." Both are spelled with conflations, flexible reading order, and underspellings, all of which are attested for T78, 514 and its variants. If this assumption is correct, T78, 514 likely stands for a conflation of *TE'* with a logogram that would most likely be *EH*, "tooth," and potentially a third glyph with a reading that begins with *a-*, as the examples prefixed by *ya-* appear to indicate. Therefore, the full *difrasismo* would consist of *y-eh-te'-(aj)*, "his/her *ehte'* (person)," and *y-a . . .-te'-(aj)*, "his/her *a . . . te'* (person)." Given the similarity of T78, 514 to the *AT* "stinger" glyph (Lopes 2005), the second half of the kenning could be *y-at-te'-(aj)*. Since all known *ya*-T78, 514 spellings occur in a single text on the Dzibanche Hieroglyphic Stairway, it is equally plausible that *ya-AT TE'* or *ya-AT EH TE'* remained a uniquely local tradition, while the rest of T78, 514 examples stand only for *EH TE'*.

The term *ehte'* probably features the Ch'olan gloss *eh*, "tooth" (Kaufman and Norman 1984, 119). Romero (2015) recently offered an extended argument for the decipherment of T514 as a logogram for "tooth," with an emphasis on its resemblance to the conventions for representing teeth in the Classic Maya visual culture. However, I disagree with Romero's idea that the ergative prefix is permanently embedded in the logogram because such practice is otherwise absent in the script. Consequently, a combination with *TE'* for "spear" may not refer to the spear's edge or its sharpness. The compound *eh-te'* should instead mean "tooth spear." Although no such term is attested to in the Colonial sources, Yukatek *julte'* "throwing spear" (Barrera Vásquez et al. 1995, 244) and *nabte'* "hand spear" (Barrera Vásquez et al. 1995, 546) are good analogies. The translation of *ehte'* as a kind of weapon would certainly fit the lexical contexts such as the personal name Ye[h]te' K'inich, "the tooth spear of the Sun God" (figure 5.3f), popular with Motul de San Jose rulers (Tokovinine and Zender 2012). Halberds or *macuahuitl*-like weapons with spear points and rows of triangular blades or shark teeth are frequently depicted in Classic Maya imagery (figure 5.3h, 5.3i). The remains of one such weapon with an obsidian point and fifty-six shark teeth were discovered in Tomb 1 at Chiapa de Corzo (Lowe and Agrinier 1960, 40–42, figure 36, plates 18f, 19c–d). Given the complex craftsmanship and potentially exotic materials required to make such "tooth spear" weapons, they might signal a contrast between the elite warriors and the commoners armed with ordinary darts and spears.

The second half of the *difrasismo* might denote a similar weapon ("stinger spear"), but it is tempting to consider a possibility that a completely different class of objects was evoked. Tzeltalan languages share a gloss *aht* "to count (as in accounting)" (Ara 1986, 246; Kaufman 1972, 94; Laughlin 1975, 48). In Colonial Yukatek, *atal* means "to be paid" or "something paid" (Barrera Vásquez et al. 1995, 18). The gloss *te'* is also somehow related to accounting in the context of tribute payments (Miller and Martin 2004, 102). According to the main inscription and a caption to the scene on Piedras Negras Stela 12 (Stuart and Graham

2003, 61–63), the captives *utzakaw te'* "added up/stacked the stick(s)." The narrative on Naranjo Stela 32 (figure 5.3g; Graham 1978, 86) details how a subordinate lord K'uk' Bahlam gave several loads of cacao beans worth of tribute to the king and "added up/stacked the stick(s)" (Stuart 2006). References to weapons would not explain these contexts. At least one specific tribute-related gloss, (*y*)*ubte'*, attested in Classic-period inscriptions (Tokovinine and Beliaev 2013, 175) and Colonial Yukatek dictionaries (Barrera Vásquez et al. 1995, 980–981), is a combination of the term for a piece of cloth and *te'*, which together denote a piece of cloth of standardized size used in tribute transactions. Another Colonial term for tribute, *ximte'*, appears to consist of a numerical classifier for cacao and *te'* (Barrera Vásquez et al. 1995, 944–945). "Adding/stacking sticks" would then likely refer to operations with accounting devices such as tallies, and *a[h]t te'*, "counting stick" or "tally," would be a near perfect lexical match. Although no ethnohistoric accounts mention tallies in the Maya area, there are archaeological examples such as the inscribed shell tallies from Comalcalco (figure 5.4) that could be bound in stacks (as indicated by grooves on the plain sides) and contained records of the owner's ritual activities (Zender 2004b, 248–263). Courtiers with stacks of objects of similar size in the headdresses are present in the depictions of Classic Maya courtly life, including tribute payment scenes (figure 5.4b). The relative paucity of such tallies in the archaeological record is probably a result of the fact that most of them were made not from shell but from more perishable material like wood.

If the proposed interpretation of the T78, 514 and related glyphs is correct, the captives were referred to as people who pertained to the weapons and the accounting devices of the captor, his "halberd (person)" and "tally (person)." The first part of the *difrasismo* evoked warfare as a means of procuring captives, while the second implied that ransom or tribute was to be paid, perhaps in contrast to a more gruesome fate referenced by another term for captives, *baak*, "(trophy) bones." At least two war narratives (see below) conclude with placing the captives and captured items in a "house of *eh te' / aht te'*," perhaps a dedicated repository of trophies and tribute.

BROADER TRENDS IN WAR-RELATED LANDSCAPE REFERENCES

Now that the categories of place and warfare references have been defined, it is possible to consider larger trends in the relationship between them over the course of the Classic period. One can also investigate spatial variability in war landscapes, provided that the available sample is large enough to explore such an option.

As is often the case with Classic Maya inscriptions, the absolute numbers are rather misleading or at least are not as helpful as one might think. War-related place references are clearly on the rise in the Late Classic period, peak during the

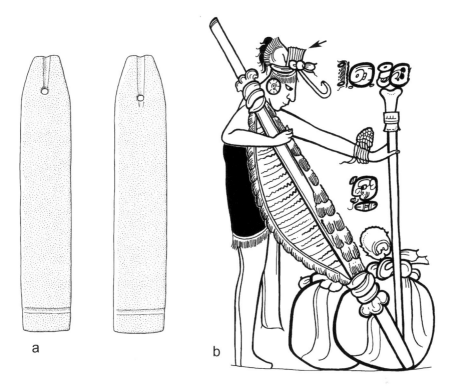

FIGURE 5.4. *Tallies in Maya archaeology and imagery: a, pendants 12A and 18A (Urn 26, Comalcalco); b, detail of the Late Classic vessel K1728.*

eighth century CE, and subsequently decline; however, this trend is a predictable outcome of the nature of the available data. Non-war references to places show the same trajectory, suggesting that it is the sample size and not changes in the relative importance of certain narrative types that causes the observable variation. Simply put, all kinds of references peak in the eighth century CE because it coincides with the absolute majority of known inscriptions.

The picture is more interesting if we consider relative frequencies of place reference types for each century (figure 5.5). In this way, one gets around the sample size factor and can see the contribution of a specific reference type to a total of place references in each century. This chart shows that the relative contribution of war-related place references to the total of place references remained fairly constant or even decreased; in other words, relatively the same quantity of places was mentioned in the narratives in connection to identifiable war-related events if we adjust for the different sample size in each century. The data do not suggest any major change in the presence of war in relation to other landscape references in Late Classic inscriptions. This finding seemingly

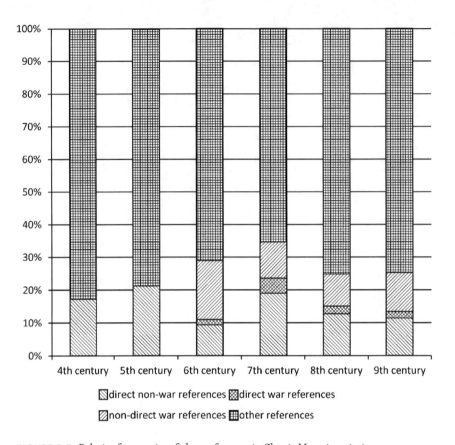

FIGURE 5.5. *Relative frequencies of place references in Classic Maya inscriptions*

contradicts the well-cited perception of the escalation of violence among Classic Maya polities, although the dataset does not deal with frequency of events but with co-occurrences of two types of references (acts of war and place names).

The absence of place names connected to war narratives during the fourth and fifth centuries CE may come down to the small number of inscriptions from this period. However, the relative frequency of non-war direct references to places as locations of events or objects of one's actions declines in the sixth century CE just as the war-related place references appear in the corpus, so there may be more going on than just different sample sizes. The sixth century CE is also interesting as most place references in war contexts appear in non-direct contexts—the names of perpetrators or victims of war-related acts. The seventh century CE sees a rise in direct references to places as objects/locations of warfare as well as other direct references to place names not related to warfare. The frequency of places in all direct references declines in the eighth and ninth

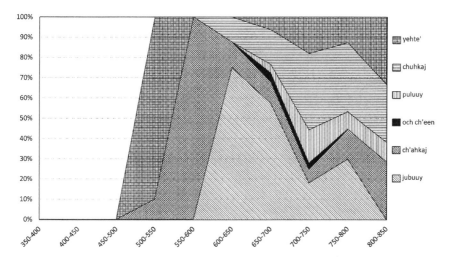

FIGURE 5.6. *Relative frequencies of place references in specific war-related clause types*

centuries CE as if the focus of the narratives once again shifts from the landscape to people and places with which they are associated.

These patterns are particularly significant if we take into account the relative frequencies of place names in specific war-related statements (figure 5.6). The sixth century CE is characterized by the near total dominance of toponyms in the names of captured individuals or their captors. The only other context is "chopping" statements. Such choices of narratives paint a landscape of raids and inconclusive military campaigns. The caveat is that perhaps there were other ways of writing about warfare that we cannot recognize as such; for example, the "arrival" of Sihyaj K'ahk' and the "entering" of Waxaklajuun Ubaah Kan "War Serpent" into the *ch'een* of Tikal, as the texts on Tikal Stela 31 and "Marker" inform us, was accompanied by the death of the previous king and followed by the accession of a new young lord with a Teotihuacan connection (Estrada-Belli et al. 2009; Martin 2003; Stuart 2000). And yet all descriptions of these events omit known references to violence and conquest: no one is captured, nothing is chopped or burned, rulers do not get overthrown, and no tribute is paid.

The seventh-century CE texts already feature all known war references in which place names may be mentioned. "Downfall" statements clearly dominate the narratives, whereas place names in captives' names decline sharply. In my opinion, this change implies a shift in the way Classic Maya written discourse dealt with landscapes and war—the new emphasis being on the outcome, the defeat of whole communities rather than raid-related destruction and captives. The known historical context is also significant because the seventh century CE was the time when Kanu'l lords of Dzibanche and Calakmul strove for dominance over most of the southern Maya lowlands (Martin and Grube 2008, 108–113). The result of their efforts was a more connected political landscape—hence a peak in direct reference to place names (war and non-war). The eventual failure of the Calakmul political project in the late seventh to early eighth centuries CE led to a progressive balkanization of the political landscape. Consequently, relative frequency of place names in relation to "downfall" declined, whereas contexts involving capture and "burning" increased. Finally, as the Classic Maya political landscape experienced a profound crisis in the Terminal Classic period, references to "downfall" of places disappeared altogether (this sample excludes the example on Yaxchilan Lintel 10 because of its unconventional paleography), and the written discourse on war and place became dominated by captives, "burning," and "chopping." Therefore, the relative frequency of reference types and specific expressions suggests a shift in the written discourse sometime in the sixth century CE when violence was mentioned for the first time in relation to places and people from specific locations. The aforementioned change was followed by another shift in which war statements became more focused on conquest and places rather than on individuals, likely associated with the Kanu'l/ Calakmul wars for regional dominance. The trend was reversed in the eighth century CE as the political landscape became more decentralized. Finally, written discourse of the ninth century CE implicated even greater balkanization and decline of conquest-oriented warfare, as places were no longer attacked to be "brought down." References to "chopping" and "burning" continued, as did mentions of places in the titles of captives.

The final set of broader trends to consider is the spatial distribution of the co-occurrences of war-related statements with place names. Regional differences in the ways of talking about landscape and warfare may be significant enough to inform our understanding of chronological patterns; for example, there appears to be no major variation in the spatial distribution of "chopping" statements (figure 5.7a). In contrast, the narratives on Dos Pilas monuments are characterized by a disproportionately high frequency of "downfall" events with place names (figure 5.7b). So even though "downfall" references are not unique to Dos Pilas, the abandonment of the site by the royal court around 761 CE (Martin and Grube 2008, 63) potentially affected the overall frequency of this type of statements in later inscriptions. References to the "burning" of places are almost exclusively restricted to Naranjo, with a few additional occurrences to the south and southwest of the site (figure 5.7c). "Ch'een entering" of places was not a preferred way of describing warfare in the region around Dos Pilas (figure 5.7d). It is possibly significant that "chopping" and "burning" of places are not mentioned at Yaxchilan or Piedras Negras: in the local discourse, places may fall, captives may be taken, but there is no emphasis on the destruction of locales in contrast to Naranjo inscriptions, where entire regions seem to be incinerated and axed.

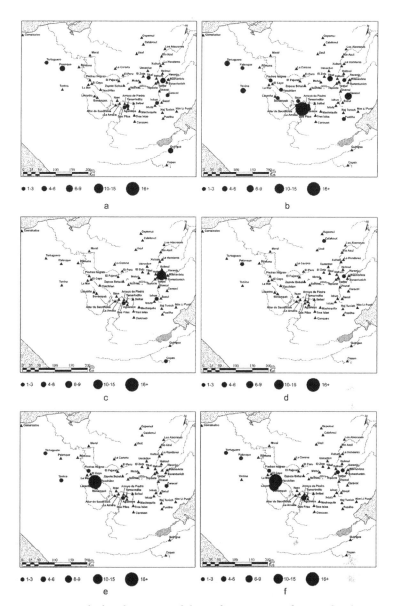

FIGURE 5.7. *Absolute frequencies of place references in specific war-related clause types:* a, ch'ahkaj; b, jubuuy; c, puluuy; d, och-ch'een; e, yeh-te'/yatte'; f, chuhkaj.

Instead, war narratives at Yaxchilan and other sites in the Usumacinta area highlight captives with place names in their titles (figure 5.7e, 5.7f). These regional differences may reflect actual spatial variation in the conduct of warfare, but just as in the case of the chronological patterns discussed above, we may be dealing with distinct traditions in the written discourse and not in military tactics or strategies.

PLACES IN THE NARRATIVES OF WAR

Who goes to war, and what goals do they pursue? It is worth emphasizing that the present chapter offers a review of the textual and visual sources, which do not necessarily reveal the actual causes of warfare (see chapter by Graham, this volume, for additional discussion). Moreover, our understanding of the Classic Maya economies, especially at the regional scale, remains woefully incomplete. That said, Classic Maya royal courts quite possibly pursued rational, long-term political and economic goals, and warfare was one of the many means of achieving these goals.

This point may be illustrated with a case of the Ik'a' lords of Motul de San José. When plotted on a map, the political network of that royal house in the eighth century CE (see Tokovinine and Zender 2012) closely overlaps the regional trade routes (figure 5.8). All of the known conflicts with Motul de San José's neighbors apparently involved access to the Upper Usumacinta and Pasion River Route and presumably further access to the Highland Verapaz Valley Route. The initial strategy of rapprochement with the courts of La Florida, Dos Pilas, and Tamarindito was likely thwarted by an increasingly assertive Yaxchilan royal house. Motul de San José rulers responded by forging an alliance with Yaxchilan that took on the Dos Pilas hegemony in the Pasion region. That attempt failed. The subsequent collapse of the Dos Pilas hegemony created a patchwork of conflicts and alliances between Motul de San José and various political actors in the Pasion region. Ultimately, Yaxchilan moved aggressively into the area and confronted Motul de San José and its allies. At no point in its history did the rulers of Motul de San José show a conflict of interest with the kingdoms to the north or east of the city. It also seems that the area under the control of Naranjo, its allies, and its clients was of no interest to Motul de San José rulers, with no record of friendly or hostile interactions. Geographic proximity alone does not explain these patterns.

As we saw in the previous section, Classic Maya perceptions and representations of war shifted between person-oriented conflict and place-oriented conquest campaigns. The same observations hold true if we turn to a micro-analysis of specific war narratives. Some of them do center on individual acts of aggression, which led to retribution such as the capture of the perpetrators. This type of narrative may be illustrated with a story on the so-called Denver and Brussels Panels (table 5.1) commissioned by Sak Tz'i' lord K'ab Chan Te' (Biro 2005, 2–8). Although the beginning of the inscription is missing, the first complete clause appears to contain a *casus belli* statement: La Mar ruler Nik Ahk

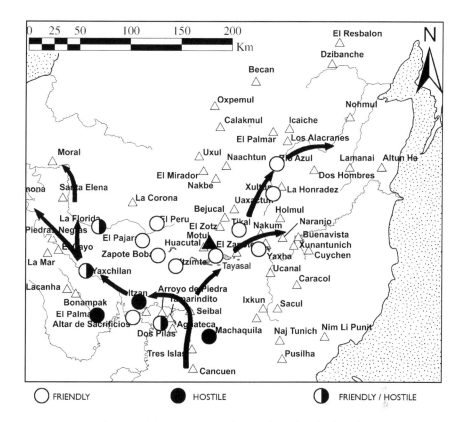

FIGURE 5.8. *Trade routes (after Demarest et al. 2014, figure 1) and political networking of Motul de San Jose rulers*

Mo' "scattered fire in the holy grounds" of Sak Tz'i' lord K'ab Chan Te' in 693 CE. The retribution comes on the following day when something that belongs to Nik Ahk Mo' is beheaded. Ak'e' lord Jun May Ahk Mo' is captured together with Yab K'awiil from K'an . . . Te'el over the next two days. Finally, four days after the initial attack, Yab K'awiil and individuals from six other locations are "summoned" (*pehkaj*) before K'ab Chan Te'. It is unclear if they are all captives or vassals, with formerly captured Yab K'awiil among them (Houston 2014). Here, the initial transgression and its agent are clearly identified in a statement with an active transitive verb. Sak Tz'i' lord K'ab Chan Te' is mentioned as the owner of the affected *ch'een*, and he then "tends to" the retribution and the conclusion of hostilities that are presumably enacted by his military captains.

The war narrative on Piedras Negras Stela 12 (Stuart and Graham 2003, 62) is rather similar in that it evokes a previous grievance, except that it places the transgression centuries before the response. The inscription mentions an Early Classic "ascent" to Pakbuul (Pomona) as some form of justification of attacks

TABLE 5.1. War narrative on the Denver and Brussels Panels

Transcription	Transliteration	Translation
DENVER PANEL		
(B5) 5 'Sip' u-CHOK K'AHK' (A6) NIK <u>AHK MO'</u> pe TUUN AJAW (B6) tu-CH'EEN-na <u>k'a-b'a</u> CHAN TE' (A7) SAK <u>TZ'I' AJAW</u>-wa BAAH ka-ba (B7) 1 PAS 1 'Ak'bal' (A8) u-? (B8) CH'AK BAAH-hi u-?	jo' 'sip' uchok[ow] k'ahk' nik ahk mo' pe['] tuun ajaw tu-ch'een k'ab chan te' sak tz'i'ajaw baah kab juun pa[h]s[aj] juun 'ak'bal' u- . . . ch'ak baah u-?	[on the day] Seven 'Sip', Pe' Tuun lord Nik Ahk Mo' scattered fire in the holy grounds of baahkab Sak Tz'i' lord K'ab Chan Te'. [At] first dawn [on the day] One Ak'bal it was his . . . , the beheading of . . . of
BRUSSELS PANEL		
(A1) NIK AHK MO' pe TUUN AJAW (B1) u-KAB-ya (A2) 2 WINIK.HAAB AJAW (B2) <u>k'a-ba</u> CHAN TE' (A3) u-2 K'IN-ni (B3) 2 'K'an' 3 'Chikchan' (A4) chu-ka-ja 1 MAY <u>AHK MO'</u> (B4) <u>a-k'e</u> AJAW yi-ta-ji (A5) ya-ba K'AWIIL-la AJ-K'AN-na <u>?-TE'</u>-la (B5) 4 'Kimi' pe-ka-ja (A6) ya-ba K'AWIIL-la AJ-K'AN-na <u>?-TE'</u>-la (B6) AJ-?-a AJ-CHAK TOOK'-la (A7) AJ-?-su AJ-pa-ni-la (B7) AJ-a-TUUN-ni AJ-a-bu-a (A8) pe-ka-ja yi-chi-NAL (B8) <u>k'a-ba</u> CHAN TE' SAK TZ'I' AJAW	nik ahk mo' pe['] tuun ajaw ukab[j]iiy cha' winikhaab ajaw k'ab chan te' ucha' k'in cha' 'k'an' hux 'chikchan' chu[h]kaj juun may ahk mo' ak'e' ajaw yitaaj yab' k'awiil aj k'an . . . te'el chan 'kimi' pe[h]kaj yab k'awiil aj k'an . . . te'el aj . . . a' aj chak took'al aj . . . s aj paniil aj atuun aj aaba' pe[h]kaj yichnal k'ab chan te' sak tz'i' ajaw	Pe' Tuun lord Nik Ahk Mo'; two score-year lord K'ab Chan Te' had tended to it. [On] the two days of Two 'K'an' [and] Three 'Chikchan' Ak'e' lord Juun May Ahk Mo' was captured; Yab K'awiil of K'an . . . Te'el had accompanied him. [On the day] Four 'Kimi' Yab K'awiil of K'an . . . Te'el, man of . . . a', man of Chak Took'al, man of . . . s, man of Paniil, man of Atuun, man of Aaba' were summoned. They were summoned before Sak Tz'i' lord K'ab Chan Te'.

in 792 and 795 CE when Pakbuul "fell down" twice and several individuals were seized and subsequently "added up their tallies" as captives of the Piedras Negras ruler and his key vassal from La Mar (Martin and Grube 2008, 152–153). In contrast to the narrative on the Denver and Brussels Panels, the lord of Pakbuul and his vassals presumably deserved to be attacked because they were from Pakbuul or descended from the families who committed the initial transgression. Retribution is depersonalized and agent-less ("Pakbuul fell down"). Although parts of the inscription on Stela 12 are missing, despite his double downfall, the ruler of Pakbuul himself was not captured and only his subordinates of *sajal* rank fell victim to the attack. The concluding statement lists significant captives, with a potential allusion to ransom or tribute payment; therefore, the end of hostilities is not dissimilar to the story of Nik Ahk Mo' and K'ab Chan Te'.

Humans are not the only agents of Classic Maya war stories, yet the participation of deities implies more than mere supernatural intervention, as gods may be patrons of places and royal households (see chapters by Christenson, and Hernandez and Palka, this volume). One such narrative is the inscription on the Hieroglyphic Stairway of the House C of the Palenque royal palace (Robertson 1991, figure 319), commissioned to commemorate the military exploits of K'inich Janaab Pakal (table 5.2). The story begins with Pakal's birth in 603 CE and his accession in 615 CE. It then goes back to 599 CE when Lakam Ha' (the ancient name of part of the archaeological site of Palenque) was devastated by its enemies. The text curiously mentions the deceased "Sky Witness" as the protagonist of the attack (see above), although it is possible that an omitted prefix means that the clause refers to a military commander of the late Kanu'l lord (Martin 2000b, 110–111; Martin and Grube 2008, 160, 164–165; Stuart and Stuart 2008, 140–141). The "chopped" place of Lakam Ha' is the focal point of the statement. The perpetrator is mentioned, but as a cause/orchestrator rather than the one who actually did the "chopping." The narrative cites links to the place names Kanu'l and "Maguey Altar" (Grube 2004a; Martin 1997a, 2005b), which identify "Sky Witness" as a member of one of the most ancient Classic Maya dynasties as if to show that if Palenque were to be desolated, it could only be arranged by one of the greatest Maya kings.

The destruction of Lakam Ha' was accompanied by a specific act of desecration when the three divine patrons of the Palenque rulers "were thrown." It was followed by an "opening" act involving Nuun Hix Lakam Chaahk and the ruler of Yaxchilan. The significance is opaque, but the text on Naranjo Stela 23 (discussed below) implies that the "opening" may refer to the desecration of ancestral graves (Grube 2000, 257–261; Martin and Grube 2008, 76). Finally, Santa Elena ruler Nuun Ujol Chaahk "filled/enclosed/buried it" (ubut'uw), presumably completing the ritual humiliation of the Palenque gods and ancestors (Polyukhovych 2012, 123; Simon Martin, personal communication, 2015). Of all the descriptions of the attack, it is the only sentence with an active transitive verb where the agent is clearly marked and named.

This last point is important in the context of the final part of the narrative. It shifts to 659 CE when Nuun Ujol Chaahk and other individuals not previously named were captured (Stuart and Stuart 2008, 158–159). A passage on one of the tablets in the Temple of the Inscriptions details the arrival of the captured Nuun Ujol Chaahk and the "eating" of enemy gods and captives by the Palenque divine patrons in the presence of the victorious K'inich Janaab Pakal impersonating the war deity Bolon Yook Te' (Guenter 2007, 49; Stuart and Stuart 2008, 169). The narrative on the Hieroglyphic Stairway (table 5.2) refers to the captives as the "tallies and halberds" (see above) of K'inich Janaab Pakal as Bolon Yook Te' at the "house of tallies and halberds," possibly the ancient name of the House C.

The narrative on the Palenque stairway is essentially a story of how an insult or damage to the gods of Lakam Ha' was avenged, with the highlighting of a

TABLE 5.2. War narrative on the Palenque Hieroglyphic Stairway

Transcription	Transliteration	Translation
(B6) 6 'Lamat' (C1) 1 CHAK ? CH'AK-ka LAKAM HA' u-KAB-ji OOX-xo ku-lu-a (D1) chi-'Altar' ya-AJAW TE' HUT-? CHAN ka-KAN-la AJAW (C2) ya-le-he 'G1' UNEN-K'AWIIL 'G3' (D2) i-PAS-ja u-?-AAN NUUN HIX LAKAM CHAAHK (C3) yi-ta-ji [ITZAM] ?KOKAAJ BAHLAM PA' CHAN AJAW ha-i (D3) u-bu-t'u-wa NUUN u-JOL CHAAHK wa-[k'a-be] AJAW (C4) i-chu-ka-ja 7 'Chuen' 4 IHK' SIHOOM-ma yi-ta-ji (D4) AHIIN CHAN-na a-ku ?AJAN a-ku (C5) ti-tz'a-? 7 ? SAK-ja-li ? (D5) u-?-?-ma EH TE'-he 9 OOK K'UH TE' (C6) K'IN JAN pa-ka-la K'UH BAAK AJAW EH TE' NAAH (D6) u-K'ABA' yo-OTOOT PAT-la-ja LAKAM HA'	wak 'lamat' juun chak [at] ch'a[h]k[aj] lakam ha' ukabij oox kula' chih 'altar' yajawte' hut . . . chan kanu'l ajaw yaleh 'G1' unen k'awiil 'G3' i-pa[h]saj u . . . aan nuun hix lakam chaahk yitaaj itzam kokaaj bahlam pa' chan ajaw haa' ubut'uw nuun ujol chaahk wak'be['] ajaw i-chu[h]kaj huk 'chuwen' chan[te'] ihk' sihoom yitaaj ahiin chan ahk ajan chan ahk . . . huk . . . sakjaal . . . u . . . [y]-eh te' [y-at te'] bolon [y]-ook te' k'uh k'in[ich] jan[aab] pakal k'uh[ul] baak[al] ajaw eh te' [at te'] naah uk'aba' y-otoot patlaj lakam ha'	[On the day] Six 'Lamat', One 'Sip' Lakam Ha' was chopped; oox kula', 'Maguey Altar' yajawte' Kanu'l lord 'Sky Witness' tended to it. 'G1', Unen K'awiil, 'G3' were thrown. Then the . . . of Nuun Hix Lakam Chaahk was opened. Pa' Chan lord Itzam Kokaaj Bahlam accompanied it. As for him, Wak'be' lord Nuun Ujol Chaahk filled/buried it. Then he was captured [on the day] Seven 'Chuwen', Four 'Ch'en'; Ahiin Chan Ahk, Ajan Chan Ahk, . . . Sakjaal . . . accompanied him; [they were] the halberds, the tallies of Bolon Yookte' god, holy Baakal lord K'inich Janaab Pakal [at] the house of halberds, the house of tallies, [which] is the name of his dwelling. It took shape [at] Lakam Ha'.

specific human perpetrator from Santa Elena; however, the retribution is cast pretty much as a divine act, and some of its victims are also enemy gods. The winning Palenque ruler assumes a specific divine identity but remains somewhat removed from the action. Who personally captured Nuun Ujol Chaahk and the others seems to be irrelevant. The final act belongs to the gods of the Palenque Triad when they eat the captives and their deities.

Some Classic Maya war narratives that embrace this divine will or divine charter framework avoid the subject of the initial perpetration altogether, as if the act of war were self-explanatory and did not require any justification. This approach may be illustrated with a story of Tikal's attack on Naranjo, as told on Lintel 2 of Temple 4 and Stela 5 at Tikal (Martin 1996, 2000b, 111–113). The inscription on Stela 5 (Jones and Satterthwaite 1982, figures 7 and 8) begins with Yihk'in Chan K'awiil's accession in 734 CE when he became king and "settled" (kajaay) at Sak Saak Lakal, the dwelling of one of Tikal's patron gods and the ch'een of the local Maize God and ancestors (Tokovinine 2013b, 30–31, 79–81). The narrative moves on to the completion of the thirteenth year of the k'atun in 744 CE, but the scene on the monument reveals Yihk'in Chan K'awiil with the defeated Naranjo ruler Yax Mayuy Chan Chaahk at his feet. Here, the monument presumably reveals something that happened between the two essential acts of rulership, settling among Tikal gods and ancestors and sustaining the renewal of time, but it does not elaborate, as if the circumstances of Yax Mayuy Chan Chaahk's capture were too insignificant.

The text on Lintel 2 (Jones and Satterthwaite 1982, figure 73) provides additional details (table 5.3). The campaign began in 744 CE when Yihk'in Chan K'awiil "descended" (Zender 2005, 13–14) from Sak Saak Lakal as Huk Chapaht Tz'ikiin K'inich Ajaw, a warrior manifestation of the Sun God that frequently carries "flint and shield." He "arrived at Tubal," a location approximately equidistant between Tikal, Motul de San Jose, and Naranjo. The "first dawn" of the following day saw the downfall of the "Wak Kab Nal person," probably the king of Naranjo identified by his Maize God (Tokovinine 2011, 96–97). The defeat happened at "the holy grounds of the Ihk' Miin god," the divine founder of the Naranjo dynasty. The holy grounds in this case are a cluster of temples at Naranjo associated with the Sa'aal place name (Tokovinine and Fialko 2007), where its king probably made his last stand. The narrative continues with the capture of Yax Mayuy Chan Chaahk's palanquin and war deity that was then housed in a special building, the same "house of tallies and halberds" as at Palenque. The story concludes with a procession in 747 CE when Yihk'in Chan K'awiil was likely carried (the verb in question is unclear) in the captured palanquin while dressed as the Maize God of the "Maguey Altar" place and of the Kanu'l kings of Calakmul (Tokovinine 2013b, 116–120), whom he defeated in 736 CE (Martin and Grube 2008, 48–49, 113).

The confrontation between Naranjo and Tikal is cast as a conflict between the gods and ancestors of each place, which does not require further justification and implies involvement from entire sociopolitical communities associated with each group of deities. Yihk'in Chan K'awiil descends from the temple of his gods/ ancestors/maize, and then the enemy lord is brought down in the holy grounds of his divine ancestor. Yihk'in Chan K'awiil's Sun God prevails over Yax Mayuy Chan Chaahk's war palanquin god. The Maize God of Tikal (Wak Hix Nal Maize God as known from other contexts) prevails over the Naranjo ruler's Maize God, just as Tikal's Maize God prevailed over the Calakmul Maize God. The defeated gods are taken and even somehow absorbed by the winner (see similar examples in chapters by Christenson, and Hernandez and Palka, this volume).

The Tikal narrative may be compared to the stories detailing Naranjo's conquests of Yaxha (Grube 2000, 257–265; 2004b, 201, 206–207; Grube and Martin 2004, 49, 72–74; Martin and Grube 2008, 76, 82). The first campaign was described on Stela 23 (table 5.4; Graham 1975, 60). It began in 710 CE with the "burning" of the ch'een of the "powerless" (ma' ch'abil ma' ak'abil) Yaxa' lord Joyaj Chaahk, who apparently escaped with his Tikal wife shortly after his accession to kingship. Naranjo ruler K'ahk' Tiliw Chan Chaahk "had tended to" (ukabjiiy) those

TABLE 5.3. War narrative on Lintel 2, Temple 4, Tikal

Transcription	Transliteration	Translation
(B3) 6 'Eb' (A4) CHUM-mu K'AN-JAL-wa (B4) EHM-ye SAK ?SAAK LAK-la (A5) 7 CHAPAHT TZ'IKIIN K'IN (B5) yi-IHK'-K'IN CHAN K'AWIIL-la (A6) K'UH ?WAYWAL (B6) HUL tu-ba-la (A7) 1 PAS (B7) 7 'Ben' (A8) 1 K'AN-JAL-wa (B8) ?JUB (A9) 6 KAB NAL-la (B9) tu-CH'EEN-na (A10) IHK' mi-?MIIN K'UH (B10) BAAK-wa-ja (A11) TZ'UNUN PIIT-ta-la (B11) ?-chi-yu (A12) SAAK-ki pi-li-pi (B12) IHK' K'IN-ni hi-HIX (A13) IHK' HUUN-na (B13) u-K'UH-li (A14) YAX ma-yu CHAN CHAAHK-ki (B14) SAK CHWEN-na (A15) ?ye-EH TE' NAAH-ji-ya (B15) KAL-ma TE'	wak 'eb' chum k'anjalaw ehmey sak saak lakal huk chapaht tz'ikiin k'in[ich ajaw] yihk'in chan k'awiil k'uh[ul] waywal hul[i] tubal juun pa[h]s[aj] huk 'ben' juun[te'] k'anjalaw jub[uuy] wak kab nal tu-ch'een ihk' miin k'uh baakwaj tz'unun piital . . . saak pilip ihk'in hix ihk' huun uk'uhuul yax mayu[y] chan chaahk sak chwen yeh te' [at te'] naahiiy kaloom te'	[On the day] Seven 'Eb', the seating of 'Pohp', holy sorcerer Huk Chapaht Tz'ikiin K'inich Ajaw Yihk'in Chan K'awiil descended from Sak Saak Lakal. He arrived at Tubal. [At] first dawn [on the day] Seven 'Ben', One 'Pohp' Wak Kab Nal [person] fell down in the holy grounds of the god Ihk' Miin. The hummingbird palanquin . . . Saak Pilip Ihk'in Hix Ihk' Huun, the god of white *chuwen* Yax Mayuy Chan Chaahk, was taken captive. It had been [at] the house of halberds, the house of tallies of the Kaloomte'.

events. Three months later, according to the same text, the bones and skull of a recently deceased Yaxa' lord, Yax Bolon Chaahk, were "opened" and "scattered on the island" (Grube 2000, 257–261). Finally, it appears that K'ahk' Tiliw Chan Chaahk "added up / stacked" the enemy deities as his "halberd and tallies." In so doing, he was accompanied by two poorly understood Naranjo gods or groups of deities (Tokovinine 2011, 98).

The second campaign against Yaxha took place in 799 CE. The longer inscription on Stela 12 (Graham 1975, 36) lists a series of "chopping" attacks unleashed on Yaxha and its dependencies by Itzamnaah K'awiil of Naranjo. Yaxha ruler K'inich Lakam Tuun "ran" (*ahni*) and sought refuge (*t'abaay*) at various locations but was eventually taken captive. His precious possessions (*ikaatz*) and his palanquin were "presented" (*nawaj*) before Itzamnaah K'awiil (Stuart 1998, 414). The narrative on Naranjo Stela 35 (Graham 1978, 92) retells the story from a different angle. The emphasis is on the patron deity of Yaxha, a manifestation of the Jaguar Lord of the Underworld, who was impersonated by K'inich Lakam Tuun on at least one occasion according to Yaxha Stela 31 (Grube 2000, 263–265; Martin 1997b). The text on Naranjo Stela 35 evokes a mythical event in which the same old jaguar fire deity was burned by "four men, four youths" and then states that Itzamnaah K'awiil "repeated" it (*ukobow*) as he tended to the beheading of

TABLE 5.4. War narrative on Stela 23, Naranjo

Transcription	Transliteration	Translation
(E9) PUL-yi (F9) u-CH'EEN (E10) ma CH'AB AK'AB-li (F10) JOY-ja-ya CHAAHK (E11) YAX-a AJAW (F11) 18 K'IN-ni (E12) a-AJAW-ni (F12) i-LOK'-yi (E13) yi-ta-ji (F13) ya-AT-na (E14) IX MUT AJAW (F14) u-KAB-ji-ya (E15) K'AHK TIL-wi (F15) CHAN-na CHAAHK (E16) K'UH (F16) SA' AJAW-wa (E17) 17 4 WINIK-ji (F17) 2 'Men' (E18) 13 YAX K'IN-ni (F18) pa-sa-ja (E19) u-BAAK-le (F19) u-JOL (E20) YAX 9 CHAAHK (F20) YAX-a AJAW (E21) CHOK ti PET-ni (F21) u-TZ'AK-wa (G1) ya-? (H1) K'UH (G2) ye-TE' (H2) K'AHK TIL-wi (G3) CHAN-na CHAAHK (H3) K'UH SA' AJAW (G4) yi-ta-ji (H4) no-NOH-la (G5) ?-na (H5) xa-MAN-na (G6) ?-na (H6) AJ-SA'-li	puluuy uch'een ma['] ch'abil [ma'] ak'abil joyaj chaahk yaxa' ajaw waxak-lajuun k'in[iiy] ajawaan[iiy] i-lok'ooy yitaaj yatan ix mut[al] ajaw ukabjiiy k'ahk' tiliw chan chaahk k'uh[ul] sa'[aal] ajaw huklajuun[hew] chan winikjiiy cha' 'men' huxlajuun[te'] yaxk'in pa[h]saj ubaakel ujol[el] yax bolon chaahk yaxa' ajaw cho[h]k[aj] ti peten utz'akaw y . . . k'uh ye[h] te' [at te'] k'ahk' tiliw chan chaahk k'uh[ul] sa'[aal] ajaw yitaaj nohol . . . n xaman . . . n aj-sa'aal	The holy grounds of the powerless Yaxa' lord Joyaj Chaahk burned. He then fled with the Mutal princess, his wife, eighteen days since he became king. Holy Sa'aal lord K'ahk' Tiliw Chan Chaahk had tended to it. Seventeen days, four months later, [on the day] Two 'Men', Thirteen Yaxk'in, the bones and the skull of Yaxa' lord Yax Bolon Chaahk were opened. They were scattered on the island. He added up/ stacked . . . god(s). It was the halberd, the tally of holy Sa'aal lord K'ahk' Tiliw Chan Chaahk. Southern . . . , Northern . . . of Sa'aal accompanied him.

the god of the "powerless" (ma' ch'abil ma' ak'abil) K'inich Lakam Tuun. The scene on the monument shows the victorious Naranjo ruler preparing to reenact the mythical torching episode on the bound K'inich Lakam Tuun.

Just as in the Tikal narratives, these attacks do not appear to have required any prior transgression as a *casus belli*. Instead, they are cast as repeats of the ancient conflicts between the deities associated with Yaxha and Naranjo; for example, Itzamnaah K'awiil appears as a mere agent of the will of the gods he embodies. Victory is clearly linked to a successful destruction and appropriation of enemy gods and ancestors in addition to the capture of enemy rulers. It is significant that Naranjo narratives are full of place names and deities, but there are very few humans apart from the attacker and the victim. The emphasis seems to be not on settling personal scores but on defeating and partially appropriating a hostile, political community objectified as its holy places and divine patrons (see chapters by Christenson, and Hernandez and Palka, this volume).

SUMMARY AND CONCLUSIONS

Despite difficulties with identifying place names and war-related statements in the Classic Maya textual record, this discussion has offered macro- and micro-level views of how war landscapes were represented in the available narratives. On the macro-level, we have seen that while the relative contribution of war narratives to other kinds of references to places remained more or less constant, the dominant types of references to places in the context of war changed over time. The seventh century CE saw the highest relative frequency of narrative contexts indicative of conquest warfare, with emphasis on places rather than individuals. The eighth century CE was marked by a decline of such contexts. Sixth- and ninth-century CE narratives are broadly similar in that the emphasis of war references was on people associated with certain places in contrast to places as locations or victims of war-related acts. These trends coincide with the observed centralization of the Classic Maya political landscape in the seventh century CE, which was preceded and followed by a less centralized geopolitical order. Data from the fourth and fifth centuries CE, associated with an episode of Teotihuacan-Tikal political centralization, stand out for the absence of identifiable landscape-war references, as if a different discourse was in place. The ninth-century CE accounts seem to reflect an increasing balkanization of the political landscape.

On a micro-level, war references to places range from stories of personal transgressions and retributions to narratives involving entire political communities embodied by their rulers and gods. A prior attack against one's holy grounds (ch'een) may have been mentioned, but other narratives cast acts of war as part of the preexisting order of things—confrontations between different regional deities in which the attacker simply fulfilled the roles of certain gods. Sometimes, as in Yihk'in Chan K'awiil's conquest of Naranjo, one can identify multiple (and partially overlapping) sets of deities associated with the winning and losing sides, including maize gods, ancestors, war gods, and local divine patrons. Destruction and appropriation of enemy gods and ancestors seemed to be an essential component of a successful conquest of a place, in addition to capturing its ruler and other members of the court.

Acknowledgments. The Classic Maya Place Name Database Project was supported by grants from FAMSI and Harvard University. The final stage of the project benefited from a Dumbarton Oaks Junior Fellowship. The endeavor would have been impossible without guidance from my mentors and colleagues William Fash, Stephen Houston, and Gary Urton. I would also like to thank Shawn Morton and Meaghan Peuramaki-Brown for the kind invitation to contribute to the volume and the editorial input that substantially improved the original manuscript. My special thanks to Elizabeth Graham, Dmitry Beliaev, and the anonymous reviewers for their comments and suggestions on this chapter. I remain solely responsible for any errors and omissions.

6

"When We Two Parted"

Remaking the Ancient Maya Political Landscape of North-Central Belize

HELEN R. HAINES AND KERRY L. SAGEBIEL

When we two parted
In silence and tears,
Half broken-hearted,
To sever for years,
Pale grew thy cheek and cold,
Colder thy kiss;
Truly that hour foretold
Sorrow to this!

LORD BYRON, "WHEN WE TWO PARTED" (EXCERPT)

Understanding the nature of the social and political organizations of ancient Maya polities has been a key focus in Maya studies for well over half a century. This debate encompasses discussion at both the inter-polity and intra-polity levels. We know that politics in the Maya world were part of a dynamic process that saw rulers create alliances, only to break these bonds to realign themselves with other factions. Sometimes these alliances were hegemonic in nature, while

DOI: 10.5876/9781607328872.c006

at other times they were hierarchical, forcibly created through warfare and conquest. Epigraphic and iconographic evidence records these conflicts between the rulers of Maya cities, and there are many monuments depicting captives taken in battle, some of which were the ruling kings of contesting cities.

Despite considerable study, there are many unanswered questions regarding the quotidian application of political power in these cases. One key issue that remains unclear is the nature, or degree, of power a conquering king held over the territory he vanquished. In some cases, such as at Tikal, we see a defeated area "falling silent" for decades, while in other areas we see rulership continuing virtually undisturbed with the kings continuing to use the title of *k'uhul ajaw*, or "divine lord," although now under the acknowledged suzerainty of a different site (see chapter by Tokovinine, this volume).

Understanding the nuances of political interactions of past cultures frequently entails the careful knitting together of often-disparate lines of evidence. The sporadic discovery of these puzzle pieces obliges us to rethink, expand, and even remake our interpretations as new information emerges. Such is the case for the region around the large and well-known site of Lamanai in north-central Belize. In this chapter we will revisit the epigraphic discussions of Stela 9, Lamanai, in light of new archaeological data from Ka'kabish. Evidence from these two sources when combined, although drawn from material excavated decades apart, provides a fuller and more nuanced understanding of the ancient Maya landscape of north-central Belize and elucidates the dynamic nature of Early Classic–period Maya politics.

REGIONAL SETTING

The region is defined on the east side by mangrove swamps along the Caribbean coast and demarcated on the west by the Río Bravo escarpment: a dramatic, roughly 80–90 m uplift (Lohse 2004, 121). The northern and southern boundaries are more geographically amorphous (figure 6.1). Although the northern boundary is generally drawn along the Río Hondo, this may not accurately reflect Maya cultural boundaries but rather be an easy geographic reference point, one that also constrains broader studies because of its role as a modern political border. While the actual southern boundary is also uncertain, there are clear differences in the ceramic stylistic attributes of the north-central area and those of the Belize River Valley (see Awe 1992; Cheetham 2005; Graham 1987b; Kosakowsky 1987; Kosakowsky and Pring 1998; Powis 2001, 2002), leading us to hypothesis that a cultural division existed between these two spheres, somewhere around the south end of the New River Lagoon.

Geographically, the area is largely flat, rising gradually from the coast to the foot of the Río Bravo escarpment. This relatively even countryside is interrupted in places by a series of limestone ridges that protrude from the landscape,

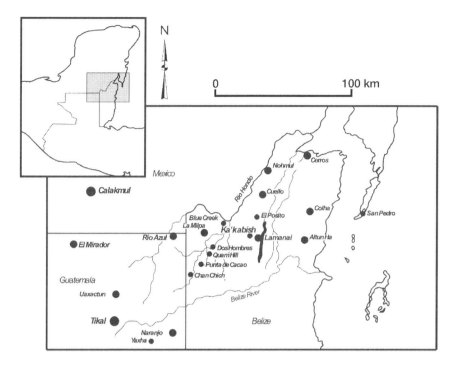

FIGURE 6.1. *Map of Northern Belize and Central Peten showing key sites*

running down the center of the region along a roughly northeast/southwest axis (Hammond 1973; Wright et al. 1959). Several long rivers, including the Río Hondo to the north, the Booth and Bravo Rivers to the west, and the Northern and New Rivers in the middle of the region, crosscut the landscape. Other large water sources include several lagoons (more prevalent near the coast), the largest of these being the New River Lagoon at the southern terminus of the New River. These diverse topographic features are important aspects for reconstructing the ancient Maya landscape.

Numerous settlements have been documented in the region, including Altun Ha, Cerros, Colha, Cuello, El Pozito, K'axob, Lamanai, Nohmul, San Estevan, and Santa Rita (Chase 1990; Chase and Chase 1988, 1998, 2004, 2005; Graham 1987b; Graham, Pendergast, and Jones 1989; Hammond 1985, 1991; Hammond, Clark, and Donaghey 1995; Hammond et al. 1987; Hester 1983; Hester, Eaton, and Shafer 1980; Hester, Shafer, and Eaton 1982, 1994; Hester et al. 1979; Levi 1993, 2002; McAnany 2004; Neivens and Libbey 1976; Pendergast 1979, 1981, 1982, 1985, 1986, 1990, 1992, 1993, 1998; Pyburn 1990, 1991; Robertson and Freidel 1986; Rosenswig 2008, 2009; Rosenswig and Kennett 2008). Many of these settlements are located either adjacent to waterways or on ridge tops, while other small and less well-known sites dot the coastline (Vail 1988). Not only were the rivers and ridges strategic locations, but riverine trade and access to the coast were integral to the economy as long-distance trade routes.

The location of ancient Maya settlements is likely a result of geophysical and environmental reasons in addition to economic or strategic considerations, as much of the coastal area is unsuitable for the construction of large centers because of its low-lying and marshy nature (Pendergast 1979, 7). A large portion of the land between the Northern River and the northern coast, from modern-day Sarteneja to just north of Belize City, consists mainly of coastal lagoons, beach ridges, and swamps and has been described as a "featureless, marshy plain" (Vail 1988, 3–4; see also Wright et al. 1959, 211, 224), a description that can be extended into the low-lying interior areas. This environment has been described as "suitable for neither habitation nor farming" (Thomson 2004, xiv). While mangrove swamps predominate along the area with black mangrove forests in the interior areas (Vail 1988, 4), patches of drier calcareous land exist on which "a 'cohune ridge' or 'broken ridge' vegetation" pattern predominates, and it is on these "islands" that most sites in the area are situated (Hammond 1981, 183).

To the west of the New River, the land becomes higher and drier, although some low-lying *bajos* are notable along the lower New River closer to the coast (Johnson 1983). Both Ka'kabish and Lamanai are located in this drier interior zone. Vegetation in the area falls into Wright's "dry tropical zone" classification, which consists of broadleaf deciduous forests (Wright et al. 1959, 29). Although a formal survey of the vegetation for Ka'kabish has yet to be conducted, pre-liminary observations have noted the presence of cohune palms (likely *Orbignya* spp.), allspice, copal, ceiba, and ficus trees. Many of these trees are also present at Lamanai (Lambert and Arnason 1978), positioned along the northwest bank of the New River Lagoon, at the headwaters of the New River. Situated roughly 10 km inland from Lamanai at approximately 270 degrees northwest, Ka'kabish is constructed atop a distinct limestone ridge. Its location on this ridge would have not only provided the inhabitants with a commanding view of the surrounding area but would have also made the site clearly visible from other locations on the landscape, including the ridge to the east on which Lamanai lies and from the edge of the Río Bravo escarpment to the west. Unlike Lamanai, which has been the site of previous archaeological research (Graham 1987b, 2004; Graham, Pendergast, and Jones 1989; Pendergast 1981, 1985, 1986, 1992, 1993, 1998; Simmons 2005, 2006; Simmons, Pendergast, and Graham 2009), Ka'kabish is considerably less well-known and has only recently become the focus of archaeological inves-tigations (Haines 2008a, 2008b, 2010, 2011a, 2011b, 2011c, 2012; McLellan 2012; Tremain 2011; Tremain and Haines 2013).

A review of the corpus of Maya texts will show that north-central Belize was largely peripheral to the political heartland, or hotbed, of the Classic period:

the Central Peten. By "peripheral" we mean there are few extant carved monuments in the region, and those that are present do not directly reference any of the Central Peten sites. Nor do we see any evidence of other sites from the Peten or elsewhere referencing cities such as Lamanai, the largest community in this part of the coastal plain in terms of the size and number of monumental constructions (Andres 2005, 17), or any other location in north-central Belize that we can determine. Unlike Caracol and sites in the Belize River Valley, which played a role on the larger "global" Maya political landscape as noted through monuments and other epigraphic inscriptions, sites in north-central Belize seem to have been largely excluded from the greater political game. As the point of our chapter revolves around the changing relationship between Ka'kabish and Lamanai as a means of broadening our understanding of conflict in the Classic period, it is to these two sites that we will devote our discussion.

OVERVIEW OF LAMANAI

Lamanai is the largest site in the region; and it is highly likely that its position near the mouth of the New River Lagoon played a factor in its prosperity, longevity, and concomitant urban sprawl, as the lagoon and river system were an important part of the ancient Maya trade network (Graham 2011; Pendergast 1977, 131, 1986, 245). Excavations at the site revealed a long history beginning in the Middle Formative period and continuing, albeit with changes in the political system, through to Historic times (Graham 1987b; Graham, Pendergast, and Jones 1989; Pendergast 1981, 1985, 1986, 1992, 1993, 1998). Several structures have been dated to the late Middle Formative period (ca. 600–400 BCE; Structures N9–56, N10–43, P89, P8–11, and P8–103 [Pendergast 1981, 42; Powis 2001, 2002]); however, it was during the Late Formative period that intensive occupation and construction began at the site. This development boom saw the construction of many monumental buildings, including the Mask Temple (N9–56) and the High Temple (N10–43), the latter of which is the largest building in the area, standing roughly 33 m tall (Pendergast 1981).

Construction activity continued throughout the Classic period and into the Postclassic (Graham 2011; Pendergast 1984, 1985, 1986). Construction projects at Lamanai during the Late Classic period tended to conserve labor by focusing on simply remodeling the front facades of large public structures (e.g., the Jaguar Temple and High Temple) rather than completely rebuilding (Pendergast 1992, 73). This parsimony may have been caused by a decline or restriction in available labor tribute (Howie, White, and Longstaffe 2010, 373; Pendergast 1992, 73). This conservation of labor may have a correlation in the small number of palaces, or elite residential structures (i.e., a probable "mega-palace group to the south-east of N10–43" [Elizabeth Graham, personal communication, 2014]), constructed during the Late Classic period and by extension a lesser number of high-ranking elite individuals to organize architectural constructions.

One location that did seem to be the focus of considerable activity in the latter part of the Late Classic through the Early Postclassic is Group N10[3], also known as the Ottawa Group. It is believed that this group, at least in the eighth century CE, was funded as a kind of administrative and possibly residential center for Lamanai rulers (Howie, White, and Longstaffe 2010, 394). In the ninth century CE, the courtyard group underwent considerable remodeling and renovation work, including the razing of a stucco frieze with rulership images before filling and raising the courtyard and changing the structures from stone to combinations of stone and perishable materials (Graham 2004, 224). It is believed that occupation of this group and other areas of the site continued into the Early and possibly Late Postclassic periods (Graham 2004).

While there are numerous monumental structures and residential buildings at the site, only two altar stones (one fragmentary) and nine stelae have been recovered. Carvings were noted on only three stelae (Stelae 1, 2, and 9) and on both altar stones, along with a "gigantic slab" (possibly part of a large low wall) on Structure N10–36 (Pendergast 1983, 3). With the exception of Stela 9, discussed below, the texts and images on these monuments are "indecipherable" as a result of "extensive abrasion and other damage" (Pendergast 1988, 1, 3). Large iconographic decorations in the form of masks were discovered on several buildings, most notably on Structures N10–9 ("the Jaguar Temple" [Pendergast 1977, 130]), N10–43 ("the High Temple"), and N9–56 ("the Mask Temple"). Based on its large site size, longevity, and presumed concomitant prosperity, coupled with its history of and investment in monumental buildings from an early date, it is perhaps unsurprising that articles referring to north-central Belize often confer on Lamanai, a priori, the role of a major, if not the only, capital city in the region (Andres 2005, 17; Mathews 1991).

The presence of an emblem glyph on Stela 9 at Lamanai, an identifier most often associated with primary or politically significant centers, lends credence to the importance ascribed to Lamanai during the Classic period. The emblem glyph is assumed to represent "a polity centered at Lamanai" (Closs 1988, 14), although the main sign has not been conclusively identified (Closs 1988, 14); nor is there comparative epigraphic data to securely ascribe it to Lamanai (Simon Martin, personal communication, 2012). This monument, the only one that retains decipherable carving of any quantity, may also shed additional, more in-depth light on the political dynamics of the early half of the Late Classic period (ca. 600–750 CE).

The Archaeological Context of Stela 9

Stela 9 is associated with Structure N10–27, a "moderately large structure" (Pendergast 1983, 1) situated along the eastern edge of one of the complexes that comprise the ceremonial precinct at Lamanai (Pendergast 1988, 1; see also

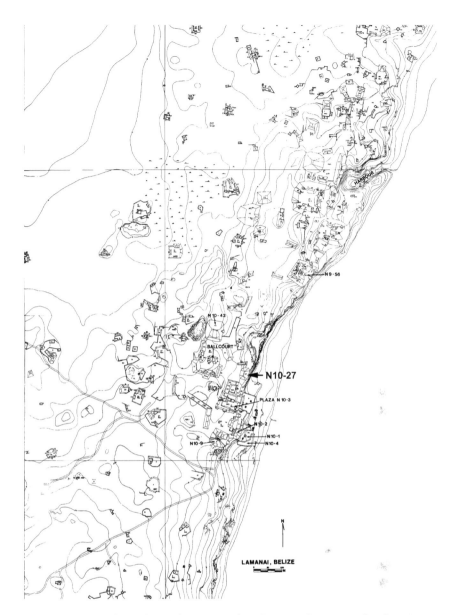

FIGURE 6.2. *Map of central area of Lamanai, Belize.* Courtesy, *Lamanai Archaeology Project.*

figure 6.2). The structure was built in at least two episodes, with the final construction displaying an architectural form referred to as the "Lamanai Building
Type" (LBT): a masonry building, rather than being placed at the summit of
the high, terraced platform, is situated partway up the face of the substructure,

perpendicular to the primary axis, and the summit is devoid of a permanent building (Loten 2006, 95; Loten and Pendergast 1984, 3; Pendergast 1981, 36, 1988, 5). This form appears at Lamanai at the beginning of the seventh century CE and continues to be constructed throughout the seventh century and into the eighth century CE (Pendergast 1988, 5).

Stela 9 was found broken, with the base of the monument discovered in situ in the central room of the LBT (Pendergast 1988, 4). The upper portion of the stela was found facedown at the foot of the short set of stairs in front of the room, buried a scant 35 cm below the surface and resting directly on the steps (Pendergast 1988, 1). Whereas the upper portion of the stela was well preserved, the lower portion was damaged, apparently because of a fire that was also responsible for fracturing the monument. Although it is conceivable that the fire was the result of a ritual gone awry, Pendergast (1988, 7) believes, and we concur, that it was more likely that the destruction of the monument was the result of a deliberate act (Graham 2004).

The theory that the destruction of Stela 9 was deliberate is evinced in diverse lines of evidence, not the least of which is the location of the upper portion of the monument. From its position in the room, it is impossible for the top half of the monument to have reached its final resting place at the foot of the stairs without human assistance (Pendergast 1988, 7). The room in which the stela was located is of sufficient size that should the monument have broken and fallen unassisted, it would have remained on the floor of the room. The lack of "striations, impact fractures, or other damage of the sort that would surely have resulted from a high-speed slide down the steps" (Pendergast 1988, 7) suggests not only that the toppling of the monument was a deliberate act but also that it was a "controlled event" (Pendergast 1988, 7; see also chapter by Hernandez and Palka, this volume, for comparative examples).

In considering the heat necessary to fracture the monument, it is clear that in order to break the thick limestone, the fire had to be "of considerable intensity" (Pendergast 1988, 4) and was therefore clearly far in excess of one needed for ritual purposes. The blaze resulted not only in severe damage to the monument itself, in the form of blackening, crazing, and spalling on the lower portion, but also to the room in which the stela was housed: the fire caused calcination of the floor around the monument and charring on the rear wall of the room. In addition, the lack of material below the fallen upper portion of the monument indicates that the structure was not only in use but was also well maintained at the time the stela fell (Pendergast 1988, 6), ruling out possible post-abandonment damage, natural collapse, or destruction caused by a forest fire. Evidence from the excavation of a midden that accumulated on the plaza and against the lowermost terrace faces of Structure N10–27 also indicates that the LBT was deliberately razed because wall collapse lay on a clean plaza surface, with no evidence of natural abandonment and decay (Graham 2004).

According to Graham (2004, 230), accumulation of the midden began "virtually immediately" after the building was destroyed and the stela burned. Midden deposition seems associated with a shift in ritual activity away from Structure N10–27 to the Ottawa Group (N10[3]) to the south (Graham 2004, 230–231). Based on the ceramic material comprising the midden, Elizabeth Graham (personal communication, 2013) posits that the destruction of the LBT occurred during the Terminal Classic Terclerp ceramic phase (750–900 CE; Graham 2004, 230–231), with a most probable date sometime around 800 CE (Graham, personal communication, 2013).

The Epigraphic Content of Stela 9

Both Michael Closs (1988) and Simon Martin have conducted epigraphic analyses of Stela 9 (figure 6.3). While the translations do not agree exactly, to be expected in light of recent advancements in epigraphic translations, they do agree on certain key aspects that are relevant to our interpretation. Three things are of particular interest in our discussion: (1) the date of the monument, (2) the regalia worn by the individual in the iconographic image, and (3) the sociopolitical titles ascribed to at least one of the individuals mentioned in the text.

The first key point on which the translations agree is the date for the creation of the monument. The inscription begins with a date recording an event in 625 CE (Simon Martin, personal communication, 2012), which is also presumed to be the date when the monument was erected. Stela 9 goes on to record a second unknown event, seventeen years prior in 608 CE (Closs 1988; Simon Martin, personal communication, 2012). Martin has also suggested that this may be the death of the previous ruler, "Sun Shark," the father of K'ahk' Yipiiy Chan Yopaat who commissioned the monument.

Along with the epigraphic text, the surviving portion of Stela 9 contains an image of a lord dressed in elaborate regalia. Martin (personal communication, 2012) speculates that this may be the dead lord or, more likely, the living king wearing heirloom regalia inherited from his father (see Reents-Budet 1988 for a detailed description of the monument). Of critical importance to our discussion is the ideological and political meaning encoded in the regalia, particularly that of the headdress. Taube (1992b, 82) has identified this headdress as a "War Serpent Headdress" and sees it as having originated at Teotihuacan, where it was used in association with the warrior complex and the Temple of Quetzalcoatl (see also chapters by Bassie-Sweet and Nielsen, this volume). The headdress appears in imagery elsewhere in Mesoamerica, including at Zapotec and Maya sites where it carries clear associations with war (Taube 1992b). Taube believes that "for the Maya, the War Serpent appears to be directly associated with rulership" and that

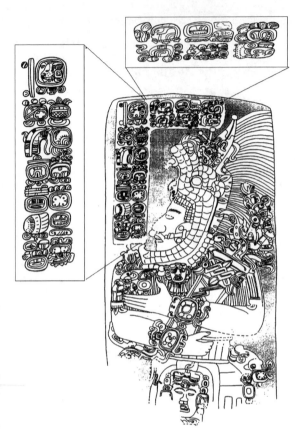

FIGURE 6.3. *Stela 9, Lamanai, Belize (Closs 1988, figure 1; Reents-Budet 1988, figure 1). Drawn by H. S. Loten, Michael Closs, and Dorie Reents-Budet. Courtesy, Lamanai Archaeology Project.*

"it is specifically worn by rulers on the Classic Maya monuments" (Taube 1992b, 82). Moreover, Taube (1992b, 83) posits that among the Maya, rather than being associated with rulership in general, this serpent and the subsequent serpent headdress are "identified with one particular aspect of rulership, that of paramount war leader." From this we might conclude that the individual depicted on Stela 9 (either the father, the son, or perhaps both) was a successful warrior, as alluded to through his presentation in this regalia.

The living ruler, K'ahk' Yipiiy Chan Yopaat, is ascribed two titles in the epigraphic text above the image: *elk'in kaloomte'* followed by *k'uhul ajaw*. The second title, *k'uhul ajaw*, implies that the individual is, as one might expect, the "divine lord" of a city or territory. The city is assumed to be Lamanai (Closs 1988; Simon Martin, personal communication, 2012), although Martin acknowledges that there is a lack of comparative epigraphic information to confirm this designation. The title of Kaloomte' is known from the Classic period, although it carried considerably more cachet in the Early Classic when it was used to denote an especially high rank attributed to only a few rulers (Simon Martin, personal communication, 2012). While the exact nature of the term is debated, it has been loosely glossed as "overlord" or "high king," indicating a paramount position above that of "divine lord" (Freidel, Escobedo, and Guenter 2007, 200; Stuart 2000, 486–487; Wren and Nygard 2005, 173), and is associated with either a military conqueror or the leader of a hegemony. The fact that here we see the title prefixed by the geographic designation for east (*elk'in*) suggests that the individual holding the title was "claiming political or ceremonial supremacy" in the eastern part of the Maya world, which is modern-day Belize (Simon Martin, personal communication, 2012).

When we combine the iconographic image—reifying the ethos of warfare and symbolizing military accomplishment—with the epigraphic text, we can postulate that the title of Kaloomte' on Stela 9 may be, at least initially, based on military activity by the previous king, then expanded upon by the later ruler either through additional conquests or political, economic, or marital alliances with other sites in Northern Belize, including the nearby site of Ka'kabish.

OVERVIEW OF KA'KABISH

Ka'kabish is located 10 km north-northeast of Lamanai. The first known archaeologist to visit Ka'kabish was David Pendergast, then at the Royal Ontario Museum, who visited the site briefly in the early 1980s while working at Lamanai. At that time, the trip took over two hours along a muddy logging road, making full-scale work at the site untenable.

In the late 1980s CE, the logging road was graded and changed into a slightly more passable limestone/*sascab* road, connecting the villages of San Filipe and Indian Church. The construction of the road directly impacted the site in two significant ways: (1) it bisected the core area of the site and divided it into northern and southern sectors, and (2) at least one building was destroyed completely, while parts of another building and the south plaza were quarried for road fill before the plundering was halted. A secondary but potentially no less significant impact of the road was the increased accessibility of the site to looters. As a result, the site is now pockmarked with trenches, with every structure having at least two and in some cases up to five (Tremain 2011).

Recent work, initiated in 2007 under the aegis of the Ka'kabish Archaeological Research Project (KARP), has documented a long history at the site. To date, the earliest occupation of Ka'kabish is dated to the Middle Formative period (ca. 800–600 BCE), with associated material recovered from a variety of locations. Like many other sites in the region that have yielded evidence of Middle Formative occupation, a considerable portion of this material comes from secondary deposits, either from within buildings or below the plaza floor. However, evidence was also recovered at Ka'kabish to suggest that at least one, if not two, structures were also built during this period.

The first of these appears to have been a low platform, approximately 36 cm high, composed of three courses of roughly shaped stones covered with a thick layer of plaster. This platform was discovered buried beneath the southeastern quadrant of the Group D plaza. Although we have yet to determine the overall dimensions of the structure, the exposed section of the north side of the building extends over 4 m in length. Identification of the northwest corner of the building indicated that the structure had rounded corners and possible masks, as suggested by a heavily deteriorated slump of stucco near that corner. Ceramics associated with the structure suggest a possible date of 600–400 BCE, although as this material came from in front of the structure, the platform may actually date to slightly earlier.

Below the floor on which this platform was situated, a large deposit of Middle Formative–period material was encountered (ca. 800–600 BCE). This material contained, among numerous sherds in the fill, an intact Consejo Red Striated vessel, which is characteristic of this period. Carved into the bedrock were three pits surrounding a long trench. The three pits contained a multitude of marine shell beads and several jade objects. The most notable was a jade "spoon" that was found in clear association with shell beads of graduating size, indicating that the object was worn as a pendant on a necklace. The central trench contained fragmented and poorly preserved human remains and several other jade objects. The preservation of the bone was such that it was impossible to determine the sex of the interred individual or his or her exact age beyond the fact that he or she was an adult. Based on the nature of the remains and the dispersal of the teeth, we believe this to have been a secondary burial and that of an important member of the community based on the nature of the mortuary objects.

To the south of this buried platform is a pyramid-temple identified as Structure D-9. Mapping work identified four consecutive phases to this structure (Tremain 2011). Radiocarbon and ceramic material taken from the second construction episode suggests a construction date of 800–600 BCE for an early phase of the temple, while ceramics from later episodes suggest that the temple was in use and being refurbished into the Early Classic period.

Elite ritual activity at Ka'kabish codifies itself more clearly in the Early Classic, as seen in the presence of several crypts and formal tombs. Of particular note is Tomb FA-6/1, located in Structure FA-6 in the northern section of the site core. This tomb is unusual for the region, consisting of a formal, corbel-vaulted room over 2 m high and roughly 1.5 m wide by 3.5 m long, with a narrow 2.5 m-long passageway extending westward. Not only is the architectural form unique to the area, but so are the decorations. The walls of the tomb were painted a vibrant red with dark red glyphs. Christophe Helmke (2010) notes the similarity in form of the glyphs to those at Río Azul and the sites in the Central Peten. Although badly damaged by looting and erosion, enough remained to suggest that the tomb was painted with a funerary text that recorded both the name of the individual along with a death statement.

Dates obtained from carbon recovered from the ceiling and within the plaster floor suggest a mid- to late fifth-century CE (ca. 430–500 CE) construction for the tomb. Samples from charred carbon circles on the surface of the floor yielded a later date (ca. 540 CE), suggesting a possible re-entry/burning event. The elaborateness of the tomb construction coupled with the painting and text are considered characteristic of royal tombs (Fitzsimmons 2009, 11; Weiss-Krejci and Culbert 1994), and re-entry events are documented for other royal tombs in the Peten (D. Chase and A. Chase 1998, 2011; Fitzsimmons 2009; Stuart 1998). This tomb, along with other smaller, less elaborate vaulted tombs, is considered indicative of a ruling elite at Ka'kabish during the Early Classic period.

Tomb FA-6/1 is not the only unusual mortuary feature at Ka'kabish. Structure D-5 was found to contain a crypt, exactly matching a tomb style previously known only from Lamanai (Pendergast 1981, 38–39). This "cocoon" crypt, like all other formal mortuary chambers to date, was looted, leaving little with which to date the construction. The two known crypts of this type at Lamanai were dated to ca. 500 CE based on Tzakol 3-type polychromes and a slab-footed cylindrical "Teotihuacan-type" vase (Elizabeth Graham, personal communication, 2013). Clearing of the looter's tunnel that provided access to the crypt at Ka'kabish yielded a wealth (over 3,000) of obsidian blade and core fragments, along with fragments of a Tzakol 3-type plate with a similar design to those from the Lamanai tombs, suggesting that the Ka'kabish tomb is roughly contemporaneous with those at Lamanai. The fact that this type of mortuary architecture has yet to be identified elsewhere indicates a distinct connection between Lamanai and Ka'kabish. This tomb, the only one so far found at Ka'kabish, also appears amid a mortuary architecture program more heavily tilted toward the painted corbel-vaulted tombs of the Tikal/Central Peten region, thus suggesting a cosmopolitan quality to the occupation at Ka'kabish.

It is at this point, the end of the Early Classic period, when the history of Ka'kabish takes an unexpected turn. To date, we have yet to encounter any construction sequence that can be clearly dated to the early Late Classic period (ca. 600–750 CE). Lapses in activity and perhaps even outright abandonment have been suggested for other sites in the region during the sixth and seventh centuries CE (Adams 1999, 143, 145). Even otherwise stable sites appear to show a decline in population during the Tepeu I period (Sullivan and Valdez 2004, 190). We do not know if Ka'kabish merely suffered a significant population decline or if it was abandoned; however, there is a distinct hiatus in construction during this period, with activity resuming later in the Terminal Classic. Evidence for initial prosperity of the site, as viewed through its construction episodes, along with the presence (albeit restrained) of an early Late Classic population followed by the resurgence of construction activity at the site, is best documented through the ceramic assemblage.

SUMMARY OF CERAMIC CHRONOLOGY AT KA'KABISH

Analysis of the Ka'kabish ceramic assemblage by Sagebiel in 2012 and 2013, which forms the basis for the discussion below, consisted of material collected from surveys and excavations in the site center, including material from two excavated *chultunob* and surveys of the settlement zone. The ceramic chronology for Ka'kabish is still in the preliminary stages, and the temporal designations are fairly coarse. The ceramics are currently lumped into general time periods and will need further refinement in the future; however, even with these preliminary analyses, certain patterns are clear.

Although there is likely some bias in the locations where excavations and other collections have been concentrated, given their somewhat limited number at the time of this analysis, to date, no Middle Formative sherds have been recovered outside of the site center. This suggests that occupation in the area at that time was concentrated on the ridge where the site center is located. During the Late Formative through Early Classic (ca. 800 BCE–550/600 CE), the ceramic data indicate a strong occupational presence in the site center and a fair amount of occupation in the settlement zone. Conversely, occupation during the Late Classic (roughly Tepeu 1 and Tepeu 2 in the Peten, ca. 550/600–750 CE) is weakly represented in both the site center and the settlement zone. Another shift occurred in the Terminal Classic and Early/Middle Postclassic, as occupation was once again fairly high, particularly in the hinterlands. There is little evidence so far of Late Postclassic or Historic-period occupation in or near the site center, although some material dating to these periods was found in the settlement zone in collections made prior to 2012 and not analyzed by Sagebiel at the time of this analysis (Aimers and Haines 2011; McLellan 2012).

Of the 227 dated contexts examined from the site center (including the *chultunob*), approximately 38.8 percent date to the Formative period, while 34.4 percent are from the Early Classic, and only 1.8 percent date to the Late Classic period (table 6.1). A noticeable increase in occupation began in the Terminal Classic (7.5% of the contexts) and continued into the Early/Middle Postclassic period (17.6% of the contexts). A similar pattern of increasing occupation is noted in the settlement zone. There, only 6.7 percent of the 60 dated contexts are Formative period. This number remained the same for the Early Classic period, increasing only slightly during the Late Classic (8.3%) and again in the Terminal Classic (11.7%). The largest period of occupation in the settlement zone is dated to the Postclassic period (66.7% of the 60 dated contexts); however, these numbers are likely a skewed representation of occupation as they are largely derived from sherds recovered from surface survey and a small number of shallow (ca. 40 cm)

TABLE 6.1. Number of ceramic contexts dating to each time period at Ka'kabish

Location	Formative	Early Classic	Late Classic	Terminal Classic	Early/ Middle Postclassic	Indeterminate	Total
Site Center*	88	78	4	17	40	11	238
% of total	37.0	32.8	1.7	7.1	16.8	4.6	–
% of ID	38.8	34.4	1.8	7.5	17.6	–	227[†]
Settlement Zone	4	4	5	7	40	14	74
% of total	5.4	5.4	6.8	9.5	54.0	18.9	–
% of ID	6.7	6.7	8.3	11.7	66.7	–	60[†]
Totals	92	82	9	24	80	25	312

* Includes *chultunob*.
[†] Total number of dated contexts (i.e., excluding contexts of indeterminate date).

1 m × 1 m test pits, which likely biases the sample toward later time periods as deeper, buried deposits were not explored.

Although the number of dated contexts is probably a better indication of occupation and certainly of construction activity (because of the bias in raw sherd counts as a result of the reuse of thousands of midden sherds typical of many of the Formative and Early Classic construction fill contexts at Ka'kabish versus the somewhat ephemeral nature of later Classic and Postclassic construction), it is also worth looking at raw sherd counts (table 6.2). Over 80 percent (81.1%) of the identifiable sherds from the Ka'kabish site center are from the Formative period, while 8.2% date to the Early Classic period. Based on these numbers, approximately 89 percent of the identifiable sherds are Early Classic or earlier. The Late Classic through Early/Middle Postclassic sherds only make up about 11 percent of the identifiable sherds. It should be kept in mind that over half (60.8%) of the sherds from the site center are unidentifiable because of poor preservation, which is in line with other collections examined by Sagebiel (2005a, 2005b, 2006; Sullivan and Sagebiel 2003).

The two *chultunob* in the site center contained several burials dating to the Terminal Classic and Early/Middle Postclassic based on ceramics, radiocarbon dates, and other artifacts (Gonzalez and Haines 2013). The number of Late Classic sherds from the *chultunob* (n = 138) is comparable to all the Late Classic sherds from the rest of the site center (n = 149) (table 6.3). These Late Classic sherds are in contexts containing ceramics from the Terminal Classic, Early/Middle Postclassic, or both and are additional evidence that in northern Belize, Terminal Classic/Tepeu 3-style ceramics were often additions to the Late Classic ceramic repertoire still in use, particularly in elite contexts (Sagebiel 2005a,

TABLE 6.2. Number of sherds dating to each time period at Ka'kabish

Location	Formative	Early Classic	Late Classic	Terminal Classic	Early/Middle Postclassic	Indeterminate	Total
Site Center*	16,768	1,692	325	962	916	32,079	52,742
% of total	31.8	3.2	0.6	1.8	1.7	60.8	–
% of ID	81.1	8.2	1.6	4.7	4.4	–	20,663[†]
Settlement Zone	65	71	38	93	258	867	1,392
% of total	4.7	5.1	2.7	6.7	18.5	62.3	–
% of ID	12.4	13.5	7.2	17.8	49.1	–	525[†]
Totals	16,833	1,763	363	1,055	1,174	32,946	54,134

* Includes sherds from *chultunob*.
[†] Total number of identified sherds.

2005b; Sullivan and Sagebiel 2003). The small number of Formative and Early Classic sherds from the *chultunob* is mostly from lower levels near or on floors and likely represents use of the *chultunob* before they were reused as tombs in the Terminal Classic and Early/Middle Postclassic. As with the sherds from the rest of the site center, a large portion (68.2%) of the sherds from the *chultunob* was unidentifiable.

From the settlement zone (see table 6.2), 17.8 percent of identifiable sherds date to the Terminal Classic, while 49.1 percent are Early/Middle Postclassic. Only 12.4 percent of sherds are Formative, while 13.5 percent are Early Classic and 7.2 percent are Late Classic in date. Once again, nearly two-thirds (62.3%) are unidentifiable. As stated above, the bias toward the Terminal Classic and Early/Middle Postclassic most likely results from the collection strategies applied in the settlement zone. The fact that Late Classic ceramic styles may still have been in use in later periods begs the question of how many of the Late Classic–style sherds from the rest of the site are actually representative of Terminal rather than Late Classic occupation. This is one of the questions that needs further examination. However, based on the relative dearth of Late Classic sherds in comparison to both earlier and later sherds, it is highly likely that a construction and possibly occupation hiatus occurred at Ka'kabish during the seventh and eighth centuries CE.

DISCUSSION

By comparing the data from both sites, we can propose new hypotheses concerning political conflict activities in this corner of the Maya world that underline the existence of martial power and conquest. Based on Taube's recent iconographic work on serpent headdresses and Closs's and Martin's epigraphic decipherments,

TABLE 6.3. Number of contexts and sherds dating to each time period from the *chultuns* at Ka'kabish

Location	Formative	Early Classic	Late Classic	Terminal Classic	Early/ Middle Postclassic	Indeterminate	Total
Contexts	–	–	–	4	17	1	22
Sherds	23	10	138	478	502	2,471	3,622
% of total	0.6	0.3	3.8	13.2	13.9	68.2	–
% of ID	2.0	0.9	12.0	41.5	43.6	–	1,151*

* Total number of identified sherds.

we can infer that at the beginning of the seventh century CE, the individual depicted on Stela 9 laid claim to authority based on military power. The use of the title Elk'in Kaloomte' by the monument's creator, K'ahk' Yipiiy Chan Yopaat, suggests that he and possibly his descendant held (or claimed to hold) considerable sway over a large part of the eastern Maya Lowlands, which likely included the site of Ka'kabish.

Along with the title Elki'n Kaloomte', the rulers on Stela 9 also claim to be a divine *ajaw*, but the main sign of the emblem glyph remains unidentified. While it is possible that the glyph represents Lamanai, evidence from elsewhere indicates that monuments of Maya rulers were erected at sites other than their primary seat of power (e.g., Caracol ruler K'ak Ujol K'inich II's stela at La Rejolla and Calakmul ruler Yukuoom Ch'een I's monument at Dzibanche, among others [Martin and Grube 2008, 95, 103]). Most relevant to us perhaps is the erection of a monument at Mountain Cow by Kan III, the ruler of Caracol (Martin and Grube 2008, 99). Mountain Cow was a small Early Classic site that was absorbed as Caracol ascended to power and came to dominate the region in the Late Classic period (Martin and Grube 2008, 99). Therefore, while it is possible that the emblem glyph and individuals originated at Lamanai, it is also possible that the monument may refer to individuals originating from another site.

At the time of Stela 9's destruction, N10–27 was not only still in use (as evident by the cleanliness of the floor and stairs below the fallen portion), but it also appears to have been undergoing remodeling and possible refurbishment (Graham 2004, 231). This suggests that the builders had plans for the structure that did not involve abandonment and supports Graham's (2004, 230) belief that the building came to an abrupt and likely unexpected end. It is also telling that the stela was not "cleaned up" (i.e., removed from view such as the destroyed Stela 31 at Tikal [Martin and Grube 2008, 39]) but was left where it fell until covered by the accumulation of fill (Graham 2004; Pendergast 1988). We know from elsewhere that monuments of important people were reset by populations during restoration work following a conflict or even entombed in later construction (Harrison 1999, 98; see also chapter by Hernandez and Palka, this volume). If, as Elizabeth Graham (personal communication, 2013) speculates, the monument had been moved from its original location and reset in the room (an argument with which we concur), then we can infer that it and the individuals portrayed were of some importance—details that make its abandonment after nearly two centuries of display even more perplexing.

It is equally intriguing that the accumulation of trash that covered the monument appears to have been produced by the occupations of the Ottawa Group. The ninth-century CE remodeling of this group that predicated the destruction of a frieze depicting a possible ruler forms an interesting counterpart to the destruction of Stela 9, as does the deliberate abrading of the images on Structure N10–36 to remove the seated figures (Pendergast 1983, 3). A possible and highly speculative reason for N10–27's sudden demise is that the destruction, along with that of N10–36, was wrought by the inhabitants of Lamanai. Leaving the broken monument where it fell, to be covered by trash, might have been a kind of testament—the end of a dynastic era—from which they were content to walk away and leave behind. Whether these incidents were defiant acts of revolt, a statement regarding popular opinion of the individuals recorded on the monument, or both may depend on a more secure identification of the individuals on the monument.

The possibility exists that rather than representing a truly "foreign" ruling family, the monument depicts members of a particular Lamanai lineage. It is also possible that this family obtained and held sway for several centuries at the site and that the destruction of Stela 9 represents their downfall and a power shift within the established Lamanai elite population. If, as is speculated, the Terminal and Early Postclassic occupants of the Ottawa Group were the rulers of Lamanai during this period, then their purely Lamanai ceramic assemblage may be less a reflection of "attempts on the part of the community leaders to maintain and reinforce their higher socio-economic position through support of the local producers" (Howie, White, and Longstaffe 2010, 394) than an attempt of a new ruling lineage to establish validity and curry favor with the local populace.

The fact that Ka'kabish was significantly affected by events occurring at the start of the Late Classic period is clearly evinced in the archaeological record. Occupation at Ka'kabish, as inferred from the cultural material, declines dramatically at the start of the Late Classic period (ca. 550/600 CE), possibly even to the point of de facto abandonment, and does not resume until the Terminal Classic period (ca. 750–900 CE). The coinciding of these two events, the start of this hiatus and the erection of Stela 9 (625 CE) with its obvious military symbolism, conquest ideology, and statements of political power, is highly suggestive. The evidence discovered thus far indicates that the individuals pictured on the

Lamanai monument gained influence over the activities at Ka'kabish during the period of or immediately preceding the stela's erection. What is still unclear is whether the cause of the hiatus at Ka'kabish was the result of conquest or political seigniory by the Stela 9 personages or whether these individuals were merely opportunistically availing themselves of a period of instability, resulting from as yet undetermined factors, to extend their influence. It is also possible that Ka'kabish was more closely tied to the Central Peten than currently perceived and that the political vacuum caused by the Tikal hiatus (Martin and Grube 2008) left the inhabitants vulnerable to the influence of rulers from other sites. Thus the actions of the Stela 9 personages may have merely exacerbated an already tenuous situation and thereby precipitated the decline through the siphoning off of resources and available labor as tribute and the possible abandonment of Ka'kabish. Regardless, the timing of the events is too fortuitous to have been mere coincidence.

The role of the Ka'kabish inhabitants in all this political mayhem remains unclear. As with the correspondence between the hiatus at Ka'kabish and the erection of Stela 9, the downfall of the monument and the resurgence of activities at Ka'kabish seem too coincidental to not be related. If, as Graham suspects (2006; see also chapter by Graham, this volume), and again we concur with her theory, Maya conquests were done not for territory but for control of tribute, with labor resources a type of tribute, then the freeing of an area from the dynastic control of a Kaloomte' lineage may have released resources back into the area, which stimulated the revival of Ka'kabish and perhaps other sites in the region. It remains unclear whether the inhabitants of Ka'kabish instigated the likely conflict/revolt that toppled the monument or if they merely benefited from the downfall of its associated dynasty.

SUMMARY AND CONCLUSIONS

Archaeological evidence at Lamanai and Ka'kabish suggests that both sites had similar initial sociopolitical trajectories: flourishing during the Late Formative period (400 BCE–250 CE) and establishing themselves as autonomous political entities with their own elite and divine rulers during the Early Classic period. By the end of the Early Classic period (ca. 600 CE), the distribution of power in the region appears to have shifted, and Lamanai became the dominant center. Although both sites continued to coexist during the Late Classic period (600–750 CE), activity at Ka'kabish (in the form of monumental construction) appears to have diminished, if not ceased completely, during the early part of this period, while construction at Lamanai during this same time persisted, if not flourishing to the same degree as before. The fact that these trajectories underwent such marked divergence at the start of the Late Classic raises questions as to what happened to cause the change. While we see similar and as yet unexplained population declines at the beginning of the Late Classic at sites to the west, such as La Milpa and Río Azul, these cities were likely more directly influenced by events at Tikal than those in eastern Belize.

The exact reason for the decline in activity at Ka'kabish is currently unclear; however, based on the evidence presented above, we can speculate that the reason for the hiatus may have been influenced, if not outrightly caused, by the rise in prominence of another site, possibly but not conclusively that of Lamanai. The ascendency of one site in the region is evinced by the claiming of the title of Kaloomte' by the ruler on Stela 9. This position as "Overlord of the East" may have been a result of the creation of a collaborative political hegemony that saw Ka'kabish willingly ally itself with Lamanai or the leader depicted on the Lamanai monument; on the other hand, it may have resulted from military conquest, as implied by the inherent symbolism of the War Serpent Headdress and the choice to render the individual in this regalia.

If Ka'kabish was indeed united with Lamanai into a larger hegemonic polity during the second half of the sixth century CE, this could explain the differences in tomb architecture at Ka'kabish between the fifth and sixth centuries CE and the seventh- to late eighth-century CE construction hiatus. The downfall of this controlling polity may be implied by the destruction of Stela 9 if we postulate that the damage occurred as the result of a retaliatory action against an unpopular ruler by an as yet undetermined protagonist. As the destruction of the monument took place at the same time as the resumption of activity at Ka'kabish, it is unclear if the inhabitants participated in this action or if they merely benefited as a result of the decentralization of power.

Although we may never know the exact nuances of the relationship between Ka'kabish and Lamanai without the addition of new texts, we can draw several new conclusions about the political landscape and conflict engagements of this area of north-central Belize, starting with the fact that Lamanai was not the only site in the region with an elite population and rulers capable of co-opting royal symbols and prerogatives. Despite its close proximity and smaller size, Ka'kabish also had an emergent kingship during the early part of the Classic period. Moreover, while Lamanai is one of the largest sites in the region and outlasted many other cities, it is a mistake to equate these attributes automatically with long-term or initial primacy. Lamanai now appears to have arisen simultaneously with at least one neighboring city and ascended to its position as a regional power later in its developmental trajectory rather than at its outset. Perhaps most important, we now have evidence that the cities in north-central Belize, despite their lack of texts, mention on monuments at cities in the Peten or elsewhere, or evidence of their overt incorporation into the larger political game, were not immune from the politics of aggression that permeated the other parts of the Maya world. Far from a placid backwater, north-central Belize was a dynamic area where cities created and re-created themselves as they competed for power on the ever-changing political landscape.

Acknowledgments. We would like to thank Elizabeth Graham, David Pendergast, and Simon Martin, who were exceedingly generous with their time, comments, and data. We would also like to thank the members of the Belize Institute of Archaeology, Jaime Awe and John Morris, for their continued support of the Ka'kabish Archaeological Research Project. This research would not have been possible without the financial support of the Social Science and Humanities Research Council of Canada.

7

Reexamining the Role of Conflict in the Development of Puuc Maya Society

GEORGE J. BEY III AND TOMÁS GALLARETA NEGRÓN

Warfare and conflict are important, if not central, topics in contemporary Maya studies. Hieroglyphic, iconographic, and archaeological evidence all show that Maya warfare was widespread, persistent, and highly elaborated (Brown and Stanton 2003; Culbert 1991; Demarest et al. 1997; Martin and Grube 2008; O'Mansky and Demarest 2007). Warfare brought down dynasties, destroyed cities, and in all likelihood contributed in significant ways to the cultural and demographic decline of Maya polities in the Late and Terminal Classic periods (700–1000 CE), both in the southern and northern Maya lowlands. Despite the intense focus on the study of Maya warfare and conflict, surprisingly little is known about its nature in the northern Maya lowlands prior to the Postclassic. The relative scarcity of epigraphy, a more limited iconographic database, and less direct evidence for conflict in the archaeological record have all contributed to this fact. Two major exceptions are Chichen Itza, its iconography and ethnohistory together suggestive of its being the capital of a bellicose society characterized by the extensive practice of warfare, and the site of Yaxuna, with its archaeological evidence of conflict (Ambrosino, Ardren, and Stanton 2003; Freidel 2007).

DOI: 10.5876/9781607328872.c007

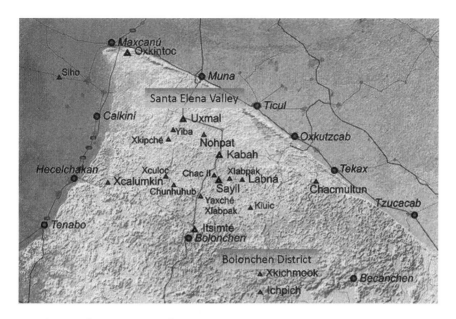

FIGURE 7.1. *The Puuc region and major Puuc sites*

Much less is known about warfare and conflict in the Puuc region, which was home to one of the most famous expressions of Maya culture, the Puuc Maya. Despite the lack of data or perhaps as a result of it, a model for the role of conflict in this region nonetheless emerged and took the shape of a particular narrative. This chapter examines recent research that is leading to a reassessment of the role and nature of warfare and conflict both in the Puuc region and between the Puuc and the larger Maya world. Although far from complete, new views dramatically alter traditional ideas on the timing, history, and processes of warfare and conflict and how they might have helped shape the social and political landscape of the Puuc.

It is important to understand that the word *Puuc* has a geographic, architectural, and ethnic meaning (Stanton and Bey n.d.) (figure 7.1). Geographically, the term *Puuc* is associated with a region located in the northwestern part of the Yucatan Peninsula. The Puuc region, also known as the Hill Country of Yucatan, is a zone that presents important differences with other geographic regions of the Maya lowlands. As Gallareta Negrón (2013, 10–13) notes, while the hilly region was traditionally divided into two districts (Dunning 1992; Kurjack and Garza 1981; Wilson 1980), Duch-Gary (1991, 49–62) offered another interpretation of the geographic composition of the Puuc region that is useful. He recognizes three zones or districts of a physiographic sub-province, denominated *"lomeríos carsotectónicos campechanos"*: (1) the low and extended mountain range (Sierrita de Ticul, the "real" Puuc Hills Range), which is the most important terrain feature of northern Yucatan (it is linear and runs in a northeast-southeast direction for about 200 km, rising up to 100 m above sea level [asl]); (2) low *"lomerios"* with plains, or "the Santa Elena and Tabi Plains," with vast and relatively plain extensions and small hills; and (3) high *lomerios* with plains (Bolonchen District), characterized by great concentrations of karst elevations in the form of domes (*uitz*) that on occasion reach heights of 80 m asl, alternating with minor extensions of plain terrains with deep red soils. Combining Duch-Gary's (1991) physiographic partition with Kurjack and Garza's (1981) position that the Puuc region does not include the *kegelkarst* region southeast of Campeche City and that its southern limit is delineated by the Akalches zone demarcates a territory defined by natural factors that is of great utility for understanding the archaeological communities on this portion of the peninsula.

Puuc also refers to an architectural style associated with Maya society in the hill country, although examples of Puuc architecture are found throughout the northern lowlands. Puuc-style architecture is characterized by complex, stone mosaic sculpture, primarily found above the medial molding on well-engineered structures of finely cut stone masonry; however, within the Puuc region the architecture varies in both time and space, and there are also examples of non-Puuc architecture, such as Chenes-style buildings and pre- and proto-Puuc-style structures. As a result, one needs to be very cautious in making assumptions about power, conflict, and culture when using the idea of "Puuc"-style architecture, especially when trying to equate it with a particular social group or time period.

The association of the region and architecture with other traits such as ceramics has resulted in a third way of conceptualizing Puuc: as an ethnic or demographic term (Stanton and Bey n.d.). This term has been used "to label the ancient Maya who lived in the Puuc Hills region, especially during the Early to Terminal Classic Periods" (Stanton and Bey n.d.), and has led to a common assumption that when Puuc-style architecture is found outside the Puuc region, it is the result of either the migration or expansion of political power of the Maya who lived there. The assumption that architecture or other traits such as ceramics reflect conflict and warfare is obviously highly problematic and should be approached with caution when attempting to understand the role of warfare and conflict of the Puuc Maya (Bey 2003). Our research approach is to examine the adaptation of Maya people to particular physiographic environmental conditions, and we do so with extreme caution regarding the correlation of architecture and ceramics with any particular ethnic group.

THE STUDY OF CONFLICT IN THE PUUC REGION

Traditionally, as with much of our thinking about the Puuc Maya, conflict has been framed in relation to events in the southern lowlands. This is seen when examining the two basic dimensions of Puuc conflict: the internal and the external. By this we mean the role of warfare and conflict within the Puuc region versus that between the region and the rest of the Maya world. Internally, the inhabitants of the Puuc region were traditionally seen as relatively peaceful when compared with those to the south. Sharer's (1994, 369) view is representative of this thinking regarding the internal dimension of conflict. As he noted:

> A high density of settlement combined with the unusually close spacing between Puuc cities might suggest a competitive social environment. Yet there are few indications that warfare plagued this region . . . The impression given, especially in contrast to the increasing martial themes evidence from much of the Late Classic and Terminal Classic lowlands to the south, is that the new cities of the Puuc managed to develop a political order with less emphasis on warfare, at least for a time. . . . Perhaps the Puuc sites were ruled by elite lineages that maintained an effective, cooperative relationship (such as a confederation) by marriage or even by political alliances. Or perhaps one site [i.e., Uxmal] managed to dominate the entire region, enforcing a relatively tranquil order for most of the Terminal Classic.

This view of southern influence and little conflict was echoed more recently by O'Mansky and Demarest (2007, 30): "In the Puuc region, great cities arose beginning in the late eighth century CE in what was previously a sparsely populated zone. The organization of Puuc society was similar to that of the southern lowlands (Dunning 1992) and the florescence of the Puuc region may be directly connected to the collapse of the southern lowlands, though slightly later. By the late ninth century CE, the city of Uxmal had come to dominate the region. Exactly how this occurred is unclear, and there is little direct evidence of warfare."

In this model, conflict and collapse in the southern lowlands serve as some type of trigger to the Puuc region, which is largely unoccupied until the late 700s CE. A rapid development of dozens of Puuc cities takes place between the late eighth and late ninth centuries CE, culminating in the appearance of a regional capital at Uxmal in the late 800s CE. A lack of evidence of internal warfare, close spacing of undefended cities, and economic prosperity suggest that the unification of the Puuc region was relatively peaceful, as was the nature of the Puuc polity.

Modification of this model has been driven to a significant degree by the research of Kelli Carmean, Nicholas Dunning, and Jeff Kowalski (2004; Kowalski 2003). They do not see the Puuc as the peaceful environment archaeologists originally conceived it to be; instead, they recognize that some type of internal conflict likely played a significant role in the unification of the Puuc region by an Uxmal-centered Maya leadership. They see the closely spaced cities as reflecting "a series of independent, small-scale, regal-ritual, dynastically focused kingdoms in the eastern Puuc—relatively newly centralized with the beginning of the Terminal

Classic—jockeying for power and status among themselves, while seeking to maintain their centralized status within their own communities in the face of the centrifugal forces of the still-strong lineage heads" (Carmean, Dunning, and Kowalski 2004, 442–443). The result is that by the late 800s CE, as Demarest (2004b, 269) points out, "rapid growth and immigration to this area, combined with status rivalry and its associated costs in labor and conflict, may have created a political environment in the late 9th and 10th centuries similar to that of the southern low-lands in the eighth century . . . [and in fact] the need for centralization of authority through alliance or conquest might have been even greater [in the Puuc] given their reliance on careful cooperative husbandry or scarce water sources."

This more recent thinking also recognizes greater sociopolitical distinction in the Puuc with an eastern and western subdivision. The scenario described above may be largely associated with the eastern Puuc, whereas in the western Puuc there is less evidence of "centralization" (read conflict). The "small regional state" centered at Oxkintok had seen its power "dissipated by the onset of the Terminal Classic," with the result being a set of "independent, very small-scale polities" (Becquelin 1994, cited in Carmean, Dunning, and Kowalski 2004, 443). Dunning (1992, cited in Carmean, Dunning, and Kowalski 2004, 443) had previously noted that "with the exception of Oxkintok, western Puuc sites are virtually devoid of the dynastic stelae found in the many major eastern Puuc sites." However, as with the traditional model, the end result is the same. Uxmal emerges in the late 800s CE at the end of this period of internal Puuc competition and warfare as the center of sociopolitical leadership. Political unification apparently takes place under the leadership of the one known great Puuc *ahau*, Lord Chac, who oversaw some type of alliance and for a short time held together the Puuc kingdoms under the organization of a regional state.

Uxmal is the centerpiece of any discussion of conflict in the Puuc. It emerges as the unifying force in the model of internal conflict and the driver in the discussion of Puuc external conflict outside the hill country (see Cobos, Guillermo, and Moll 2014 for a recent review of this discussion). Uxmal and the nearby sites of Kabah and Mulchic have long been recognized for evidence of militarism in their art and iconography. There are a number of stelae at Uxmal depicting warriors: Stela 2, Stela 3, Stela 4, Stela 7, Stela 11, and the most famous of the Uxmal monuments, Stela 14 (figure 7.2). At the time they were identified by Blom (1934), they were all located on the so-called Stela Platform northwest of the Nunnery. Unfortunately, only the ruler on Stela 14 has been identified. Inscriptions on the stela identify him as Chan Chak K'ak'nal Ajaw, more commonly known as Lord Chac (Kowalski 1985, 2007), where he is depicted standing triumphantly with weaponry and defeated captives. Lord Chac is thought to have ruled Uxmal during the late ninth and early tenth centuries CE and was responsible for many of the major Terminal Classic Puuc-style constructions at the site, including

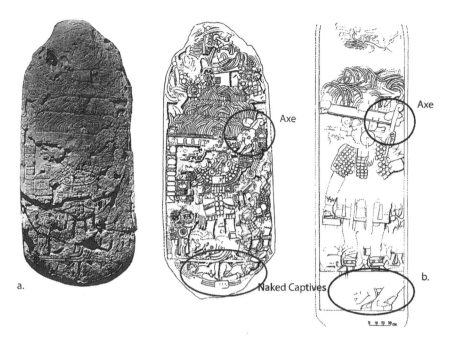

FIGURE 7.2. *Uxmal stela: a. Stela 14, b. Stela 11*

the Nunnery and at least the last construction stage of the Governor's Palace. References to Venus in the Nunnery, as well as war serpents and captives, and the depiction of Lord Chac over the central doorway of the Governor's Palace as the center of the universe (with a Venus reference) all further establish him as a warrior king and mighty conqueror.

Regardless of whether the other stelae are also of Lord Chac, it is clear that militarism and the display of captives was a common theme on them, suggesting that Terminal Classic authority at Uxmal projected warfare as a central idea in the city's public narrative. In fact, it appears that the Stela Platform served as a giant war memorial celebrating a series of conquests most likely of neighboring centers in the Puuc region. Uxmal also stands as the one major center in the Puuc with a wall system surrounding the site center, providing additional evidence of the role of conflict in its sociopolitical life. The wall has an irregular, elliptical plan, with the north-south axis approximately 1 km long and the east-west axis about 600 m long. The walls surround most of the major structures associated with the site center of Uxmal. The best-preserved sections of the wall are located on the west and south sides (Barrera Rubio 1980). Because the wall system is attached to a number of buildings, it has been suggested that it was not planned but was constructed relatively quickly. This point has been used to argue as evidence for increasing conflict during the Terminal Classic period.

The site of Kabah, linked directly to Uxmal by an 18 km-long *sakbe* and thought to be a satellite of the city, has both lintels and jambs clearly showing military activity. The carved doorjambs from Room 21, located on the eastern side of the Codz Pop, were first documented in the 1930s CE (Pollock 1980). In 2013, Lourdes Toscano Hernandez and Gustavo Novelo Rincon discovered two additional doorjambs in a north room of the Codz Pop (Room 1 of Structure 2C6). The Room 21 jambs show Maya warriors dancing with weapons and also attacking and stabbing naked captives or defeated enemies. These jambs have been dated to 859 CE while the new ones are dated fourteen years later, to 873 CE (Stuart and Rubenstein 2014).

At the site of Mulchic, located less than a dozen kilometers from Uxmal and very close to Kabah, a damaged but important sequence of murals was located inside one of the standing vaulted buildings of the site (Barrera Rubio 1980; Lyall 2011; Piña Chan 1964). The murals, dated to 853 CE (Lyall 2011, 97), indicate a range of activities similar to those found at Bonampak, including a "battle between two groups, the taking of prisoners, a procession of priests and preparation for the sacrifice of the prisoners, and a scene showing their execution" (Barrera Rubio 1980, 173). Piña Chan (1964) and Lyall (2011) also concluded that the artists applied southern lowland painting conventions. As Barrera Rubio (1980) pointed out, the battle is between Maya and provides evidence of hostility between communities in the region—one can assume he means the Puuc region. Despite the similarity in style to the Bonampak murals, the activities indicate a set of military and post-battle activities similar to what we recognize in the southern Maya lowlands.

An additional mural at the site of Chacmultun, located at the northeastern edge of the Puuc overlooking the east end of the Santa Elena Valley, also depicts military activity. In a description of the mural, Barrera Rubio (1980, 175) notes that one scene "depicts warriors carrying decorated spears as standards and some men with trumpets, all of them inactive, except for one at the extreme left, who is throwing a spear." A second scene illustrates a "military skirmish in which warriors on the left seem to be escorting two individuals who carry staffs of authority. The troops in the forefront, however, appear to be on the defensive, fleeing from the attack. Their enemy on the right has taken prisoners, giving the impression that they had succeeded in attacking by surprise." Warriors are depicted carrying plain and decorated spears, banners, curved sticks, and shields. Barrera Rubio suggests that these murals likely date between 600 and 900 CE, indicating that they may predate the Uxmal stela and Kabah doorjambs.

A final mural fragment depicting a group of armed warriors is found at the site of Ichmac, located several kilometers southwest of Uxmal and apparently within its immediate sphere of influence (Tejeda Monroy 2014). What is especially interesting about these murals is that the sequences of battles and associated activities appear to be a fairly common theme in the mural painting of Puuc sites, given that the remains of four of the best-preserved sets of murals in the Puuc all present narratives of war and conflict. They are clearly versions of similar interior treatments, as is seen at Bonampak in the south, and are part of a tradition of painting and glorifying warfare and conflict that is just as developed as, and in some ways strikingly similar to, those found in southern centers. They are also all found within what is considered the central sphere of influence of Uxmal and, except for Chacmultun, are less than 18 km from the city.

CONFLICT IN THE PUUC IN THE LIGHT OF RECENT RESEARCH

A policy of conflict and militarism associated with Puuc Maya communities is no longer in doubt for archaeologists studying Uxmal and the Puuc region. The idea the Puuc inhabitants developed a political order with less emphasis on warfare than in other parts of the Maya world is simply incorrect. The data, particularly from iconography and architecture, support a model in which conflict and militarism played a central role in the sociopolitical life of the region. But despite battle scenes, bellicose lords, and the institution of militarism being highly elaborated, the details by which Uxmal forged a regional political state remain unclear. Lord Chac's Uxmal is assumed to be the end result of that process, but how long before him did consolidation begin? How many of the warrior/captive stelae found at Uxmal are associated with Lord Chac and how many represent prior rulers? Was militarism largely restricted to the 30–40 years associated with Lord Chac, or did conflict mark Puuc politics for a long period of time prior to his reign? It is still not even clear if Uxmal unified the entire Puuc region under its centralized leadership, with some archaeologists holding on to the idea that "the territory controlled by the Uxmal state may have been no larger than about a 30 km radius around the site proper. . . . the entire Santa Elena area" (Carmean, Dunning, and Kowalski 2004, 444). If the Late and Terminal Classic landscape consisted of nothing more than a small city-state defined by Uxmal, its immediate vassals, and a larger landscape of, at best, loosely affiliated petty kingdoms, the role and nature of conflict would no doubt be quite different than the one that seems to be emerging from the most recent analyses.

An examination of the most recent research from Uxmal and the Puuc adds further detail to the models of conflict presently offered and begins to address remaining questions such as those posed above. In the remainder of this chapter, we highlight some of the most recent data and ideas associated with the region, considering their impact on earlier models as regards the role of conflict in the Puuc.

The nature of Lord Chac's militaristic policy in the late ninth and early tenth centuries CE, centered at Uxmal, is coming into better focus (Cobos, Guillermo, and Moll 2014; Ringle 2012). It had been proposed that "Uxmal's ruler 'Lord Chaak' established a formal military alliance with the Itzá during the Terminal Classic period" (Kowalski 2003, 243), and recent research has continued to expand on this idea of outside influence. Based on his analysis of the Nunnery Quadrangle, Ringle (2012) presents evidence for the adoption by the leadership of Uxmal at this time of an ideological system focused on the incorporation of "Mexican" or "Toltec" iconography, architectural traits, and associated behaviors. He argues that Uxmal served as another of the Epiclassic Tollans, much as did Chichen Itza to the east.

Ringle (2012) proposes that the "Toltec" system, with its political, religious, and economic dimensions, was overlaid onto the traditional Maya system, with evidence for this seen in the architecture and iconography of the Nunnery (and also the Governor's Palace and Ball Court). The west building of the Nunnery is interpreted as a place where kings were made, legitimizing the rulers of Puuc cities through Uxmal's authority. The larger political entity Uxmal had created was celebrated in the south building, which served as a special new form of *popol nah*, where each room represented a particular Puuc community. The east building is now firmly established as a building dedicated to warfare (which had been posited by Schele and Mathews [1998] and others). Ringle makes a strong case based on iconography that there were as many as six institutionalized military positions in place and that the military was a well-organized central organ of the state. He argues, again based on iconography, that the military may have allowed social mobility for non-elites, as was the case in the central highlands during the Late Postclassic. His analysis concludes that the Puuc region was likely unified politically, with militarism serving as a central component in the organization and stability of the state. He also suggests that the polity was organized in a way that would have encouraged and supported an externally focused policy of military expansion.

Cobos and colleagues (2014) argue for more than simply the incorporation of Mexican ideological traits or an Itzá alliance. They propose that after Lord Chac became the ruler of Uxmal, he conquered Kabah and initiated a new political phase across the Puuc region. The centerpiece of this new phase involved Uxmal establishing "strong political and commercial ties along with cooperation programs (such as regional military collaboration)" with Chichen Itza (Cobos, Guillermo, and Moll 2014, 62). They see a number of traits supporting this analysis, such as the appearance of Sotuta trade ware at Uxmal and a Chichen Itza warrior depicted next to Lord Chac on Stela 14 (Kowalski 2003, 239, 2006, 306–308; Proskouriakoff 1950, 164). The authors posit that "from the first half of the tenth century until the middle of the eleventh century, Uxmal benefited from its alliance with Chichen Itza and . . . this alliance was used to consolidate Uxmal's supremacy in Western Yucatán" (Cobos, Guillermo, and Moll 2014, 62).

The idea of Uxmal as a larger regional power had been suggested by others, though Cobos provides the most complete argument for a regional alliance between it and Chichen Itza. Carmean and colleagues (2004) suggested that as Uxmal codified its local or regional authority, it may have made a bid for broader regional power, perhaps by enlisting the aid of non-Puuc allies such as Chichen Itza. Freidel and his colleagues also pushed this idea, arguing that Yaxuna "came into conflict with some of the Puuc polities, and groups of Puuc people occupied the site, demonstrated by the construction of Puuc-style palaces on the North Acropolis and Southeastern Acropolis" (Kristan-Graham and Kowalski 2007, 41). Equating Puuc buildings with Puuc conquest in this manner would suggest that the Uxmal polity extended its control across much of the northern Maya lowlands, at least as far as Ek Balam and Culuba to the east. We would strongly caution against this based simply on the distribution of Puuc architectural style.

Two of the most significant changes in our understanding of the prehistory of the Puuc, dramatically transforming our consideration of the role of conflict, are the recognition that there was a significant population in the Puuc region much earlier than previously thought and that large sites (communities) existed well before the rise of the Classic centers of the late eighth century CE. New research by Ringle (2014) and Smyth and Ortegon Zapata (2008) and others has shown that the Puuc had as long a history of in situ cultural development as any area in the Maya world and that by the late Middle Formative, huge monumental architecture (some of the largest constructions in the history of the northern Maya lowlands) was being built. Our work at Kiuic has established that the site was founded prior to the appearance of Mamon pottery, at approximately 900 BCE, and continued to develop up until its abandonment around 950–1000 CE—a period of almost two millennia (Andrews, Bey, and Gunn 2018). Although Kiuic is the only site ^{14}C dated to this early time period in the Puuc, we now know that early Middle Formative (900–600 BCE) occupation is found elsewhere in the Puuc, and we have established that by the late Middle Formative (600–300 BCE) the entire Santa Elena Valley and Bolonchen District were occupied (Ringle, Bey, and Gallareta Negrón in press). Some sites were small, such as Paso del Macho (although it has a ball court), while others like Yaxhom, Xcoch, and Xocnaceh were major centers at this time. The main acropolis at Xocnaceh was 90 m × 100 m and 8 m high by the Middle Formative, and the site of Yaxhom, located at the eastern edge of the Santa Elena Valley (known locally as the Valle de Yaxhom), was dominated by an acropolis 145 m on a side that had a height of up to 9.5 m (figure 7.3). Both of these acropoli had several platforms and pyramids atop them, some as high as 21 m. Yaxhom actually consists of at least two other outlier sites with megalithic architecture (Nucuchtunich and Nohoch Cep) and a major human-modified *aguada* (Xpotoit). Surrounded by a berm of 3 m, the *aguada* was about 275 m long. Assuming a depth of 3 m, Ringle calculates the *aguada's*

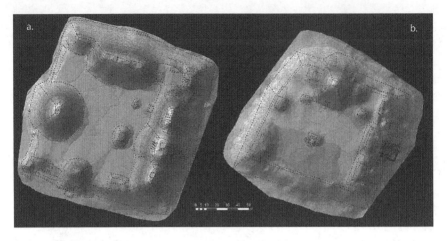

FIGURE 7.3. *Middle Formative Puuc acropoli: a. Yaxhom, b. Xocnaceh*

capacity to have been about 50 million liters. Using the conservative consumption figures of 17–26.7 l/day favored by Becquelin and Michelet (1994; Ringle and Tun Ayora 2013), approximately 1,868,500–2,935,000 person/days of water could have been stored in the fully filled *aguada* and possibly significantly more.

Both the traditional and more recent models for the role of conflict in the development of Puuc society were based on the assumption that the Puuc was "sparsely populated" until the eighth century CE and that political kingdoms were only newly centralized around the late eighth century CE. Since we now know that the Puuc region was widely occupied by the Middle Formative and enormous centers had begun processes of centralization as early as 600 BCE, much of the traditional or modified model for conflict has to be completely recalibrated and reconsidered. The Terminal Classic landscape was the end product of almost 2,000 years of in situ development, and the role of conflict was also likely the end product of this same history. The variation in site size and composition has led us to conclude that by the Middle Formative, a regional hierarchy had developed with several very large centers at the top and numerous medium and small centers scattered throughout the Puuc. Also, since excavations at any of the major Maya centers in the Puuc produces Middle and Late Formative components, it is probable that almost all of the major centers have very long local histories of development. It is unlikely that the evolution of huge centers and the organization of the Puuc into a hierarchical settlement landscape in the Formative, as well as the in situ development of many of the sites that came to dominate the landscape in the Late and Terminal Classic, occurred without conflict.

Brown and Garber (2003) argue persuasively that evidence for conflict or warfare is found in the southern lowlands as early as the Middle Formative at sites

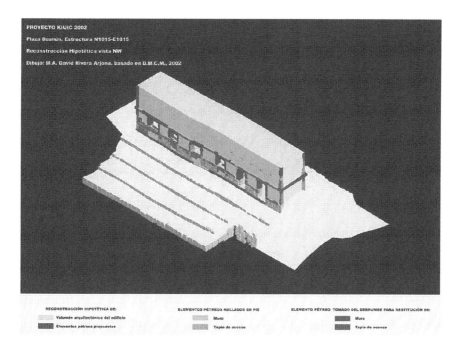

PROYECTO KIUIC 2002

Plaza Dzunun, Estructura N1015-E1015

Reconstrucción Hipotética vista NW

Dibujo: M.A. David Rivera Arjona, basado en D.M.C.M., 2002

RECONSTRUCCIÓN HIPOTÉTICA DE:

Volumén arquitectónico del edificio

Elementos pétreos propuestos

ELEMENTOS PÉTREOS HALLADOS EN PIE

Muro

Tapia de acceso

ELEMENTO PÉTREO TOMADO DEL DERRUMBE PARA RESTITUCIÓN DE:

Muro

Tapia de acceso

FIGURE 7.4. *Example of a* popol nah *at Kiuic*

like Blackman Eddy. Reilly and Garber (2003, 147) argue that warfare imagery is "implicit and couched in supernatural were-jaguar imagery within the Formative period Olmec style." Elsewhere, Marcus and Flannery (1996, 104) argue that "evidence of the destruction of building 28 [at San Jose Mogote] combined with iconographic evidence from Monument 3 indicates that the pattern of raiding, temple burning, and ritual sacrifice of captives evident in the later periods was present as early as 600 BCE." There is little doubt that conflict played some role in the evolution of the Puuc society of the Middle Formative, and any model that hopes to explain conflict in the Puuc must begin by focusing attention on the evidence and ideas associated with this time period.

We also now recognize that the pattern of settlement associated with the late eighth and ninth centuries CE, the time period of "relatively newly centralized kingdoms" according to earlier models, was largely in place by 550 CE. Around this time, we find the construction of the first Classic-period *popol nahs* in the Puuc. These slab-vaulted council houses found at numerous Puuc centers, such as Labna, Kiuic, Huntichmul, Dzula, Nohpat, Xcanacruz, Sabbache, and Chac II, were probably built between 550 and 600 CE (figure 7.4). As discussed previously by Bey and Ringle (1989; Ringle and Bey 1992), a *popol nah*, together with a "temple" and often a small altar in the shared plaza between them, formed the core

FIGURE 7.5. *Early Puuc vaulted building from Kiuic's Yaxche Palace, circa 700–800* CE

of many northern Maya civic centers. We have called these groups in the Puuc "Early Puuc Ceremonial complexes" (Ringle, Bey, and Gallareta Negrón 2006). We find them at the majority of sites we have examined in the Puuc and are confident that more *popol nahs* remain to be identified. In the Bolonchen region of the Puuc, the settlement landscape starts taking on the shape we associate with the Terminal Classic in the mid-sixth century CE, with *popol nahs* and associated Early Postclassic complexes springing up every 6 to 7 km. The *popol nahs* served as the council houses for emerging elites in these sites, the heads of lineages who made day-to-day decisions about the internal and external affairs of the communities; however, within 100 years (by 700 CE) the Early Postclassic complexes became the centers of early palaces ruled by a dynastic ruler. These early palaces are characterized by proto-Puuc or Early Puuc–style architecture, defined by columned vaulted rooms decorated primarily with stucco rather than the cut stone mosaic of the "classic" Puuc period.

At Kiuic, where we have undertaken a detailed excavation of the evolution of one of these palaces (called the Yaxche Group), we identified the Formative plaza of Kiuic, which developed into an early Early Postclassic complex by 550 CE and by 700 CE into a palace with three plazas and a central royal residence facing the *popol nah* (figure 7.5). By 800 CE, Kiuic's early palace had transformed into a ceremonial complex dominated by a 10 m pyramid burying the early residence of the Kiuic royal family. This ceremonial complex is connected by a *sakbe* to a new and much larger palace complex constructed in the colonnette and mosaic style of 800s and 900s CE.

The time period after 800 CE in the Puuc is marked by an explosion of growth in terms of the number of new structures and the scale (size) of architecture. What we see taking place at Kiuic happens throughout the Puuc region, in some cases such as Labna in a very similar fashion (figure 7.6). The size and density of both vaulted buildings and communities in the Puuc is impressive, and as part of this transformation, Uxmal/Kabah emerges as the capital of a new level

FIGURE 7.6. *Terminal Classic palace at Labna, 800–950 CE, Puuc mosaic style*

of sociopolitical integration. The process, which undoubtedly included the development of the practices of ninth- and tenth-century CE Puuc conflict, is therefore rooted in the evolution of the Puuc landscape in the sixth and seventh centuries CE. It is not, as traditional models purported, a result of the collapse in the south or the immigration of these southerners to a sparsely inhabited landscape but rather of internal processes that included practices of conflict that had their roots in the Formative.

Much of the prior discussion of warfare in the Puuc has focused on the stelae from Uxmal, the murals at Mulchic, and the doorjambs at Kabah: evidence from the region's political heartland. But a quick look at sources such as Pollock (1980) reveals that iconographic references to warfare in the Puuc were not restricted to the "capital." Despite the fact that Carmean, Dunning, and Kowalski (2004, 443) play down the role of the western Puuc in the conflicts of the Late and Terminal Classic (they characterize the region as composed of "myriad independent, very small polities . . . virtually devoid of the dynastic stelae found in the many major eastern Puuc sites"), iconographic references to conflict seem just as common in the western Puuc as in the eastern Puuc (figure 7.7).

The iconography of conflict outside the Uxmal central zone primarily consists not of actual depictions of conflict but of depictions of kings or lords of Puuc sites in bellicose poses with shields and weapons, sometimes with captives and sometimes dancing. Among eastern Puuc sites we find warrior figures sculpted in the earliest throne room of Labna, dated by Gallareta Negrón at around 750 CE. A review of Pollock (1980) reveals a number of western Puuc sites with warrior imagery (figure 7.8).

1. CACABBEEC: A stela with a warrior holding a spear and a shield with Tlaloc on it (532, figure 894).

2. HALAL: A jamb with a possible warrior with a knife and a bag, pierced nose, and a butterfly pectoral (552, figure 925).

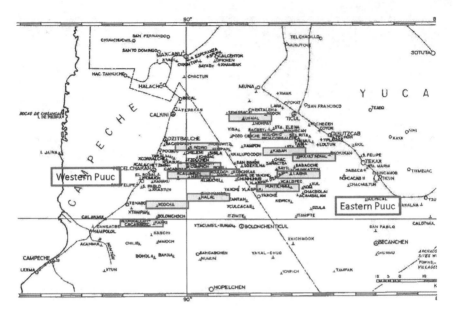

FIGURE 7.7. *Puuc sites with conflict-oriented iconography*

3. XCOCHA: A sculpted doorway column with a warrior with a shield and a two-bladed axe (508, figure 849). A sculpture on the west column of the Building of the Glyphic Band with a warrior with shield and spear (511, figure 856). A sculpted doorway from a building in the Southeast Group of a warrior with a doubled-bladed axe and shield (514, figure 863). A man with a shield and spear associated with the Southwest Group (514, figure 864).

4. SAN PEDRO: On the North Hilltop Group there is a warrior in profile with a spear and shield (472, figure 789).

5. XCALUMKIN: On the Initial Series Building there are sculptures on the jambs of the entrance to the east room, which are warriors with spears (or batons) and shields (425, figure 713). On the middle building of the Hieroglyphic Group there are sculpted jambs with two dancing warriors, one with a shield and barbed flint weapon (442, figure 741). On the south building of the Hieroglyphic Group there are two sculpted jambs with dancing warriors with shields and axes (449, figure 751).

6. XCULUC: Two sculpted columns of warriors with axes (shields?) (380, figure 629).

An initial survey and analysis of these depictions indicate that they are found mostly on jambs and columns of buildings stylistically associated with the Early Puuc style that emerged around 700 CE, not the later Puuc Mosaic style. This is

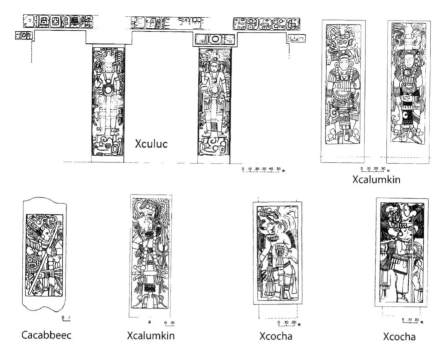

FIGURE 7.8. *Eastern Puuc conflict iconography (adapted from Pollock 1980)*

confirmed at Xcalumkin, where associated hieroglyphic texts are dated at 724 CE (Lintel 2) and 751–771 CE (Column 1). They are associated with the time period when the *popol nahs* and EPCs were replaced by early palace groups, as were established at Labna, Kiuic, and Huntichmul. As discussed above, this was probably also the time period associated with the appearance of Late Classic kingship. These events would have predated the great late eighth-century CE expansion associated with Uxmal and the appearance of stelae and Puuc mosaic architecture and before the purported migration of collapsing southern Maya into the Puuc region.

Attention should also be paid to depictions of Chac (Chahk; see also chapter by Bassie-Sweet, this volume) in a discussion of conflict in the Puuc region. Typically discussed in reference to rain and the constant preoccupation of Puuc Maya with managing rainwater, Chac was associated with warfare as well (Taube 1992a). According to Taube (1992a, 24), "The lightning axe wielded by these figures is frequently portrayed as a battle weapon . . . a shield often accompanies the lightning axe (see mural of south wall, Mulchic)." As Taube points out, the warrior king of Uxmal takes the name of Chac. In fact, if we look at the early eighth-century CE depictions of warrior kings in the Puuc, they are often shown with a battle axe and shield, almost undoubtedly a reference to their relation to

Chac as a war god. When we see Chac and kings impersonating Chac, as on all three of the carved stelae we have recovered from Huntichmul (one of which is dated to 849 CE) (Ringle, Bey, and Gallareta Negrón 2009), we cannot discount the possibility that the dancing kings are not simply associating themselves with rain but with war as well.

The lack of fortifications in the Puuc, with the exception of Uxmal, was one of the facts archaeologists used to consider that the Puuc polities "managed to develop a political order with less emphasis on warfare, at least for a time . . . Perhaps the Puuc sites were ruled by elite lineages that maintained an effective, cooperative relationship (such as a confederation) by marriage or even by political alliances" (Sharer 1994, 369). However, social tensions between polities can be marked in other ways besides walls and fortifications. As LeBlanc (2003, 278) noted for the southwestern United States, "When warfare intensified in the Southwest, polities formed with broad no-man's lands between them." It appears that the Puuc polities also created no-man's lands between them. Even though they are closely spaced together, Gallareta Negrón's 12 km × 1 km survey among Labna, Huntichmul, and Kiuic (which gives us hitherto unknown detail and clarity of regional occupation in the Puuc) shows clearly demarcated zones where permanent occupation is virtually nonexistent, as well as checkpoints and small defensive features at the edge of polities along least-cost routes (Gallareta Negrón, Bey, and Ringle 2013). This survey indicates that these no-man's lands existed by the early eighth century CE. The survey has also recorded features that can be interpreted as boundary markers, as well as checkpoints, a surveillance unit on the top of a hill, and stone "shields" formed by upright slabs located on elevated ground adjacent to the least-cost route and alternate roads, in the close vicinity of the checkpoints. Those outposts represent if not warfare directly, the military defense against potential invaders or transgressors.

The Puuc region underwent a severe demographic collapse at the end of the Terminal Classic period (approximately 925–1050 CE). The almost total and permanent abandonment of most Puuc settlement, except for minor post-monumental occupations at sites like Uxmal (Bey, Hanson, and Ringle 1997) and Huntichmul (Hill and Galvan 2009), is still not well understood. Climatic shifts in the form of severe episodes of drought are presently favored by many archaeologists to have played a significant role in the abandonment and political disintegration of the Puuc region (Cobos, Guillermo, and Moll 2014; Hoggarth et al. 2016); however, we still lack a set of secure dates anchoring these shifts to demographic and political decline in the Puuc region. Hoggarth and colleagues (2016, 30) summarize the paleoclimatic evidence for drought in Yucatan and argue that the Yok Balum speleothem (from Belize) provides the most fine-grained dataset for understanding "the climatic context for the collapse of political systems at Chichen Itza and other northern lowland centers." Using it in conjunction with ^{14}C and hieroglyphic dates (see Hoggarth et al. 2016 for a review of their methodology), they conclude that there were two waves of political collapse in the northern Maya lowlands, each associated with periods of climatic stress. The first wave runs from 850 to 925 CE and is associated with the collapse of the Puuc political system, while the second occurs around 1000 CE and is associated with the decline of Chichen Itza (Hoggarth et al. 2016, 31). Cobos and colleagues (2014) also use paleoclimatic data (although not the Yok Balum speleothem data) to argue for the abandonment of Uxmal. They recognize that drought conditions began earlier but place the tipping point in the mid-eleventh century CE, later than the first wave posited by Hoggarth and colleagues.

The relationship between proposed droughts and conflict during either of these hypothesized periods of collapse is not known, although based on our present understanding, several suggestions may be offered. The collapse occurs at the time when militarism appears to be the most organized and structurally complex in the Puuc. Uxmal could have used military force as a way to extract resources and force compliance of its citizens and the polities under its control. Murals and sculpture provide evidence that the Puuc Maya practiced organized warfare at least within the region and had a tradition of depicting battles and military operations similar to that seen in the southern lowlands. If faced with climatic stress, as suggested by Hoggarth and colleagues (2016) and Cobos and coauthors (2014), the use of force as a way to try and prop up a destabilized state is not out of the question. The equation is made more complex if we assume that, as Cobos and others suggest, Uxmal had a formal alliance with Chichen Itza. This alliance could have provided Uxmal with more potential to use militarism as a tool for stability even as the political system faced greater stress as a result of climatic shifts. The same ten sources of obsidian found at Chichen Itza have also been identified at Uxmal (Braswell, Paap, and Glascock 2011), leading Cobos and coauthors (2014, 63) to suggest "its participation in the same exchange system in which Chichen Itza was engaged." If so, Uxmal was likely linked in to the Chichen Itza military industrial complex associated with obsidian weapon production. Access to obsidian through its alliance with Chichen Itza could have provided Uxmal with an important military advantage over other kingdoms under its control.

Conversely, increased organization and influence of the military instituted by Lord Chac and shaped by "Toltec" ideological changes could have been a source of destabilization as the Puuc region experienced climatic shifts. If used internally, military force could have upset long-standing patterns of resource distribution, supporting certain groups at the expense of others and exacerbating stress. It may even have resulted in levels of sustained conflict at a time when cooperation would have been most necessary to sustain the regional polity. The idea of Uxmal's success serving as a source of regional instability has been considered by Carmean and colleagues (2004). They hypothesized that Uxmal may have added a degree of internal instability to the region by mounting an attempt to establish political and military sovereignty over its nearby Puuc neighbors. Evidence for this attempt comes in the form of an apparent decline in the construction of new (post-850 CE) monumental architecture chiefly in those sites closest to Uxmal (Xkipche and Xcoch), while construction continued at sites clearly tied to Uxmal's ascendancy (e.g., Nohpat, Kabah, and Labna). This strategy, combined with the polity's external ambitions, resulted in "an increasingly precarious population-to-cultivable-land ratio . . . [a] move [that] may have thrown the entire region into a tail spin from which it never recovered" (Carmean, Dunning, and Kowalski 2004, 445). If Uxmal's military success contributed to increasing instability, internal conflict may have further exacerbated crises that appeared as a result of climatic shifts and reduced agricultural output.

SUMMARY AND CONCLUSIONS

Traditionally, archaeologists argued for a late period of population growth in the Puuc (post-800 CE), related to the collapse of the southern Maya lowlands. Perhaps as a result of this process of late development, it was commonly believed that the Puuc was distinct from other parts of the Maya world in that conflict played a minor role in its cultural evolution and success (O'Mansky and Demarest 2007; Sharer 1994). In the last decade or so, this model has been modified to take into account the idea that internal conflict and warfare were likely important in the consolidation of the Puuc, with various kingdoms jockeying for power and ultimately an effort to centralize power being directed from Uxmal.

Uxmal is the centerpiece of any contemporary discussion of Late/Terminal Classic conflict in the Puuc. There is a strong opinion held by archaeologists that Uxmal developed into the regional capital of the Puuc region, unifying the area. Conflict played a central role in this process, as seen in various battle murals and iconography of warriors, including the warrior *ahau* Chac. Lord Chac practiced a policy that further elaborated the role of conflict by institutionalizing a highly structured "Toltec"-style military organization. Some archaeologists argue that Uxmal at this time had extended its policy-making outside the Puuc region through an alliance with Chichen Itza that included participation in its obsidian procurement system. It has even been argued that Puuc kingdoms were involved in military activity as far as eastern Yucatan, at such sites as Yaxuna.

New research, carried out by the authors and others, provides information indicating that conflict at Uxmal and other Puuc sites in the Late/Terminal Classic represented the end of a long period of conflict and militarism in the region. This new research proves that the region had already developed monumental architecture, a varied settlement landscape, and social complexity by 700–600 BCE. Although specific evidence of warfare is lacking in the Middle

Formative Puuc data, evidence for it elsewhere in the Maya world at this time suggests that the evolution of communities like Yaxhom and Xocnaceh did not take place without some level of conflict.

It is now recognized that the Late/Terminal Classic sociopolitical landscape of the Puuc region did not take shape in the late eighth century CE as previously thought but that it did so at least by the mid-sixth century CE. By the early eighth century CE, rival kingdoms had emerged led by warrior kings. Militarism in the early Late Classic was a common motif, especially in the western Puuc, with warriors commonly portrayed on the columns and jambs of vaulted structures. Although they lacked walls, these polities were defined by no-man's lands, reflecting the social boundaries and political tensions existing between them. By the second half of the ninth century CE, Uxmal appears to have forged the Puuc region into a unified political entity, and by the end of the ninth century CE it had incorporated a Mesoamerican or "Toltec" ideology into the preexisting Maya one. This new ideological system supported a well-defined military organization that served as one of the major institutions of the regional state. Conflict in the tenth century CE was the end process of almost 2,000 years of warfare and compromise among the Puuc Maya.

The relation between the almost total demographic collapse of the Puuc region at the end of the Terminal Classic period (925–1050 CE) and the role of conflict is still poorly understood. Sociopolitical complexity, militarism, and population were likely the greatest right at the time of abandonment, and the failure to sustain Puuc culture in the region may be associated with climatic shifts in the form of droughts. Yet research at Kiuic and Escalera al Cielo (a suburban community at the edge of Kiuic) shows no evidence of warfare at the time of abandonment; rather, the evidence suggests that the inhabitants of the community undertook a planned abandonment with anticipation of reoccupation (Simms et al. 2012). It remains uncertain whether militarism served as a stabilizing or destabilizing force during this catastrophic event.

PART II

Conflict in Broader Mesoamerica

8

Hearts and Torches

Possible Teotihuacan Military Entradas in
North-Central and Western Mesoamerica

JESPER NIELSEN

The tremendous importance of Teotihuacan culture in the Central Mexican highlands in the Late Formative (ca. 200 BCE–100 CE) and Classic (ca. 100–600 CE) periods has long been recognized (e.g., Millon 1973, 1992). However, in terms of mapping and understanding the extent of the influence of this powerful imperial state in the fourth and fifth centuries CE, archaeologists, epigraphers, and art historians have only just begun. Numerous parts of Mesoamerica remain where the potential economic, political, and cultural interactions and exchanges with the ancient metropolis have yet to be adequately investigated (Cowgill 2003, 324). The aim of this chapter is to present a preliminary iconographic analysis of some remarkable examples of imagery that strongly suggest Teotihuacan presence in the north-central and western portions of Mesoamerica—more precisely, the Bajío region in the state of Querétaro and in the state of Michoacan to the west of the Valley of Mexico. I will also briefly refer to comparable iconographic and epigraphic evidence found elsewhere in Mesoamerica where it has been suggested that a possible Teotihuacan empire had succeeded in taking power in an attempt to control the flow of

DOI: 10.5876/9781607328872.c008

local resources and extract tribute (Nielsen 2003). In so doing, I exemplify what can be called an "imperial iconography" centered on the display of a relatively small but well-defined group of Teotihuacan objects and elements of dress that include spearthrowers; darts; square shields; the so-called shell-platelet head-dress, or a headdress with human hearts; back mirrors; and torches. Scholars have intensely debated how to interpret such images, along with other material indicators of Teotihuacan culture, including *talud-tablero* architecture, green Pachuca obsidian, and stuccoed and painted tripod vessels.

Are the aforementioned objects and elements evidence of an actual Teotihuacan military presence? Or should they rather be seen as the result of local non-Teotihuacano rulers who, for internal political reasons, emulated these foreign symbols as a means of strengthening their own power (Nielsen 2003, 1–8; see also Braswell 2003a and Cowgill 2003 for an overview of previous and current studies of Teotihuacan-Maya interaction)? I would like to stress the complexity and multi-directionality of Teotihuacan's interaction with different regions of Mesoamerica (Helmke and Nielsen 2013) and recent research on bone and teeth from graves at both Teotihuacan and the Maya world has revealed new and fascinating insights into the complexities of migrations of groups and individuals among these two regions (e.g., White, Price, and Longstaffe 2007; White et al. 2000, 2002; Wright 2004, 2005). As will be exemplified in the present chapter, the iconographic evidence, along with the epigraphic records from the Maya area, suggest a military expansion and incursions into several areas and indicate that for a relatively brief span of time (perhaps in the range of fifty years) Teotihuacan controlled what may have been the greatest empire in the history of Mesoamerica (Cowgill 2003, 316; Nielsen 2003).

TEOTIHUACANOS ABROAD: TRADERS, IMPERIALISTS, OR BOTH?

The first time archaeologists discovered an unprecedented amount of Teo-tihuacan *talud-tablero* architecture and artifacts outside of Central Mexico was during the excavations undertaken by the Carnegie Institution at the Late Formative (ca. 200 BCE–300 CE) and Early Classic (ca. 300–600 CE) Maya high-land site of Kaminaljuyu in Guatemala (Kidder, Jennings, and Shook 1946, 218–240, 250–256). Since then, the findings in the burials of Mounds A and B southeast of the Acropolis have generated a continued debate over the links between Kaminaljuyu and Teotihuacan (Braswell 2003b; Cheek 1977; Nielsen 2003, 161–188). Among the spectacular finds from the burials were stuccoed and painted tripod vessels and vases with Teotihuacan-style motifs, Fine Thin Orange ceramics, back mirrors with Teotihuacan iconography, as well as so-called Storm God jars.

A few decades later, the excavations of the Tikal Project (1956–1970 CE) at the Northern Acropolis at Tikal provided further evidence of Teotihuacan influences and those from a series of inscribed monuments from the Central Peten (e.g., Tikal Stela 31, the Tikal Ballcourt Marker, and Uaxactun Stela 5). Epigraphers have since managed to recount some of the central events, including the arrival of Teotihuacanos in 378 CE and the subsequent installment of a Teotihuacan-affiliated ruler, Yax Nuun Ahiin, who was the son of "Spearthrower Owl" (Jatz'o'm Kuy), believed to have ruled in Teotihuacan from 374 to 439 CE (Stuart 2000, 467–490; see also Proskouriakoff 1993, 4–15). In this case, a Teotihuacan military takeover is documented in historical texts and not simply implied from the spread of imperial iconography. Researchers still debate what language was dominant at Teotihuacan, and early variants of Totonac, Mixe-Zoque, Otomi, and Nahuatl have all been mentioned as candidates. Importantly, the inscription from Tikal Stela 31 records at least one word in Nahuatl, strongly suggesting that at least some of the Teotihuacanos spoke an early form of that language (for a summary of current views on language[s] at Teotihuacan, see Nielsen and Helmke 2011, 345–349).

In the 1990s CE, new evidence of strong links to Teotihuacan was discovered in a series of tombs from the Acropolis of Copan (Bell, Canuto, and Sharer 2004a; Sharer et al. 2005; Stuart 2005a). As a result of these discoveries, several researchers now agree that Teotihuacan succeeded in conquering and controlling several important Maya cities in the late fourth century CE, and this incursion into the Maya region is commonly referred to as the Teotihuacan *entrada* (Martin and Grube 2008, 29–35; Stuart 2000; see also Estrada-Belli et al. 2009). It has also been suggested that Teotihuacan had economic and political interests in Veracruz at sites such as Matacapan, Piedra Labrada, and Soyoltepec (Nielsen 2003, 78–79; Santley 1989; Yarborough 1992).

Looking toward the southwest of Mesoamerica, a number of archaeological sites in present-day Guerrero (e.g., Acatempan, Petatlan, Tepecoacuilco, and Texmilincan) have Teotihuacan-style monuments showing warriors with spear-throwers, darts, and torches, as well as other diagnostic features (Manzanilla López 2008; Nielsen et al. 2019a; Reyna Robles 2002; Taube 2011, 93–98, figsures 5.13a, 5.14a–b, 5.16a, 5.17a, 5.18a–c) (figure 8.1). The clear traces of Teotihuacan influence are found further south along the Pacific Coast at Cerro Tortuga in Oaxaca (Rivera Gúzman 2011); in Chiapas at Cerro Bernal, Los Horcones, and Fracción Mujular (García-Des Lauriers 2007; Navarrete 1986; Taube 2000a, 40–44, figure 33); and into southern Guatemala where Teotihuacan-style artifacts such as richly decorated tripod vessels, *candeleros*, and incense burners have been found at Escuintla, Tiquisate, Lake Amatitlan, Montana, and Los Chatos (Berlo 1984; Bove and Medrano Busto 2003; Hellmuth 1975; Nielsen 2003, 189–199). More recently, the previous interpretations of the relationship between Teotihuacan and the Zapotec capital of Monte Alban as one based on diplomacy and peaceful trade have also been challenged, and new evidence suggests a significant Teotihuacan

FIGURE 8.1. *Small Teotihuacan-style stela from Guerrero (presently in the Museo Tamayo) with imperial iconography: warrior wearing shell-platelet headdress and goggles and holding darts and a burning torch. Drawing by Nicolas Latsanopoulos.*

presence and even militarism at this city (Taube 2011, 91–93, figure 5.11c–e; Winter 1998; Winter, Martínez López, and Herrera Muzgo 1999) (figure 8.2).

In comparing the spread and consistency of the suggested imperial iconography of Teotihuacan with that of the Late Postclassic Mexica, upon whose status as an imperial power is agreed, one is struck by a stark difference regarding the available data. The extent of the Mexica empire is documented primarily, though not exclusively, through written sixteenth-century CE accounts (versus archaeological [e.g., architecture, ceramic styles] or iconographic [representations of Mexica warriors] evidence) left by imperial representatives in the tribute-paying provinces. In the case of Teotihuacan, we are left only with archaeological and iconographic evidence; therefore, the discussion at hand focuses on the questions of the kind and amount of archaeological/iconographic traces hegemonic empires can be expected to leave behind (Smith and Montiel 2001). At present, it appears that we actually have better archaeological and iconographic evidence for the existence of a Teotihuacan empire than of the Mexica empire (Nielsen 2003, 61–86, 2006a). Based solely on the iconographic and epigraphic records, I believe there is sufficient evidence to suggest the existence of a short-lived but widespread hegemonic

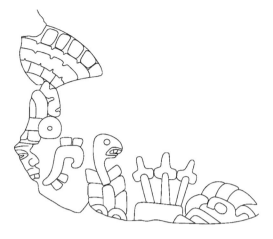

FIGURE 8.2. *Fragment of column from the North Platform (Vertice Geodesico) at Monte Alban with Teotihuacano warrior with square shield, spearthrower, and darts. Drawing by Javier Urcid and Elbis Domínguez.*

Teotihuacan empire. As outlined above, we are now in a position to identify a number of specific sites and areas that seem to have been under Teotihuacan control or imperial influence. As Kenneth Hirth and Jorge Angulo Villaseñor (1981, 137) noted, "Teotihuacan materials are not evenly distributed throughout Mesoamerica but occur in greatest frequency along natural corridors of trade and communication as well as in areas of important scarce resources."

Addressing the main topic of the present chapter, Teotihuacan influence has been noted at a number of sites in the states of Hidalgo, Querétaro, Guanajuato, and Michoacan (Brambila Paz and Crespo 2002; Braniff 2000; Castañeda López 2008; Díaz Oyarzábal 1980; Ekholm 1945; Faugère 2007; Saint-Charles Zetina, Viramontes Anzures, and Fenoglio Limón 2010, 26–34, 65–112). Frequently, local stylistic features and chronological indicators suggest indirect influence or Epiclassic (ca. 600–900 CE) emulations of Classic architecture and iconography, as can be seen at Plazuelas and Peralta in Guanajuato and Tingambato in Michoacan. This is not the case with the recently discovered murals at the archaeological site of El Rosario in the state of Querétaro, 140 km northwest of Teotihuacan, which are the first examples of Teotihuacan-style murals and elaborate iconography discovered that far north of Teotihuacan (Saint-Charles Zetina, Viramontes Anzures, Fenoglio Limón 2010; Nielsen et al. 2019b) (figure 8.3); hence, they are extremely important in terms of understanding Teotihuacan influence and possible imperial interests in a wider region of Mesoamerica that encompasses the modern states of Guanajuato, Querétaro, and Michoacan. Coupled with a renewed interest in Teotihuacan's relations with western Mexico (Gómez Chávez 1999; Gómez Chávez and Gazzola 2007) and Michoacan (Filini 2004), the murals allow us to say much more about what should perhaps eventually be termed north-central and western *entradas*. The fact that the Teotihuacanos depicted in the murals from El

FIGURE 8.3. *The North Wall of the Pórtico de los Cuchillos, Structure 1, El Rosario.* Courtesy, *Proyecto Arqueológico El Rosario.*

Rosario carry shields, darts, and flaming torches and speak of darts and bleeding hearts is rather suggestive; these elements strongly suggest a Teotihuacan military takeover to control whatever resources could be gained from the San Juan del Río Valley and its surroundings.

THE TEOTIHUACANO WARRIORS AT EL ROSARIO

The unique, polychromatic, Teotihuacan-style murals from El Rosario embellish the portico, referred to as the Pórtico de los Cuchillos, of the first construction phase of Structure 1, which is situated at the center of the site (Fenoglio Limón, Viramontes Anzures, and Saint-Charles Zetina 2010; Nielsen and Helmke 2015; Saint-Charles Zetina, Viramontes Anzures, and Fenoglio Limón 2010). Based on stylistic and stratigraphic evidence, this phase has been dated to what corresponds to the Tlamimilolpan and Xolalpan phases at Teotihuacan (200–650 CE). The most well-preserved murals adorn the North, Northeast, Southeast and South Taluds of the portico walls. The remnants of the feet of a standing figure on the *tablero* of the North Wall show that the murals were once significantly larger. The *talud* murals are dominated by four striding Teotihuacan warriors with shields and darts placed among hill signs qualified by obsidian blades, probably signifying that they arrived to, or acted in, a place seemingly named "Obsidian Mountain" (Saint-Charles Zetina, Viramontes Anzures, and Fenoglio

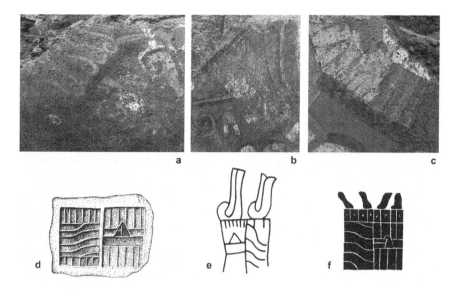

FIGURE 8.4. *Torches from El Rosario and Teotihuacan: a, detail from the North Wall at El Rosario showing torch with characteristic Teotihuacan-style flames; b–c, the remaining parts of the torches on the Southeast and Northeast Walls at El Rosario; d, mold for ceramic ador-nos for theater-style censers with set of torches; e–f, pairs of burning torches from Teotihuacan (a–c, courtesy, Proyecto Arqueológico El Rosario; d, adapted from Von Winning 1987: II, figure 18c; e, after Taube 2000b, figure 10.5a; f, after Linné 1934, figure 24).*

Limón 2010, 129–131; see also Nielsen and Helmke 2008, 462, 473). In the following section I focus on the torches carried by the warrior figures as well as the bleeding hearts attached to the speech scroll of the figure on the Southeast and North Taluds. I review these elements in the context of themes commonly found in Teotihuacan iconography in areas outside the city itself.

The Torches and Their Significance

In three cases, warriors are shown holding torches in front of them (figure 8.4a–c). On the North Wall, the torch is shown with Teotihuacan-style flames; while these are missing on the Southeast Wall because of the decay of the mural, a comparison between the two bundled elements makes it evident that this is also a representation of a torch. On the Northeast Wall, only a fraction of the torch is preserved, but again one may note the same way of representing the lower portion of the torch, as well as identical coloration. Presumably, the warrior on the badly damaged South Wall originally held a similar torch. In Teotihuacan iconography, torches take on an easily recognizable shape, consisting of wrapped bundles of wooden sticks with stylized flames emanating from the top (figure

8.4d–f). The distinct manner of representing a torch bundle as consisting of two parts or pairs is not uncommon in the iconography of Teotihuacan (Taube 2000a, figure 10.5a; Von Winning 1987: II, figures 18c, 25c) and serves as a diagnostic feature further suggesting that the El Rosario murals were painted by Teotihuacanos. What is equally striking about the El Rosario torches is that they fall into the pattern of Teotihuacan-style iconography that has been observed in several regions of Mesoamerica, including the Maya region, as well as the Gulf Coast, Oaxaca, and Guerrero (see chapters by Bassie-Sweet, Abtosway and McCafferty, and Koontz, this volume, for additional discussion of Teotihuacan-style iconography in the Maya, Mixtec, and Veracruz regions, respectively). We repeatedly find Teotihuacano warriors carrying the characteristic helmets and headdresses (e.g., the War Serpent and shell-platelet headdresses), weaponry (spearthrowers, darts, and square shields), and torches that are so emblematic of the Teotihuacan state military apparatus (see Nielsen 2003, 87–97).

I have previously suggested that these torches, rather than merely denoting Teotihuacanos setting foreign cities or temples ablaze (which remains a possibility), are related to the Mesoamerican concept of "Toma de Posesión" (Nielsen 2003, 88–93, 2006a). In the Late Postclassic Central Mexican tradition, the ceremony of the Toma de Posesión was crucial for the legitimization of a new ruler. First and foremost, the ceremony represented the act of founding a new dynasty, town, or settlement, but it could also refer to the appropriation of new land. Essentially, it was a sequence of rituals marking the beginning of a new era. Michel Oudijk (2002, 102) has provided the most in-depth study of this ritual sequence, and he noted that it consisted of several different elements:

1. Shoot arrows at the four cardinal points
2. Perform the New Fire ritual as well as other related rituals and ceremonies
3. Order four lords to the land into possession
4. Demarcation of the land
5. Divide the land among the lords and nobles.

It is well-known that Mesoamerican cultures had a fairly common standard repertoire for showing the military conquest and acquisition of new territory. The most frequent way of doing this in Central Mexico and Oaxaca was the straightforward display of military power; for example, a warrior grasping the hair of the defeated enemy, toponyms pierced by darts, or a burning/destroyed temple structure (Marcus 1992a, 353–411). By showing the aggressors engaged in drilling a new fire, a conquest or takeover could be depicted in a subaltern way; thus, the fire drilling and torches signaled military and political superiority and dominance, and we must assume that in many instances such Toma de Posesión ceremonies did in fact take place after the conclusion of military actions proper. As a powerful symbol of transformation and re-centering, the flaming torch symbolized the installation of a new ruler, the founding of a new town, and the arrival of a new order (Nielsen 2006a; see also Jansen and Pérez Jiménez 2007, 49–50, 85–86).

Increasing evidence suggests that New Fire ceremonies were also celebrated at Teotihuacan. A number of stone reliefs found near the Pyramid of the Sun have scenes of fire drilling carved on them, and a large stone representing a year bundle, similar to Aztec sculptured stone *xiuhmolpillis*, was discovered near the pyramid (Berrin and Pasztory 1993, 173, cat. no. 8; Fash, Tokovinine, and Fash 2009; Von Winning 1979). The Teotihuacan-style inscription on Stela 1 from Piedra Labrada in Veracruz also bears a striking resemblance to the New Fire ceremony celebrated in the year 7 Eye Reptile, with a lit torch resembling those from El Rosario lying atop the calendrical sign (Helmke and Nielsen 2011, 17–18; Nielsen and Helmke 2018, 77–83; Taube 2000a, 45). Recall that the Mexica associated the Pyramid of the Sun with the beginning of time as well as fire rituals: myths that may well have had their roots in Classic Teotihuacan traditions (Boone 2000). When viewed together, the available evidence strongly suggests that New Fire rituals played a prominent role in Teotihuacan religious and political life, both at home and abroad.

Worth emphasizing are the examples of high-ranking Teotihuacanos with flaming torches in their headdresses that are represented outside Teotihuacan. Elsewhere, Christophe Helmke and I (Nielsen and Helmke 2014) have suggested that these are most likely part of an important title that identifies the person wearing the headdress as a "firehouse-keeper." The clearest example of this appears on a finely carved stone slab from Soyoltepec in Veracruz, showing an individual wearing a Feathered Serpent headdress and brandishing two burning torches in his hands (Bolz 1975, lxx) (figure 8.5a). The torches reappear in his headdress but are crossed and set below the roof of a building. As suggested by William Fash and his coauthors (2009, 221), there is evidence that a "firehouse" (possibly the Pyramid of the Sun or its Adosada platform) played center stage in much of Teotihuacan's ritual and political life and that dynasties even in distant parts of Mesoamerica actively sought to demonstrate a link to such a structure and the power and status with which it was associated. This can be seen at Maya cities such as Tikal, Holmul, and Copan, where Maya texts mention a house marked by two crossed torches (now read as *wiin te' naah*) (e.g., Estrada-Belli and Tokovinine 2016, 159–161; Fash, Tokovinine, and Fash 2009, 201–220; Stuart 2000, 490–493). Assuming that the "firehouse-keeper" title referred to on the Soyoltepec monument was derived from the "firehouse" at Teotihuacan, it follows that the individual portrayed was a representative or emissary of the same place.

Two additional examples of the torch headdress should be mentioned. The first appears on the famous Stela 31 at Tikal (dedicated in 445 CE) and is the one Maya monument that has provided the most crucial evidence of Teotihuacan's influence

FIGURE 8.5. *Teotihuacan-style headdresses incorporating torches: a, Early Classic monument from Soyoltepec, Veracruz; b, detail from Tikal Stela 31; c, Cherán-style vase from Michoacan (a, drawing by Jesper Nielsen after Bolz 1975, LXX; b, adapted from Jones and Satterthwaite 1982, figure 51a; c, photo by Marie-Areti Hers,* courtesy, Instituto Nacional de Antropología e Historia).

in the Maya area. On the left side of the stela is a portrait of Yax Nuun Ahiin I, son of "Spearthrower Owl" and likely the fourth ruler (374 to 439 CE) of a Teotihuacan dynasty (Stuart 2000, 467–490). Worth noting about the image of Yax Nuun Ahiin I are the small Teotihuacan-style torches stuck in his headdress, which are practically identical to those seen at Piedra Labrada, Soyoltepec, and El Rosario (figure 8.5b). While there seems to be no visual reference to a house in Yax Nuun Ahiin's headdress, it is very plausible that this is a Maya artist's rendition of a Teotihuacan headdress, identifying its wearer as a representative of the "firehouse."

Another version of this unusual headdress appears on an unprovenanced poly-chrome vessel from Michoacan (possibly from the site of Querendaro) and is one of the most interesting examples of Teotihuacan-style iconography from this region (Carot and Hers 2011, 16–17, figure 4; Filini 2004, 68–69) (figure 8.5c). On it we see a human figure repeated three times, separated by bands with a repeated glyphic compound (discussed below). Eduardo Matos Moctezuma and Isabel Kelly (1974) first compared the imagery with murals from Tepantitla and Teopancaxco at Teotihuacan, and more recently, Agapi Filini (2004, 68–69) briefly discussed the vessel and in particular the half star appearing on the fig-ure's dress, which she correctly noted has been attributed with both aquatic and martial associations. The half star was closely associated with warfare, sacrifice, and death in Teotihuacan and later Central Mexican cultures (Baird 1989). In the murals from Teopancaxo, halved stars appear in combination with the so-called trilobe (water or blood) sign (Langley 1986, 296–297) (figure 8.6a–b). This is possibly a reference to war, since we know that the Classic Maya logogram for "war" combines a star with water pouring down (Helmke and Nielsen 2014). We also find examples of the star-and-trilobe glyph represented in the Maya region (Copan and Tikal) in iconographic and archaeological contexts that point toward contacts with Teotihuacan (figure 8.6c–d).

Other iconographic elements on the Michoacan vessel deserve additional attention. First, although the vessel itself and the execution of the imagery are attributed to the local Cherán style, the Teotihuacan-style iconography is skill-fully imitated. The richly clad Teotihuacano holds a distinctive incense pouch, and a speech scroll with flowers attached—possibly denoting singing—emanates from his mouth (Nielsen 2014). Most important, the Teotihuacano wears a huge feathered headdress with three unlit torches stuck into it, indicating that he, too, was a "firehouse-keeper." Although the vase was a local product, its imagery suggests that the artist and his community or town experienced the arrival of emissaries associated with the Teotihuacan "firehouse." Whether this implies an actual Teotihuacan imperial presence and *entrada* in this part of Michoacan is less certain, but it does demonstrate how widespread specific titles and icono-graphic themes related to Teotihuacan warfare and state institutions were in the Early Classic period. As discussed below, additional evidence suggests a Teotihuacan presence in Michoacan, in particular in the Cuitzeo Basin in the northern part of the state.

To briefly reiterate, the drilling of a New Fire or the bringing of torches representing the New Fire to newly conquered or otherwise subjugated areas or towns was a vivid symbolic act expressing the change of power relations. As shown, individuals (sometimes of exceedingly high rank, as in the case of Yax Nuun Ahiin) carrying a Teotihuacan title directly associated with a "firehouse" are documented far away from Teotihuacan and suggest the presence of ethnic

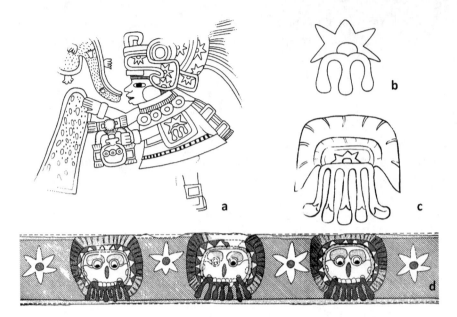

FIGURE 8.6. a, *Warrior-priest from the mural in Room 1 at Teopancaxco (Teotihuacan) adorned with a half star with a "trilobe" sign beneath it; b, detail of the warrior-priest from Teopancaxco showing half star in combination with the "trilobe" sign; c, feather-rimmed half star with elaborate water or blood droplet on stuccoed and painted tripod from the Sub-Jaguar Tomb at Copan; and d, stars combined with skulls with blood droplets gushing from their mouths. Teotihuacan-style stuccoed and painted tripod from Burial 48 at Tikal. a–c, drawings by Christophe Helmke; d, adapted from Culbert 1993, figure 30b.*

Teotihuacan imperial emissaries in these areas. The flaming torches brought forth by the Teotihuacan warriors in the El Rosario murals thus served as powerful symbols that a new, strong political order had arrived in the San Juan del Río Valley.

The Bleeding Hearts

It has been noted that the headdress of the individual on the North Talud of the Structure 1 portico at El Rosario includes bleeding hearts, presumably human hearts, and that this is a trait that can be seen in headdresses at Teotihuacan (Fenoglio Limón, Viramontes Anzures, and Saint-Charles Zetina 2010; Saint-Charles Zetina, Viramontes Anzures, and Fenoglio Limón 2010, 120; see also Latsanopoulos 2005); however, this motif reappears three times in relation to the warriors on the Southeast and North Taluds. On the Southeast Talud, a heart with several large droplets of blood is shown attached to the speech scroll emanating from the warrior (figure 8.7a). Affixed to the speech scroll is also the

FIGURE 8.7. *Speech scrolls with hearts and darts: a, El Rosario Southeast Wall speech scroll with feathered eye, bleeding heart, and dart butt; b, dart butts as part of glyphic collocation (Glyph 3) at the Plaza de los Glifos, La Ventilla; c, the lower speech scroll from the North Wall at El Rosario with "trispiral" sign and a heart. Drawings by Christophe Helmke.*

butt of a dart, and almost identical examples of this element are found as part of composite glyphic signs in the text of the Plaza de los Glifos at La Ventilla (Cabrera Castro 1996, 403–405; Nielsen and Helmke 2011) (figure 8.7b).

The bleeding heart and dart suggest that the speech scroll denotes a reference to warfare and heart sacrifice, and presumably the warriors verbally announced their role as bringers of war and the demand for human sacrificial victims and hearts. Elsewhere I have suggested that the speech scroll could refer to a specific genre of war song, akin to those documented in the Mexica *Cantares Mexicanos* (Nielsen 2014). On the North Talud, another heart and so-called trispiral or triskele motif are attached to the speech scroll just below the flaming torch (figure 8.7c). As early as 1956, Laurette Séjourné (1976 [1956], 119–120) identified the "trispiral" motif as representing a stylized human heart in cross-section (see also Langley 1986, 298), and at Teotihuacan the bleeding heart and the trispiral version often appear together and clearly substitute for each other, as at El Rosario (Cabrera Castro 1995, figure 18.4). In sum, the close association between the torches and the hearts underscores the martial and sacrificial theme of the scenes.

Àngel Iván Rivera Guzmán (2011) published a spectacular Teotihuacan-style stela (Monument 2) from the site of Cerro Tortuga on the coast of Oaxaca (figure 8.8). The nearly 3 m-tall stela shows a Teotihuacan warrior with an emblem combining a shield, a blood-dripping dart, and a raptor (possibly an owl) on his chest. Of special interest to the present discussion is the figure's speech scroll that includes a stylized heart with dripping blood (the so-called trilobe motif) (Rivera Guzmán 2011, 437). The stela from Cerro Tortuga thus provides a comparable example of a monumental artwork in Teotihuacan style, with a warrior figure speaking or singing of bleeding human hearts in a region far from Teotihuacan

FIGURE 8.8. *Detail of Monument 2 from Cerro Tortuga (Oaxaca) with Teotihuacano warrior with speech scroll. Note also the similarity of the dart butt to that attached to the speech scroll from El Rosario. Redrawn by Jesper Nielsen after Rivera Guzmán 2011.*

proper. While the stela is more clearly influenced by local styles of iconography and writing compared to the El Rosario murals, it is an important addition to the picture of a widespread Teotihuacan imperial iconography centered on themes related to warfare. The prominent role of human hearts in the El Rosario mural program suggests that one of the intended messages of the imagery was to highlight the militaristic and sacrificial aspects of the Teotihuacan state (Sugiyama 2005, 220–243). What we see, and what the local visitors to Structure 1 were to have witnessed, is not a proclamation of water-bringing feathered serpents, maize-carrying Storm Gods, or esoteric mythological scenes but straightforward references to conquest and death in the area of the "Obsidian Mountain."

GO WEST: INDICATIONS OF TEOTIHUACAN PRESENCE IN MICHOACAN

Leaving Querétaro and turning our attention toward the region west of the Central Mexican highlands, today mainly covered by the state of Michoacan, we find growing evidence of Teotihuacan influence or even direct presence in the late fourth and fifth centuries CE. Compared to most of the other regions of Mesoamerica mentioned previously (except perhaps for Guerrero), considerable expanses of Michoacan remain relatively unexplored archaeologically. Many archaeological sites have been looted, and for decades, archaeological and historical research has focused on the Late Postclassic Tarascan culture at impressive and easily accessible sites such as Tzintzuntzan (Filini 2004, 1–4; Olmos Curiel 2006).

It has long been recognized that Classic-period sites show clear traces of the spread of Teotihuacan architectural forms, ceramic styles, and iconographic features. Teotihuacan-looking stucco paintings have been reported from El Otero (Jiquilpan) in the western part of the state, and wonderful pseudo-cloisonné vessels from the same site display obvious iconographic inspiration from Teotihuacan, as discussed by Marie-Areti Hers (2013, 219–240). Teotihuacan-style ceramics and an alabaster mask, along with *talud-tablero* structures, have been found at Huandacareo and Tres Cerritos. At the site of Loma Santa María on the outskirts of Morelia, an Old Fire god ("Huehueteotl") sculpture was found along with *talud-tablero* architecture, green obsidian, and other Teotihuacan-related artifacts (Cárdenas García 2013; Gómez Chávez and Gazzola 2007, 125–128; Matos Moctezuma and Kelly 1974; Oliveros 1975; Pollard 2000, 62–64; Williams 2009). Excavations by the Michoacan Project (1983–1986) at Loma Alta in Lake Zacapu also suggest relations with Teotihuacan (Carot 2001; Carot and Hers 2011, 15), and among the most revealing discoveries were an Old Fire god sculpture and a Cherán-style vase fragment with a wonderful warrior figure in pure Teotihuacan style (Carot 2013, 169–172; Carot and Hers 2011, 15–19, figures 5–6). Impressive *talud-tablero* structures are also known from Tingambato, and while an exact dating remains problematic, these are now thought to date from the Epiclassic period (Melchor Cruz Hernández and Landa Alarcón 2013; Pollard and Cahue 1999; Williams 2009).

Filini (2004) has documented and studied the presence of Teotihuacan in the Cuitzeo Basin, and her contributions to the subject are by far the most comprehensive and detailed studies of Teotihuacan influence in this part of Mesoamerica (see also Carot and Hers 2011; Filini and Cárdenas García 2007). Her work systematically discusses Teotihuacan-related ceramics found in the basin and lists all the iconographic motifs and themes derived from Teotihuacan that she was able to identify in the archaeological assemblage (Filini 2004, 38–41, 54–73). According to Filini, Teotihuacan war symbolism predominates in the local adaptations of Teotihuacan motifs, yet although martial themes are most common, Teotihuacan's role in Michoacan appears to have had different levels of intensity at different sites (a pattern that has also been noted for the Maya area; see Nielsen 2003, 251–253). This indicates varying degrees of interaction with and knowledge of the Teotihuacan state apparatus and its visual representations.

Filini (2004, 112) notes: "The inhabitants of the Cuitzeo Basin locally reproduced Teotihuacan symbols of power, deposited Teotihuacan-related artifacts as burial offerings, and added Teotihuacan architectural details on a number of terraced platforms." To Filini (2004, 113), the evidence suggests that sites in the Cuitzeo Basin maintained a relative degree of autonomy, interpreting them as belonging to a "semi-periphery" in contrast to a "primary periphery," and she argues that they "deliberately transformed Teotihuacan elements into the local fabric."

It has also been suggested that Teotihuacano traders and emissaries were en route to other areas of western and northern Mesoamerica, thus using the Cuitzeo Basin only as a corridor, just as it has been argued that they may have had interests in local cinnabar sources (Gómez Chávez and Gazzola 2007, 126–127). As discussed earlier, there is reason to assume that the Teotihuacan empire employed a number of different strategies, from actual conquest and military presence to threat and marriage alliances, to establish control over desired resources (Berdan and Smith 1996; Nielsen 2003, 63–70) and that each strategy would have left different traces in the archaeological record. Furthermore, as was the case with the Maya region, Teotihuacan symbols, imagery, and material culture spread around the locations that were most directly affected by Teotihuacan culture; hence, most of the examples that can be designated as Teotihuacanoid or Teotihuacan-inspired imagery and ceramics should not be seen as evidence of direct Teotihuacan influence. I do not disagree with Filini's conclusion that most of Teotihuacan's influence in the Cuitzeo Basin, and in Michoacan in general, seems to have been of an indirect nature and that the iconography is integrated into local styles and themes; however, I still find it worthwhile to consider some of the motifs she did not identify or discuss—in this case, the aforementioned torch headdress. As I have suggested, this headdress may be indicative of a more permanent military presence, perhaps centered at a site yet to be discovered (here we only have to remind ourselves about our perspective on the Teotihuacan presence in Querétaro before the excavations at El Rosario; see, for example, Braniff 2000, 39–40; Filini and Cárdenas García 2007, 139).

Returning to the possible Querendero vessel, showing the Teotihuacano emissary with the likely "firehouse-keeper" title, I wish to briefly discuss the vertical bands of two repeating glyphic signs: an eye with a "trilobe" underneath (figure 8.9a–b). The exact significance of this collocation is undetermined, and while a Westerner may immediately associate the two signs with crying or weeping, it could well be an abbreviated reference to a bleeding heart, since hearts are commonly depicted with an infixed eye—possibly as a reference to the glistening wet surface of the heart (in general, liquids are often marked by similar eyes in Teotihuacan iconography). We saw an example of such an eye with a blood "trilobe" on the stela from Cerro Tortuga (see figure 8.8), and this interpretation would fit an overall context of warfare and sacrifice. Significantly,

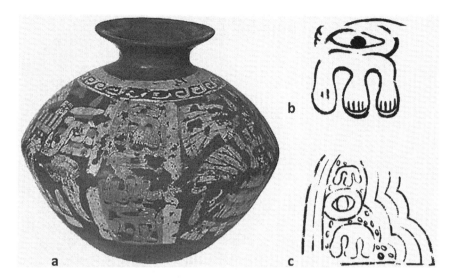

FIGURE 8.9. *Possible references to bleeding hearts in: a, vertical band of repeating glyphs on Cherán-style vase from Michoacan; b, one of the glyphs from Cherán-style base; and c, glyph infixed in mountain sign below Teotihuacano warrior on Mural 2 from Xelha (Quintana Roo). a, photo by Marie-Areti Hers, courtesy, Instituto Nacional de Antropología e Historia; b–c, drawings by Christophe Helmke based on photos by Marie-Areti Hers and Ricardo Alvarado.*

the combination of the "trilobe" with an eye also appears along with a magnificent Teotihuacan warrior, complete with square shield, spearthrower, and jaguar-butterfly headdress, in the large Mural 2 from the Maya site of Xelha on the Caribbean coast of Mexico (Helmke and Nielsen 2014, 90–91; Nielsen 2003, 217–218; Staines Cicero 1995, 58) (figure 8.9c). We thus find remarkable consistency in the motifs and representations of Teotihuacan warriors, from some of the westernmost parts of Mesoamerica to its borders in the east.

Finally, two slate mirror backings from the Cuitzeo Basin should be mentioned (Filini 2004, 58–59, 69). As has been demonstrated by Karl Taube and others, such mirrors are known to have been worn by Teotihuacan warriors or warrior-priests and are one of the most characteristic features representing Teotihuacanos abroad (Nielsen 2006b; Taube 1992c). One of the mirrors from Querendaro is embellished with a so-called Mexican Year Sign (or trapeze-ray sign) (Langley 1986, 293–294; Von Winning 1987 II, 25–27), a floral design, and what are most likely stylized torches (Filini 2004, 69, figure 5.17) (figure 8.10a). The Teotihuacan Year Sign is also found outside of Teotihuacan at sites such as Kaminaljuyu (Kidder, Jennings, and Shook 1946, figure 207) and at Copan, where it appears on one of the Teotihuacan-style mirrors from the Early Classic Margarita Tomb in the Margarita substructure beneath Temple 16 (Bell et al.

FIGURE 8.10. *Mirror backings with Teotihuacan-style iconography and comparisons with Teotihuacan imagery: a, slate mirror backing from Quenrendaro, Michoacan, with large, central year sign; b, stuccoed and painted slate backing of Mirror 1 from the Margarita Tomb in Copan with year sign qualifying a mountain sign; c, Teotihuacan-style stela from Acatempan (Guerrero) with warrior standing on top of a toponym composed of the year sign; d, slate mirror backing from Alvaro Obregón, Michoacan, with raptorial bird with liquid dripping from the beak; and e, mural from Tetitla's Portico 25 showing eagle or owl with drops of blood gushing from its open beak. a and d, after Filini 2004, figures 5.17, 5.3u; b and e, drawings by Jesper Nielsen; c, drawing by Karl Taube, after Taube 2011, figure 5.13a.*

2004; Nielsen 2006b) (figure 8.10b). Here it serves as the qualifying element of a mountain sign that almost certainly refers to a place name (see Helmke and Nielsen 2014; Nielsen 2006b, 3–5, figure 2). The year sign occurs in a comparable context on an Early Classic stela from Acatempan in Guerrero (Taube 2000a, 9, figure 6d) (figure 8.10c), where a Teotihuacano warrior, complete with goggles, spearthrower, and a square shield, is shown standing atop the year sign with an affixed "root" sign. As first suggested by Taube, this probably served as a locative suffix, thereby indicating that the Teotihuacano either came from or arrived at the "year-sign-place." The second mirror, from Alvaro Obregón, is engraved with a raptorial bird with drops of blood or water dripping from its beak (Filini

2004, 58, figure 5.3u) (figure 8.10d). While the style of the execution of the motif is local, the iconography is clearly inspired by Teotihuacan imagery and suggests a reference to one of the two alleged military orders or sodalities at Teotihuacan: one associated with raptorial birds (eagles or owls), the other with felines or canines (Millon 1988; Nielsen 2004) (figure 8.10e). A possible iconographic reference to these orders can also be found on Stela 4 from Los Horcones on the Pacific Coast of Chiapas (Navarrete 1986, 15–16, figures 8–9).

The Teotihuacan-style torches, along with the year sign and the raptorial birds, are common in Teotihuacan iconography outside of Central Mexico, and Filini's (2004, 66) observation that "the kind of signs present in the Cuitzeo Basin are different for other areas of Mesoamerica that were interacting with Teotihuacan at approximately the same time" must be questioned. In fact, I suggest that the Teotihuacan iconographic repertoire encountered in the Cuitzeo Basin is strikingly similar and conforms to the group of motifs I have collectively designated as Teotihuacan imperial iconography.

SUMMARY AND CONCLUSIONS

In this brief treatment of some of the most revealing iconographic elements from the murals of El Rosario, I suggest that the images record and commemorate the arrival of armed Teotihuacano warriors carrying the flaming torches that probably signaled ritual activities akin to those that later figured in the "Toma de Posesión" ceremonies. Apparently speaking or singing about war and heart sacrifice, they announce the purpose of their presence. Viewed as a whole, El Rosario Structure 1 and its murals can be compared to other structures presumably erected at select sites, such as Kaminaljuyu in Guatemala, Copan in Honduras, and possibly also in Morelos and elsewhere (Nielsen and Helmke 2014). I take these as architectural indications of a Teotihuacan imperial expansion and the subsequent local emulations of the original temples of the capital city, perhaps commissioned by imperial representatives. El Rosario Structure 1 thus appears to have constituted an architectural entity that simultaneously served to impress and intimidate the local non-Teotihuacano population, as well as to provide the necessary spatial surroundings to conduct rituals associated with the Teotihuacan state and imperial ideology.

In terms of dating the murals, we know that the Teotihuacan *entrada* into the central Maya lowlands area occurred in 378 CE, and it is likely that a north-central *entrada* and possibly incursions into Michoacan as well took place in roughly the same time period, sometime between 350 and 450 CE when Teotihuacan imperial presence outside of the Central Mexican highlands appears to have reached its peak. The iconography of the El Rosario murals is undergoing continued study (Nielsen et al. 2019b) that, it is hoped, will cast further light on their meaning as well as their chronology. Additional archaeological investigations at El Rosario also have the potential to help clarify the exact nature of Teotihuacan's presence at the site, as well as the motivations and strategies involved. So far, we can conclude that the iconographic program of the murals conforms to the thematic pattern of Teotihuacan imperial iconography, strongly suggesting a Teotihuacan *entrada* and subsequent establishment of an enclave in this important part of the Bajío region. To quote the excavators of the murals at some length (Saint-Charles Zetina, Viramontes Anzures, and Fenoglio Limón 2010, 112): "El patrón arquitectónico característico de Teotihuacan paracer reproducirse en el Rosario; las analogías que observamos tanto en la disposición especial de los recintos porticados como los materiales y sistemas constructivos, nos indicant una clara relación entre la gran urbe y este pequeño centro ceremonial del Centro Norte. No obstante, dicho patron no constituye el único element que remite a Teotihuacan: la iconografía, las tradiciones rituals y los materiales nos dan indicios de la llegada de grupos teotihuacanos a esta región." (The characteristic architectural pattern of Teotihuacan is reproduced at el Rosario; the analogies that we observe both in the special disposition of the arcaded enclosures, as well as in the material and constructive systems, indicate a clear relationship between the great city and this small ceremonial center of the Central North. However, this pattern is not the only element that refers to Teotihuacan: the iconography, ritual traditions, and materials give us indications of the arrival of Teotihuacan groups in this region.)

A preliminary survey of the iconographic indications of Teotihuacan influence in Michoacan also revealed a number of recurring motifs and themes, suggesting that specific sites or areas of this region also witnessed the incursion of Teotihuacano representatives; however, none of the examples known at present are clearly the work of Teotihuacan artists or Teotihuacan-trained artists, as seems to be case at El Rosario. They incorporate Teotihuacan elements into local styles and represent emulations or copies of Teotihuacan artifacts and imagery. The circumstances under which such emulations were produced, as well as the possible provincial enclave in Michoacan from where such Teotihuacan-inspired material culture emanated, are yet to be determined, but the remarkable objects found near Querendaro point to the region west of Lake Cuitzeo as a potential focal area for Teotihuacan presence. It is hoped that future excavations in the Cuitzeo Basin and other parts of Michoacan will help us better understand and explain Teotihuacan's involvement in western Mexico.

Acknowledgments. First, I would like to express my sincere thanks to Karen Bassie-Sweet, the organizer of the session The Art of War (Mesoamerican Style) at the 45th Annual Chacmool Archaeological Conference at the University of Calgary in 2012 where an earlier and shorter version of this chapter was presented, for inviting me to participate and for her warm hospitality. Second, my warm thanks to the editors of the present volume, Shawn Morton and Meaghan Peuramaki-Brown, and to my friends and collaborators at INAH in Querétaro—Fiorella Fenoglio Limón, Carlos Viramontes Anzures, and Juan Carlos Saint-Charles Zetina—for their tremendous support and generosity over the past few years. Warm thanks also to Agapi Filini for her kind help in things related to Michoacan; to Iván Rivera, Nicolas Latsanopoulos, and Javier Urcid; and to Christophe Helmke for making valuable comments, correcting my English, and preparing the figures. Finally, *un abrazo* to my dear old friend Toke Sellner Reunert for accompanying me on my first trip to El Rosario in 2011.

9

Mixtec Militarism

Weapons and Warfare in the Mixtec Codices

MATTHEW ABTOSWAY AND GEOFFREY McCAFFERTY

The study of indigenous warfare in Mesoamerica has long focused on the Maya and Aztec because of their historical prominence, art historical and historical details, and general popularity. The Aztec in particular have gained a fearsome reputation in popular culture as a result of the extensive publication of their ritual violence and warfare, even appearing in popular war/strategy videogame franchises. In contrast, the inhabitants of the Mixteca Alta of modern-day Oaxaca have received little attention because of their less prominent role in the Spanish Conquest and relative remoteness. However, archaeologists and art historians do have a rich source of cultural knowledge about these peoples in the form of the pictorial manuscripts, or codices, painted in the Late Postclassic period (1100–1522 CE) that recorded historical and genealogical information spanning hundreds of years. Of relevance to this chapter, the Mixtec codices also record a wealth of information on the material culture of the ancient Mixtecs. This study focuses on the lengthiest of the Mixtec codices, the *Codex Zouche-Nuttall* (Nuttall 1975), with the goal of gaining insight into Mixtec warfare through the weapons depicted therein. Other codices, such as the *Codex Bodley* (Jansen and Pérez

DOI: 10.5876/9781607328872.c009

Jiménez 2005) and the *Codex Selden* (Caso 1964), provide additional perspectives on the observed patterns, while Nahua pictorial manuscripts, such as *El Lienzo de Tlaxcala* (Chavero 1979), provide contrasts. The sparse archaeological record of the Mixteca Alta provides on-the-ground insights.

THE MIXTEC AND CONFLICT

The production of the Mixtec codices coincided with the Postclassic Natividad period (1100–1522 CE) in the Mixteca region. Set in an era marked by political instability and shifting alliances, the high frequency of weapon and conquest imagery is scarcely surprising. Located in the western highlands of the modern state of Oaxaca, the Mixteca Alta geography is broken up by rugged mountains and fertile valleys that reinforced the social fragmentation and resulting warfare that characterized the time of the codices (Spores 1974).

The term *Mixtec warfare* has come to define the internal battles that occurred between polities of the Mixteca, as opposed to the external conquests of cultures such as the Aztec (Gorenstein 1973, 15). These conflicts are depicted in detail throughout the *Codex Zouche-Nuttall* and are particularly frequent during the life of "Lord 8 Deer Jaguar Claw," the most famous protagonist in the existing manuscripts who lived in the tenth century CE. Bruce Byland and John Pohl (1994, 106) have noted that these codical accounts have a remarkable correlation with archaeological observations and as such offer insights into Mixteca cultural practices. The intra-Mixteca warfare of the codices demonstrates that the political centers that are referred to as the "Mixtec" today did not view themselves as a single political unit in the past. Instead, they were likely a people loyal to their regional centers in place of a cohesive larger regional unit (Lind 1979, 7; see also chapters by Hernandez and Palka, Haines and Sagebiel, and Bey and Gallareta Negrón, this volume, for similar discussions for the Maya world).

The nature of internal and external Mixtec conflict was a complex combination of conventional and ritual warfare. At the time of the Spanish arrival, records indicate that no standing armies were maintained; rather, a captain was empowered to raise one as necessary, much in the manner of a Western militia (King 1988, 19). Ritualized warfare is a well-known phenomenon in Pre-Colombian Mesoamerica, especially among the Aztec, and was certainly practiced by the Mixteca as well. Some accounts suggest that cohorts of six warriors and a captain would venture forth to meet the similarly composed opposing force with the goal of capturing individuals for sacrifice (King 1988, 19). The Mixtec codices record a number of such sacrifices (e.g., *Codex Zouche-Nuttall*, 69, 81).

The Mixteca fought in defense of these centers and for personal gain through the conquest of neighboring cities, towns, and villages. In this setting, marital alliances became another valuable political tool for forging ties between geographically isolated communities, with at least 200 such agreements known from the Mixtec codices (Spores 1974, 305).

In the Mixtec codices, projectiles lodged in toponyms denote conquest, an artistic convention that dates back to at least the Terminal Formative period (300 BCE–200 CE) as demonstrated in the "conquest slabs" of Building J at Monte Alban (Winter 2011, 407; see chapters by Tokovinine and Nielsen, this volume, for discussions of Maya toponyms and Teotihuacan conflict symbolism, respectively). In Pre-Columbian times, conquest of a region entitled the victors to certain privileges; for example, the Chichimeca alliance with the Tolteca-Chichimeca during the latter's war against Cholula included the stipulation that the Chichimeca would be "paid" in land grants and lordship titles upon victory (Matthew and Oudijk 2007, 55–56). In regions of Central Mexico, it was common for a conquered people to be pressed into military service by imperialist conquerors as a way of replenishing the ranks. This type of indentured servitude may have been embraced by some as a means of achieving social mobility through the land grants and riches attainable in further conquest (Matthew and Oudijk 2007, 14). Similar shifts in allegiance occurred at the regional level as well. The small tributary villages that owed allegiance to major centers, such as Tilantongo, would reroute tribute to the victor if their major center was conquered, thus sparing themselves direct involvement in a conflict (Gorenstein 1973, 15).

Archaeological evidence for Mixtec warfare is frustratingly rare. Some sites, especially during the Classic period (200–900 CE), were relocated to fortified ridge tops (Byland and Pohl 1994, 58). During survey reconnaissance in the Tamazulapan Valley, high frequencies of projectile points (probably from *atlatl* darts) were recovered from the frontier between the Teposcolula and Tejupan districts, suggesting that this region may have had a long history of boundary disputes. In the remainder of this chapter, examples of "Mixtec warfare" will be drawn from the vivid details offered by the codices, especially in relation to weaponry and military tactics represented (for a good Maya comparative of military tactics, see Kettunen 2011).

WEAPONS OF THE *CODEX ZOUCHE-NUTTALL*

> It is war that shapes peace, and armament that shapes war.
> J.F.C. FULLER (CIYED IN HEINL 1981, 13)

Our study of Mixteca militarism began with a page-by-page frequency and contextual analysis of weapons depicted in the *Codex Zouche-Nuttall* (figure 9.1; table 9.1). As individual weapons were encountered, a spreadsheet row was created and populated with data relevant to that particular instance. Categories included the page of the weapon's occurrence, the handedness, point type and style, shaft style, decorations, and additional comments. Weapons with shafts were

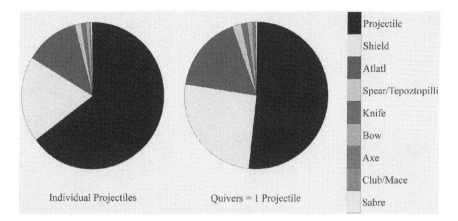

FIGURE 9.1. *Relative abundance of weapon types*

TABLE 9.1. Weapon percentages; *Codex Zouche-Nuttall* distribution

Weapon	% w/ Projectiles*	% w/ Quivers[†]
Projectile	64.76	51.83
Shield	18.75	25.82
Atlatl	12.23	16.85
Spear/*tepoztopilli*	1.46	2.01
Knife	1.06	1.47
Bow	0.66	0.92
Axe	0.40	0.55
Club/mace	0.27	0.37
Sabre	0.13	0.18

* Based on projectiles counted individually.
[†] Based on quivers counted as a single projectile occurrence.

frequently decorated with sequences of colored elements, which were recorded as a list of one- and two-letter color codes that began at the top and ended at the bottom of the weapon. This method of codical analysis promised quantifiable results, as totals and percentages of weapons, point styles, and decoration could be compared and contrasted.

Spears and *Tepoztopilli*

Known to have been used by the Aztecs, *tepoztopilli* is a Nahuatl word for a composite bladed thrusting/slashing weapon. Their hardwood shafts stretched up to 2 m in length and terminated in either oval or triangular points edged with prismatic obsidian blades (Pohl and Robinson 2005). *Tepoztopilli* are nearly ubiquitous

FIGURE 9.2. *Mixtec spears (redrawn from Nuttall 1975, 75).*

throughout the *Lienzo de Tlaxcala* (Chavero 1979), arming both the allies and enemies of Cortés. These spear-like weapons are rendered in the *Lienzo* (in a European style) precisely as described, while comparable weapons in the *Codex Zouche-Nuttall* are distinctly Mixtec. Rather than illustrating flat blades, the Mixtec artists chose to depict triangular points along the edges of their spears (figure 9.2). These projections are always white, perhaps indicating the fine white chert available in the Mixteca Alta as opposed to obsidian. The triangular shapes may represent the sharp edges of multiple blades. These blades were likely held in place, as in Aztec composite bladed weapons, with pitch or tree resin (Pohl and Robinson 2005).

The shafts of spears are nearly always bare when compared to the arrows and darts depicted by Mixtec artists. The most elaborate examples of the former appearing in the *Codex Zouche-Nuttall* are resplendent: their yellow fringes and decorative circles are mounted just below the weapon's head, leaving the shaft of the weapon exposed. Eleven spears were identified, with only one deviation from the yellow-fringed decoration: a lone green-fringed example. The shafts themselves exhibit similar uniformity with red, yellow, or brown, presumably representing hardwood. One example features a jaguar pelt wrapping a section of the shaft, though still bearing the common yellow fringe (Nuttall 1975, 68). This seems to be related to the costuming of Lord 8 Deer and not necessarily to the function of the spear. Operating the weapon required unrestricted access to the entire length of the shaft, eliminating opportunities for adornment by functional necessity.

To explain the absence of complex decor on spears/*tepoztopillis*, we must consider how they were used and by whom. Aztec weapons of the same type have been well documented, as has Tenochtitlan's military structure (Pohl and Robinson 2005). For these reasons as well as chronological considerations, they provide suitable analogues for analyzing these weapons. When compared to projectile weaponry, the Aztec *tepoztopilli* required little training to operate. Younger and less experienced warriors would be equipped with them and positioned behind the front lines, with their 7-foot *tepoztopilli* striking out from relative safety (Pohl and Robinson 2005). It is therefore possible that the lack of elaborate decoration is related to the lower status of untried Mixtec warriors as compared to veteran campaigners and nobility.

In figure 9.2, the central warrior wields a *tepoztopilli*-like weapon, though it is missing the distinctive triangular composite bladed projections. Three of these weapons were identified in the *Codex Zouche-Nuttall* and appear to be tipped with a bifacial stone point. The *Codex Selden* (p. 6) shows two individuals engaged in close-quarters combat with a similar type of thrusting weapon. These weapons also appear to have single points (bearing flake scars) in place of the composite "business end" of a spear. This interpretation is supported by apparent haft bindings visible in both examples, which are unnecessary and thus absent in composite weapons. This style of spear appears throughout the *Codex Selden* and is often shown at the climax of a thrusting motion when the point pierces flesh and armor. In the *Codex Selden*, two examples with this blade are shown affixed to a much shorter shaft, creating a weapon akin to a large knife or long dagger. Ross Hassig (1988, 92) describes similar weapons, some also hafted to wooden handles, relegating them to ceremonial contexts. The *Codex Selden* capture scene would seem to suggest a more martial purpose, at least among the Mixtec.

Knives

The *Codex Zouche-Nuttall* does not offer additional examples of the probable daggers depicted in the *Codex Selden*. All eight knives recorded in the frequency and context analysis were wielded in ceremonial circumstances, namely sacrificial, and not in direct combat. The blades are depicted with a common flint knife shape, mounted on a short shaft painted either white or red. The artists chose not to illustrate hafting, most likely because of the small scale. Three distinct blade styles were recognized, the red tip being the most common with five appearances in the *Codex Nuttall*. One knife blade has a red tip with a single red stripe across its breadth, and another is entirely red. In a departure from the expected flint knife pattern, one example has alternating stripes of red and brown down its entire length, including the blade. The precise significance of these stylistic variations is unclear and may represent distinct lithic types or simply artistic license.

Macuahuitl

The *macuahuitl*, so famously wielded by Mexica warriors, is conspicuously absent from the *Codex Selden*, *Codex Bodley*, and *Codex Zouche-Nuttall*. Shaped roughly like a modern cricket bat, the Aztec *macuahuitl* was on average 1 m in length, with obsidian prismatic blades embedded in both edges (Pohl and Robinson 2005). This weapon features prominently throughout the *Lienzo de Tlaxcala*, most frequently wielded in one hand. The *Lienzo* (Chavero 1979, 34) appears to demonstrate the lethal capabilities of the *macuahuitl*'s edge, as one defending warrior falls near the newly severed arm while a fellow warrior has been decapitated.

The absence of *macuahuitls* in the Mixtec group codices is striking and begs the question of whether the Mixtec used the weapon to the same degree as the Aztec (if at all). Archaeological evidence of the *macuahuitl* in the Mixteca Alta is scant, as it is for all the weapons studied herein; however, the prerequisite technologies were clearly not lacking, as depictions of composite weapons (*tepoztopilli*) are found throughout the Mixtec group codices. While relatively simple to manufacture, wielding the "Aztec Sword" effectively required a great deal of training, ascribing the weapon a high status in the Aztec armory (Hassig 1988, 94). As will be discussed below, the *atlatl* also required experience and skill to master. Often the armament of choice among lords and deities in the *Codex Zouche-Nuttall*, it is possible that the *atlatl* displaced the *macuahuitl* as the symbolic weapon of the Mixtec upper echelon.

Axes

Axes are found in only three instances in the *Codex Zouche-Nuttall*, each one appearing with a different-colored blade. It is possible that green blades represent greenstone, while the yellow and tan denote a copper composition; however, the sample size is too small to be certain. Befitting their utilitarian farming origins, the axe shafts are entirely devoid of decoration and are illustrated as hardwood.

Turning once more to the Aztec realm for comparison, Ross Hassig (1988, 92) has identified axes more frequently with individuals apparently costumed for combat. John Pohl and Charles Robinson (2005, 18) agree, arguing that Aztec warriors commonly carried axes for close-quarters combat. Intriguingly, the *Codex Zouche-Nuttall* (p. 20) (figure 9.3) portrays a battle scene in which an axe-wielding warrior is shown pierced through the leg by an *atlatl* dart, perhaps launched by the pictured enemy. It is clear that among Mixtec artists, axes were considered a suitable combat weapon and not exclusively symbolic or utilitarian.

Clubs

Upon consultation of the *Codex Selden*, accompanied by Pohl's (2002, 2003) scene-by-scene narrative, it was possible to identify a war club in the *Codex Zouche-Nuttall* that corresponds to that identified in the *Selden* (p. 13). Two boast feather elements akin to a variety frequently adorning *atlatls*, while the others exhibit rectangular elements that may symbolize blades. The projections in figure 9.4 represent something besides composite blade tools, as they are depicted

FIGURE 9.3. *Battle scene with axes (redrawn from Nuttall 1975, 20).*

FIGURE 9.4. *"4 Lizard" with war club (redrawn from Nuttall 1975, 66).*

as circular in both codices and are probably representations of teeth projecting from a jawbone (likely deer). What is known is that these weapons served more than ceremonial functions, as demonstrated by the spray of blood emanating from 4 Lizard's club (Nuttall 1975, 66).

The *Lienzo de Tlaxcala* contains numerous warriors wielding a variety of clubs. Pohl and Robinson (2005) describe a generalized hardwood club, which matches the *Lienzo de Tlaxcala*'s depictions, called a *cuauhololli*. These are ubiquitous throughout Mesoamerica and almost certainly existed in the Mixteca region. It is possible that these cheaply made and easily obtained weapons did not coincide with the elite image the *Nuttall* artists were determined to depict and were therefore largely omitted.

Bows

It is a measure of Hollywood's influence that when one pictures a battle between steel-clad conquistadors and Mesoamericans, the bow and arrow invariably comes to mind; therefore, it may not be surprising that the *Lienzo de Tlaxcala* illustrates bow-wielding warriors with arrows in flight throughout its many battles (figure 9.5). This study of the *Codex Zouche-Nuttall* was only able to identify five examples of the bow. In fact, bows account for less than 1 percent of the weapons cataloged, possibly even fewer, as two red-and-white striped members of this category may simply be components of a carried pack. When compared with the many *atlatls* noted, representing 17 percent of the total, bows appear to be underrepresented (refer to table 9.1). Bows do appear in several places in the *Codex Bodley*, although they lack any detail beyond shaft and string (Jansen and Pérez Jiménez 2005). A toponymical element in the *Codex Selden* (p. 4) includes the upper half of a strung un-flexed bow rendered with greater detail. The upper end appears to be bound, possibly for reinforcement, with several small ornamental feathers attached. Originally a hunting tool and lacking the association with deities that the Mixtec *atlatl* enjoys, the bow and arrow most likely did not merit prominence in the codices. The shortage of bows in the *Zouche-Nuttall* as compared to other projectile weapons, specifically *atlatls*, will be addressed in greater detail when projectile identification is discussed.

Atlatl

The Mesoamerican *atlatl* is often confused with a "spearthrower." While the principle of increasing the effective length of the arm to amplify throwing power is the same, the execution is far more complex. At the core of this difference is the projectile. A spearthrower launches an inflexible wood spear, whereas an *atlatl* launches a flexible reed projectile that stores the spring energy of the throw to increase power and accuracy (Chacon and Mendoza 2007). It is for this reason that Donald Slater (2011, 371) has proposed "dart-thrower" as an alternative term; however, as this study frequently makes specific reference to the Aztec arsenal, the Nahuatl *atlatl* was deemed most appropriate. Aztec examples were approximately 2 feet long, with a dart groove in the upward-facing side and a spur at the far end sitting parallel to the shaft (Pohl and Robinson 2005). Two loops position the forefingers, leaving the thumb and two remaining digits to grasp the dart. By some estimates, the use of an *atlatl* increases the force applied on the dart by as much as twenty times what a human arm can produce. The Aztecs evidently held this weapon in high esteem, perhaps because of the amount of training required to become proficient (Pohl and Robinson 2005).

The *atlatl* seems to have been held in equally high regard, if not more so, by the Mixtec. Identifying depictions of this type closely mirrored the parameters described by Slater (2011, 372), with finger loops, distal spurs, and decorative elements (considered in that order). The *Codex Zouche-Nuttall* contains ninety-two *atlatls* (17% of the total), overshadowed only by the shields and projectiles themselves (figure 9.6). As *atlatls* were a readily identifiable weapon type, analysis of this large corpus revolved around decorative elements. Throughout the *Codex Zouche-Nuttall* they appear to decorate the entire shaft in unique and novel

FIGURE 9.5. *"7 Snake" wielding a bow with an* atlatl *(redrawn from Nuttall 1975, 10).*

FIGURE 9.6. *"Lord 3 Water" with* atlatl, *darts, and shield (redrawn from Nuttall 1975, 42).*

manners; however, no clear pattern has emerged. Many *atlatls* shared design elements with an example from Aztec Tenochtitlan's "Stone of the Warriors" (Hassig 1988, 78, figure 8). Twenty-five of the *atlatls* displayed a decorative element originally identified as a spotted yellow feather. Upon comparison with jaguar skins depicted in the *Codex Zouche-Nuttall*, it was observed that this was in fact a small section of that animal's pelt. Thanks to experiments conducted with modern reconstructions by Slater (2011, 384), we can state that even these most elaborate and novel of the *atlatl* designs (including a "double-barreled" example) were functional weapons in their own right.

Atlatls appear to be completely absent from the *Codex Bodley* and the *Lienzo de Tlaxcala*. In both cases, as mentioned under the "Bows" heading, the bow and arrow appear to take their place. There has been a long-held yet untested belief that the bow and arrow may have been a late introduction into Mesoamerica circa 500 CE (Brown and Stanton 2003, 282). It is thought that the Aztec bow was acquired from earlier migrations of the Chichimecs from the arid lands of northern Mexico (Pohl and Robinson 2005, 17). The differential representation of *atlatls* and bows may relate to such a cultural practice.

Pohl and Robinson (2005) emphasize that *atlatls* are often associated with serpent imagery in Mesoamerica and that some surviving examples are carved to that effect. As noted above, reed *atlatl* darts flex when launched, compressing and then releasing spring energy as they push off the spur of the *atlatl*. What many sources fail to mention is that once airborne, the flexing does not stop; rather, the dart continues to flex and usually rotates in flight. This is strikingly obvious in slow motion but visible to the naked eye, and it seems clear that Pre-Columbian Mesoamericans must have been aware of this trait and even encouraged it. Modern *atlatl* enthusiasts "tune" their darts' flex by shortening or lengthening the reed portion of the shaft and then reinserting the hardwood foreshaft. Producing *atlatl* darts was an act with clear avian symbolism, so much so that the Aztec associated their crafting with the festival of Quecholli (Hassig 1988, 79). The Aztec hunting feast Quecholli falls in the solar month of the same name, which translates to "bird of rich feathers" and may specifically refer to the roseate spoonbill (Conan 2007, 78). Arrows and darts would be created in several distinct steps over ten–eleven days, offered to ancestors and Huitzilopochtli before culminating in a ritual hunt and procession led by vassals of Mixcoatl (Conan 2007, 81). While we cannot be certain that a Mixtec equivalent of Quecholli was practiced, the *Zouche-Nuttall* does associate the *atlatl* with high-status individuals such as Lord 8 Deer and various deities. Both darts and *atlatls* are highly decorated, especially compared to other weapons such as *tepoztopilli*, appearing in the *Zouche-Nuttall* with a wide variety of colored fringes and feathers.

The symbolic significance of the *atlatl* should not be understated when considering Classic- and Postclassic-period Mesoamerica. Possibly beginning in the Formative but certainly by the Classic, *atlatl* and dart are associated with deities such as Tlaloc at Teotihuacan and throughout the Maya region (Slater 2011, 375; see also chapters by Bassie-Sweet and Nielsen, this volume). Tlaloc representations or impersonators appear several times throughout the *Zouche-Nuttall* but lack *atlatls* or darts. It would certainly be interesting to find that the Mixtec *atlatl* was associated with other deities, perhaps Quetzalcoatl or Mixcoatl. There are some indications of a serpent connection that extend beyond the feathered serpent carvings and include the behavior of the dart mid-flight (Baugh 1998, 41). The *atlatl* dart's motion through the air is quite serpentine as it spins and flexes, combined with the fletching and any additional decor, and it becomes a perfect metaphor for the Feathered Serpent. Naturally, the codices do not explicitly state this, and some speculation is required. However, as figure 9.7 illustrates, the association of *atlatl* darts with serpents does exist in the *Zouche-Nuttall*. It may be the relation to Quetzalcoatl that explains the high status and frequency of *atlatls* in the *Codex Zouche-Nuttall*.

Projectiles

When quivers of projectile points are tallied as a single weapon, they account for 283 instances (52%) of a total of 546 weapon depictions in the *Codex Zouche-Nuttall* (figure 9.7). When the projectiles within quivers are considered individually, the total weapon count rises to 752, including 487 projectiles (65%; table 9.1). By contrast, shields only represent 19 percent of the 752 total but rise to 26 percent of the 546 depictions. At first glance these numbers appeared remarkably high, prompting the questions of why Mixtec artists would choose to depict so many projectiles relative to weapons. The obvious, and arguably the most likely, explanation is that a single *atlatl* or bow would require multiple projectiles to be an effective weapon, a fact of which the creators of the *Zouche-Nuttall* were clearly aware.

For the purposes of the weapon distribution study, projectiles were divided into three categories: Arrow, Arrow/Dart, and Dart. Distinctions were made on the basis of association with other weapons and with further consideration taken if a projectile forms part of a naming or dating element or depicts conquest. To be placed in the Dart category, a projectile was required to be associated with an *atlatl*, whereas an Arrow would naturally be found with a bow. The Arrow/Dart category was created to house any projectile point not illustrated in either context, including conquest signifiers or dating and naming elements.

Arrows were confidently identified only once in the *Codex Zouche-Nuttall* (Nuttall 1975, 11), where a quiver with two arrows is carried in the same hand as a bow by Lord 7 Monkey, who lacks an *atlatl* or shield (figure 9.8). Potentially valuable detail is lacking in this image, as the arrows, unfortunately, are mostly obscured by the bow and quiver; however, the points are visible and are roughly half the size of the dart points carried by an *atlatl*-wielding Lord 8 Snake, shown just below and to the left of Lord 7 Monkey (depicted at the same scale). While acknowledging that Mixtec artistry is not renowned for naturalistic renderings, projectile points do appear at roughly the same scale throughout the *Codex Zouche-Nuttall*, with the exception of these probable arrow points. The Arrow heads themselves are triangular in shape and of the Red Tip with 1 Stripe subcategory created for this analysis. These identifiers were noted frequently among the Dart and Arrow/Dart categories; thus, they are not unique to arrows, although the shaft to which they attach certainly are. The artist chose to draw a separate brown segment of shaft tapering to the diameter of the base of the

FIGURE 9.7. *Serpent-adorned arrow/*atlatl *dart (redrawn from Nuttall 1975, 76a).*

FIGURE 9.8. *"Lord 7 Monkey" carrying a bow (redrawn from Nuttall 1975, 11).*

points. This segment is not the lower portion of the quiver—two separate shafts are discernable—and likely represents a different binding style.

The *Codex Bodley* is completely lacking in *atlatls*; therefore, it is not surprising that Maarten Jansen and Gabina Aurora Pérez Jiménez (2005) interpret all projectiles as arrows. Bows are depicted prominently in several panels, providing support for an arrow interpretation. The arrows of the *Codex Bodley* are distinctly different from those of the *Nuttall*. *Bodley* arrow shafts are depicted running well into the body of the point, whereas the single *Codex Zouche-Nuttall* arrow's shaft does not extend beyond the base of the point. The distinctive flared section of shaft noted in the latter codex is also absent in all *Codex Bodley* arrows.

The *Codex Selden* contains a single arrow that can be identified with confidence. While projectiles appear as components of place names in several locations, it is only on page 12 that a projectile is found in direct association with a bow. In this regard, the *Selden* and *Nuttall* codices are similar. On the other hand, the projectile point has more in common with *Codex Bodley* arrows, as the shaft once again extends beyond the base of the point proper and some distance into the body. The possibility exists that this reflects hafting techniques, though it may only be a stylistic difference.

The 140 weapons that occupy the Dart subcategory of projectiles yielded interesting patterns that could permit more specific identification of the ambiguous members of the Arrow/Dart group. As with all hafted weapons, shaft decorations were recorded as color codes, with short descriptions when necessary. Initial attempts to interpret these results were frustrated by the diversity of shaft styles and colors. The difficulty stemmed from the center portion of most darts being obscured by shields, quivers, and body parts. A pair of identical darts that would otherwise have been matched by color code became distinct varieties in the database if a single color was obscured or negated. A place name in the *Codex Zouche-Nuttall* (p. 82) finally provided the key to a pattern within the shaft color code. One element of that toponym is a single horizontal dart that is, importantly, large and detailed. This dart (figure 9.9) exhibits many of the same characteristics as the Style 2 Arrow/Darts that are discussed in more detail in the following section. These include a large black or brown central feather with two tan feathers on both sides and fringes below. Taken alone, these decorative elements cannot conclusively identify this projectile as an *atlatl* dart, as they could equally be interpreted as arrow fletching.

The most significant elements for potential Arrow/Dart identification are located on the shaft proper (figure 9.9). The brown-red section of shaft that attaches directly to the point is apparently bound to the yellow length that forms the largest shaft section. This yellow section likely illustrates the reed or cane that was used in light, flexible projectiles. The former, darker section represents the foreshaft of an *atlatl* dart, which is frequently constructed from hardwoods in modern replicas.

Archaeological evidence of these techniques in Pre-Columbian Mesoamerica comes from the Tehuacan Valley Survey. Two 1.5 cm-diameter *carrizo* cane fragments were found, which MacNeish and colleagues (1967, 160) identified as the main shafts of *atlatl* darts. Diagnostic evidence came in the form of "scars from interior rubbing," with gum and fibers found near the extremity in one piece (MacNeish, Nelken-Terner, and de Johnson 1967, 160). The interior rubbing and end cutting is consistent with the insertion of a foreshaft (noted in figure 9.9). The gum and fibers are most likely remnants of binding, also illustrated in the *Codex Zouche-Nuttall*, which served to keep the cane from splitting when

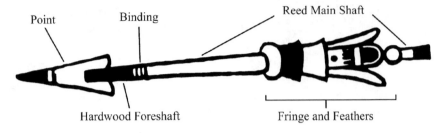

Point   Binding   Reed Main Shaft

Hardwood Foreshaft   Fringe and Feathers

FIGURE 9.9. *Atlatl dart details (redrawn from Nuttall 1975, 82).*

the hardwood foreshaft was inserted. MacNeish and colleagues (1967, 161) also identified four arrow shafts, also of cane, that were smaller in diameter than the *atlatl* shafts, ranging from 0.5–1.0 cm. The distal ends were not prepared to receive a foreshaft and were instead notched to receive a projectile point directly (MacNeish, Nelken-Terner, and de Johnson 1967, 161).

Based on the presence of this foreshaft with binding and its clear depiction in the *Codex Zouche-Nuttall*, it is possible to identify *atlatl* darts among the ambiguous Arrow/Dart category. The vast majority of projectiles in this group were representative of conquest and thus were missing their tips and frequently the diagnostic foreshaft as well. That said, 34 of the total (n =7 7) have color codes ending in Br (brown) or R (red), indicating that those examples are *atlatl* darts, and the remaining 33 could likely be safely identified as similar. As previously mentioned, two distinct styles of Arrow/Dart were observed: Style 1 having at least one "main feather" located centrally on the shaft and lacking fringes and Style 2 having at least one fringe in addition to the main feather and frequently two tan feathers transversely as well. Unfortunately, there was no observable correlation between styles and arrow or dart groups as was initially hoped. Both styles contain multiple clear examples of foreshafts and are therefore subcategories of "*atlatl* dart of unknown significance."

Addressing the projectile points of the *atlatl* darts became our next concern. As mentioned, many instances of the Arrow/Dart group have missing or obscured points and were therefore rendered unsuitable for the following analysis. Four projectile point types were identified attached to *atlatl* darts (table 9.2). Three of the categories are self-explanatory, though the Triangle/Circle type is somewhat unusual: the main body of the point is triangular, but a small curl or circle projects on one side near the base. It is possible that this is meant to represent a bone point, as Hassig (1988, 79) describes for the Aztec, or it may very well be artistic license. The next subdivision indicates point style and notes such elements as color, stripes, and spots when present. The most common point type and style in the *Codex Zouche-Nuttall* is the Triangular/Red Tip 1 Stripe variety, represented by 86 of the 140 identified darts (count by quiver, not projectile; table 9.2). The

TABLE 9.2. Dart point shapes and styles

Dart	140
ABSENT	8
(blank)	8
JAGGED TRIANGULAR	3
Red Tip	1
Red Tip 1 Spot	2
TRIANGLE / CIRCLE	3
Red Tip	1
Red Tip 1 Stripe	2
TRIANGULAR	126
Red Tip	1
White 1 Spot	1
Blank	1
Not visible	1
Red Tip	22
Red Tip 1 Spot	8
Red Tip 1 Stripe	86
Red Tip 1 Stripe 1 Spot	3
White	2
White, 1 Spot	1

red tips and stripes serve to indicate, as they do with flint knives, that the point is stone (see chapter by Bassie-Sweet, this volume, for other examples). It is possible that the different styles indicate different lithic materials; perhaps future work in the Mixteca will illuminate the matter.

Hassig (1988, 79) identifies a variety of dart point types among Aztec *atlatl* projectiles, each with a specific purpose. The point styles in the *Codex Zouche-Nuttall* that may indicate a specific projectile point type in the archaeological record are those that have "spots." Only 10 percent of darts recorded have these unique "spots" on the outside edge of the point, at roughly one third of the height. Those of the Dart category only occur with a single "spot," as points overlap in quivers, obscuring the opposite edge. Four darts of the Arrow/Dart category do indeed show "spots" on both sides of their points. It is possible that these are in fact side notches, and their location well away from the base of the point could indicate the type. While numerous comprehensive ceramic typologies exist, there is no complete lithic typology for the Mixteca Alta at the time of this writing. Instead, the Tehuacan Valley Survey was relied on to bridge this void (MacNeish, Nelken-Terner, and de Johnson 1967).

It is often difficult to reconcile codical depictions of projectiles with specific archaeologically recovered models. Among the catalog of projectile points compiled by the Tehuacan Valley Survey (MacNeish, Nelken-Terner, and de Johnson 1967), two types match the deep basal notches and roughly medial side notches observed in the *Codex Zouche-Nuttall*. The first is the Teotihuacan point, which was present throughout Mesoamerica beginning in the Classic period and peaked in popularity during the Postclassic period (MacNeish, Nelken-Terner, and de Johnson 1967, 75–76). The second candidate is the Texcoco point, known from the Postclassic Valley of Mexico, Puebla, and Oaxaca (MacNeish, Nelken-Terner, and de Johnson 1967, 76–77). The relative depth of the projectile point's notches as well as the overall dimensions differ between these types. Teotihuacan points often exhibit deep basal notches, which resonates with most depictions in the *Codex Zouche-Nuttall*, while Texcoco points do not exhibit this characteristic extreme. This may provide some weight to the explicit identification of depicted points as being of the "Teotihuacan type"; however, the Texcoco point is 1.4 cm longer and thus more likely to arm an *atlatl* dart over an arrow (MacNeish, Nelken-Terner, and de Johnson 1967, 75–77). Excavations at the Mixtec site of Tututepec uncovered projectile points with similarities to both types; however, the side notches are shallower and closer to the point than those from the Tehuacan Valley Survey (Levine 2007). Despite these issues, it does seem possible that, pending further excavations in the area and improved lithic documentation, archaeological and codical *atlatl* points may be reconciled.

Shields

Shields are ubiquitous throughout the *Codex Bodley* and *Codex Selden*. They are even more numerous in the *Codex Zouche-Nuttall*, second only to projectiles, with 141 instances recorded (26% of the total catalog, based on quivers counted as a single projectile; table 9.1). A staggering 53 distinct styles were recorded, with many appearing only once throughout the entire manuscript. Perhaps unexpected to those accustomed to Western military history, a shield is nearly always wielded even in combination with the projectile-launching *atlatl*. There are several possible explanations for this observation, the first being that the *atlatl* only requires a single hand to operate, freeing the other arm to carry a shield and a hand to grasp the darts. This specific scene is depicted with remarkable frequency throughout the *Codex Zouche-Nuttall*. Another explanation may relate to high variability in shield customization. Combined with costuming and body paint, a unique shield assists in identification of specific individuals in the codices and on the battlefield.

The most numerous single style appeared 15 times throughout the *Codex Zouche-Nuttall* and was typified by a yellow center crossed by curved white lines (much like a tennis ball) finished with a blue outline. The vast majority of shields were permutations of this theme, replacing the center or outline color and with or without the "tennis ball stripes." The most common center color is yellow and may actually depict the bare reed structure of the shield, as Aztec shields were commonly produced (Pohl and Robinson 2005). These *otlachimalli* would have had cotton padding on the reverse to provide protection from projectiles and impact (Hassig 1988, 86). Unlike the ceremonial *mahuizzoh chimalli*, the *Codex Zouche-Nuttall* artists depict functional and effective shields.

During the shield frequency and contextual analysis, it was noted that handedness was not important to the artists of this codex. That is, there was found to be a nearly perfect 50/50 distribution of the same weapon (of any type) held in the left hand versus the right hand of *Nuttall* individuals. In addition, careful examination of both hands of weapon-wielding individuals in the *Codex Zouche-Nuttall* demonstrated that based on the anatomical position of the hand, many have two left or two right hands! The same was found to be true of the feet. The significance of this pattern, if any, is unknown at this time.

THE UNORTHODOX

Blowgun

The *Codex Bodley* (p. 38) contains the only discernable example of a blowgun encountered during this study: Lord 2 Rain is shown with a cylindrical object to his lips, directed toward a bird in a tree (Jansen and Pérez Jiménez 2005, 93). The deteriorated state of the *Codex Bodley*, and indeed of this image, may lead one to believe that Lord 2 Rain is instead wielding a large spear, if close inspection did not reveal the sack of clay pellets in his left hand. From historical records and archaeological contexts, it is known that blowguns were often used to hunt small game in the Maya region, including birds (Ventura 2003). An ornate blowgun with a bag of clay pellets was also gifted to Hernán Cortés upon his arrival in Veracruz (Díaz del Castillo and Carrasco 2008, 201). While there is currently no evidence of blowguns being used in Mixtec warfare, the presence of other utilitarian implements on the battlefield, such as axes, indicates that their use is a possibility that should not be ignored.

Composite Bladed Mace

This interesting weapon is found in the *Codex Zouche-Nuttall* (p. 68) (figure 9.10) and is carried by Lord 8 Skull. Initial interpretation questioned whether it was a ceremonial object, as it is depicted accompanied by a "Venus Staff." Sometimes referred to as a quincunx, the Venus Staff is usually associated with fire drills and cult bundles that, when combined, indicate a founding ceremony, not warfare (Boone 2008, 99); however, it has been suggested that this item would have been borne into battle as the standard of Tilantongo, perhaps explaining its association with this unusual weapon (Pohl 1991, 47). Finding no similar weapons illustrated in the *Codex Selden* or the *Codex Bodley*, the unidentified weapon was compared with the *tepoztopilli* examples previously discussed (see figure 9.2). The dark-colored shaft likely indicates that it is constructed of hardwood, much like the *tepoztopilli*, while the triangular points portray a composite prismatic bladed edge as found on the latter. One would be tempted to call this a "Mixtec Sabre" were it not for the large blade mounted horizontally in the upper shaft. These all appear to be functional features, and as the weapon is entirely lacking in decoration, it is likely a utilized weapon and not ceremonial in nature.

One of the difficulties presented by the drawing style in the *Codex Zouche-Nuttall* is that three-dimensional objects are flattened, lacking any of the shading that denotes height to modern viewers. This is apparent with Lord 8 Skull's weapon, which may be round or flat in cross-section: a distinction that could illuminate the way it was used (figure 9.10). If it were known to have a round

FIGURE 9.10. *Unusual club/mace (redrawn from Nuttall 1975, 68).*

cross-section, it would likely be categorized as a mace or club. The lower end of the staff is rounded in profile and is akin to the lower extremities of the axe and war club depictions, which would presumably have a rounded cross-section.

Armor

An analysis of armor elements in the Mixtec codices was not undertaken. Individuals of the *Codex Zouche-Nuttall* appear to wear decorative costume in place of the less elaborate cotton *ichcahuipilli* (Hassig 1988, 88). As this is a depiction of elites, it is possible to speculate that these extremely elaborate costumes were worn into battle while commanding an army; however, it seems more likely that in combat a simplified version was adopted, or it was abandoned for traditional protection. It is also entirely possible that these individuals did not enter the fray at all but, like Aztec generals, managed the battle using signals from a safe location behind their lines (Pohl 1991, 10).

Fortifications

An understanding of the environment and settlement patterns of the Mixteca Alta is necessary to discussions of hilltop fortified sites in Mesoamerica. Building on the works of Alfonso Caso (1938), the Central Mixteca Alta Settlement Pattern Project aimed to achieve full coverage of the Nochixtlan, Teposcolula, and Tlaxiaco regions of Oaxaca (Balkansky et al. 2000, 368; Spores 1967). This region contains sites associated with many of the place names in the *Codex Zouche-Nuttall*;

therefore, knowledge of its settlement relates directly to the codical narratives (Byland and Pohl 1994). While this comprehensive work encompasses the Early Cruz through the Terminal Natividad (1500 BCE–1522 CE) periods in great detail, for the purposes of this analysis we draw only on data from the Late Flores through the Terminal Natividad (ca. 800–1522 CE) (explained below).

The Late Flores period (800–1100 CE) witnessed a decrease in population levels compared to the earlier Las Flores (ca. 200–500 CE). Up to six sizable and well-defended urban centers existed during this period in the Nochixtlan Valley. Defensible high-altitude sites abandoned during the previous period were often reoccupied, including Cerro Jazmín, which would grow to rival Monte Alban in size (Balkansky et al. 2000, 377). It has been argued that the considerable continuity over time and the fragmentation of Monte Alban demonstrate that cities were free from the influence of powers beyond the Mixteca Alta (Balkansky et al. 2000, 379). The following Natividad period is contemporary with the aforementioned accounts of Lord 8 Deer Jaguar Claw in the *Codex Zouche-Nuttall*. Settlements during this period were noted to be growing in population, with less new monumental construction occurring in Tilantongo (Balkansky et al. 2000, 382). Tilantongo likely did not require new monuments thanks to political continuity with the previous period, consistent with the codical 8 Deer account (Balkansky et al. 2000, 380). Both valleys and hilltops were occupied during the Natividad period, and the Nochixtlan Valley experienced the largest increase in population at this time. Increased centralization is visible, by both comparing the topographical site maps and noting the disparity in public architecture between primary and secondary polities (Balkansky et al. 2000). Incidentally, it is during the codexical period of the Natividad that monumental architectural styles are most diverse. The combination of increased centralization with diverse monumental style confirms the lack of external political influence in the Mixteca Alta at this time. Individual urban centers concentrated power over their respective valleys, attempting to increase wealth and influence through trade, marital alliance, and warfare, precisely as suggested by the narrative of the *Codex Zouche-Nuttall*.

Tepexi el Viejo is a Late Postclassic site located in the Mixteca of southern Puebla that was excavated by Shirley Gorenstein in the 1970s CE. Gorenstein (1973, 14) acknowledged that little archaeological research had been conducted on Mixtec monumental architecture at the time of her writing and that stonework appears largely in private collections. The fortifications at Tepexi el Viejo consist of two major components: the geography of the site combined with a system of walls. The three canyons, which leave only one side open to direct assault, dramatically improved the defensibility of the Tepexi hilltop (Gorenstein 1973, 20). The walls themselves can be divided into two distinct categories: a non-freestanding earth retaining wall and a freestanding double-faced wall. The former was constructed between the different levels of this site, as it is divided by height. Not surprisingly, the heights of these walls match the height difference between the current level and the next, ranging between 1.5 m and 10 m (Gorenstein 1973, 21). As with all walls at this site, those that retained earth were composed of irregular pieces of caliche nearly a meter in length, with successive layers added to create depth. Evidently, a type of adobe was mixed with potsherds to create a rough mortar between these successions of horizontal layers. Exterior defensive walls were constructed in the same fashion and ranged between 4 m and 15 m in height (Gorenstein 1973, 26).

More recently, Verenice Y. Heredia Espinoza (2007) published a volume titled *Cities on Hills: Classic Society in Mesoamerica's Mixteca Alta*. This extremely detailed survey of Las Flores-period hilltop sites in the Mixteca Alta will certainly prove valuable to future research on the subject at hand; unfortunately, these data lie outside the chronological window of the *Codex Zouche-Nuttall* and understandably focus on domestic production more than fortification.

A depiction of a hilltop fortress was uncovered in the Mapa de Texupa that was included with the Colonial-period description of the town (Bailey 1972, 454). Joyce W. Bailey (1972, 456) studied this document, noting that the steep hill adjacent to the town featured several defensive walls ringing the summit. Furthermore, small faces were depicted behind the uppermost walls, while arrows or darts ring this wall and point inward, confirming the defensive purpose of these constructions. An archaeological survey of the Tejupan area visited the hilltop fortress and documented the ruins of defensive walls as well as numerous projectile points (Byland 1980, 283).

Hilltop fortifications may serve as an explanation for the large number of projectile weapons in the *Codex Zouche-Nuttall* when compared to close combat weapons. When only offensive weapons are considered (ignoring shields and only considering projectile launchers and not projectiles themselves), bow- and *atlatl*-range weapons account for nearly 75 percent of the remaining total. Lacking records of the normal composition of a Mixtec army, we again turn to the Aztecs for comparison. With Aztec armies arrayed at a range of about 50 yards, projectiles from archers and *atlatls* as well as insults would fly forth toward the enemy, encouraging them to engage (Pohl 1991, 11). Once engaged, the *maquahuitl*- and *tepoztopilli*-bearing warriors would be maneuvered by their general in an attempt to outflank or encircle the enemy. A major goal of Aztec combat was the securing of prisoners, with close combat clearly affording more opportunities than ranged warfare (Pohl 1991, 12). Mixtec tactics, in contrast, developed out of centuries of battles among royal lineages, with the goal of deposing a rival and marrying his lineage to one's own (Pohl 1991, 36). As a result, the goal of a Mixtec warrior was to kill rather than maim and capture his opponent, a goal that can be accomplished from a distance (Pohl 1991, 38). From both the attacking and defending positions, a wall up to 10 m in height negates the effectiveness of even the 7-foot *tepoztopilli*. The most effective, and often the only, means to attack or defend these fortifications would have been with ranged weapons such as the sling, bow and arrow, and *atlatl*. The symbolism of the *atlatl* combined with its elite associations would make it the clear choice for Mixtec artists to depict in their codices populated with heroes and deities.

SUMMARY AND CONCLUSIONS

Studies of Aztec military methods and technology provide a valuable source of comparative data for exploring other Mesoamerican cultures (see further discussion in chapter by Koontz, this volume). By working from the known to the unknown, it is possible to glean information pertaining to Mixtec weapons and warfare from the *Codex Zouche-Nuttall*. Beginning with the preference for projectile weaponry to the conspicuous absence of the *macuahuitl*, some basic connections can be made between the hilltop fortifications of the Mixteca Alta and types of weaponry. The tools of war may also be seen as indicators of social status; for example, *atlatls* have been interpreted as symbols of status and power for many Mesoamerican civilizations since the Formative period (1800 BCE–200 CE) (Slater 2011, 374). Perhaps the most conclusive outcome is the confirmation that what have been variably called spears, arrows, and reeds are in fact *atlatl* darts.

As with any interpretation based on visual representations of the past, the sword of artistic license hangs over many of the assertions made throughout this study. This situation can only be remedied by archaeological survey and excavation, combined with continuing ethnohistorical studies. Future archaeological research could focus on lithic assemblages of the Mixteca, paying particular attention to projectile points. Further codical studies may apply the same numerical analysis and categories to other records, such as the *Lienzo de Tlaxcala* and the remaining Mesoamerican codices, to better understand how perceptions of warfare varied by culture and time.

10

Classic Veracruz Military Organization

REX KOONTZ

Scholars have long focused on the role of the Classic (ca. 250–900 CE) Meso-american ballgame in managing conflict throughout the Mexican Gulf Coast, especially at the large site of El Tajín (Aguero and Daneels 2009; Wilkerson 1991). Warfare and its relation to the ballgame play important roles in these arguments, and yet the organization and context of war is often ignored in favor of interpretations of the symbolism embodied in the game and its attendant rituals. Scholars have ably developed the analogy between the Mesoamerican game and warfare, often using Tajín (flourished ca. 350–1000 CE) and other Classic Veracruz evidence to bolster their claims; however, we still know little about how the game and war may have been articulated in the larger context of a regional Mesoamerican capital with significant martial activities. A key, yet little discussed, part of this articulation is the organization of military groups and their place in the polity.

Although little work has been done on the problem of Classic Veracruz military organization to date, it is safe to assume that the larger Classic Veracruz polities, implicated as they were in a highly competitive military environment,

DOI: 10.5876/9781607328872.c010

had the need for significant military organization. This chapter gathers the evidence, largely iconographic, for military organization at El Tajín and in related Classic Veracruz polities. Following in the theme of this volume, my view is largely emic, in that I am discussing iconographic statements on military organization and not the archaeological evidence on the ground. I argue that much of this iconographic evidence for military organization exists outside the traditional themes of the ballgame and its rituals, appearing instead in iconographic programs that until now have received less attention than the ballgame material. Especially important to the question of military organization is the iconography that defines the central pyramid as a central sacred mountain for the polity and how rites around that mountain may have been one way to perform the organization of the polity's military forces. Through comparisons with later central sacred mountain iconography and ritual, I argue that several key aspects of Postclassic (ca. 900–1521 CE) military organization have analogies in earlier Gulf Coast societies and that these structural continuities may be the result of a general Mesoamerican tendency to organize the military through martial cults with long-lived deity and ritual associations.

STUDYING PRE-COLUMBIAN MILITARY ORGANIZATION

Since the early 1990s we've seen an explosion of scholarship on the history of warfare in Mesoamerica (Hassig 1992; Sugiyama 2005; Webster 2000). Much of this literature is concerned with the history of military campaigns and shifting alliances. The emerging decipherment of Maya hieroglyphic documentation of military campaigns during the Classic period has given the study of warfare much new data and a new impetus (Brown and Stanton 2003; Martin and Grube 2008; Schele and Freidel 1990). This chapter is not a contribution to the history of military engagements in Mesoamerica. I am not concerned here with wars declared or battles fought. Instead, I examine the social organization of warriors as seen through the iconographic evidence found in Classic Veracruz centers. The focus is largely but not exclusively on El Tajín, the largest and most important Late Classic capital in Veracruz, Mexico.

There is little immediately relevant documentation on Gulf Coast military organization with which to anchor our task, nor is there extensive documentation of the specifics of indigenous military organization in the larger Mesoamerican archive. This makes the study of military organization in Pre-Columbian Mesoamerica a vexed issue from a number of vantage points. Much of the archival material that would speak to military organization comes to us from Spanish sources on Central Mexican Postclassic peoples (see Hassig 1988, 1992; see also chapter by Abtosway and McCafferty, this volume, for a study of Central Mexican Mixtec warfare through the use of Late Postclassic codices). In all of these documents, there is not a single unified and coherent description of Aztec military ranking and organization; instead, there is an abundance of scattered detail on military organization contained in descriptions of other subjects. That said, it may be helpful here to review some of the most important and well-studied Mesoamerican evidence for military organization before taking on the rich but little-studied evidence from Classic Veracruz.

The most striking example of possible archaeological evidence for military organization comes from the burials at the Temple of the Feathered Serpent at Teotihuacan. Dozens of sacrificial victims were laid into the foundation of this building, all dressed in Teotihuacan warrior garb and many wearing human trophies in the form of maxillae (Sugiyama 1989; Taube 1992b). Evidence from the dental enamel and bone of the sacrificial victims shows that they originated in several locations outside of Teotihuacan, but before their sacrifice many of these individuals had spent considerable time in the city (White, Price, and Longstaffe 2007; White et al. 2002). These data suggest that Teotihuacan could muster trained warrior groups with distinctive insignia (see chapter by Nielsen, this volume). As a counterargument to the identification of these figures as Teotihuacan warriors, it is possible but unlikely that the figures were chosen from foreign captives and were kept for many years to serve as this dedicatory sacrifice.

Returning to the Late Postclassic evidence, even the fascinating images of the *Codex Mendoza* (Berdan and Anawalt 1992, folio 65) that treat military rank and accomplishment are woefully incomplete, naming only those military ranks and achievements typical of the highest nobility. In other places in the same document, military costume indicative of rank is seen in the context of tribute arrangements. These costumes were not described with an eye toward documenting Pre-Columbian military organization but instead to map out tribute arrangements.

Another problem with Aztec sources on military organization is the quickening development of Aztec military organization in the period prior to the Conquest. Other Central Mexican polities did not organize their military in the same fashion as the Aztecs, suggesting some innovation in that area (unsurprising given the rapid rise of Aztec military might) (Hassig 1988, 27). Thus it is unclear whether the Aztec system, specifically the Mexica variant, may be allowed to stand as a typical Late Postclassic military organization, much less a typical Mesoamerican system; however, there are basic elements that may be seen across most, if not all, Mesoamerican military systems.

In what is the most synthetic statement on ancient Mesoamerican military organization to date, Ross Hassig (1992) categorizes all Mesoamerican military organization according to the amount of social mobility available to warriors. An aristocratic military organization, in which the warrior class was firmly tied to elite status, was viewed as the traditional model for Mesoamerica, and there was little or no room for non-elites in this system. Compared to later, more meritocratic military organization, the aristocratic type would have greatly limited the size of the army. Hassig views the Classic Maya military system as a good example of this, with the military forming a small noble force.

According to Hassig (1992), greater social mobility developed in more meritocratic military societies. The Late Postclassic Aztec system was arguably such a meritocratic military organization, where warriors could rise through the ranks as they performed successfully. The *Codex Mendoza* (folio 65) shows the types of costumes that were made available to the warrior after each capture, surely indicating the increasing rank as well as increased prestige. In this way, the meritocratic system could provide space for a large number of non-elite warriors who hoped to rise socially through their military performance. At the same time, this system could accommodate many more warriors than an elite-focused system. But how and when did such a meritocratic system develop in Mesoamerica? These are questions that have yet to be asked for the most part, let alone answered. In sum, Hassig's aristocratic and meritocratic categories allow us to focus on certain key aspects of military organization, but the historical depth of those categories in ancient Mesoamerica is subject to debate.

Other differences in warrior costumes found in Late Postclassic public art were probably more indicative of narrative strategies than of military organization. The Mexica warriors found on the well-known "Stone of Tizoc" wear Toltec military costume ornaments, including the butterfly pectoral, a headdress with upright feathers, and the triangular skirt apron, eschewing the contemporary Mexica battle gear (Umberger 1996, 100–101). They are juxtaposed with simply dressed figures sporting bows and arrows, both of which indicate Chichimec peoples and more generally refer to uncivilized peoples when compared to the civilized Toltec. The Mexica themselves could identify with one of these groups or the other, depending on the sort of narrative desired (Umberger 1987, 70). How these categories worked in the actual military organization of the Mexica or others is still an open question. What is probable is that we are not given a glimpse of Mexica military organization here but instead are dealing with combat framed as a battle of social identities and supernatural powers (the latter evident in the presence of an engaged Tezcatlipoca or his impersonator; similar ideas are echoed in the Maya contexts discussed in the chapters by Tokovinine, and Hernandez and Palka, this volume).

When we come to the Classic Maya, the glyphic and iconographic records are even more socially compressed. The overwhelming majority of glyphic warfare passages focus on the ruler's actions. Surviving mural programs from the Late Classic (ca. 600–850 CE; Bonampak, Mulchic) and the Terminal Classic or Early Postclassic (ca. 850–1050 CE; Chichen Itza) give the viewer a particular vantage on what may be battlefield practice, but much recent scholarship argues for the specific ritual context of many of these images (Coggins and Shane 1984; Ringle

2009). A ritual context has also been argued for the related battle imagery of Cacaxtla (Miller 1998, 192). While significant information can be gleaned from these images, they were clearly not meant to depict military organization and should be used with a firm grasp of the larger iconographic context, a goal beyond the confines of this chapter. What we can say with some confidence is that these murals and later documentary evidence highlight the importance of elite warriors in all aspects of warfare, at least as framed by the artists and scribes of the Classic period.

Drawing solely on the elite would have significantly limited military actors and their organizations. Other scholars have tried to develop more precise hypotheses on the military population of similar Mesoamerican polities. David Webster (2000, 99) estimates that the Classic Maya polity of Copan could have fielded between 500 and 600 men in the late eighth century CE. The populations of Copan and El Tajín were comparable at that point in time (see Webster 2001, 169; for Classic-period densities in the Tajín region, see Daneels 2012, 356), and both polities wielded considerable political and military power in their region; thus it is probable that Tajín had a military of similar size. How could such a fighting force be organized, and what sorts of iconographic and archaeological evidence might speak to that organization?

THE TAJÍN REALM AND THE PROBLEM OF ITS MILITARY ORGANIZATION

While scholars have been working on the iconography and archaeology of the military in the Maya and Central Mexican areas for some time, this has not been the case on the Gulf Coast. The city of El Tajín was unique among human settlements in the region during the period ca. 600–1000 CE. By the Late Classic period, a large part of the north-central Veracruz region shared an architectural style and a ceramic assemblage (figure 10.1). The center of this architectural and ceramic array was the site of El Tajín, which by this period had a population of perhaps 20,000 and a monumental central district of pyramids, ball courts, and range structures that dwarfed anything in the region. Both the physical extent of the realm and public iconography in the capital suggest that the Tajín polity developed a significant military organization as it rose to regional power. Several scholars, including Michael Kampen (1972), Sara Ladrón de Guevara (2005), and I (Koontz 2009), have identified rites directly related to warfare in the public iconography of El Tajín, but until recently none of us have gone further and investigated possible military organization of the polity.

There is good reason for the lack of investigation of our theme in Classic Veracruz studies in general and studies of El Tajín in particular. We have seen how difficult the study of military organization has been even when we have documentary sources. For our initial approach to the Tajín materials, we are limited

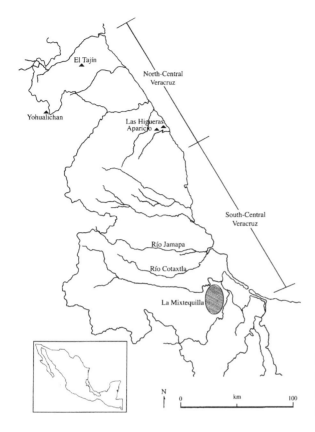

FIGURE 10.1. *Map of Classic Veracruz area with the Tajín-dominated region*

to the iconographic and archaeological. What material evidence can we marshal for military organization in the region? We have no archaeological data at Tajín comparable to Kenneth Hirth's (1995) at the contemporary site of Xochicalco, where he proposed defensible city wards, each the responsibility of a military unit. We also have little elite architecture that we can as yet firmly define as military in the sense of a warrior house or an armory. Neither do we have military status or office identified glyphically. Glyphic evidence at El Tajín is limited mainly to name tagging, as it is in the great majority of Late Classic Veracruz visual culture (Koontz 2009). The imagery does provide us with several examples of warfare accouterments and costumes, allowing us to place these activities in relation to the panoply of rites described in the public sculpture at the site.

The contemporary examples of military organization at Xochicalco and among the Maya (alluded to above) strongly suggest that there were complex military organizations at Tajín's peer polities. These cases also make clear that there is much we do not know about military organization during the period. In the case of Tajín, what we do have, which I have argued previously and will

FIGURE 10.2. *El Tajín, South Ballcourt, Southeast Panel, with supernatural donation of arms. Late to Terminal Classic period.*

expand upon here, is iconographic and archaeological evidence of military banners and their manipulation in central rites in the heart of the city (Koontz 2009, 20–35). The banners and their associated rites may provide some insight into the military organization employed by the Tajín polity during its time as a regional power.

SUPERNATURAL DONATION OF WEAPONRY

While many authors have pointed out the symbolism associated with warfare in the Classic Veracruz ballgame and its attendant rituals, there are few examples of iconography that can be firmly tied to actual warfare practices (as opposed to warfare-related rites, of which there are many). Like the contemporary Maya, the Classic Veracruz peoples were not interested in depicting actual battle scenes (Miller and Martin 2004, 164). They focused instead on the return of a success-ful military expedition with its attendant sacrificial rites. The most often cited example that may fit this category is ball court decapitation sacrifice, assumed to have been carried out on a captured enemy warrior following a successful battle.

Much Tajín ball court iconography has to do with this decapitation sacrifice and related rites that were part of the ballgame sequence throughout Classic Veracruz. However, a panel from El Tajín's main ball court depicts a rite that seems directly related to martial matters (figure 10.2). On the left is a supernatu-ral emerging from a zoomorphic maw while holding three long spears. He offers these spears to the human in the center of the composition. I have argued that this is a variation on the Classic-period iconographic theme of the supernatural

FIGURE 10.3. *Figure processing with red banner, Las Higueras, Veracruz, Late Classic period.*

donation of weaponry (Koontz 2009, 47–49). Like the Teotihuacan warrior head-dress (Sugiyama 1989; Taube 1992b) and the Maya flint/shield motif (Schele and Miller 1986), this scene grounds the polity's weaponry in the sacred (see chapters by Bassie-Sweet and Nielsen, this volume); therefore, the ballgame and ball court ritual at Tajín did have some articulation with military organization beyond the often cited use as a metaphor for war or arena for conflict management.

BANNERS

While the supernatural donation of arms is a widely depicted theme in Meso-america by the Classic period, El Tajín and related Classic Veracruz sites exhibit other military iconography that is not so widespread. Central is the war banner or standard. In this mural fragment (figure 10.3) from the important Late Classic program at nearby Las Higueras, we see a figure processing to the right with a trailing red-and-white device. Several other Higueras figures hold very similar rectangular banners on large poles, with only the color varying from device to device. The banner manipulated by the Higueras figure is comparable to the rectangular banner worn by later Mexica warriors (such as in *Codex Mendoza*, folio 67r), suggesting that the earlier Higueras examples could also be military devices (Koontz 2009, 28).

Given the prime iconographic position of the Higueras banners and what I will argue are equally important placements for Tajín banners, it is pertinent to establish the relationship between ancient Mesoamerican war banners and this chapter's larger theme of military organization. Banners would not be an unusual way to indicate military organization in Mesoamerica. Many ethnohistoric reports from the Gulf Coast region and across much of the rest of Mesoamerica document the entangled use of banners in the organization of military units on the eve of the Spanish Conquest (Hassig 1988, 57; see also chapter by Nielsen, this volume). It is clear from these early accounts that banners were a chief method of forging battle group identity and signaling movement or other strategy. Much of the rest of this chapter will turn to the examination of banners in Tajín archaeology and art and what they may be able to tell us about military organization in the capital.

Identifying Banner Use at El Tajín

The evidence for banner manipulation rites is found mainly in Tajín's Central Plaza, specifically at the base of the Pyramid of the Niches and at the summit of the adjoining Mound 4. I have argued this at length elsewhere (Koontz 2009, 15–30) and will synthesize here. The iconographic argument focuses on Mound 4, shown in the upper (northern) part of the figure 10.4 map (figure 10.4.) The Mound 4 we see today was designed during the apogee of Tajín as a fairly typical pyramidal base, and it was certainly in place at the same time as the other important elements found in the Central Plaza, including the Pyramid of the Niches. Surmounting the rather plain base of Mound 4 was an elaborately decorated temple. When this temple was deliberately demolished near the end of Tajín's florescence, the major interior sculpture was broken in half and thrown down the north side of the structure, where it was buried with debris, to be discovered in the early 1970s CE by José García Payón (1973).

Known as the Mound 4 Panel, this major sculptural element was easily pieced together soon after its discovery (figure 10.5). It is carved on four sides: the upper side along with three of the four short sides. The location of the carving suggests that the piece was meant to stand against a wall, with the carved short sides facing out and the main carved surface facing up (Koontz 2009, 20; Ladrón de Guevara 2006). A similar orientation is illustrated at the bottom center of the panel, where a flat panel is supported with two legs. I argue that this is an illustration of how the panel was used.

The general structure of the Mound 4 Panel composition is highly symmetrical. A large feathered device defines the central axis of the panel (discussed below). On either side of the central device are two figures. Both outside figures carry a decorated bag associated with ritual activity throughout Mesoamerica, while the interior figures manipulate cloth objects and a fire bundle. All of these objects and activities suggest a ritual environment. The fire bundle on the right central figure and the decorated bag on the outside figures are found throughout Tajín iconography and may be mapped in more precise terms. For the moment, what is important is simply establishing a ritual environment for the scene.

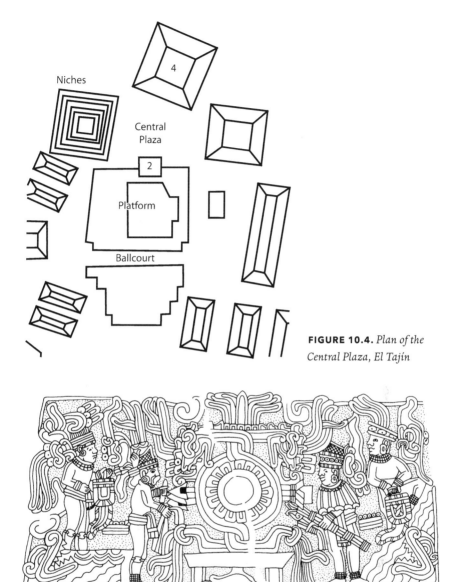

FIGURE 10.4. *Plan of the Central Plaza, El Tajín*

FIGURE 10.5. *Mound 4 panel, main carved face, Late Classic period*

The focal point of the rite is the central pole that springs from the turtle's back in the lower center, moves through the bench, and emerges as a petaled disk surrounded by intertwined serpents. I have argued at length (Koontz 2009, 88–95) that closely related variants of this pole configuration are found throughout Tajín

FIGURE 10.6. *The Central Plaza and Pyramid of the Niches seen from the summit of Mound 4 with an inset of the Mound 4 panel on the right, El Tajín, Late Classic period*

imagery as important war banners, including figures who manipulate simplified but clearly related versions of the disk and intertwined serpent banners. These two banners, manipulated by Tajín figures in other public programs, seem to function as stripped-down versions of the two central elements in the Mound 4 Panel.

In addition to serving as the most important iconographic statement on banner iconography, there is little doubt that the Mound 4 Panel itself was used as a base for such a banner. The central petaled area was drilled through the rock, creating a very regular cylinder 17 cm in diameter. Recall that the panel was probably placed this side up, in a configuration similar to the panel shown in the lower central portion of the iconography. Just as the pole depicted on the face of the Mound 4 Panel passes through the illustrated panel to emerge supporting the petaled disk, so, too, would a banner pole pass through the Mound 4 Panel itself.

With an idea of how the Mound 4 Panel functioned, let us now return to the Central Plaza. Recall that the panel was placed in the temple structure at the summit of Mound 4 where this image was taken (figure 10.6). The locus of the banner rite in the temple superstructure would have been small and restricted, especially when compared with what I will argue were the teeming masses below on the plaza. In fact, not only would the ritual participants at the summit be separated from these masses, their position would yield a vista that surveyed the crowd.

The summit of Mound 4 was not the only place in the area in which banner rites were held. Directly in front of the Pyramid of the Niches is a series of

FIGURE 10.7. *Prismatic blocks (3 of 15) in front of the Pyramid of the Niches, El Tajín, Late Postclassic period*

prismatic blocks (figure 10.7). Each block contains a single hole drilled into the center of its upper face. These holes are directly comparable in size to the one found in the center of the Mound 4 Panel, and it is very likely that they served the same purpose: banner bases. Further, one might assume that the banner rites at the foot of the Pyramid of the Niches and the summit of Mound 4 were part of an integrated ritual spectacle, just as the later Mexica used banners on the plaza and at the summit of their central temple in the Panquetzalitzli banner rites documented in greatest detail in Sahagún (1981, 141–150).

The Mound 4 Panel, with its elaborate depiction of what I have identified as a banner rite, would have surveyed any plaza banner rite from the summit (figure 10.6); however, the other banner rites were experienced from the plaza floor. I turn now to ritual participants/audiences at the plaza level and how their experience of the banner rite would have compared to that described for those few on the summit of Mound 4.

Banner Rites and Military Organization

If one accepts the iconographic identifications above, then the center of Tajín hosted significant banner rites both on the summit of Mound 4 and in the Central Plaza. Banners were traditionally associated with the most important units of military organization in Mesoamerica, at least during the Postclassic period (Hassig 1988, 57). This clears the way for us to relate banner rites and military organization; however, beyond this straightforward relation, the move from such an insight to more interpretative readings of the Tajín banner rites is not clear. In an attempt to pry greater meaning from banner rites and their performance in particular spaces, we turn to several associated facts about the performance of Mesoamerican rites in general and of banner rites in particular.

We have strong reason to believe from several ethnohistoric reports, as well as some Pre-Columbian inscriptions and images, that only priests, other elites, and those necessary to the rites were allowed onto the summits of the raised architecture during public performances. Where did the "regular" people experience the pageantry? Fray Diego Durán's (1971, 88) informants describe the gathering of a huge popular crowd at the foot of the main pyramid during the later Mexica banner rites. This later ethnohistorical evidence, coupled with the logic of the physical layout at Tajín, strongly suggests that there was a large Central Plaza crowd in attendance during the banner rites.

While both the Mound 4 participants and those in the Central Plaza may have been witness to the same events, in almost every respect the experience of the banner rites for those in the Central Plaza would have been significantly different from that of the participants high on the summit of Mound 4. The banner bases at the foot of the pyramid would have served to orient the viewers, but instead of a small crowd and one elaborately carved jewel-like base, there are over a dozen monumental plain prismatic bases and several thousand participants that could have reasonably attended in the Central Plaza. It is possible that these banner rites used the rectangular banner, so popular in Classic Veracruz iconography, in the processions from Las Higueras identified above (see figure 10.3).

The imageless banner bases and extended space of the Central Plaza (see figure 10.7), the locus of one experience of the banner rite, must be seen in relation to the experience of those on the summit, with the elaborately carved single-banner base in the closed, restricted, and raised space of the Mound 4 superstructure (see figure 10.6). Not only is the ritual context very different, but the Mound 4 Panel banner type is also very different from the rectangular banner type seen in Higueras and elsewhere. The elite banner depends on arrays of feathers decorating intertwined serpents, or feathered serpents. Further, the Mound 4 base is carved in the finest Classic Veracruz scroll style, while the banner bases in the plaza received no carved decorative treatment. Access to Classic Veracruz style was a mark of the elite throughout the region, seen in a closely related set of scroll styles employed in burials with carved yokes and other ballgame paraphernalia, as well as in finely wrought ceramics and decoration on palace structures. It is this style that is foregrounded in the restricted banner rite at the summit of Mound 4.

Other, perhaps more obvious markers of elite-ness at the summit of Mound 4 are the small restricted nature of the space and the raised position of the participants in relation to those on the plaza floor. Most important for us, the elite group is able to gaze upon the proceedings below. As Stephen Houston and Karl Taube (2000, 287–290) point out in their important treatise on the archaeology of the senses in ancient Mesoamerica, sight was agentive in ways the other senses were not. When Late Classic Maya rulers looked down on ritual acts, they were participating in and even legitimating those acts in a real, active sense. Maya writing records the active gaze of these rulers with the specific *yichnal* expression, while the accompanying imagery positions the field of vision as emanating from above; thus when a ruler's active vision (and other active senses) encompassed a set of ritual acts and personages, the ruler could be seen as legitimating those persons and acts through the active sensing of the event. If we may borrow this analogy from the Late Classic Maya, then the contemporary Tajín elite stationed on the small platform at the summit of Mound 4 would have been in just such a position to "see" the rites in the Central Plaza in the same active, legitimating sense.

In contrast, what is given to the vista of the plaza participants is the combination of niche and flying cornice in the Pyramid of the Niches. Interestingly, the niche and flying cornice architectural style is not contiguous with the Classic Veracruz scroll style: the former was restricted to Tajín and its hinterland, while the latter indicates a much wider elite interaction sphere in which Tajín nobles participated and eventually developed their own variant. In this way, the Pyramid of the Niches, with its ultra-distinctive niche and flying cornice architecture, functioned as a sort of polity emblem, as George Kubler (1973) suggested long ago. The Classic Veracruz scroll style, in contrast, referenced a related but distinct interaction sphere that marked elites throughout the region. The banner rites may therefore be evidence of two distinct levels of ritual experience: a popular one with more than a dozen banners raised at the foot of the pyramid and a private and elite rite occurring directly above at the Mound 4 Panel inside the temple atop the pyramid.

DISCUSSION

While the evidence above can in no way give us a nuanced account of military organization at El Tajín or in Late Classic Veracruz, a reading of banner performances does open a dialogue with several interpretative possibilities. The identification of a two-tiered banner rite suggests that the military had more than one level of organization: a regional elite stratum (centered on the Mound 4 rite) somehow intercalated with a secondary tier of additional nobility (whose banners were raised in front of the Pyramid of the Niches). This is purely speculative at this juncture, although there are other programs at the site (Mound of the Building Columns) that show an entire array of different identities and ranks participating in what are clearly warfare-related rituals, including banner rituals (Koontz 2009, 69–104). The murals of Las Higueras, mentioned earlier in terms of their detailed depiction of banner rites, also illustrate a wide array of identities in relation to warfare-related ritual.

Continuing on a more speculative path, the military organization I have outlined here for apogee-period Tajín meshes well with some recent ideas on the organization of the Tajín polity. Annick Daneels (2012, 356) has suggested that the settlement patterns in and around El Tajín point to that site as the head of a segmentary state. Regardless of whether the organization was purely segmentary, Daneels rightly places emphasis on understanding the several important sites located near Tajín that contain in miniature all the elements necessary for a polity in the region, including monumental pyramids linked to ball courts. How were these smaller but critical units integrated into the center? One part of the response could be the military organization outlined here, with the secondary elite governing the next level of settlement with their own pyramids and ball courts but brought to the center through the elite military rites at the summit of Mound 4 that are described above. In addition, we know that these regional elite also had access to the finest portable sculpture (Wilkerson 1970), which could possibly have been used as another strategy of incorporation. Overall, it is difficult to imagine how one could prove such organizational patterns from the current archaeological data, but the iconographic data explored here would encourage us to begin to gather pertinent data in the future.

Just how these iconographic programs at El Tajín, Las Higueras, and elsewhere can be correlated in terms of dress, device, and other markers of rank and office has yet to be studied on a regional level, although several recent works deal with individual sites in a holistic fashion (Koontz 2009; Ladrón de Guevara 2005; Morante López 2005). Such an analysis would be a valuable next step in any further discussion of the iconographic and archaeological evidence for military organization. This chapter has focused on the analysis of banner rites and military organization in the Tajín region during the Late Classic period, proposing that there was a two-tiered military organization, at least in terms of the way that organization was performed in well-attested Mesoamerican banner rites.

SUMMARY AND CONCLUSIONS

To conclude, I suggest that there is a historical dimension to this complex and to the military organization to which it likely refers. The stela shown here (figure 10.8) may be an Early Classic example of the banner complex in the region. The frontal presentation and lack of narrative is unlike the later iconography of militarism seen on the Mound 4 Panel (see figure 10.5) and elsewhere, but in each case there are similar key military symbols and items, especially the banner.

FIGURE 10.8. *Early Classic (Cacahuatal phase, 350–600 CE) stela from Classic Veracruz*

The figure holds a banner in his right hand, and the petaled disk in the center is very much like the petaled disk banner found in the center of the later Mound 4 Panel and elsewhere at the site. Here, a single individual manipulates the banner without relation to other roles. This iconic presentation, a frontally facing figure relating only to the viewer and not to other figures in a narrative, suggests that these earlier banner images stressed the power of a paramount ruler and not the interconnected court of the later narrative images. The mosaic serpent heads with upturned snouts on the headdress strongly suggest close ties with Teotihuacan, or at least with the warfare cult based on such headdresses found at the latter site. Although little more can be said from the sparse Early Classic remains now known from the region, it is probable that the Late Classic banner rites discussed here grew out of this earlier matrix that focused on the paramount who controlled these banners and who had some connection with Teotihuacan or a related site.

PART III

Discussion

11

Organized Violence in Ancient Mesoamerica

TRAVIS W. STANTON

Scholars of ancient societies around the world continue to debate the term *warfare*, and little consensus has been reached since anthropology began to question its meaning more seriously during the 1960s CE (e.g., Fried, Harris, and Murphy 1968; Otterbein 1968). While there is a high level of agreement that warfare is a form of organized violence,[1] some researchers put more emphasis on different factors, including scale (Fry 2007, 13–17; Reyna 1994) and degree of premeditation (Kelly 2000, 3–5; Monks and Osgood 2000), often leaving scholars to talk to each other in vague terms as if the meaning of warfare was common sense. Further complicating our comprehension of "warfare" as a variable human behavior, it is clear that the differences in its meaning and importance among the different fields of archaeology, as well as individual researchers, have greatly impacted the questions we ask; for example, a perusal of the literature on ancient warfare still shows the heavy influence of military history in some parts of the world with its focus on arms and battlefield tactics (e.g., Gnirs 1999; Yates 1999). Granted, the historicities of strategy and combat are important topics. The fact that Hannibal defeated the much larger Roman Army on the fields of Cannae in 216 BCE by

DOI: 10.5876/9781607328872.c011

drawing the troops into a restricted area that neutralized their great numbers matters (Cottrell 1992). Yet the repeated focus on these types of studies leaves a feeling that large-scale organized violence only impacted the combatants and the political trajectories of their leaders. This line of research tends to ignore the messy, disorganized, and widespread impacts of "organized violence." Who were the other affected parties (e.g., local refugees, Roman and Gaul suppliers of the combatants, families of kidnapped child soldiers, taxpayers), and how did they cope with both the short- and long-term repercussions of the violent event? How were certain Mediterranean societies organized to form conquest empires during the first millennium BCE? Did large-scale sanctioned violence have an effect on other types of violence, including gladiatorial combat and domestic abuse? As several researchers have noted (Carman 1997; Knüsel and Smith 2014a; Valckx Gutiérrez, Stanton, and Ardren 2011), these are the types of questions whose answers will provide a more profound view of organized violence in the past.

There is a growing literature of conflict research that is more focused on the social complexities of violence. For example, work on the experience of violence has become more common in the archaeological literature (Carman 1997; Knüsel and Smith 2014a). Gender studies focused on warfare have also become more prominent in the literature in several world areas (Davis-Kimball and Behan 2002; De Pauw 1998; Goldstein 2001; Hanks 2008; Knüsel and Smith 2014a; Tung 2012, 2014; Valckx Gutiérrez, Stanton, and Ardren 2011; Western and Hurst 2014). Yet where does Mesoamerica fit in terms of the research currently being conducted? What are the questions we have been asking, and what are those we should be asking?

In some ways, this volume is a reflection of trends in the study of Mesoamerican warfare (see also Hassig 1988, 1992; Stanton and Brown 2003). Many of the usual suspects are present, such as the Maya (Bassie-Sweet; Bey and Gallareta Negrón; Christenson; Haines and Sagebiel; Hernandez and Palka; Tokovinine), with the heavy emphasis on Classic-period (ca. 300–1000 CE) hieroglyphs and iconography (Bassie-Sweet; Haines and Sagebiel; Tokovinine), the martial nature of a possible Teotihuacan conquest state (Nielsen), the Epiclassic (ca. 550–900 CE) (Koontz), and Postclassic (ca. 900-contact CE) Oaxaca (Abtosway and McCafferty). Ritual (Hernandez and Palka; Nielsen), iconography (Abtosway and McCafferty; Bassie-Sweet; Koontz; Nielsen), and settlement patterns (Bey and Gallareta Negrón; Haines and Sagebiel) take prominent roles in one or several chapters. Yet some of the themes we often see, such as the Mexica (e.g., Hassig 1988) or the economic repercussions of warfare (e.g., Chase and Chase 1996), are notably muted in favor of themes we do not often see in Mesoamerica, such as analyses of place and conflict (Hernandez and Palka; Tokovinine), non-Postclassic northwest Mexico (Nielsen), and a study of arms (Abtosway and McCafferty) that has been fairly elusive in Mesoamerica since the work of Hassig (1988; see also

Aoyama 2005; Sheets 2003; Slater 2011) despite its prominence in other parts of the world. For the rest of this brief chapter I will explore several avenues of research into organized violence and how they have been, or could be, applied to Mesoamerican data.

ORIGINS OF CONFLICT AND VIOLENCE

Though not a central theme in this volume, one of the primary questions that has called the attention of anthropologists and archaeologists working across the globe regarding warfare and violence concerns their origins (e.g., Estabrook and Frayer 2014; Guilaine and Zammit 2001; Kelly 2000; Livingstone-Smith 2007; Otterbein 2004; "operational approaches" in Peuramaki-Brown, Morton, and Kettunen, this volume). Some hold that violence is genetically programmed and that the human propensity to wage war is somehow related to our evolutionary past (e.g., Livingstone-Smith 2007; Wrangham 1999; Wrangham and Peterson 1996), shared with some modern species of primates such as chimpanzees (see de Waal 1989; but see also Mitani, Watts, and Amsler 2010). Yet trying to demonstrate such arguments using archaeological data has been nearly impossible, given in part the extremely low frequency of early finds that could be interpreted (arguably in many cases) as evidence for human-against-human violence (e.g., Thorpe 2003). While precious little archaeological research has been attempted on violence in early archaeological contexts in the Americas, many of the same hurdles facing archaeologists in the Old World are present: few data in general and the equifinality in explaining them. Despite the fact that anthropologists agree that violence occurs, or occurred, in all modern and recent societies (the Inuit being one of the last cultures thought not to express organized violence as a behavior over the last couple of centuries [Burch 1974; see also Keeley 1996; Thorpe 2005]), trying to understand its "emergence" in the archaeological record has been a hotly debated subject (Knüsel and Smith 2014b).

There has been surprisingly little archaeological research on early violence in Mesoamerica. MacNeish (1964) reported on the remains of two children, one cremated and the other whose head had been severed, roasted, and the brains removed, that have been considered to be evidence of possible human sacrifice from the El Riego phase of the Archaic (ca. 8650–5700 BCE) in Tehuacan. Claims of Early (ca. 1200–1000 BCE; Coe and Diehl 1980) and Middle Formative (ca. 1000–400 BCE; Pijoan Aguadé and Mansilla Lory 1997; Pijoan Aguadé and Pastrana 1989) cannibalism have also been taken as possible evidence of early violence (LeBlanc 2003), although these data could just as well relate to mortuary practices. Yet compelling evidence for human sacrifice at El Manati does suggest an early origin for later sacrificial behavior (Ortíz Ceballos and Carmen Rodríguez 1999). Evidence for desecratory termination rituals (Brown and Garber 2003), possible martial iconography (Angulo Villaseñor 1987; Marcus and

Flannery 1996; Reilly and Garber 2003), and settlement patterns (see chapter by Bey and Gallareta Negrón, this volume; Marcus and Flannery 1996) from the Middle Formative has also been marshaled to indicate that organized violence and not just human sacrifice was present at this early time; however, I do not think we should be surprised that organized violence was present by this time, if not much earlier, even if the data concerning this behavior are sparse.

To think there was no level of organized violence, even by the Initial Formative (ca. 1700–1200 BCE), would lead us down the path toward a problematic search for that one peaceful society of the ancient world. The question here is really: what was the nature, or more likely diverse natures, of early organized violence throughout Mesoamerica during the early periods? Further, how did they set the tone for expressions of organized violence during later periods when data on the subject are more prevalent? Put in other terms, how and why did the widespread adoption of human torture, sacrifice, and raiding for captives come about? While such practices can be documented in myriad societies throughout the world (e.g., Verano 2014), the way Mesoamerican peoples generally practiced and presented them in text and image was unique, and we know very little about the reasons why these particularities emerged from early Mesoamerican societies. Bey and Gallareta Negrón (this volume) make a strong case for early conflict in the Puuc region that showcases the importance of understanding later conflict in the context of a deep cultural sequence. Furthering this type of research will be critical for understanding the later cultural constructions of violence and warfare in Mesoamerica that are much more common in the literature, as well as the relationship between violence and emerging rulership in a period—to take a quote from Cobb and Giles (2009, 105) out of its original Mississippian context, "when individuals were able to leverage cosmology and ritual to usurp the fetters of kinship and community." The performance of violence by emerging Formative elites may have been one of the many essential tools used to accrue power in a diverse and competitive social landscape.

RITUAL, RELIGION, AND WARFARE

Endless research has been written up on the relationship between ritual/religion and warfare/sacrifice in ancient Mesoamerica (e.g., Boone 1984; Conrad and Demarest 1984; Hassig 1988, 1992), often giving the impression in the popular media that Mesoamerican peoples were obsessed with ripping out peoples' hearts (see Ardren 2009). While there is no doubt that warfare and sacrifice were, in many and complex ways, interrelated to religious and ritual behavior among Mesoamerican peoples, there is still a tremendous amount of work to be done on the subject.

We can start by dividing our conceptualizations of the links between ritual/religion and warfare/sacrifice into several lines of interpretation. First, there are many rituals portrayed in iconography, mentioned in text, or materialized in archaeological contexts that concern organized violence; the Late Classic iconography found among the river kingdoms of the western Maya lowlands typifies such patterning (e.g., Miller 1986; Tate 1992). Koontz's (this volume) discussion of banner rituals at El Tajín is also an excellent example. Deftly discussing the importance of these rituals as an organizing principle of this site's military force (both as creating separate identities for sodalities and as signaling systems for tactical movements on the battlefield, much like use in other societies), Koontz explores how the study of warfare-related rituals can go beyond an understanding of the performance of "violence theater"[2] but can hold clues to how violence was organized and conducted, themes not often explicitly demonstrated in Mesoamerican iconography. In fact, I would argue that ritual behavior has just begun to be understood in terms of what it can inform us concerning violence and warfare; for example, the placement of the banners in such a prominent area of the site bespeaks the importance of these activities in the larger sociopolitical arena at El Tajín. Such public rituals would have had an enormous impact concerning peoples' interpretation of the built landscape.[3] Given the general Mesoamerican trend, at least during the Classic and Postclassic, of emphasizing warfare-related rituals in iconography, the use of war banners and the performance and glorification of violence theater in such prominent areas of sites like El Tajín could be used as a starting point for exploring cultural ideals concerning warfare and violence. Further, it could be used to explore the agency of non-combatants who in one way or another were active participants in the negotiation of violence in diverse Mesoamerican societies. This is an exciting line of research that should give a better understanding of the social context within which organized violence occurred.

Second, it is apparent that what we term as warfare was not just an earthly affair for ancient Mesoamerican peoples. The outcomes of at least some violent events were determined by otherworldly figures who were not just "on the side" of the victors but who engaged in battle among themselves. Reilly and Garber (2003) discuss the possibility that such conceptions go back at least to the Middle Formative among the Gulf Coast Olmec and can be seen in the form of *nagual* figures. Yet it is not really until the Classic period that patron deities related to warfare become easier to spot in the iconographic and epigraphic records, specifically in the Maya region. Bassie-Sweet (this volume) makes a good argument that Tlaloc was adopted by the Classic Maya as a version of Chahk and a patron god of war. Given the importance of the Teotihuacan war complex outside the Basin of Mexico (e.g., see chapter by Nielsen, this volume; Schele and Freidel 1990), this appropriation by some Maya is not surprising. Yet what were the factors that led certain individuals or groups to adopt particular patron gods of war over others? As Christenson (this volume) notes in his description of the Tz'utujil adoption of Santiago as their patron god following their defeat by the Spanish, emulation could certainly be a factor. Yet there must have been a host of other reasons these deities were chosen. Further, what would happen if two of the same deities fought each other? While the answer to the first question remains elusive, Tokovinine (this volume) mentions that there were "local" Maize Gods and that the Maize God from one site could defeat his counterpart from another. This was not a simple question of whose side the deity was on but was rather a result of the fact that each deity was an individual. This is clearly apparent in any analysis of modern and historical Virgin and Christ figures in Mesoamerica; while embodying the same concepts, they can visit and socially interact with one another as separate entities. I suggest that in the past they could also have fought against each other as different otherworldly individuals representing the same idea.

Interestingly, the fact that the Lake Petén Itzá Maya shot arrows at an oracular image used to petition success in battle against the Spanish after the fighting went poorly for them (Hernandez and Palka, this volume) suggests that humans could also inflict harm on these deities. In fact, research into termination rituals indicates that deities were not immune to human violence directed at them (see chapter by Hernandez and Palka, this volume; Pagliaro, Garber, and Stanton 2003; Stanton, Brown, and Pagliaro 2008). As Tokovinine (this volume) describes, the three patron deities of Palenque were thrown down and, in his terms, desecrated after a violent event at the end of the sixth century CE. This ritual destruction was likely cleaned up and the deities and sacred spaces healed, but this recorded event touches on a point emphasized by Hernandez and Palka (this volume) that sacred objects and spaces were profaned not just as an affront to the losers but because they were thought to be powerful weapons of war—a point I will discuss in more detail below.

A third idea we can explore concerning the relationship between ritual/ religion and warfare / sacrifice is that some religious beliefs may have been structured to promote a culture of violence and warfare; for instance, although we can criticize the idea that Classic Maya warfare was only an elite affair aimed at capturing warriors for sacrifices, the fact remains that many, if not all, Classic-period political-religious systems in Mesoamerica required human sacrifice through capture, structurally incorporating a need for sustained violence (see Freidel 1986; see chapter by Koontz, this volume). Further, the Mexica claim that the sun (and a number of other deities) required human sacrifice was not a new concept during the Postclassic—although the scale at which the Mexica practiced the sacrifice of captured warriors appears to have been taken to new levels—and as Conrad and Demarest (1984) argue, it provided an ideology for conquest warfare (see Headrick 2003 for a Teotihuacan comparison). While these examples shed important light on the role of religion as a structuring principle of violence in ancient Mesoamerica, much still needs to be understood about how such structures came into being and varied in time and space.

A fourth line of inquiry concerns the poorly researched possibility that ancient Mesoamericans used violence as a tool to convert peoples to new religious beliefs or to manifest differences in religious beliefs. While we know a good deal about Mesoamerican religious systems, there is surprisingly very little evidence pointing toward wars of religious conflict and conversion, so common in other parts of the ancient world. One possibility to explore is whether the Epiclassic spread of the Feathered Serpent Cult was undertaken using organized violence. Much has been discussed concerning the increase in the iconography of warfare during the Epiclassic (see Ringle, Gallareta Negrón, and Bey 1998) but not necessarily concerning organized violence as a tool to spread the ideology. Another possibility to explore might be the increase of Central Mexican iconography in other areas of Mesoamerica during the apogee of Teotihuacan where there is ample evidence of the spread of imagery related to violence (see chapter by Nielsen, this volume). While both of these Mesoamerican horizons include evidence for violence and the spread of new ideologies, there is little evidence to indicate that this violence was caused by actual clashes of religious ideologies or the conversion of people to a different way of interpreting the cosmos. This would be an interesting area for further research, given the large datasets available to investigators.

LANDSCAPE AND WARFARE

Settlement patterns (e.g., Hirth 1978; Parsons 1971) and defensive features (e.g., Silverstein 2001; Webster 1976) have long played an important role in our understanding of Mesoamerican warfare. People's choices in terms of where to live and how they constructed their built environment often reflected deep concerns for their safety, among a host of other factors. As Bey and Gallareta Negrón (this volume) demonstrate, these concerns could be far older than we often consider (see also Flannery and Marcus 1996). The chapter on Puuc settlement really drives home the fact that archaeologists need to marshal more and diverse data on early conflict to be able to discuss "origins of warfare" questions in Mesoamerica.

Haines and Sagebiel (this volume) also aptly demonstrate how settlement pattern data can complement iconographic and epigraphic evidence for increased conflict—in this case, evidence for the abandonment of Ka'kabish during the time the ruler of Lamanai chose to project an image of bellicosity. The Lamanai case is not unique. There is ample evidence that large cities where warfare-related iconography permeated the public view, such as Chichen Itza and Teotihuacan, grew in population at the expense of neighboring communities (Sanders, Parsons, and Santley 1979; Stanton and Magnoni 2013; Vallejo 2011). Yes, it is likely that organized violence was a major factor in those population displacements, but as Haines and Sagebiel (this volume) note, migration can be influenced by a wide host of factors, including the level of dependency on other allies (in this case, certain Central Peten communities) or economic opportunities that may or may not be linked to the militaristic activity in the region.

Beyond settlement patterns, this volume breaks new ground in the treatment of landscape and warfare. I found Tokovinine's (this volume) discussion of the association of the "entering the *ch'een*" phrase with captive taking very informative and much in line with Hernandez and Palka's (this volume) treatment of the Zacpeten sacred center. As mentioned above in the discussion of termination rituals, certain parts of the landscape could be, as Freidel (1998) once termed them, "ensouled." These animate areas of the landscape were powerful and, as Hernandez and Palka (this volume) argue, could be used to wage otherworldly war against the enemy. Thus there was a need to protect the space and the deities that inhabited it from harm—something the people from Lamanai were unable to do considering the damage inflicted on Stela 9 (see chapter by Haines and Sagebiel, this volume). Returning to the El Tajín banners discussed by Koontz (this volume), the presence of patron war deities in such sacred precincts would have layered even more war-related meanings onto these public spaces, further anchoring the idea of sanctioned violence to the center of a community's identity. Moreover, while capturing a site center might not have resulted in the political incorporation of the losing community into larger conquest states (some known exceptions and tribute relationships aside), the capture of the site center must have been a strategic goal for large-scale conflict; this is beautifully alluded to on the Hieroglyphic Staircase of House C at Palenque (see chapter by Tokovinine, this volume). While such work in the Maya region benefits from hieroglyphic texts, it will be interesting to see such ideas explored in other Mesoamerican contexts in the future.

ECONOMICS OF CONFLICT

I think one would be hard pressed to find examples of organized violence categorized as warfare that do not have intended economic consequences, despite the motivations professed by those involved in the conflict, and even fewer that do not have unintended consequences. In Mesoamerica, there are clear examples of the economics of conquest. The hiatus of Tikal and growth of Caracol after the "star-war" event of 562 CE is a much-discussed case in the Maya area (Chase 1991; Chase and Chase 1996), while the economic boom of the Mexica empire through strategies of coercion and conquest is a widely researched example from Central Mexico (Berdan et al. 1996). Yet the economics of conflict and warfare remains an understudied topic that should gain more interest in Mesoamerica as we begin to more clearly understand how the associated economies functioned (see, for example, Bey 2003; Dahlin et al. 2007; Foias and Bishop 1997; Howie 2005; Masson and Freidel 2002; Pool and Bey 2007; Skoglund et al. 2006).

In this volume, the economics of warfare is broached by Nielsen, who touches on a widely debated topic: the martial nature of the Teotihuacan state and its economic interests abroad (e.g., Braswell 2003c; Schele and Freidel 1990). His argument focuses on the spectacular mural at El Rosario, Querétaro, with its Teotihuacan imagery of warriors, weapons, and torches—common iconographic elements found at many other sites with Teotihuacan "influence" throughout Mesoamerica. While evidence for Teotihuacan influence during the Early Classic continues to mount (e.g., Garcia-Des Lauriers 2007; Winter 1998, 2010), I suspect that those cautious about this military expansion will continue to argue for trade (specifically, armed caravans pertaining to individual apartment compounds and not a Teotihuacan state) instead of conquest to explain the mural (e.g., Manzanilla 2011). I think what we can agree on is that the cultural elements strongly associated with the city of Teotihuacan during the Early Classic spread along important economic trade routes (e.g., Carballo and Pluckhahn 2007) and that, as Nielsen (this volume) correctly points out, they are heavily weighted toward symbols of war and conquest. While it remains difficult to prove the idea of hegemonic empire building, the reality that organized violence was a major part of the spread of these cultural elements, at least in some areas I think, is hard to deny. Yet the lack of consensus as to the type, scale, and even motives of that violence hinders our ability to grapple with how it articulates with a Teotihuacan economic system beyond simple statements that link the motives of violence to a need to control trade routes and access to resources. As is well illustrated by the Mexica case (e.g., Berdan et al. 1996), the past reality is likely to have been much more complex. In any event, until a better consensus is reached as to how to interpret these frustratingly tempting data, analogies to the Mexica or other societies' ways of using organized violence to shape economic systems will remain hotly debated.

THE EXPERIENCE OF VIOLENCE

There is no doubt that any form of organized violence elicits a wide range of highly charged emotions and feelings: anger, sorrow, elation, horror, pain, fear, and relief top a long list I could mention. As archaeology has moved in directions that more strongly privilege the experience of ancient peoples (e.g., Joyce, Meskell, and Turner 2003), archaeologists studying warfare have attempted to better contextualize one of the most extreme forms of human experience (Carman 1997; Vandkilde 2003; "cognitive" and "experiential" approaches in Peuramaki-Brown, Morton, and Kettunen, this volume). Yet there has been a relative lack of research within this interpretive framework in Mesoamerica, despite rich archaeological data and a series of fascinating social questions that could be asked of them.

Archaeologists working in Mesoamerica face an interesting problem. On the one hand, the fact that violence, sacrifice, and warfare have been so sensationalized has resulted in a tendency for some to shy away from the study of these topics (see Demarest 2007), rightfully acknowledging that ancient Mesoamericans led rich lives textured by many other activities; on the other hand, the same images of violence, sacrifice, and warfare that are often used to propagate these sensational visions of ancient Mesoamerican society do in fact suggest that there were certain attitudes toward violence that need to be further explored. Beyond the obvious and generalized experiences organized violence can elicit from people (e.g., pain, horror), I think one of the more interesting questions deals with how these experiences were colored by diverse Mesoamerican attitudes toward violence and pain. In contrast to many other ancient societies that used excessive images of violence in public contexts to demonstrate the prowess of their rulers and armies, there is a general feel for Mesoamerican art that indicates that pain, sacrifice, and death went far beyond political statements. Could the prevalence of these themes in the iconography be some indication that ancient Mesoamericans naturalized them to some degree? I would find it hard to believe that such extensive (both temporally and spatially) emphasis on these concepts did not have a profound impact on shaping people's outlooks and attitudes toward, and, ultimately, experiences of, violence (see Campbell 1992).

We get glimpses of Mesoamerican attitudes toward violence in studies that reference trophy taking (e.g., Tiesler et al. 2017; cf. Chacon and Dye 2007; Otterbein 2000b; M. J. Smith 2014, 118); for example, Helmke and his colleagues (2012), in a paper given at the symposium that led to this volume, discussed the practice of raiding for captives for the acquisition of trophies. They mentioned that the ability of a warrior to capture an enemy or at least demonstrate the killing of an enemy through the acquisition of a part of the body as a trophy[4] "implies the presence of societies cultivating the warrior ethos and positively valuating successful warriors, who kept count of their kills."[5] I concur and suggest that there are other data indicating similar attitudes toward warriors in Mesoamerica, such as the Mexica hair-cutting ceremonies that followed a young warrior's first successful capture and the widespread practice of gladiatorial boxing throughout Mesoamerica (Taube and Zender 2009), that can be brought to bear in these types of studies. How widespread in time and space were such attitudes? How much resistance was there to such social constructions, and from whom? These are fruitful questions for future work on a subject that begs further research.

THE PEOPLE WHO PRACTICED WAR AND OTHER FORMS OF VIOLENCE

Warfare and other forms of organized violence require attention to strategy and logistics as well as people, although as we have seen in Mesoamerican archaeology, it is often unclear who actually did the fighting. While I believe that some areas of warfare studies need to move out of their traditional focus on arms, warriors / soldiers, and battlefield tactics (e.g., Farris 1992; Raaflaub 1999), this is not to say, as Abtosway and McCafferty (this volume) demonstrate, that they are not important themes that beg attention; for example, Koontz (this volume) argues that the fighting force for El Tajín would have been around 500 to 600 warriors based on the idea that the elites were the ones who did the fighting (cf. Freidel 1986, 107). Webster (2000, 99; see also Inomata and Triadan 2009, 65) has argued against this logic for the Classic Maya. How we rectify such disparate views of battlefield participation among Classic-period societies in the eastern lowlands of Mesoamerica will greatly change our views of warfare. There is an incredible difference between fielding 500 versus tens of thousands of warriors: an important point when conceptualizing the attack by Tikal on Naranjo (see chapter by Tokovinine, this volume). The problem lies with the iconography of elite warriors in eastern Mesoamerica in general and the epigraphy of the Classic Maya specifically. While these data focus on the role of elites in warfare, does this focus give us a broad view concerning how warfare was really practiced, or does it tell us more about how the elite wanted their perceived roles to be commemorated?

While excavating a household that we today classify as a Late Classic commoner residence at Yaxuna, Yucatán, during the 1992 field season, Dave Johnstone recovered an approximately forty-year-old male with a cranium and first four cervical vertebrae of a twenty- to twenty-five-year-old male on top of the primary individual's left femur (Stanton et al. 2010, 233; Tiesler et al. 2017). The burial is interpreted as a commoner warrior who was buried with a war trophy. When thinking about the elite warrior argument, I always come back to this case and ask myself if this commoner could have been an anomaly, and every time I reach the answer that no, he probably was not. Despite a continued adherence to the elite warfare model, I think commoner combatants may have been common throughout the entire Maya sequence, as in other parts of Mesoamerica. Abtosway and McCafferty (this volume) make a strong case for the indigenous downplaying of the role of lesser, or commoner, combatants in the Mixtec area, even though they were an important part of the fighting force. As in the Greek "hero-warrior" complex, the commoners in Mesoamerica will not likely be afforded space in iconographic programs to commemorate their actions, and there may be very few who were actually buried with objects that could identify them as warriors (possibly even more so if organized violence was not their primary profession or activity).[6] We know about commoner participation and the potential for social mobility of Mexica warriors because of the Spanish documents. Yet as Webster (2000) points out, we also know about the participation of Maya commoners in battles because of similar documentation.

Granted, these fairly similar portrayals of commoner participation in organized violence during the Postclassic do not explain the difference in the iconographic treatment of warriors between eastern and western Mesoamerica during the Classic; however, they do suggest that we should be careful in limiting all organized conflict to elites in the eastern lowlands and instead conceptualize it as a multi-textured social landscape in terms of conflict.

One logical area of analysis that will help us tease out who not only participated in battlefield combat but who also suffered physical violence in general is the field of bioarchaeology. While not included in this volume, bioarchaeologists working in Mesoamerica have recently stepped up studies of evidence for warfare and sacrifice, with interesting results (e.g., Chávez Balderas 2014; Serafin, Peraza Lope, and Uc González 2014; Serafin, Uc González, and Peraza Lope 2014; Tiesler and Cucina 2006, 2012). Such studies are helping to contextualize the use of weapons such as those described by Abtosway and McCafferty (this volume) by placing the frequency and contexts of wounds that may have been caused by such objects in perspective. While we may find objects with frequency in the iconography, some may be for show or to scare people into not attacking. The arms that may have been actually used more in battle may have been those that do not show up often in the iconography (cf. Knüsel and Smith 2014b, 8)—food for thought as we begin to cross datasets in future analyses. Finally, bioarchaeology will not just help clarify who was physically harmed by organized violence and how—although as Knüsel and Smith (2014b) caution we must be careful regarding questions of equifinality (e.g., accidents)—it should also provide tangential data on health that will help us understand the impact of sustained violence on non-combatants (cf. Wright 1997) as well as occupational stress data that may help us identify full-time warriors.

Archaeologists working in Mesoamerica seem to be caught in a constant tendency to view evidence for human-against-human violence, specifically bioarchaeological evidence of trauma, as warfare or ritual sacrifice that was sanctioned by the elites; this is something we need to reconsider. We know very little of Pre-Columbian conflict resolution, and what we do know comes primarily from elite or Contact-period contexts. Did commoners come to blows within their own cities? Could raids be conducted without the prior sanction of royal leaders? Was corporate group feuding a persistent problem? Given the importance of revenge as a reason for violent conflict (e.g., Maschner 1997) and how violence often escapes the control of legitimate authorities in modern societies, we must keep an open mind as to how we interpret our data.

FINAL COMMENTS

As this volume shows, there is much still to be learned not only about ancient Mesoamerican warfare but also about violence and the culture of violence that was prevalent in this part of the ancient world. Given the resistance to studies of prehistoric warfare across the world in the postwar period (Keely 1996), particularly acute in the Maya area prior to the first cogent discussions of the Bonampak murals, we have come a long way as a field in a relatively short period of time. Yet we have still only begun to scratch the surface of studies of organized violence in Mesoamerica. I feel as though I have asked a lot of questions in this chapter, but I also believe the key for the future will be to continue to look beyond the historical particularities of our archaeological cases and frame our data to address important social questions concerning organized violence in general. This volume makes important contributions in that direction, and I look forward to seeing continued work in the near future.

Acknowledgments. I thank Traci Ardren and two anonymous reviewers for their comments. I maintain responsibility for the final version.

NOTES

1. See Walker (2001) for a discussion of the definition of violence.

2. Meaning ritual performances associated with violent behavior often done in the safety of the home community and not to be confused with the idea of violence and warfare as performance in and of itself (cf. Whitehead 2005).

3. The public treatment of captives and the display of whole and parts of bodies, commonly used as both actors and props in Mesoamerican violence theater, would have had a great impact on people's perceptions of these places as well as shaping how all sorts of attitudes and social relationships were negotiated. While much work has been conducted on human sacrifice in this area of the world, much remains to be done on theorizing violence and corporality (cf. Novak 2014).

4. Given the importance of human remains to ancestor veneration in Mesoamerica, the acquisition of human trophies may have had complex and layered meanings (cf. Western and Hurst 2014, 172). In fact, the stealing of important human remains in order to defile them (cf. Hernandez and Palka, this volume) or holding them hostage, such as the *huacas* taken to Cuzco by the Inka (Lane 2010, 575), may complicate the archaeological record.

5. Although not all societies with a well-developed tradition of valuing the role of the warrior practiced systematic trophy acquisition (e.g., Kjellström 2014).

6. Remember that artifacts in burials do not always indicate activities in life (cf. Hanks 2008).

12

"This Means War!"[1]

ELIZABETH GRAHAM

The contributions to this volume probe our perceptions of the nature of conflict and competition in Mesoamerica. The chapters also illuminate the range of social, cultural, and ideological factors the social sanctioning of conflict entails. I have initially avoided using the term *war* to turn attention to our own emic perspective. It is curious, as the *Oxford English Dictionary* (OED) comments, that there was no word for "war" as late as early historic times in the Germanic languages from which, of course, English derives. The OED does not supply chronological dates for "early historic times," but other information in the entry references the period when the literate Romans spread out across Europe because the Romans had a word for what we now think of as war, which was *bellum*. The closest equivalent in the Germanic languages was *werre*, which—from its hypothesized Proto-Indo European roots to its Old Saxon and other Germanic derivatives—meant *confusion, trouble, disorder, discord, strife, struggle, disturbance, perplexity*, but not, oddly enough, "hostile contention by means of armed forces," as war is defined in the OED. As far as I can tell by adding information from the *American Heritage Dictionary* (AHD), the words *guerre* in French and *guerra* in

DOI: 10.5876/9781607328872.c012

Spanish were derived from a Frankish root, *werra*, and by about the 1100s CE or so, all of these terms were used in the way we might use "war" today.

This ambiguity in the roots of European terms now used to refer to hostile contention by means of armed forces suggests that ideas about how to deal with competition—especially competition manifested as conflict—were much more varied than in our modern concept of war. Did rivals agree on concepts of winning or losing that they applied to their group, or did conflict entail predominantly individual agendas that permitted individuals from either side to benefit? Concomitantly, were there different words to describe these situations? Were there different rules of engagement in different sorts of competition so that only some competitions were manifested in conflict and only particular kinds of conflict entailed socially sanctioned killing?

Clearly, we cannot avoid using the term *war* (and its closest equivalents in other languages, e.g., *krieg* or *guerra*). Since the twelfth century CE, it has come to cover a widely recognized manner of resolving rival claims to power or resources through socially sanctioned methods of arming, fighting, and killing. War clearly has meaning for us, and it behooves us to use it to describe conflict and competition, which I hope to explain, as in the anthropology of war (Fried, Harris, and Murphy 1968) or war before civilization (Keeley 1996) or an origin of war (Kelly 2000) or a beginning of war (Otterbein 2004) or a cultural context of warfare (Nielsen and Walker 2009). We should keep at the forefront of our minds that we hold many ideas about war—such as the extensive killing we take for granted as part of warfare or the concept of surrender—which may not have applied to competition and conflict in the Maya world. It is also possible that the Maya socially sanctioned arming or fighting or killing in ways we might not at first recognize as war—such as the killing of an opponent away from and after the armed engagement. Where we can document conflict in hieroglyphic texts, we assume that rules of engagement were like ours by employing concepts of winning and losing, which we apply to one "side" or the other. I do not argue that our concepts cannot illuminate Maya actions; I argue that the fit may not be as tight as we would like. Thinking about the history and cultural roots of our own terms and concepts helps generate questions we might not otherwise ask about how people in the past thought about or behaved in their world (Graham 2009).

In addition to exploring the roots of terminology, we can look to competition as a broader heuristic category (recognizing that humans compete in complex ways over a range of perceived needs and wants). We might hypothesize that individuals in social groups, even those with obligatory sharing, will compete for or expect access to resources (some individuals, for example, eat more than others). Individuals will also organize into groups (factions) to compete with other groups for resources (Brumfiel and Fox 1994). Our word *competition* serves well to categorize a phenomenon that recognizes a degree of friction yet does not necessarily entail violence and can even include play (Huizinga 2014 [1950]). One could make the case that a key factor is whether the competition is intra-group or inter-group, as it is inter-group competition that is more closely associated with warfare (e.g., Fausto 2012; Graeber 2014, 28–34; Webster 2000, 72). On the other hand, intra-group competition can often involve violence; the prime function of Mughal warfare is said to have been to bridge the *inner* frontiers of empire (emphasis from Gommans 2002, 3). Even intra-community competition can become violent, although violence on this level, particularly when it results in the death of a perceived rival or competitor *within* the community, is not generally socially sanctioned (Webster 2000, 72).

Conflict entails the idea that in some competitions, usually those involving organized groups, both bodily harm and killing are socially sanctioned, and our term *war* covers this nicely (Webster 1975, 2000). Where individuals represent groups, terminology can be trickier. Some competition could conceivably involve a "theater" of struggle in which individuals who represent a group compete in front of an audience. Where killing is not socially sanctioned—although bodily harm might be, as in boxing (Taube and Zender 2009)—we would call this "sport"; however, on some theaters of struggle, killing may well have been socially sanctioned. A version of the Mesoamerican ballgame in which elite men from rival armed groups compete could conceivably fit into this category. Here, terminology is critical because the killing, even though it is played out as theater in order to have been witnessed by the community, is most likely to have been socially sanctioned as *war*.

Our vocabulary separates war and sport because sports today generally do not involve socially sanctioned killing, whereas warfare does. Yet warfare can have an element of game, as has been ascribed to pre-modern warfare (Huizinga 2014 [1950]), which through "competitiveness and playfulness, as well as through . . . shared rules and conventions, brought together various parts of society" (Gommans 2002, 3). Reflecting what Gommans (2002, 205–206) calls the fluid politics of the Mughal Empire, Mughal warfare is said to have been characterized by openness and flexibility and even play (Subrahmanyam 2012, 22). Such complexity in elements of war should inspire us to reevaluate the socially sanctioned killing we have come to associate with modern concepts of war. The manner and extent to which violence was socially sanctioned in armed conflict may distinguish not only our understanding of warfare from what was going on in Mesoamerica but also practices among warring Mesoamerican groups (Aoyama and Graham 2015).

Given the perspective described above, we would not expect to find a one-to-one correlation between our term *war* and references to conflict in Mayan texts, which indeed is the case (see chapter by Tokovinine, this volume). In addition to the existence of more than one way competition and conflict were played out, we might also expect a range of terms or modes of expression that would reflect what we lump together as winning or losing. The almost insuperable hurdle involves knowing what the rules of engagement were; the language of the inscriptions as well as changes in weaponry over time suggest that the rules of engagement did not remain static (Aoyama and Graham 2015). Suffice it to say at this point that attempting to discern the rules of engagement as well as the criteria involved in winning or losing is at least as important as knowing, for example, that Tikal claimed victory over the ruler of Calakmul (Martin and Grube 2008, 44).

The chapters in this volume shed a great deal of light on the complexities of both text and iconography in matters that relate to competition and conflict. I discuss the chapters and their implications according to various themes, which I hope will highlight new directions of research. I first consider *winning* and what it might mean for one community or city to "conquer" or subdue or overcome another. What are the implications of winning, and how might they be manifested in texts and titles? The next logical step is to consider the *rules of engagement*. Much of what I say remains speculative, but speculation is important in providing the means of articulating new hypotheses that can be tested by further investigation. Related to rules of engagement is the meaning attributed to *objects and images*. What sorts of *metaphors* we can expect and what meaning we can attribute to tropes—as reflected in lordly titles as well as in claims on the power or influence of various deities or spirits—are themes of importance and worth expanding in the context of conflict. The focus on individuals, either lords or gods, leads us to consider the degree to which conflict is *a family affair* (involving those we know rather than those we do not care about). I consider the role of *history and culture* in both conflict and its resolution with regard to how we interpret the origins of cultural icons and symbols as well as elite titles. Finally and not least important, I consider the assumptions that underlay *socially sanctioned killing* in the past with the implication that the term and the concept of *human sacrifice* must be consigned to the dustbin.

WINNING

We often understandably frame the results of conflict as conquest (victory) or defeat (e.g., Demarest 2004a, 102; Martin and Grube 2008; O'Mansky and Dunning 2004, 94; Schele and Miller 1986, 29; Stuart 2000, 482; Valdés and Fahsen 2004, 140) because there are indications in texts—such as the taking of captives, the loss of a life, or a shift in power-holding—that one group or community or center gained at the expense of another. Yet it is difficult to picture either the details of the engagement or the full nature of the results and their significance. How was it judged that a particular group "won" (Schele and Miller 1986, 218)?

Hernandez and Palka (this volume) make the point that the way war and culture are intertwined is vital in understanding how conflict is conducted. Where everyday life in cities and towns continued after war events, as seems to have been the case among the Maya in Classic times, there had to exist agreed-upon rules concerning armed engagements as well as on how losing was determined and what winning entailed. Where there are statements of conquest in the inscriptions, we should expect that the social and economic implications—such as the details of power and wealth transfer—accorded well with such rules. Where warfare was extremely disruptive to communities, as occurred in the Terminal Classic (e.g., Demarest et al. 1997; Inomata 1997), there is every reason to consider that we are looking at conflict in which there was cultural disjunction between the opposing sides and armed struggle entailed more than traditionally agreed methods of power and wealth appropriation. To draw from Hernandez and Palka, warfare cannot be considered above cultural considerations.

Admittedly, criteria for winning in Mesoamerican warfare are obscured by our lack of detailed knowledge concerning how people or groups self-identified within the larger categories we use of "Maya" (Henderson and Hudson 2015) or "Mixtec" or "Mexica." We have identifiable glyphs on stelae that reflect identities of families and dynasties (Schele and Miller 1986, 137) who engaged in conflict, but use of terms such as *Maya warfare* or *Maya religion* or *Maya populace* masks the very diversity that would have been associated with factions and groups at the heart of the initiation of conflict. The history of conflict between France and England or between Boudicca and the Romans would never be understood if it was assumed that self-identification as "European" was a factor in stimulating aggression. For lack of knowledge of names of subgroups or ethnic factions or areas, we perforce use "Maya," but for the purpose of generating hypotheses, this should not prevent us from *envisioning* the dynamics of warfare as involving a variety of cultural groups and allegiances (Aoyama and Graham 2015). Insight comes from Abtosway and McCafferty (this volume), who observe that the intra-Mixteca warfare described in the codices reflects people loyal to their regional centers and not to a cohesive larger regional unit. What did people from a particular Mixtec center hope to win? According to Abtosway and McCafferty, they were motivated by personal gain.

Even if we envision that the sites we excavate functioned as centers of polities and hence as rallying points for agents, engagements also involved confederations, as in the case of the several centers that identified as "Pomona" in conflicts with Piedras Negras; confederations were also in operation in large parts of southeastern Peten (Laporte 2001; Webster 2002, 165). Without a term equivalent to our "war" in the inscriptions (see chapter by Tokovinine, this volume; see also Schele and Miller 1986, 209–222), we are left with a variety of references that seem to reflect the results of conflict and hence the nature of a "win" but that are metaphorical and culturally specific—therefore difficult for us to understand. Before I discuss these references, it is important to frame the political landscape from which the references might draw meaning.

Framing the Political Landscape

Martin and Grube (2008, 21) have proposed that the political landscape of the Classic Maya is better expressed by interaction between and among the various states/polities/centers than by a territorial map. I have made a similar argument on the basis of the knowledge we have of community interaction at the time of the Spanish Conquest and on studies of indigenous and Spanish fighting tactics during the Conquest (Graham 2006, 2011, 29–46; Graham, Simmons, and White 2013). If competition and conflict among the Classic Maya were more about shifting dominant and subordinate relationships than about the taking of territory, then it helps to envisage how competition and conflict might have operated under these conditions. How would people or polities increase wealth or resources without actually appropriating territory?

An appropriate model—*pace* to those who consider pre-industrial civilizations to have been starkly different from us—is the modern world, in which nation-states and their political rulers, Vladimir Putin excepted, generally do not engage in conflict for territory (i.e., to annex Iraq or Guatemala to the United States or the United Kingdom). Nation-states and their political chiefs engage in conflict over rights to resources, such as oil or minerals or crops. The resources are owned today by multinationals, and politicians (at least in terms of the government offices they hold) are subject to the power of the multinationals. Politicians are often offered jobs in these companies when they retire from office, become stakeholders in corporations, or both. Thus government officeholders, heads of companies, corporate executives, landed gentry, wealthy investors—although they can be from different countries—all have a stake in the present economic system because the profits from resource exploitation accrue to them, if not strictly speaking as a class, as an elite group with shared interests (Graham 2012). They may not share all aspects of culture because they may be British or Brazilian or Saudi Arabian or Greek or Russian or Chinese, but they share enough in the way of values to sanction the economic system, even when—and perhaps because—the system frequently involves conflict as a means of resource appropriation or retention.

This idea, albeit in a slightly different form, was first introduced by Michael Smith (1986) in a landmark paper in which he emphasized that despite their image as bloody and brutal, the Aztecs' success did not depend on military coercion. The Aztec system, if I may provisionally call it that, was successful because the elites from highland Mexico, Morelos, Puebla, Oaxaca, or the Gulf Coast—who would have self-identified locally—had a stake in the economic system of tribute/taxpayers and tribute/tax receivers (Graham 2014; M. J. Smith 2014). Those at the upper end of the scale received tribute/taxes and those lower down the social scale paid tribute/taxes. Warfare among elites—that is, among the *tlatoque* of city-states or *altepetl* against *altepetl*—was usually a last resort and if carried through, shifted resources among elites. The claims of the Mexica of the fear and awe in which they were held by foreign and subject rulers were propagandistic; there was, in fact, tacit agreement among elites to uphold a system in which their common interests transcended political boundaries.

Such a system is dependent on frequent communication and shared experiences among the people of cities and city-states, great time depth to such communication, wide-ranging commercial networks, and a great deal of intermarriage. One has to imagine a "global" Mesoamerica (a world system? [Blanton and Feinman 1984]) in which the flow of people from northern regions southward and eastward, and vice versa, had been going on for a very long time. Since Formative times, marine trade networks facilitated the circum-peninsular movement of goods, and the networks were well integrated with riverine and overland routes. Foot travel, rather than a limitation (Sanders and Webster 1988, 529), can be a strong stimulus to local commerce. I say this based on my experience living in London, where commercial and industrial sectors of the city are everywhere integrated with residences. Although public transport is excellent, roads are congested; as a result, people walk considerable distances, even late at night or in the early hours of the morning. Vendors have sprung up along these routes selling food and drink; because people are walking (and not traveling from point to point in a bus or tube), they are apt to buy food or drink more than once en route, and there are lots of vendors. Small grocery stores also stay open late, some all night.

This phenomenon got me thinking that foot travel must have stimulated, not limited, opportunities for commerce, at least at the local or inter-community level. Although it is often argued that paved roads, wheeled vehicles, and pack animals are an advantage in travel and transport, there are good reasons to put this claim into context. For one thing, the Maya did not know they were at a disadvantage; therefore, *not* having a cart or a horse would not have limited their vision of where they could go or what commercial transactions were possible. It is also true, as anyone who works in the Neotropics knows, that paved roads, wheeled vehicles, and beasts of burden are a mixed blessing given the huge and costly effort of upkeep. History also shows that the advantages of owning horses, cattle, or wheeled vehicles accrued to the better-off; for example, in early Ireland prior to the coming of Christianity, horse-drawn transport was an aristocratic monopoly (Leighton 1972, 171). In the rest of Western Europe, goods could be carried by animals such as mules or in ox-drawn carts, but animals and carts were limited and their use costly; other than goods, apparently only "the criminal, the aged, the sick, and women were transported by wagon" (Leighton 1972, 172). Kings, nobles, bishops, and abbots rode horseback; priests walked or rode asses; the masses walked (Leighton 1972, 172).

In Mesoamerica, in places where water-borne travel or transport was not possible, *everyone* had to walk or take foot travel into account (as in the case of merchants who needed to transport goods or rulers whose status meant they should be carried). Thus there existed a profusion of opportunities to provide food, drink, supplies, apparel, gear, medicines, transport services (porters), and rest stops to walking travelers of all stripes: individuals, families, messengers, pilgrims, and merchants' "caravans." It is no stretch of the imagination to envision not impenetrable jungle but a landscape crisscrossed with paths and bustling with activity in Classic times, especially since we know that trade, which involved the movement of goods over long and short distances, was a key force in Maya history (Graham 1987a).

What does this have to do with winning wars? Despite what might be called ethnic or linguistic differences, the networks of people, communication, and trade argue strongly for a Mesoamerica in which, at least to some degree, cultural values were shared. We know this was true of elites (Smith 1986), but some measure of commonality may also have existed at other levels as the result of the involvement of large segments of the population in exchange and commerce—inter-regionally, intra-regionally, and locally—as envisioned above. The time depth of contact with a variety of cultures other than one's own would have had (at least) two outcomes: (1) elites throughout Mesoamerica were likely to have consisted of a proportion of individuals who were related and shared kinship connections, and (2) the commercial sector would have had a reasonable amount of power.

Conditions in Mesoamerica were ripe for conflict that involved appropriating resources in ways that did not necessarily have to involve land acquisition. One does not need to own (in our terms) land in a situation in which one has acquired the rights to its resources. If everyone in a group agrees on the rules about who as part of the group has rights to resources through tribute/taxes, one needs only to compete with others in the group for a piece of the pie (see, e.g., García Loaeza 2014, 222–223). Attempts to kill people in order to incorporate the land on which they live can also be counterproductive in situations in which people's labor and the established infrastructure are the bases of the economy. The need is only to kill or capture or subdue the *right* people in socially sanctioned ways if one is to appropriate their wealth, which can include rights to land and its products. Abtosway and McCafferty (this volume) cite a Postclassic example (see their citation to Matthew and Oudijk 2007) in which the Chichimeca allied themselves with the Tolteca-Chichimeca during the war against Cholula. The alliance included the stipulation that the Chichimeca would be paid in land grants and lordship titles. One is reminded of the Mexica rise to power because of their alliances with the Tepanecs of Atzcapozalco (Smith 2011, 46–49), in which the Mexica newcomers sought titles that would give them access to resources through tribute.

Economics—the acquisition of wealth or control of resources—plays a critical role in warfare (Webster 1975, 468–469); however, Scherer and Verano (2014, 4), in the introduction to their hugely informative edited volume on war in Pre-Columbian Mesoamerica and the Andes, state that "nevertheless, to understand why people go to war we must look beyond material gain." In support, they cite a recent survey of the reasons for enlistment among US infantry battalions. Only one reason given by those who enlisted was financial ("money for college"), while the other top choices were adventure, serving the country, patriotism, and the desire to be a soldier. Somehow Scherer and Verano neglected to take into account the fact that all of the soldiers in the army receive salaries. A survey that truly looked beyond material gain would have to offer men or women the opportunity to fight and possibly be killed in Afghanistan or Iraq but without pay or any benefits to either them or their families. I doubt that anyone would volunteer to fight solely as an adventure, to serve the country, to be patriotic, or to serve as a soldier without any salary or benefits. In earlier centuries, as in the case of the British Navy in the late eighteenth and early nineteenth centuries CE, many of the ship's hands were conscripted when they were either drunk or asleep on land. The "pay" in those days was a share of the loot when another ship was captured.

It is hard to imagine that anyone anywhere would fight repeatedly for no economic reward. Among the Classic Maya, conflict must have involved gain for those who fought. But what was the mechanism of wealth transfer if land was not appropriated? Miller and Martin (2004, 166) discuss the economic dimensions of captive taking in suggesting that a "prisoner of note represented a much wider set of obligations and resources—be it a ransom that could be extorted or tribute that could be demanded." I have long proposed that captive taking among elites *was* the mechanism of wealth transfer (Graham 2006, 2008, 2009, 2011, 40–43; Graham, Simmons, and White 2013). By this I do not mean that ransom (as understood in Western European warfare) was involved (McAnany 2010, 278–283) or that the case was one of tribute having to be demanded; instead, tribute or tax payments, including access to land, through the act of capture were accorded the victor (Gorenstein 1973, 15). The capture itself embodied resource redistribution. I admit that this is speculative, but we need to look to models, perhaps to feudal Japan (Ikegami 1995), where, in the context of codes of honor, ransom was rare and enslaving captives was out of the question (Ikegami 1995, 102). Instead, individual samurai warriors' triumphs over as many combatants as possible (exemplified by the accumulated severed heads of opponents) brought maximum wealth—through redistribution of land by their lords—to the individual (Ikegami 1995, 101–103). Connecting captive taking, resource redistribution, and codes of honor also makes sense of the images of live captives on monuments and portable objects, on the naming of captives and the preoccupation with their identities (Scherer and Golden 2014, 59), and on the contradictions in representing captives as humiliated figures yet also as individuals with noble status (Houston, Stuart, and Taube 2006, 203). Among the samurai, capture entailed a particular kind of social and personal humiliation that could only be remedied—or made honorable—by death (Ikegami 1995, 24–26, 102–103). The cultural and social implications of capture explain the humiliated figures on stelae ("bruised, beaten" [Scherer and Golden 2014, 59]). At the same time, receiving tribute and taxes was the right of the upper classes, and the ideology of the various cultural and ethnic groups reinforced this right; hence, captors were compelled to display the (shared) elite status of their captives.

I should make clear that captive taking could not have occurred on an individual basis—that is, each person out for himself alone. What I propose is that captive taking was part of the rules of engagement, and we have also to envision the existence of a network of political and social relationships among the armed fighters. The ruler was the nexus of the network, and it is not illogical to assume that some warriors fought under the direct overlordship of the ruler, whereas others may have had loyalties and obligations to nobles who were also obligated to the ruler in some way. A hierarchy of political, social, and economic obligations must have already been in place before a conflict. Individuals could be credited with capturing other individuals, but capture was also a political and social act, one with complex implications. Captors may have had rights to only part of the wealth of the captive, as it would have been expected that the captor would pass on gains to his lord or to the ruler. Perhaps the ruler made all the decisions; perhaps rules of honor governed the captor's behavior toward his captive and the captive's family. To turn again to Japan, a victorious samurai commander could pardon captive warriors if they elected to become his vassals (Ikegami 1995, 102). I cannot say, of course, exactly how much tribute or tax would have been transferred or how resources were redistributed, although it may be possible to construct various models that can be tested. The important point is that captive taking, although it appears on the surface to have been acts between individuals, could have worked as a mechanism of wealth transfer organized by a political entity.

Metaphorical References Reflecting the Results of Conflict

I now turn to a discussion of some of the conflict expressions as described by Tokovinine (this volume).

- *Ch'ahkaj* ("chopped") is used in expressions of conflict against a named place or against the holy grounds (*ch'een*) of a royal family or dynasty; in one instance it refers to more sweeping changes (where the land, or *kab*, of the southern, eastern, northern, and western lords was chopped), and in another it is used uniquely to refer to head chopping to describe the outcome of conflict between the rulers of Quirigua and Copan.

- *Jubuuy* is a reference to what we call "downfall"; it is a verb typically used in the expression "bringing down the flint and shield," such as the defeat of Calakmul's ruler Yich'aak K'ahk, who was said to have his "flint and shield" brought down by actions instigated by the ruler of Tikal. Nuun Ujol Chaahk of Tikal had his "flints and shields" brought down in 679 CE in an action with Dos Pilas; the death of Waxaklajuun Ub'aah K'awiil at the hands of Quirigua's king, K'ahk' Tiliw Chan Yopaatis, is described as a demise by "flint and shield" (Martin and Grube 2008, 57, 111, 205).

- Entering the *ch'een* (described above) is used in the example of the Naranjo ruler standing on a captive from Yootz, the *ch'een* (holy grounds) of which the Naranjo ruler is said to have entered. According to Tokovinine, "entering the ch'een" occurs for the first time on the Tikal "Marker."

- *K'ahk' och ch'een*, or "fire *ch'een* entering," occurs on Yaxchilan Stela 18 and Naranjo Stela 24 and in the case of a stucco frieze in Yaxchilan Structure 21 (see Helmke and Brady 2014, 205–209); its use reflects an expression with apparent roots in Central Mexican (Teotihuacan?) culture and history.

- *Puluuy*, or "burning," is used in the case of Lady Six Sky of Naranjo's "burning" of Bital and Tubal (Martin and Grube 2008, 76) but is attested at other sites.

- "Drilling fire" describes an action taken by Motul de San José at Itzan in which a local noble was captured (Tokovinine and Zender 2012).

- *Chuhkaj* translates as "she/he was seized."

- The use of *te* (as in eh-te' or at-te') describes captives (see Martin 2004).

- "He/she/it arrived" (*hul-iy* or *hul-li-ya*) is used to account for Sihyaj K'ahk's presence at Uaxactun and Tikal (Macleod 1990; Martin 2003, 12–13; Stuart 2000, 476–477).

These expressions seem to represent forms of "winning" or at least a change in the power hierarchy ("arrival"). Why are they so numerous? Expressions that describe the outcome of competition and conflict are numerous in all languages and are often metaphorical. "Downfall" in English is a good example, "fire" has come to mean engaging a weapon, and blowing the souls out of one another has been used to describe fighting (Ruskin 1909, 96). Lakoff (1991) observes that the natural way to justify war entails metaphorical definition, not least because metaphors constitute "powerful forms of language that can influence how a concept is perceived and understood" (Hartmann-Mahmud 2002, 427); hence, of all the activities engaged in and described by the Classic Maya, the nature of war and conflict may be the most difficult to which to ascribe meaning.

Aside from the difficulties inherent in metaphorical understanding, we are likely to be dealing with people who shared some aspects of culture but not others; hence, winning is expressed and perhaps enacted in different ways, as suggested also by Tokovinine. We apply the term *Maya* to all the groups who use the expressions above because the elites shared a writing system and some cultural values, but this does not mean that the people involved failed to see themselves as associated with distinctive communities whose members shared a culture or history that included particular expressions of domination. Expressions such as *k'ahk' och ch'een* or "fire *ch'een* entering" may have roots in Central Mexican culture and conflict history (Brady and Colas 2005; Helmke and Brady 2014).

Words such as *te*, in referring to captives, may reflect the particular nature and extent (summing up) of wealth appropriation, which is consonant with my hypothesis that a greater number of captives will result in a greater share of wealth, either directly by appropriation of the captive's tribute or indirectly through the granting of rights by the captor's overlord. The association with "spears" is interesting because it accords well with the idea that elite fighting codes among the Maya emphasized hand-to-hand combat with lances or spears (Aoyama and Graham 2015). Entering the *ch'een* could conceivably have entailed an appropriation of titles and all that went with it (tribute rights over swaths of territory) and hence access to resources in a way that was a step above the capture of lone individuals. The capture of a ruler with the intention of causing his death may have involved a particular metaphorical expression (e.g., bringing down the flint and shield). In cases in which rulers were not killed but instead made vassals, other expressions might have been used. Some expressions, such as the drilling or scattering of fire, may simply derive from rituals that can (but may not always) symbolize conflict or its end result, as in our use in English of "fire" or "burning." I should make clear that as a non-epigrapher I make no claims to translation of these expressions; I simply propose that they represent what we would expect in any situation in which conflict has a deep history and winning has the potential to be realized in a number of ways, ranging from encounters outside cities between large groups to encounters inside cities between individuals on ball courts.

RULES OF ENGAGEMENT

The rules by which competition or conflict is waged are even more difficult to pin down than "winning" because such rules are rarely, if ever, made explicit, even today. Individuals internalize such rules and are often unaware of their cultural relativism until a group with other rules is encountered, and even in these situations it is often difficult for an individual to change his way of thinking (see Graham, Simmons, and White 2013). One way to extract data that might help in constructing hypotheses to test would be to study changes in weaponry over time and space (Aoyama and Graham 2015). In this volume, Abtosway and McCafferty's chapter is a goldmine of information on weapons associated with warfare. One weapon of interest that reflects rules of engagement is the bow and arrow. Abtosway and McCafferty question the assumption that the bow and arrow is a late introduction to Mesoamerica, but with regard to the Maya, bow-and-arrow technology—if not a late introduction per se—was not widely adopted until quite late. At sites with which I am familiar in Belize, the small side-notched points that reflect bow and arrow use do not appear in quantity until the Late Postclassic or even the Spanish Colonial period (Graham 2011, 252; Simmons 1995). Aoyama reports arrow points at Copan as early as the Classic period (Aoyama 1999) and at Aguateca in the Terminal Classic (Aoyama 2005), although the quantities are relatively small compared to larger-sized points (*atlatls*, thrusting spears). Abtosway and McCafferty suggest that the differential representation of *atlatls* and bows and arrows relates to cultural practice or, in my terms, rules of engagement.

What is called for with regard to the adoption of both side-notching (of any size point—spears, *atlatls*, or arrows) and the bow and arrow in the Maya lowlands is scrutiny of the archaeological record for occurrences at particular sites at particular times. With regard to the practices of notching, Abtosway and McCafferty make reference to MacNeish and colleagues' catalog of projectile points, particularly the "Teotihuacan point" that is said to have been present throughout Mesoamerica from the Classic through the Postclassic periods (MacNeish, Nelken-Terner, and de Johnson 1967, 75–76, figure 62). What MacNeish and colleagues (1967, 76) actually state is that the Teotihuacan points in Mexico seem to appear in the Classic period but are not common until Postclassic times. If one examines the illustrations of the Teotihuacan points (MacNeish, Nelken-Terner, and de Johnson 1967, figure 62), they vary in size: some are flat-based, others have a notch taken out of the base, and others have distinctive side notches. These features are likely to be important reflections of hafting practices. If one views the chronological display of points (MacNeish, Nelken-Terner, and de Johnson 1967, 54, figure 34), small side-notched points (arrowheads), which form the bulk of the Teotihuacan points, do not appear until the Venta Salada period—which has a huge time span from ca. 700 CE until the Conquest—and hence are not fully "Classic."

No small side-notched arrow points appear in the burials associated with the Temple of the Feathered Serpent or the Pyramid of the Moon at Teotihuacan, although arrow points without side-notching are indeed present. Such variation in weaponry almost surely reflects cultural practice, as Abtosway and McCafferty propose. The time at which particular cultural practices appear in the archaeological record is also important. When cultures clashed, it is possible that, as with the Mayas and Spaniards in the sixteenth century CE, the conflict was not between groups who were closely related culturally (Webster 2000, 72) but between groups whose rules of engagement—and hence the kinds of violence or even methods of killing that were sanctioned—differed (Graham, Simmons, and White 2013).

Bey and Gallareta Negrón (this volume) comment on ways in which the lack of fortifications in the Puuc, with the exception of Uxmal, has been interpreted and note that some have equated the lack of fortifications with lack of conflict. Lack of fortifications is more likely to reflect rules of engagement, and there is no reason to assume that lack of a defensive wall is an indication of absence of warfare. Even a substantial construction such as Hadrian's Wall is thought to have served multiple functions: a symbol of power or imperial identity (Hingley 2008, 26; Poulter 2008, 103), a frontier mark (Collingwood 1921), a barrier or elevated walk to guard against raiding and to regulate licit and illicit traffic (Bidwell 2008, 129; Collingwood 1921; Poulter 2008, 103), and a defensive feature equivalent to a kind of fort wall (although this seems to have proved the most difficult to substantiate [Bidwell 2008]). Bey and Gallareta Negrón make the excellent point—although they qualify their statement slightly—that conflict can be seen as contributing to the stability of a state. This seems counterintuitive, but it depends on whether rules of engagement are shared among the communities and settlements of the region.

Koontz (this volume) argues that the organization of military groups and their place in the polity might provide clues to larger-scale military organization and hence indirectly to rules of engagement. Although his analysis is meant to apply to Classic Veracruz, which he describes as a "highly competitive military environment," the organization of the individuals who do the fighting or who at least have a role in conflict situations is important in understanding the nature of warfare anywhere in Mesoamerica. An important point that Koontz makes with regard to the Mexica, which applies also to the Maya, is the idea that military organization is likely to have changed through time. At the same time, Koontz suggests that there are "basic elements that may be seen across most, if not all, Mesoamerican military systems." *Why* this should be true is a complex matter. Did the Gulf Coast civilizations set the stage in the second millennium BCE so that the basic rules of engagement were theirs and were simply copied by the less powerful? Or, as seems to be the case in many places in world history (see, e.g., Subrahmanyam 2012, 22–23 for Afghan, North Indian, and East India Company game-changing tactics), did those groups who fought according to rules of engagement, in which winning meant killing the most people, triumph consistently (the Spaniards being an excellent example) so that incrementally, over time, rules that sanctioned the most killing became shared?

Is it possible to document changes in the rules of engagement in the archaeological record (outside detailing changes in weaponry)? Haines and Sagebiel (this volume) discuss the site of Ka'kabish, where settlement dates from at least the Middle Formative to the Postclassic period, although occupation of the site center differs in details from occupation of the settlement zone. Unlike Lamanai, Ka'kabish appears to have declined dramatically in the early Late Classic period, ca. 600–750 CE. Haines and Sagebiel suggest that the individuals named and events recorded on Lamanai Stela 9, which date to the early part of the seventh century CE (Closs 1988; Martin 2016; Pendergast 1988; Reents-Budet 1988), may reflect regional power concentration at the site. During this period, construction efforts continued in the site center at Lamanai but were discontinued at Ka'kabish, whereas in the Late Classic to Terminal Classic transition both sites witnessed a flurry of activity.

More data will be required to be able to paint a fuller picture, but their scenario is an intriguing possibility. I suggest, based on archaeological evidence in the form of midden accumulation around and against the Structure N10-27 platform terrace faces (Graham 2004), that Stela 9 with its early seventh-century CE dates was moved from an unknown original position and re-erected during the first half of the eighth century CE in the central room of the building athwart the stairs of Structure N10-27. Pendergast (1988), on the other hand, sees no reason to assume that the stela was not originally erected in the room in 625 CE and that the building and the stela stood in place for 150–200 years. The case described by Pendergast implies that the stela represents the lineage in power from the beginning of the seventh century through the first half of the eighth century CE; if re-erected, the same could be true, but there is also the option that Lamanai's eighth-century CE rulers had another reason to make the most of a claim of legitimacy based on a relationship of some sort (blood or affinal ties) or simply a recognition of the sequence of office holding (Martin 2003, 29) to the individuals named on Stela 9.

The ruler or ruling group that came to power at Lamanai in the second half of the eighth century or the early ninth century CE did so in an environment that is likely to have included conflict. Fire damage to the stela (Pendergast 1988), combined with cessation of construction as the building was being modified, dismantling of the upper portions of the building, and slow and deliberate burial of the terraces by midden deposition, all suggest a kind of aggressive behavior that involved changes in cultural priorities. The midden that accumulated reflected a deliberate "dump" of fragmented ceramics, many of which were from fine-ware vessels that may have originated in various ceremonies associated with the N10[3] ("Ottawa") plaza/courtyard group (Howie 2012). The Terminal Classic ceramics in the midden display aspects of continuity in Late Classic styles (Graham 1987b) and production (Howie 2012). With regard to the Ottawa Group at this time, there were significant changes in construction techniques and orientation of buildings (Graham 2004; Pendergast 1985, 1986)—activities that paralleled Ka'kabish's resurgence. It is interesting that the more drastic change in fine-ware surface treatment at Lamanai occurred in the late tenth to early eleventh centuries CE with the manufacture of the Buk-phase Zakpah ceramics (Aimers 2009; Aimers and Graham 2013; Walker 1990), although continuity is reflected in production expertise (Howie 2012). There are no texts on these ceramics that can be recognized, at least thus far, as linked to war, but the question remains: Was conflict responsible for a change in the individuals at the top of the community's hierarchy, and did new ritual practices and tastes require changes in the appearance of pottery?

OBJECTS AND IMAGES

Hernandez and Palka (this volume) provide both detail and insight in their discussion of the role of meaningful objects and places in war. Consulting divine beings, often represented by images as in the cases of Cozumel and Noh Peten, seems to have been an important part of Maya (and many other cultural groups') behavior in times of crisis. Thus it is not difficult to understand the importance of the shrine dedicated to the Virgin in Cancuc in Chiapas in the revolt of 1712 or the talking cross in the Guerra de Castas. The discussion of the Jakaltek association of lightning with war nicely dovetails Bassie-Sweet's and Bey and Gallareta Negrón's references (this volume) to Chahk. The idea that notions of the sacred and their material manifestations influenced Maya warfare seems well supported by what we know of conflict, both ancient and modern. In fact, the outcome of armed conflict could well have been viewed by all those involved as determined by the sacred. In European history, the waging of war was often seen as a way "to obtain a decision of holy validity" (Huizinga 2014 [1950], 91).

The important and often neglected idea that landscapes can be objectified as symbols is exemplified by Hernandez and Palka's proposal that the mass (secondary) burial at Zacpeten is archaeological evidence for an attack on spiritual forces and disruption of communication with the deceased. Even if the mass burial should turn out to reflect a different sort of event, their example works powerfully in getting us to think of how people might use a ritual landscape to convey a message of dominance.

Objects and images are clearly meaningful, but what we see as an object, such as a statue or effigy that is not part of our cultural repertoire, would in Maya eyes be a symbol not just of a deity or spirit but of all that the deity stands for in its long relationship with individuals and the community, as in the case of Catholic saints (Graham 2011). The destruction of the statue of Saddam Hussein in Firdos Square described by Hernandez and Palka symbolized triumph because it stood for the downfall of Saddam Hussein, his regime, and its history. We attribute agency to objects, yet in the case of the Maya, because we are outsiders, we must be extremely cautious in treating objects themselves as powerful. Villagutierre Soto-Mayor (1983 [1701], 315) seems to attribute such power to an object in his description of an Itzaj "idol," which he reports (from the Spanish point of view) as being consulted by the Maya at a time of war. From the Maya point of view, the ritual or cultural practice of "consultation" would very probably be found to be inextricable from political or economic or religious motives for conflict. In the same way, the statue of Saddam Hussein was not erected by his supporters because the image itself had power but rather because the image symbolized a history of his dominance; its destruction symbolized the end of that dominance. I agree that success in war is related to the preservation of a community's sacred places and images, but the destruction or preservation of a sacred place or image is a reflection or consequence of the complex dynamics of competition or conflict. Destruction or preservation of an image is more a symptom than a cause.

THEIR OWN METAPHORS

I think we can, with little opposition, proceed on the assumption that the Maya, and indeed all Mesoamerican peoples, had as part of their conceptual systems a wealth of metaphors that they used to make sense of their experience (Lakoff and Johnson 1980). Assuming that many meanings were conventional, shared, and preserved in ritual (Lakoff and Johnson 1980, 109, 234–235), we should be able to develop hypotheses concerning what representations symbolize and test to see whether these interpretations continue to be supported over time. On the other hand, people, including artists, are influenced by other cultures over time, and individuals themselves can add degrees of interpretation. Probably the most we can do is establish flexible rather than rigid frameworks of interpretation and repeatedly test their strengths.

Bassie-Sweet's discussion (this volume) of the Classic Maya gods of flint and obsidian, Chahk and Tlaloc, respectively, integrates into a comprehensible package what can seem to be disparate connections of these deities to materials (flint, obsidian), products (fire, in both cases), celestial phenomena (thunder/rain, meteors), and human action. The idea that action can only take place through some kind of material medium reinforces the importance of making these connections (Graeber 2001, 83). We might reverse this (*pace*) and state that the medium or range of media cannot be understood without taking the action into account. Bassie-Sweet proposes that Tlaloc was associated with war. If we consider, as discussed in the opening section of my chapter, that our concept of "war" has roots in a range of ideas broader than simply hostile contention by armed forces, then we can expand on Bassie-Sweet's insight and suggest that Chahk and Tlaloc are ideas that arise out of people's attempts to categorize or conceptualize friction or conflict more broadly in the material world (e.g., like the old meaning of *werre* as confusion, disorder, disturbance, perplexity). Flint and its association with fiery, noisy thunder and obsidian and its association with the burning up of meteors can then both be seen to serve as metaphors for behaviors that include, but can be broader than, our notion of warfare.

Bassie-Sweet's proposal that the Early Classic lineages acquired Tlaloc effigies from Teotihuacan as emblematic of patron war gods and that the Wi'te'naah (also Winte'naah) structures in the Maya area, closely associated with Tlaloc imagery, were temples dedicated to Tlaloc and his avatars is closely argued. How did lineages in the Maya area acquire Tlaloc associations? Some sort of conflict seems to have been involved—with westerners initiating the conflict with the Maya. Who were these westerners? They could have come from ruling lineages or families originating in Teotihuacan, or perhaps they represented a broader spectrum of people with socio-cultural affiliations to Teotihuacan and its area of influence. Once they intermarried with individuals from whatever city or area was targeted, it stands to reason that only particular families could claim an association with the western lineage(s), which would indeed complicate developing hierarchies among the ruling elite. Such interactions would also introduce a level of competition that could have formed the roots of conflict in which rules of engagement were disputed.

Other intriguing implications arise from the idea that the title of Kaloomte'—or at least the title as it would come to be known and advertised in the Maya area—was restricted in its distribution. Could the title as conceptualized have originated outside the Maya lowlands? The first time the title is known is through its association with Sihyaj K'ahk' at Tikal (Martin and Grube 2008; Stuart 2000), and Bassie-Sweet highlights its association with Tlaloc imagery and hence with war and conquest. With the distinctive history of the Tlaloc iconography and the Kaloomte' title, we may be looking at a particular kind of war. By this I mean that conflict, in the sense implied by the Kaloomte' title, may have entailed rules of engagement that were not universal and differed from rules of conflict in places where individuals (of other lineages?) would or could not claim to have "entered Wi'te'naah" or to have used the Kaloomte' title; however, to have been meaningfully read or recognized among elites, the significance of the title had to have some history in the lowlands, and we ought to consider (even without direct evidence) the existence of a good deal of Formative highland-lowland interaction.

Bassie-Sweet also discusses the overlap between Tlaloc and God L, both associated with obsidian, but she states that it is Tlaloc who is associated with war and God L with merchants. Perhaps the connection is not so distinct, and the imagery she describes also represents links among merchants, acquisition of resources, and conflict or disruption. We might then consider that the title of Kaloomte' reflects a rank associated with success or conquest that historically (having developed in its region of origin) conflated conflict (or achievement) with acquisition of new resources and perhaps also with a particular pattern of resource redistribution. In Western history, we have only to look at the activities of the East India Company to remember how closely interconnected are conflict and trade (Dalrymple 2002; Robins 2012).

Place names have significance on several levels, but there is little question that the metaphors used by the Maya for places and titles are difficult for a cultural outsider to interpret. Tokovinine's discussion (this volume) revolves around frequencies of place names in the context of warfare. Although his discussion is not centered on warfare, this is an advantage because warfare is not a phenomenon that can fruitfully be considered apart from socio-cultural phenomena.

Tokovinine (2013b) has identified toponyms that may be linked to specific locales within Maya cities and towns, and his research leaves little question regarding the importance of power of place in Maya narratives and indeed in Maya life. Identifying place names seems not to be without problems; for example, Oox-kul, one of the names associated with "Sky Witness" who attacked Palenque, lacks, according to Tokovinine, the morphological attributes of a toponym and does not appear outside the context of the Kanu'l lords. It is possible that it was once a toponym, perhaps even a narrowly circumscribed one, but that it became a title, although this would be difficult to prove on present evidence. I mention it because the use of these names over time, whatever their origin, is likely to reflect changing hierarchical relationships among lords and rulers, and the stimulus to such changes is as likely conflict as anything else.

Tokovinine highlights that the most frequent land categories are *kab* and *ch'een*, with the latter referring to places that are considered "holy" or special to particular lineages and are linked to ancestral grounds and the former referring more broadly to people or places under the sway of a particular ruler or lineage. Places are not usually classified as *kab*, but *kab* may belong to places in the way social and political entities can be associated with places. This seems to me to imply strongly that even where places can be identified, they are intimately linked to people, which reinforces the idea that the taking of territory or land per se was not visualized or actualized as a dynamic in Maya conflict.

Ch'ahkaj may refer, based on Tokovinine's description, to an effect of conflict rather than to conflict itself. This would explain its dissociation from military victory. It is an enigmatic term and may have to do with the abrupt ending or curtailing of the power of a lineage or the manner in which such an ending occurred. "War" may have been only one of the possible conditions under which *ch'ahkaj* could occur; alternative conditions might have been other socially sanctioned categories of competition or conflict. With *jubuuy*, the implication (my suggestion and not Tokovinine's) is that a large number of the enemy lords were captured—hence the phenomenon of a "fall" or "toppling" of the rule of a king—so that the community would have had to undergo considerable restructuring at the hands of the victors.

IT'S A FAMILY AFFAIR

Let us consider for the moment the possibility that place names and people's names may not be entirely distinguishable from each other. As in the cases of the royal houses of Europe, place names can be family names, individuals can be named after places, and reference to places may reflect history rather than geography (see discussion in Martin 2014, 207–211). A good example is one of the oldest royal houses of Europe, the House of Wettin (Helbig 1980). "Wettin" in the "House of Wettin" refers both to a place (or at least a "mythical" place in that it was once long ago a municipality but is now a town) and to a dynasty. In this particular case, the family who ultimately built the dynasty originated in a place called "Wettin" in what is now Germany, and they came to be called "Wettins." Through time (they ruled for almost a millennium), the title "Wettin" did not come close to covering the territories over which the family had power. In 1422 CE, one of the Wettins, Frederick IV, received the Duchy of Saxe-Wittenberg from the then-emperor. Frederick's title had been Frederick IV of the House of Wettin, Margrave of Meissen, and Landgrave of Thuringia, but with the new duchy he became Frederic I, Elector of Saxony. What is interesting is that Frederick used the Saxony title and applied it to all of his domains, even those that were in Thuringia. He took this step because the Saxony title was a ducal title, the most prestigious title the family possessed; all family members and their descendants used the title, even though many of them held land (or had rights to resources from land) that was in Thuringia and not in Saxony. We can imagine that it gets even more complicated through time as titles are passed on and lands are split between sons.

Being able to read the proper nouns in any text (titles, names, dynasties, houses, or places) is only a beginning. Whether a noun is a title or a place or a "house" or some or all of these things can only become known as more knowledge is accumulated regarding local and regional histories. Titles do not always represent control of place; for example, the title of "Elector" in the case I have described meant that the titleholder had a vote in the election of the Holy Roman Emperor. Another fascinating example is "Duchy," a term used almost exclusively in Europe. Apparently, duchies are no longer sovereign, meaning that the title of "Duke" does not come with rule of a territory (although it can come with rights to income), except in the single case of the Grand Duchy of Luxembourg. The Duchy of Cornwall generates income for the Duke (the Prince of Wales) but he has no political power in or over Cornwall. What can we learn from these examples? We need simply to keep in mind how complex the sociopolitical landscape can be. More knowledge can only come from more texts, but we should nonetheless continue to ask questions based on a wide range of possibilities, some of them generated by known histories of ruling families elsewhere in the world. How many Classic-period lineages owed their prestige and economic clout to claims of relationship to founding lineages? Were various individuals and families—including perhaps families outside the lowlands—scrambling since Formative times either to share rights through marriage or to acquire rights through conflict? Was social exclusion one of the strategies used by lowland dynasties to dominate access to resources and services? If so, was supporting a change in the rules of engagement a justifiable reaction?

HISTORY, CULTURE, AND EMPIRE

Several points have been made about the passage of time and its potentially confounding effect on our attempt to understand terms that refer to people, to the claims they make through their titles, and to the ways they describe their actions or achievements. Culture and beliefs were also factors; if combatants did not share cultural values, they might not focus on the etiquette of titles or at least on the etiquette of the rules of the enemy. In some cases, different sorts of conflict or competition, and hence references to conflict, competition, or places, may have depended on the cultural practices and values of who was fighting. Our use of the term *Maya* is balanced in favor of an expectation of uniformity. It also encourages us to think about who or what was "foreign" strictly in terms of places, when long-term family and lineage ties may have made foreigners of locals.

Nielsen's chapter (this volume) argues for the existence of a Teotihuacan empire, and his discussion encourages us to think deeply about Mesoamerican interaction. He describes Teotihuacan as an imperial state that held sway in the fourth and fifth centuries CE, and he is not alone (see Coe 2012, 30, 140). The reality that power was amassed by people and families who originated—or at least built a historical base—in the Central Mexican highlands is not doubted. The lack of an overarching political system structurally different from the cities it controlled and the absence of a state-managed economy or extensively managed territorial boundaries (Blanton et al. 1993, 17, 223–224) indicate that if Teotihuacan can be said to have ruled an empire, then, like the Aztec Empire, it was hegemonic, as Nielsen makes clear. The nature of Teotihuacan hegemony has been somewhat elusive in that military takeover has been harder to prove than cultural influence. Nielsen has added significantly to the data from Tikal and Copan on *entradas* by proposing that aspects of Teotihuacan iconography in some places in Mesoamerica—he uses El Rosario in Querétaro as an example—reflect military takeovers and not just Teotihuacan influence. Teotihuacan influence takes a number of forms—ceramics, architectural preferences, design styles, weaponry—and the significance of the presence of these features outside of Teotihuacan has long been a subject of debate (Braswell 2003a). Nielsen describes images of individuals who carry shields, darts, and flaming torches and who seem to be speaking or singing about war and death. He argues that the flaming torch signifies the installation of a new ruler, and its appearance in men's headdresses marks the presence of Teotihuacanos outside of Teotihuacan. His case is more detailed and subtle than I have represented it here, but the important point is that he sees the iconographic evidence he has marshaled as adding to the existing evidence for wider Teotihuacan military action and hence as support for the existence of a short-lived but powerful Teotihuacan empire.

His case is strong and closely argued, and if hegemons are defined as powers that seek dominance but not the establishment of boundaries around appropriated territory, then Teotihuacan fits the bill. My only comments are that references to "human sacrificial victims" should be reevaluated in light of the possibility that rules of engagement in warfare involved death by heart removal and that we consider that those who brought Teotihuacan culture and values—warriors or merchants or eligible marriage partners—to areas outside of Central Mexico may have come from "Teotihuacanized" families in the broader region rather than solely from Teotihuacan.

To address the question of the dynamics of such an empire, we would need to consider a number of points already discussed. The main one is that not just Maya but also Mesoamerican political systems were based on interpersonal obligations (taxes, tribute, income from commerce) rather than on direct annexation of territory and attendant resources. If the Central Mexicans were, in deeper history, originally migrants from regions to the north of the Valley of Mexico, their own power politics may have been different from what they found in Mesoamerica, but they would have been heavily influenced—particularly in order to access positions of power—by much older traditions already in place and developed earlier along the Gulf Coast. The imperial iconography described by Nielsen is distinctively "Teotihuacano" on the one hand—spearthrowers, darts, square shields—but the extensive use of shell in headdresses reflects influence from people with ready access to marine resources.

Like *Maya*, the term *Teotihuacano* can be a hindrance. Experimentally, we might consider erasing from our minds the idea of a Teotihuacan ruling family sending out sons in pursuit of empire and instead try to imagine Teotihuacan and its rulers over time. Whatever families were in power in Central Mexico, they had increasing numbers of descendants who married into other families—some from Teotihuacan itself, some from outlying cities, some perhaps from as far away as the Gulf Coast—representing the commercial reach of the great city. Perhaps at some point, most of the alliances close to home had already been made, which meant that new opportunities lay largely in venturing into territories farther afield. Those mentioned by Nielsen include Kaminaljuyu, Tikal, Copan, Guerrero, the Pacific Coast of Oaxaca, Monte Alban, Chiapas, southern Guatemala, Hidalgo, Querétaro, Guanajuato, and Michoacan. This spread alone suggests that we are looking at enterprising individuals or groups—and by this I mean warriors as well as merchants—and not an imperial army. Indications are that these individuals shared a range of cultural values that were manifested metaphorically in material things. Those noted by Nielsen are spearthrowers, darts, square shields, the shell-platelet headdress, a headdress with human hearts, back mirrors, and torches. Individuals who shared these cultural emblems and hence practices need not have been part of a united front, and in fact it is highly likely that they were not. Both Nielsen (2003, 251–253) and Filini (2004), among others, have observed that Teotihuacan's role appears to have had different levels of intensity in different places.

The idea that the Teotihuacan imprint results from the spread of individuals seeking fortune and power is strongly suggested by Nielsen's observation of the short-lived but widespread Teotihuacan phenomenon. If individuals, their retinues, and ultimately their (new) families and descendants were the "culprits" displaying Teotihuacan-related cultural symbols rather than individuals who represented state interests in seeking to widen territorial boundaries, then short-lived influence is just what we would expect. The trade, tribute, and commercial advantages acquired during this period of opportunity could well have continued for years. Residence of cultural Teotihuacanos in Oaxaca or Michoacan or at Tikal or Copan, as well as variation in their places or families of origin, would result in the selective display of images—even if most images were martial—and eventually the disappearance of some, but perhaps not all, of the Teotihuacan symbols that were characteristic of an earlier era in Central Mexico and its region of influence. The idea of individual or small-group acts of acquisition or aggression integrates well with Nielsen's suggestion that the symbol of the flaming torches represents a ceremony that legitimized new rule. As Nielsen proposes, the ceremony would have marked a point in time when resources and services supplied through tribute and taxes under the old order were redirected to the advantage of a new ruler or ruling order. Where the torch-headdress is displayed, as in the case of Yax Nuun Ahiin I at Tikal and as worn by the figure on the polychrome vessel from Michoacan, the power of its symbolism seems, over time, to derive from its use by descendants as a title rather than from its direct attribution to a Teotihuacan emissary.

Accoutrements such as dart throwers, darts, and shields certainly represent conflict, and it is difficult to deny that aggression figured in Teotihuacan's dominance. Nielsen quotes Hirth and Villaseñor (1981, 137), who draw a connection between Teotihuacan presence and areas of desirable resources. If rights to resources and trade were the goal, several methods are likely to have been used to bring about change in favor of the outsiders. Outsiders came with knowledge of their home territory and its commercial links and would have been very likely to maintain ties to people in Central Mexico or the Gulf Coast who circulated materials that would have been valued by Maya rulers and their families and were not accessible in Peten or Honduras. Marriage into a Maya ruling family was probably the most desirable option. Even if only trade connections were established in the first instance, it is hard to imagine that anyone hailing from Teotihuacan or the surrounding region who resided in a Maya community for any length of time would not have married locally. Trade connections with people from Central Mexico, the Gulf Coast, and other areas almost certainly preceded the better-known Teotihuacan connections recorded in texts, perhaps by many years. Consequently, whoever arrived at Tikal in the fourth century CE was not a total stranger (Stuart 2000).

By the fourth and fifth centuries CE, if local rulers chose for one reason or another to resist commercial intrusion of individuals or groups from Central Mexico, conflict may have been the only option, although the nature of the conflict leaves us with questions about rules of engagement. Adoption of Teotihuacan or Central Mexican symbolism—if not the result of marriage alliance in which the child took on the symbolism of the parent's culture—suggests not only that Maya (and other Mesoamerican) forces lost whatever battles were waged but also that they may have been forced to change their rules of martial engagement in the process, in which case new weapons, such as darts and spearthrowers, were adopted (Aoyama and Graham 2015). Although we might not expect the imagery used by conquerors to be internalized by the conquered, this would depend on how Mesoamerican groups interpreted victory and loss. Christenson (this volume) provides an example in the Tz'utujil adoption of Santiago and the Virgin Mary as protectors; he reports a conversation in which a traditional Tz'utujil priest admitted that Santiago and Mary were once foreigners but were now Tz'utujils and spoke only Tz'utujil.

Bey and Gallareta Negrón (this volume), like Nielsen, discuss militarism in art; in their case the region is the Puuc. They emphasize the great time depth of occupation in the Puuc region, especially the scale of Middle Formative architecture. They observe that some sites were "small," but perishable architecture was almost certainly an important element of towns and villages of the time, hence zones of occupation may have extended well beyond the recognized masonry-built cores. The implications of early settlement are, as the authors emphasize, that conflict would have had a role in the history of the region. Bey and Gallareta Negrón put to rest—one hopes permanently—the idea that the Puuc rise was made possible by collapse in the south. Instead, post-800 CE growth reflects internal processes that included conflict with roots in the Formative. In addition, the rulership thought to have evolved in the ninth century CE actually manifested itself in the early eighth century CE—before the purported migration of southerners.

SOCIALLY SANCTIONED KILLING

It seems to have become almost universally accepted, as articulated by Hernandez and Palka (this volume), that in addition to being a way to increase power, war was also "a source of captives that were central to ancient Maya religion, which required the sacrifice of human blood to spiritual forces" (see also Schele and Miller 1986, 14). Part of the wide support in our field for the idea that the Maya practiced human sacrifice comes from the very fact that we accord viability to the term *religion*. We agree that something called "religion" subsumes motivations that can be heuristically separated from politics or economics or greed (Graham 2011, 66–71) and then use the term to subsume a practice that *we*, following the sixteenth-century CE friars, see as "human sacrifice." There is no known ancient Mayan (or Nahuatl) word or combination of words that can be definitively interpreted as human sacrifice (Graham and Golson 2006); neither did the Maya conceptualize "religion" as a category (Pharo 2007). We are so accustomed to "religion" as a concept that we do not question its use, yet an argument can be made that the term arose in the West in a growing multicultural milieu as a means of categorizing and making sense of the practices of an "other." This does not make it wrong so much as historically and culturally contingent.

Competition in the Maya world can be assumed to have materialized, at least in one form, as conflict, particularly war. War involves socially sanctioned killing, which is not unusual globally today or in history. War provides, in fact, the most widespread rationale for killing people without being accused of a crime. To remove any room for moral doubt, societal leaders bring in a god or a fight against "evil," and killing becomes a duty. If we can for a moment get out of our heads that there was ever any such thing as human sacrifice (the socially sanctioned killing of an individual to please or placate gods [see Watts et al. 2016]), we might see that textual and pictorial evidence presents a good case for tying the fate of captives among the Maya to the social sanctioning of killing as part of conflict in wars over resources. Add to this the points made above about resource appropriation being dependent on tribute, taxes, and services historically owed to individuals (rather than based on direct control or ownership of land), and the common depictions of captives and captive taking are support for the argument that killing people was a sanctioned consequence of conflict over resources, the rights to which were embedded in individual entitlements—all almost certainly elites who had histories (through marriage or wars) of accumulating or appropriating such entitlements. Such conflict was most often played out on the field as war but may have also been played out in certain circumstances on the ball court, as discussed above and suggested by Koontz (this volume) in his emphasis on the importance of the way the ballgame and warfare articulated along the Mexican Gulf Coast.

Koontz notes that much attention has been given to ball court iconography associated with decapitation. He draws attention to a panel in El Tajín's main ball court that depicts a rite that relates to martial matters. The panel has a supernatural emerging with three spears from a zoomorphic mouth and handing the spears to a human in the center of the composition. Koontz interprets this as supernatural donation of weaponry, but an alternative or complementary interpretation is that it symbolizes the gods' legitimization and hence social sanctioning of killing in war.

Koontz also discusses the distinctive war banner or standard associated with El Tajín. Rites involving the display of banners or standards, such as the ballgame, are thought to have been linked to the return of a successful military expedition. Koontz presents a strong argument for the presence of banner rituals at both elite and non-elite levels, involving the plaza of the Pyramid of the Niches and its associated architecture, and suggests that such rituals reflect more than one level of military organization. He admits that such an association cannot yet be proved, but military organization was almost certainly complex, and banner rites and their associated iconography seem excellent candidates for generating viable hypotheses about levels of military organization and their significance. What is also intriguing in his discussion is the linking of the imagery of an individual holding a banner on an Early Classic stela with Teotihuacan. Thus Teotihuacan or individuals who shared the cultural values of Teotihuacan loom large as the source of a particular kind or kinds of conflict practices.

WHERE DO WE GO FROM HERE?

This volume explores Maya conflict, often through explicit reference to the epigraphic and iconographic record, and hence is an attempt at an emic perspective on warfare. It may then be asked why I, an archaeologist, am contributing, for I am by no means an epigrapher or an art historian. The editors specifically intended to include contributions that drew on archaeological materials, ancient texts, and images to provide a view of conflict from the Maya perspective. I am not Maya, but I have attempted, based on the points made by contributors to the volume, to approach warfare by asking the most basic questions about why people fight in groups, why they fight other groups, what constitutes winning, and how all this meshes with people's life goals such as prosperity, wealth, and, in some cases, power.

I draw from the chapters in the volume to propose several ways forward. In the first instance, we should continue to broaden our ideas about what constituted conflict and competition in societies and cultures other than our own. Turning to Asian warfare would be a good start because at least in what are known today as China and Japan, the term *religion* did not exist until contact with the West (Bowie 2000, 22n23), and the role of the warrior and his defeat or capture have significance very different from such roles in Western warfare. Literature on South Asian warfare includes studies of a range of social, political, strategic, and individual motivations behind fighting, which are often simplified in later accounts as "religious" (Gommans 2002; Subrahmanyam 2012). Study of the region might provide models that would stimulate new questions about Maya warfare.

Perhaps the most important way forward would be to cease employing the terms *sacrifice* or *human sacrifice* as if they were explanatory. If we know that an individual was killed, we should simply use the word *killed* and cite the evidence. In many circumstances we will find, as has been the case in cave research, that there is often no clear evidence that people were killed, let alone killed for the purpose of placating a deity (Wrobel, Helmke, and Freiwald 2014). Use of the term *human sacrifice* brings with it assumptions that are rarely questioned, and elaborate scenarios are built on such assumptions (e.g., Girard 1972; Watts et al. 2016). To provide an example of the difference a word or two can make, the statement "the practice of sacrifice, dismemberment, and display of war captives is well documented in the ethnohistoric literature" (Berryman 2007, 380) could as accurately be expressed as: the practice of killing those captured in conflict and dismembering and displaying their body parts is well documented in the ethnohistoric literature.

I have drawn in this chapter on archaeological evidence, texts, and images to propose that the killing so widely described as human sacrifice was sanctioned instead as an inevitable part of what we today would call war. The fact that the killing did not take place on the "battlefield" does not exclude it from the category of conflict or war; it simply excludes it from our own metaphors. Once "human sacrifice" is laid aside and we take on more fully the idea (as hypothesis) that wealth is embedded in individuals and their relationships—including the tribute and taxes owed to them—and once we have explored non-Western models of what it means to be captured in war, we can begin to look at the naming and depictions of captives primarily as a reflection of economic and political goals. This is not to deny that some sort of spiritual or otherworldly underpinning was involved but only that "religion" was the icing on a cake that was already baked.

Although I do not have expertise in deciphering texts, it may not be out of order to emphasize that despite the common language of Maya inscriptions, we are likely to be dealing with groups in the lowlands that self-identified not as "Maya" but according to their home city, town, or village (Restall 1997); according to their family connections or group affiliations; or according to their status in society. There were probably a number of bases for hostilities. Without explicit details in texts, it is difficult to know how to improve analytical strategies, except to keep in mind that cultural variation in either space or time is possibly responsible for variable references to conflict or its consequences (see chapter by Tokovinine, this volume). Thinking about rules of engagement is also important. Where groups agreed on rules of engagement, we might expect texts (perhaps upholding a tradition in titles) and archaeology (continuing construction in cities and common weaponry) to reflect this; however, rules were subject to change as the result of contacts with new people and cultures. In the case of culture clash through technology or tactics, the side that has the stronger rationale for killing or disabling the larger number of people—an area in which supernatural and moral sanctioning looms large—will come out ahead. Thus older cultural traditions in fighting must either mesh with the new or be rejected, a process that continues in our own times. We can therefore enrich our understanding of Maya warfare from texts, iconography, and archaeology by continuing to broaden our ideas about what has come to constitute conflict and competition in our own culture, society, and history.

NOTE

1. "Of course you realize, this means war!" Bugs Bunny, *Bully for Bugs*, 1953. Warner Bros., Looney Tunes, directed by Chuck Jones, written by Michael Maltese.

References

Adams, R.E.W. 1999. *Rio Azul: An Ancient Maya City*. Norman: University of Oklahoma Press.

Aguero, A., and A. Daneels. 2009. "Playing Ball—Competition as a Political Tool." In *Blood and Beauty: Organized Violence in the Art and Architecture of Mesoamerica and Central America*, ed. H. Orr and R. Koontz, 117–138. Los Angeles: Cotsen Institute of Archaeology, University of California.

Aimers, J. J. 2009. "Bring It On: Using Ceramic Systems at Lamanai." *Research Reports in Belizean Archaeology* 6: 245–252.

Aimers, J. J., and E. Graham. 2013. "Type-Variety on Trial: Experiments in Classification and Meaning Using Ceramic Assemblages from Lamanai, Belize." In *Ancient Maya Pottery: Classification, Analysis, and Interpretation*, ed. J. J. Aimers, 91–106. Gainesville: University Press of Florida.

Aimers, J. J., and H. R. Haines. 2011. "The Pottery of Ka'Kabish." Paper presented at the 76th Annual Meeting of the Society for American Archaeology, Sacramento, CA, March 30–April 3.

DOI: 10.5876/9781607328872.c013

Alach, Z. 2011. "The New Aztecs: Ritual and Restraint in Contemporary Western Military Operations." *Advancing Strategic Thought Series*. DTIC Document. http://oai.dtic.mil/oai?verb=getRecord&metadataPrefix=html&identifies=ADA547492. Accessed October 20, 2014.

Alvarado, P. de. 1924. *An Account of the Conquest of Guatemala in 1524*. Ed. S. J. Mackie. New York: Cortes Society.

Ambrosino, J. N., T. Ardren, and T. W. Stanton. 2003. "The History of Warfare at Yaxuna." In *Ancient Mesoamerican Warfare*, ed. K. M. Brown and T. W. Stanton, 109–124. Walnut Creek, CA: Altamira.

Andres, C. R. 2005. "Building Negotiation: Architecture and Sociopolitical Transformation at Chau Hiix, Lamanai, and Altun Ha, Belize." PhD dissertation, Indiana University, Bloomington.

Andrews, E. W. 1970. *Balankanche, Throne of the Tiger Priest*. Middle American Research Institute Publication 32. New Orleans, LA: Tulane University.

Andrews, E. W., G. J. Bey III, and C. Gunn. 2018. "The Earliest Ceramics in Yucatan." In *Pathways to Complexity: New Ideas on the Rise of Maya Civilization*, ed. K. M. Brown and G. J. Bey III, 49–86. Gainesville: University of Florida Press.

Angulo Villaseñor, J. 1987. "The Chalcatzingo Reliefs: An Iconographic Analysis." In *Ancient Chalcatzingo*, ed. D. C. Grove, 132–158. Austin: University of Texas Press.

Anonymous. 1935 [ca. 1700]. *Isagoge Histórica Apologética de las Indias Occidentales*, vol. 8. Guatemala City: Biblioteca Goathemala.

Aoyama, K. 1999. *Ancient Maya State, Urbanism, Exchange, and Craft Specialization: Chipped Stone Evidence from the Copán Valley and the La Entrada Region, Honduras*. University of Pittsburgh Memoirs in Latin American Archaeology 12. Pittsburgh, PA: Department of Archaeology, University of Pittsburgh.

Aoyama, K. 2005. "Classic Maya Warfare and Weapons: Spear, Dart, and Arrow Points of Aguateca and Copan." *Ancient Mesoamerica* 16 (2): 291–304.

Aoyama, K., and E. Graham. 2015. "Ancient Maya Warfare: Exploring the Significance of Lithic Variation in Maya Weaponry." *Lithics: Journal of the Lithic Studies Society* 36: 5–17.

Ara, D. d. 1986. *Vocabulario de Lengua Tzeldal Según el Orden de Copanabastla*. Fuentes para el Estudio de la Cultura Maya 4. México, DF: Universidad Nacional Autónoma de México.

Ardren, T. 2009. "Twenty-First Century Reinventions of Alexander, Xerxes, and Jaguar Paw: A Critique of Apocalypto and Popular Media Depictions of the Past." *Archaeological Review from Cambridge* 21: 149–158.

Arkush, E., and C. Stanish. 2005. "Interpreting Conflict in the Ancient Andes: Implications for the Archaeology of Warfare." *Current Anthropology* 46 (1): 3–28.

Armillas, P. 1951. "Mesoamerican Fortifications." *Antiquity* 25 (98): 77–86.

Ashmore, W. 1991. "Site-Planning Principles and Concepts of Directionality among the Ancient Maya." *Latin American Antiquity* 2 (3): 199–226.

Astor-Aguilera, M. A. 2010. *The Maya World of Communicating Objects: Quadripartite Crosses, Trees, and Stones*. Albuquerque: University of New Mexico Press.

Avruch, K. 1998. *Culture and Conflict Resolution*. Washington, DC: United States Institute of Peace Press.

Awe, J. J. 1992. "Dawn in the Land between the Rivers: Formative Occupation at Cahal Pech, Belize and Its Implications for Preclassic Occupation in the Central Maya Lowlands." PhD dissertation, University of London, London, England.

Bailey, J. W. 1972. "Map of Texupa (Oaxaca, 1579): A Study of Form and Meaning." *Art Bulletin* 54 (4): 452–472.

Baird, E. T. 1989. "Stars and War at Cacaxtla." In *Mesoamerica after the Decline of Teotihuacan ad 700–900*, ed. J. C. Berlo and R. A. Diehl, 105–122. Washington, DC: Dumbarton Oaks Research Library and Collection.

Balkansky, A. K., S. A. Kowalewski, V. Perez Rodriguez, T. J. Pluckhahn, C. A. Smith, L. R. Striver, D. Beliaev, J. F. Chamblee, V. Y. Heredia Espinoza, and R. Santos Perez. 2000. "Archaeological Survey in the Mixteca Alta of Oaxaca, Mexico." *Journal of Field Archaeology* 27 (4): 365–389.

Bardawil, L. 1976. "The Principal Bird Deity in Maya Art: An Iconographic Study of Form and Meaning." In *The Art, Iconography, and Dynastic History of Palenque, part 3*, ed. M. Greene Robertson, 181–194. Pebble Beach, CA: Pre-Columbian Art Research, Robertson Louis Stevenson School.

Barrera Rubio, A. 1980. "Mural Paintings of the Puuc Region in Yucatán." In *Third Palenque Round Table, 1978, part 2*, ed. M. Greene Robertson, 173–182. Austin: University of Texas Press.

Barrera Vásquez, A., J. R. Bastarrachea Manzano, W. Brito Sansores, R. Vermont Salas, D. Dzul Góngora, and D. Dzul Poot. 1995. *Diccionario Maya: Maya-Español, Español-Maya*. 3rd ed. México, DF: Editorial Porrúa.

Bassie-Sweet, K. 1991. *From the Mouth of the Dark Cave*. Norman: University of Oklahoma Press.

Bassie-Sweet, K. 1996. *At the Edge of the World*. Norman: University of Oklahoma Press.

Bassie-Sweet, K. 2008. *Maya Sacred Geography and the Creator Deities*. Norman: University of Oklahoma Press.

Bassie-Sweet, K. 2011. "Change Your God, Change Your Luck." Paper presented at the 2011 Chacmool Archaeological Conference, University of Calgary, Calgary, Canada, November 9–13.

Bassie-Sweet, K. 2012. "Thunderbolt and Meteor War Gods of the Maya." Paper presented at the 2012 Chacmool Archaeological Conference, University of Calgary, Calgary, Canada, November 8–11.

Bassie-Sweet, K. 2013. "The Iconography of the Gods from the Popol Vuh and Classic Period Maya Art." Workshop presented at the Minnesota Maya Society, Hamline University, Minneapolis.

Bassie-Sweet, K., and N. A. Hopkins. 2018. *Maya Narrative Arts*. Boulder: University Press of Colorado.

Bassie-Sweet, K., N. A. Hopkins, and J. K. Josserand. 2012. "Narrative Structure and the Drum Major Headdress." In *Parallel Worlds: Genre, Discourse, and Poetics in Contemporary, Colonial, and Classic Maya Literature*, ed. K. M. Hull and M. D. Carrasco, 195–220. Boulder: University Press of Colorado.

Bassie-Sweet, K., N. A. Hopkins, R. M. Laughlin, and A. Brizuela Casimir. 2015. *The Ch'ol Maya of Chiapas*. Norman: University of Oklahoma Press.

Baugh, R. A. 1998. "Atlatl Dynamics." *Lithic Technology* 23 (1): 31–41.

Becquelin, P. 1994. "La Civilizacion Puuc Vista desde le Región de Xculuc." In *Hidden among the Hills: Maya Archaeology of the Northwest Yucatan Peninsula*, ed. H. J. Prem, 58–70. Acta Mesoamericana 7. Möckmühl, Germany: Verlag von Flemming.

Becquelin, P., and D. Michelet. 1994. "Demografia en la Zona Puuc: El Recurso del Método." *Latin American Antiquity* 5: 289–311.

Bell, E. E., M. A. Canuto, and R. J. Sharer, eds. 2004. *Understanding Early Classic Copan*. Philadelphia: University of Pennsylvania Museum of Archaeology and Anthropology.

Bell, E. E., R. J. Sharer, L. P. Traxler, D. W. Sedat, C. W. Carrelli, and L. A. Grant. 2004. "Tombs and Burials in the Early Classic Acropolis at Copan." In *Understanding Early Classic Copan*, ed. E. E. Bell, M. A. Canuto, and R. J. Sharer, 131–157. Philadelphia: University of Pennsylvania Museum of Archaeology and Anthropology.

Berdan, F. F., and P. R. Anawalt. 1992. *The Codex Mendoza*. Berkeley: University of California Press.

Berdan, F. F., R. E. Blanton, E. Hill Boone, M. G. Hodge, M. E. Smith, and E. Umberger, eds. 1996. *Aztec Imperial Strategies*. Washington, DC: Dumbarton Oaks Research Library and Collection.

Berdan, F. F., and M. E. Smith. 1996. "Imperial Strategies and Core-Periphery Relations." In *Aztec Imperial Strategies*, ed. F. F. Berdan, R. E. Blanton, E. Hill Boone, M. G. Hodge, M. E. Smith, and E. Umberger, 209–217. Washington, DC: Dumbarton Oaks Research Library and Collection.

Berlo, J. C. 1984. *Teotihuacan Art Abroad: A Study of Metropolitan Style and Provincial Transformation in Incensario Workshops*. BAR International Series 199. Oxford, England: British Archaeological Reports.

Berrin, K., and E. Pasztory. 1993. *Teotihuacan: Art from the City of the Gods*. London: Thames and Hudson.

Berryman, C. A. 2007. "Captive Sacrifice and Trophy-Taking among the Ancient Maya." In *The Taking and Displaying of Human Body Parts as Trophies by Amerindians*, ed. R. J. Chacon and D. H. Dye, 377–399. New York: Springer.

Beutelspacher, C. R. 1994. *A Guide to Mexico's Butterflies and Moths*. México, DF: Minutiae Mexicana.

Bey, G. J., III. 2003. "The Role of Ceramics in the Study of Conflict in Maya Archaeology." In *Ancient Mesoamerican Warfare*, ed. M. K. Brown and T. W. Stanton, 19–30. Walnut Creek, CA: Altamira.

Bey, G. J., III, C. A. Hanson, and W. M. Ringle. 1997. "Classic to Postclassic at Ek Balam, Yucatan: Architectural and Ceramic Evidence for Defining the Transition." *Latin American Antiquity* 8: 237–254.

Bey, G. J., III, and W. M. Ringle. 1989. "The Myth of the Center." Paper presented at the 54th Annual Meeting of the Society for American Archaeology, Atlanta, GA, April 5–9.

Bidwell, P. 2008. "Did Hadrian's Wall Have a Wall-Walk?" In *Understanding Hadrian's Wall*, ed. P. Bidwell, 129–143. South Shields, England: Arbeia Society.

Biro, P. 2005. *Sak Tz'i' in the Classic Period Hieroglyphic Inscriptions*. Mesoweb. www .mesoweb.com/articles/biro/SakTzi.pdf. Accessed October 21, 2014.

Blanton, R. E., and G. Feinman. 1984. "The Mesoamerican World System." *American Anthropologist* 86 (3): 673–682.

Blanton, R. E., S. A. Kowalewski, G. M. Feinman, and L. Finsten. 1993. *Ancient Mesoamerica: A Comparison of Change in Three Regions*. Cambridge, England: Cambridge University Press.

Blom, F. 1934. "Short Summary of Recent Explorations in the Ruins of Uxmal, Yucatan." In *Proceedings of the 24th International Congress of Americanists*, 55–59. Hamburg, Germany: International Congress of Americanists.

Bolz, I. 1975. *Sammlung Ludwig Altamerika*. Recklinghausen, Germany: Verlag Aurel Bongers.

Boone, E. H., ed. 1984. *Ritual Human Sacrifice in Mesoamerica: A Conference at Dumbarton Oaks, October 13th and 14th, 1979*. Washington, DC: Dumbarton Oaks Research Library and Collection.

Boone, E. H. 2000. "Venerable Place of Beginnings: The Aztec Understanding of Teotihuacan." In *Mesoamerica's Heritage: From Teotihuacan to the Aztecs*, ed. D. Carrasco, L. Jones, and S. Sessions, 371–395. Boulder: University Press of Colorado.

Boone, E. H. 2008. *Stories in Red and Black: Pictorial Histories of the Aztec and Mixtec*. Austin: University of Texas Press.

Boot, E. 2004. *Vocabulary in the Ch'olti' Language: A Transcription of the "Bocabulario Grande" by Fray Francisco Morán (1695)*. Foundation for the Advancement of Mesoamerican Studies, Inc. http://www.famsi.org/mayawriting/dictionary/boot/cholti _moran1695_revised.pdf. Accessed January 30, 2018.

Bove, F. J., and S. Medrano Busto. 2003. "Teotihuacan, Militarism, and Pacific Guatemala." In *The Maya and Teotihuacan: Reinterpreting Early Classic Maya Interaction*, ed. G. E. Braswell, 45–79. Austin: University of Texas Press.

Bowie, F. 2000. *The Anthropology of Religion*. Oxford, England: Blackwell.

Bowles, S. 2009. "Did Warfare among Ancestral Hunter-Gatherers Affect the Evolution of Human Social Behaviors?" *Science* 324: 1293–1298.

Brady, J. E., and P. R. Colas. 2005. "Nikte' Mo' Scattered Fire in the Cave of K'ab Chante': Epigraphic and Archaeological Evidence for Cave Desecration in Ancient Maya Warfare." In *Stone Houses and Earth Lords: Maya Religion in the Cave Context*, ed. K. M. Prufer and J. E. Brady, 149–166. Boulder: University Press of Colorado.

Brambila Paz, R., and A. Ma. Crespo. 2002. "El Centro Norte de Mesoamérica: Su Organización Territorial en el Clásico." In *Ideología y Política a Través de Materiales, Imágenes y Símbolos: Memoria de la Primera Mesa Redonda de Teotihuacan*, ed. M.E.R. Gallut, 547–562. México, DF: Consejo Nacional Para la Cultura y las Artes, Instituto Nacional de Antropología e Historia.

Braniff Cornejo, B. 2000. "A Summary of the Archaeology of North-Central Mesoamerica: Guanajuato, Querétaro, and San Luis Potosí." In *Greater Mesoamerica: The Archaeology of West and Northwest Mexico*, ed. M. S. Foster and S. Gorenstein, 35–42. Salt Lake City: University of Utah Press.

Braswell, G. E. 2003a. "Introduction: Reinterpreting Early Classic Interaction." In *The Maya and Teotihuacan: Reinterpreting Early Classic Maya Interaction*, ed. G. E. Braswell, 1–43. Austin: University of Texas Press.

Braswell, G. E. 2003b. "Understanding Early Classic Interaction between Kaminaljuyu and Central Mexico." In *The Maya and Teotihuacan: Reinterpreting Early Classic Maya Interaction*, ed. G. E. Braswell, 105–142. Austin: University of Texas Press.

Braswell, G. E., ed. 2003c. *The Maya and Teotihuacan*. Austin: University of Texas Press.

Braswell, G. E., I. Paap, and M. D. Glascock. 2011. "The Obsidian and Ceramics of the Puuc Region: Chronology, Lithic Procurement, and Production at Xkipche, Yucatan, Mexico." *Ancient Mesoamerica* 22 (1): 1–20.

Bricker, V. R. 1981. *The Indian Christ, the Indian King: The Historical Substrate of Maya Myth and Ritual*. Austin: University of Texas Press.

Briggs, C. L. 1996. *Disorderly Discourse: Narrative, Conflict, and Inequality*. Oxford, England: Oxford University Press.

Brinton, D. G. 1894. "Nagualism: A Study in Native American Folk-Lore and History." *Proceedings of the American Philosophical Society* 33 (144): 11–73.

Brown, M. K., and J. F. Garber. 2003. "Evidence of Conflict during the Middle Formative in the Maya Lowlands: A View from Blackman Eddy, Belize." In *Ancient Mesoamerican Warfare*, ed. M. K. Brown and T. W. Stanton, 91–108. Walnut Creek, CA: Altamira.

Brown, M. K., and T. W. Stanton, eds. 2003. *Ancient Mesoamerican Warfare*. Walnut Creek, CA: Altamira.

Brumfiel, E. M., and J. W. Fox, eds. 1994. *Factional Competition and Political Development in the New World*. Cambridge, England: Cambridge University Press.

Bullard, W. R. 1970. "Topoxté: A Postclassic Maya Site in Peten, Guatemala." In *Monographs and Papers in Maya Archaeology*, ed. W. R. Bullard, 245–307. Papers of the Peabody Museum of Archaeology and Ethnology, vol. 61. Cambridge, MA: Harvard University Press.

Burch, E. S., Jr. 1974. "Eskimo Warfare in Northwest Alaska." *Anthropological Papers of the University of Alaska* 16: 1–14.

Byland, B. E. 1980. "Political and Economic Evolution in the Tamazulapan Valley, Mixteca Alta, Oaxaca, Mexico: A Regional Approach." PhD dissertation, Pennsylvania State University, State College.

Byland, B. E., and J.M.D. Pohl. 1994. *In the Realm of 8 Deer*. Norman: University of Oklahoma Press.

Cabrera Castro, R. 1995. "Atetelco." In *La Pintura Mural Prehispánica en México, 1: Teotihuacan*, vol. 1, ed. B. de la Fuente, 202–256. México, DF: Universidad Nacional Autónoma de México.

Cabrera Castro, R. 1996. "Caracteres Glíficos Teotihuacanos en un Piso de La Ventilla." In *La Pintura Mural Prehispánica en México, 1: Teotihuacan*, vol. 2, ed. B. de la Fuente, 401–427. México, DF: Universidad Nacional Autónoma de México.

Calnek, E. 1988. *Highland Chiapas before the Spanish Conquest*. Papers of the New World Archaeological Foundation, vol. 55. Provo, UT: Brigham Young University.

Campbell, J. C. 1992. "Wife-Battering: Cultural Contexts versus Social Sciences." In *Sanctions and Society: Cultural Perspectives on the Beating of Wives*, ed. D. A. Counts, J. A. Brown, and J. C. Campbell, 229–249. Boulder: Westview.

Carballo, D. M., and T. Pluckhahn. 2007. "Transportation Corridors and Political Evolution in Highland Mesoamerica: Settlement Analyses Incorporating GIS for Northern Tlaxcala, Mexico." *Journal of Anthropological Archaeology* 26: 607–629.

Cárdenas García, E. 2013. "Mesoamérica y la Tradición Cultural del Occidente Mexicano: Una Introducción a la Arqueología Regional." *Arqueología Mexicana* 21 (123): 29–36.

Carlsen, R. S. 1996. "Social Organization and Disorganization in Santiago Atitlán, Guatemala." *Ethnology* 2 (1): 141–160.

Carlsen, R. S. 1997. *The War for the Heart and Soul of a Highland Maya Town*. Austin: University of Texas Press.

Carmack, R. M. 1973. *Quichean Civilization*. Berkeley: University of California Press.

Carmack, R. M. 1981. *The Quiche Mayas of Utatlan: The Evolution of a Highland Kingdom in Highland Guatemala*. Norman: University of Oklahoma Press.

Carmack, R. M., and J. L. Mondloch. 1983. *Título de Totonicapán*. México, DF: Universidad Nacional Autónoma de México.

Carman, J., ed. 1997. *Material Harm: Archaeological Studies of War and Violence*. Glasgow, Scotland: Cruithne.

Carmean, K., N. Dunning, and J. K. Kowalski. 2004. "High Times in the Hill Country: A Perspective from the Terminal Classic Puuc Region." In *Terminal Classic in the Maya Lowlands: Collapse, Transition, and Transformation*, ed. A. A. Demarest, P. M. Rice, and D. S. Rice, 424–449. Boulder: University Press of Colorado.

Carot, P. 2001. *Le Site de Loma Alta, Lac de Zacapu, Michoacan, Mexique*. BAR International Series 920. Oxford, England: British Archaeological Reports.

Carot, P. 2013. "La Larga Historia Purépecha." In *Miradas Renovadas al Occidente Indígena de México*, ed. M.-A. Hers, 133–214. México, DF: Universidad Nacional Autónoma de México / Instituto Nacional de Antropología e Historia.

Carot, P., and M.-A. Hers. 2011. "De Teotihuacan al Cañon de Chaco: Nueva Perspectiva sobre las Relaciones entre Mesoamérica y el Suroeste de los Estados Unidos." *Anales del Instituto Investigaciones Estéticas* 33 (98): 5–53.

Carrasco, D. 2008. "Introduction: The Dream of the Conquistador and a Book of Desire and Destruction." In *The History of the Conquest of New Spain*, by B. Diaz del Castillo, ed. D. Carrasco, xi–xxvii. Albuquerque: University of New Mexico Press.

Caso, A. 1938. *Exploraciones en Oaxaca, Quinta y Sexta Temporadas, 1936–1937*. México, DF: Instituto Panamericano e Geografía e Historia.

Caso, A. 1964. *Interpretation of the Codex Selden 3135 (A. 2)*. México, DF: Sociedad Mexicana de Antropología.

Caso Barrera, L., and M. Aliphat Fernández. 2002. "Organización Polítca de los Itzas Desde el Postclásico Hasta 1702." *Historia Mexicana* 51 (4): 713–748.

Castañeda López, C. 2008. "Plazuelas, Guanajuato." *Arqueología Mexicana* 16 (92): 44–47.

Chacon, R. J., and D. H. Dye, eds. 2007. *The Taking and Displaying of Human Body Parts as Trophies by Amerindians*. New York: Springer.

Chacon, R. J., and R. G. Mendoza. 2007. *Latin American Indigenous Warfare and Ritual Violence*. Tucson: University of Arizona Press.

Chagnon, N. A. 1988. "Life Histories, Blood Revenge, and Warfare in a Tribal Population." *Science* 239 (4843): 985–992.

Chagnon, N. A. 2009. *Yᴁnomamö*. 6th ed. Belmont, CA: Wadsworth.

Chapman, J. 1994. "Destruction of a Common Heritage: The Archaeology of War in Croatia, Bosnia, and Hercegovina." *Antiquity* 68 (258): 120–126.

Chase, A. F. 1991. "Cycles of Time: Caracol in the Maya Realm." In *Sixth Palenque Round Table, 1986*, ed. M. Greene Robertson and V. M. Fields, 32–42. Norman: University of Oklahoma Press.

Chase, A. F., and D. Z. Chase. 1989. "The Investigation of Classic Period Maya Warfare at Caracol, Belize." *Mayab* 5: 5–18.

Chase, A. F., and D. Z. Chase. 1996. "The Organization and Composition of Classic Lowland Maya Society: The View from Caracol, Belize." In *Eighth Palenque Round Table, 1993*, ed. M. J. Macri and J. McHargue, 213–222. San Francisco: Pre-Columbian Art Research Institute.

Chase, A. F., and D. Z. Chase. 1998. "Late Classic Maya Political Structure, Polity Size, and Warfare Arenas." In *Anatomía de una Civilización: Aproximaciones Interdisciplinarias a la Cultura Maya*, ed. A. C. Ruiz, M.Y.F. Marquínez, J.M.G. Campillo, M.J.I. Ponce de León, A. L. García-Gallo, and L.T.S. Castro, 11–30. Madrid, Spain: Sociedad Española de Estudios Mayas.

Chase, A. F., and D. Z. Chase. 2007. "Late Classic Ritual Variation in a Maya Community: Continued Investigation of Structure in and near Caracol's Epicenter, 2007 Field

Report of the Caracol Archaeological Project." Report submitted to the Institute of Archaeology, Belmopan, Belize.

Chase, A. F., D. Z. Chase, and M. E. Smith. 2009. "States and Empires in Ancient Mesoamerica." *Ancient Mesoamerica* 20 (2): 175–182.

Chase, D. Z. 1990. "The Invisible Maya: Population History and Archaeology at Santa Rita Corozal." In *Precolumbian Population History in the Maya Lowlands*, ed. T. P. Culbert and D. S. Rice, 199–214. Albuquerque: University of New Mexico Press.

Chase, D. Z., and A. F. Chase. 1988. *A Postclassic Perspective: Excavations at the Maya Site of Santa Rita Corozal, Belize*. Monograph 4. San Francisco: Pre-Columbian Art Research Institute.

Chase, D. Z., and A. F. Chase. 1998. "The Architectural Context of Caches, Burials, and Other Ritual Activities for the Classic Period Maya (as Reflected at Caracol, Belize)." In *Function and Meaning in Classic Maya Architecture*, ed. S. D. Houston, 300–332. Washington, DC: Dumbarton Oaks Research Library and Collection.

Chase, D. Z., and A. F. Chase. 2004. "Santa Rita Corozal: Twenty Years Later." *Research Reports in Belizean Archaeology* 1: 243–255.

Chase, D. Z., and A. F. Chase. 2005. "The Early Classic Period at Santa Rita Corozal: Issues of Hierarchy, Heterarchy, and Stratification in Northern Belize." *Research Reports in Belizean Archaeology* 1: 111–131.

Chase, D. Z., and A. F. Chase. 2011. "Ghosts amid the Ruins: Analyzing Relationships between the Living and the Dead among the Ancient Maya at Caracol, Belize." In *Living with the Dead: Mortuary Ritual in Mesoamerica*, ed J. L. Fitzsimmons and I. Shimada, 78–101. Tucson: University of Arizona Press.

Chavero, A. 1979. *El Lienzo de Tlaxcala*. México, DF: Innovacion.

Chávez Balderas, X. 2014. "Sacrifice at the Templo Mayor of Tenochtitlan and Its Role in Regards to Warfare." In *Embattled Bodies, Embattled Places: War in Pre-Columbian Mesoamerica and the Andes*, ed. A. Scherer and J. Verano, 173–199. Washington, DC: Dumbarton Oaks Research Library and Collection.

Cheek, C. D. 1977. "Teotihuacan Influence at Kaminaljuyu." In *Teotihuacan and Kaminaljuyu*, ed. W. T. Sanders and J. W. Michels, 441–452. University Park: Pennsylvania State University Press.

Cheetham, D. 2005. "Cunil: A Pre-Mamom Horizon in the Southern Maya Lowlands." In *New Perspectives on Formative Mesoamerican Cultures*, ed. T. G. Powis, 27–38. BAR International Series 1377. Oxford, England: British Archaeological Reports.

Chinchilla Mazariegos, O. F. 2006. *A Reading for the "Earth-Star" Verb in Ancient Maya Writing*, vol. 56. Barnardsville, NC: Center for Maya Research.

Christenson, A. J. 2007. *Popol Vuh: The Sacred Book of the Maya*. Norman: University of Oklahoma Press.

Christenson, A. J. n.d. *K'iche'-English Dictionary and Guide to Pronunciation of the K'iche'-Maya Alphabet*. Foundation for the Advancement of Mesoamerican Studies, Inc.

http://www.famsi.org/mayawriting/dictionary/christenson/quidic_complete.pdf. Accessed January 30, 2018.

Chuchiak, J. F. 2009. "De Desciptio Idolorum: An Ethnohistorical Examination of the Production, Imagery, and Functions of Colonial Yucatec Maya Idols and Effigy Censers, 1540–1700." In *Maya World Views at Conquest*, ed. L. G. Cecil and T. W. Pugh, 135–158. Boulder: University Press of Colorado.

Clausewitz, C. Von. 1976 [1832]. *On War*. Trans. M. Howard and P. Paret. Princeton, NJ: Princeton University Press.

Closs, M. P. 1988. *The Hieroglyphic Text of Stela 9, Lamanai, Belize*. Research Reports on Ancient Maya Writing, vol. 21. Washington, DC: Center for Maya Research.

Cobb, C. R., and B. Giles. 2009. "War Is Shell: The Ideology and Embodiment of Mississippian Conflict." In *Warfare in Cultural Context: Practice, Agency, and the Archaeology of Violence*, ed. A. E. Nielsen and W. H. Walker, 84–108. Tucson: University of Arizona Press.

Cobos, R., A. A. Guillermo, and R. G. Moll. 2014. "Ancient Climate and Archaeology: Uxmal, Chichen Itza, and Their Collapse at the End of the Terminal Classic Period." *Archaeological Papers of the American Anthropological Association* 24 (1): 56–71.

Coe, M. D. 1973. *The Maya Scribe and His World*. New York: Grolier Club.

Coe, M. D. 1978. *Supernatural Patrons of Maya Scribes and Artists*. Cambridge, MA: Academic.

Coe, M. D. 2012. *The Royal Cities of the Ancient Maya*. London: Thames and Hudson.

Coe, M. D., and R. A. Diehl. 1980. *In the Land of the Olmec: The Archaeology of San Lorenzo Tenochtitlán*. Austin: University of Texas Press.

Coe, M. D., and J. Kerr. 1998. *The Art of the Maya Scribe*. New York: Harry Abrams.

Coggins, C., and O. C. Shane, eds. 1984. *Cenote of Sacrifice: Maya Treasures from the Sacred Well at Chichén Itzá*. Austin: University of Texas Press.

Collingwood, R. G. 1921. "The Purpose of the Roman Wall." *Vasculum* 8: 4–9.

Conan, M. 2007. *Sacred Gardens and Landscapes*. Washington, DC: Dumbarton Oaks Research Library and Collection.

Conrad, G. W., and A. A. Demarest. 1984. *Religion and Empire: The Dynamics of Aztec and Inca Expansion*. Cambridge, England: Cambridge University Press.

Cottrell, L. 1992. *Enemy of Rome*. Boston: Da Capo.

Cowgill, G. L. 2003. "Teotihuacan and Early Classic Interaction: A Perspective from Outside the Maya Region." In *The Maya and Teotihuacan: Reinterpreting Early Classic Maya Interaction*, ed. G. E. Braswell, 315–335. Austin: University of Texas Press.

Culbert, P. T. 1991. *Classic Maya Political History: Hieroglyphic and Archaeological Evidence*. A School of American Research Book. Cambridge, England: Cambridge University Press.

Culbert, P. T. 1993. *The Ceramics of Tikal: Vessels from the Burials, Caches, and Problematic Deposits*. Tikal Report 25, part A. Philadelphia: University of Pennsylvania Museum of Archaeology and Anthropology.

Dahlin, B. H., C. T. Jensen, R. E. Terry, D. Wright, and T. Beach. 2007. "In Search of an Ancient Maya Market." *Latin American Antiquity* 18: 363–384.

Dalrymple, W. 2002. *White Mughals: Love and Betrayal in 18th-Century India*. London: HarperCollins.

Daneels, A. 2012. "Developmental Cycles in the Gulf Lowlands: Collapse and Regeneration." In *Oxford Handbook of Mesoamerican Archaeology*, ed. C. Pool and D. Nichols, 348–371. Oxford, England: Oxford University Press.

Davis, J. L. 2000. "Warriors for the Fatherland: National Consciousness and Archaeology in Barbarian Epirus and Verdant Ionia, 1912–22." *Journal of Mediterranean Archaeology* 13 (1): 76–98.

Davis, R. H. 1999. *Lives of Indian Images*. Princeton, NJ: Princeton University Press.

Davis-Kimball, J., and M. Behan. 2002. *Warrior Women: An Archaeologist's Search for History's Hidden Heroines*. New York: Warner Books.

Deloria, V. 1969. *Custer Died for Your Sins: An Indian Manifesto*. Norman: University of Oklahoma Press.

Demarest, A. A. 2004a. "After the Maelstrom: Collapse of the Classic Maya Kingdoms and the Terminal Classic in Western Peten." In *The Terminal Classic in the Maya Lowlands: Collapse, Transition, and Transformation*, ed. A. A. Demarest, P. M. Rice and D. S. Rice, 102–124. Boulder: University Press of Colorado.

Demarest, A. A. 2004b. *The Ancient Maya*. Cambridge, England: Cambridge University Press.

Demarest, A. A. 2007. "Ethics and Ethnocentricity in Interpretation and Critique: Challenges to the Anthropology of Corporeality and Death." In *The Taking and Displaying of Human Body Parts as Trophies by Amerindians*, ed. R. J. Chacon and D. H. Dye, 591–617. New York: Springer.

Demarest, A. A., C. Andrieu, P. Torres, M. Forné, T. Barrientos, and M. Wolf. 2014. "Economy, Exchange, and Power: New Evidence from the Late Classic Maya Port City of Cancuen." *Ancient Mesoamerica* 25 (1): 187–219.

Demarest, A. A., M. O'Mansky, C. Wolley, D. Van Tuerenhout, T. Inomata, J. Palka, and H. Escobedo. 1997. "Classic Maya Defensive Systems and Warfare in the Petexbatun Region." *Ancient Mesoamerica* 8 (2): 229–253.

De Pauw, L. G. 1998. *Battle Cries and Lullabies: Women in War from Prehistory to the Present*. Norman: University of Oklahoma Press.

de Waal, F. 1989. *Peacemaking among Primates*. Cambridge, MA: Harvard University Press.

Díaz del Castillo, B., and D. Carrasco. 2008. *The History of the Conquest of New Spain*. Albuquerque: University of New Mexico Press.

Díaz Oyarzábal, C. L. 1980. *Chingú: Un Sitio Clásico del área de Tula, Hidalgo*. México, DF: Colección científica, Instituto Nacional de Antropología e Historia/Secretaría de Educación Pública.

Dillon, B. J. 1982. "Bound Prisoners in Maya Art." *Journal of New World Archaeology* 5: 24–45.

Duch-Gary, J. 1991. *Fisiografía del Estado de Yucatán*. Texcoco: Universidad Autónoma de Chapingo.

Duncan, W. N. 2009. "The Bioarchaeology of Ritual Violence at Zacpetén." In *The Kowoj: Identity, Migration, and Geopolitics in the Late Postclassic Petén, Guatemala*, ed. P. M. Rice and D. S. Rice, 340–367. Boulder: University Press of Colorado.

Dunning, N. 1992. *Lords of the Hills: Ancient Maya Settlement in the Puuc Region, Yucatan, Mexico*. Monographs in World Archaeology 15. Madison, WI: Prehistory.

Durán, D. 1971. *Book of the Gods and Rites and the Ancient Calendar*. Civilization of the American Indian Series 102. Norman: University of Oklahoma Press.

Early, J. D. 2006. *The Maya and Catholicism: An Encounter of Worldviews*. Gainesville: University Press of Florida.

Eidelson, R. J., and J. I. Eidelson. 2003. "Dangerous Ideas: Five Beliefs That Propel Groups Toward Conflict." *American Psychologist* 58 (3): 182–192.

Ekholm, G. 1945. "A Pyrite Mirror from Queretaro, Mexico." *Notes on Middle American Archaeology and Ethnology* 53 (2): 178–181.

Espinoza, V.Y.H. 2007. *Cities on Hills: Classic Society in Mesoamerica's Mixteca Alta*. BAR International Series 1728. Oxford, England: British Archaeological Reports.

Estabrook, V. H., and D. W. Frayer. 2014. "Trauma in the Krapina Neaderthals: Violence in the Middle Paleolithic?" In *The Routledge Handbook of the Bioarchaeology of Human Conflict*, ed. C. Knüsel and M. J. Smith, 67–89. London: Routledge.

Estrada-Belli, F., and A. Tokovinine. 2016. "A King's Apotheosis: Iconography, Text, and Politics from a Classic Maya Temple at Holmul." *Latin American Antiquity* 27 (2): 149–168.

Estrada-Belli, F., A. Tokovinine, J. M. Foley, H. Hurst, G. A. Ware, D. Stuart, and N. Grube. 2009. "A Maya Palace at Holmul, Guatemala and the 'Teotihuacan Entrada': Evidence from Murals 7 and 9." *Latin American Antiquity* 20 (1): 228–232.

Evans, C. 2014. "Soldiering Archaeology: Pitt Rivers and 'Militarism.'" *Bulletin of the History of Archaeology* 24 (4): 1–20.

Farris, W. W. 1992. *Heavenly Warriors: The Evolution of Japan's Military, 500–1300*. Cambridge, MA: Harvard University Press.

Fash, W. L. 2001. *Scribes, Warriors, and Kings*. London: Thames and Hudson.

Fash, W. L., A. Tokovinine, and B. Fash. 2009. "The House of New Fire at Teotihuacan and Its Legacy in Mesoamerica." In *Art of Urbanism: How Mesoamerican Kingdoms Represented Themselves in Architecture and Imagery*, ed. W. L. Fash and L. López Luján, 201–229. Washington, DC: Dumbarton Oaks Research Library and Collection.

Faugère, B., ed. 2007. *Dinámicas Culturales Entre el Occidente, el Centro-Norte y la Cuenca de México, del Preclásico al Epiclásico*. Zamora, Mexico: El Colegio de Michoacán.

Fausto, C. 2012. *Warfare and Shamanism in Amazonia*. Cambridge, England: Cambridge University Press.

Fenoglio Limón, F., C. Viramontes Anzures, and J. C. Saint-Charles Zetina. 2010. "Iconografía y Cuchillos Curvos: Espacios Rituales de Sacrificio y Guerra en El Rosario, Querétaro." Unpublished manuscript in possession of the authors.

Ferguson, R. B. 2001. "Materialist, Cultural, and Biological Theories on Why Yanomami Make War." *Anthropological Theory* 1 (1): 99–116.

Filini, A. 2004. *The Presence of Teotihuacan in the Cuitzeo Basin, Michoacán, Mexico: A World-System Perspective*. BAR International Series 1279. Oxford, England: British Archaeological Reports.

Filini, A., and E. Cárdenas García. 2007. "El Bajío, la Cuenca de Cuitzeo y el Estado Teotihuacano." In *Dinámicas Culturales Entre el Occidente, el Centro-norte y la Cuenca de México, del Preclásico al Epiclásico*, ed. B. Faugère, 137–154. Zamora, Mexico: El Colegio de Michoacán.

Fitzsimmons, J. L. 2009. *Death and the Classic Maya Kings*. Austin: University of Texas Press.

Flannery, K., and J. Marcus. 2012. *The Creation of Inequality: How Our Prehistoric Ancestors Set the Stage for Monarchy, Slavery, and Empire*. Cambridge, MA: Harvard University Press.

Foias, A., and R. L. Bishop. 1997. "Changing Ceramic Production and Exchange in the Petexbatun Region, Guatemala: Reconsidering the Classic Maya Collapse." *Ancient Mesoamerica* 8: 275–292.

Fox, J. W. 1978. *Quiche Conquest: Centralism and Regionalism in Highland Maya State Development*. Albuquerque: University of New Mexico Press.

Freidel, D. 1986. "Maya Warfare: An Example of Peer-Polity Interaction." In *Peer-Polity Interaction and Sociopolitical Change*, ed. C. Renfrew and J. Cherry, 93–108. London: Cambridge University Press.

Freidel, D. 1998. "Sacred Work: Dedication and Termination in Mesoamerica." In *The Sowing and the Dawning: Termination, Dedication, and Transformation in the Archaeological and Ethnographic Record of Mesoamerica*, ed. S. B. Mock, 189–193. Albuquerque: University of New Mexico Press.

Freidel, D. 2007. "War and Statecraft in the Northern Maya Lowlands: Yaxuna and Chichen Itza." In *Twin Tollans: Chichen Itza, Tula, and the Epiclassic to Early Postclassic Mesoamerican World*, ed. J. K. Kowalski and C. Kristan-Graham, 345–376. Washington, DC: Dumbarton Oaks Research Library and Collection.

Freidel, D., H. L. Escobedo, and S. P. Guenter. 2007. "A Crossroads of Conquerors." In *Gordon R. Willey and American Archaeology*, ed. J. A. Sabloff and W. L. Fash, 187–208. Norman: University of Oklahoma Press.

Freidel, D., L. Schele, and J. Parker. 1993. *Maya Cosmos: Three Thousand Years on the Shaman's Path*. New York: William Morrow.

Fried, M. H. 1967. *The Evolution of Political Society: An Essay in Political Anthropology.* New York: Random House.

Fried, M. H., M. Harris, and R. Murphy, eds. 1968. *War: The Anthropology of Armed Conflict and Aggression.* Garden City, NY: Natural History Press.

Fry, D. P. 2007. *Beyond War: The Human Potential for Peace.* Oxford, England: Oxford University Press.

Fry, D. P., and K. Björkqvist, eds. 2009. *Cultural Variation in Conflict Resolution: Alternatives to Violence.* Oxford, England: Psychology Press.

Fry, D. P., and P. Söderberg. 2013. "Lethal Aggression in Mobile Forager Bands and Implications for the Origins of War." *Science* 341: 270–273.

Gallareta Negrón, T. 2013. "The Social Organization of Labna, a Classic Maya Community in the Puuc Region of Yucatan." PhD dissertation, Tulane University, New Orleans, LA.

Gallareta Negrón, T., G. J. Bey III, and W. M. Ringle. 2013. *Proyecto Arqueológico Regional de Bolonchén, Temporada de Campo 2012.* México, DF: Informe Técnico al Consejo de Arqueología del Instituto Nacional de Antropología e Historia.

Galtung, J. 2000. *Conflict Transformation by Peaceful Means (the Transcend Method).* New York: United Nations Disaster Management Training Programme.

Garcia Barrios, A. 2006. "Confrontation Scenes on Codex-Style Pottery: An Iconographic Review." *Latin American Indian Literatures Journal* 22 (2): 129–152.

García-Des Lauriers, C. 2007. "Proyecto Arqueológico Los Horcones: Investigating the Teotihuacan Presence on the Pacific Coast of Chiapas, Mexico." PhD dissertation, University of California, Riverside.

García Loaeza, P. 2014. "Fernando de Alva Ixtlilxochitl's Texcocan Dynasty." In *Texcoco: Prehispanic and Colonial Perspectives*, ed. J. Lee and G. Brokaw, 219–242. Boulder: University Press of Colorado.

García Payón, J. 1973. "El Tablero de Montículo Cuatro." *Boletín del Instituto Nacional de Antropología e Historia* 7: 31–34.

Gat, A. 2006. *War in Human Civilization.* Oxford, England: Oxford University Press.

Gilchrist, R. 2003. "Introduction: Towards a Social Archaeology of Warfare." *World Archaeology* 35 (1): 1–6.

Girard, R. 1972. *Violence and the Sacred.* London: Continuum.

Gluckman, M. 1955. *Custom and Conflict in Africa.* Oxford, England: Basil Blackwell.

Gluckman, M. 1963. *Order and Rebellion in Tribal Africa.* New York: Free Press.

Gnirs, A. 1999. "Ancient Egypt." In *War and Society in the Ancient and Medieval Worlds*, ed. K. Raaflaub and N. Rosenstein, 71–104. Cambridge, MA: Harvard University Press.

Goffman, E. 1974. *Frame Analysis: An Essay on the Organization of Experience.* New York: Harper and Row.

Goldstein, J. S. 2001. *War and Gender: How Gender Shapes the War System and Viceversa.* Cambridge, England: Cambridge University Press.

Golitko, M., J. Meierhoff, G. M. Feinman, and P. R. Williams. 2012. "Complexities of Collapse: The Evidence of Maya Obsidian as Revealed by Social Network Graphical Analysis." *Antiquity* 86: 507–523.

Gómez Chávez, S. 1999. "Presencia del Occidente de México en Teotihuacan: Aproximaciones a la Política Exterior del Estado Teotihuacano." In *Ideología y Política a Través de Materiales, Imágenes y Símbolos: Memoria de la Primera Mesa Redonda de Teotihuacan*, ed. M.E.R. Gallut, 563–625. México, DF: Consejo Nacional Para la Cultura y las Artes/Instituto Nacional de Antropología e Historia.

Gómez Chávez, S., and J. Gazzola. 2007. "Análisis de las Relaciones Entre Teotihuacán y el Occidente de México." In *Dinámicas Culturales Entre el Occidente, el Centro-Norte y la Cuenca de México, del Preclásico al Epiclásico*, ed. B. Faugère, 113–135. Zamora, Mexico: El Colegio de Michoacán.

Gommans, J. 2002. *Mughal Warfare: Indian Frontiers and High Roads to Empire, 1500–1700*. London: Routledge.

Gonzalez, T. A., and H. R. Haines. 2013. "Exploring the Ritual Function of Chultuns: A Taste from Ka'Kabish." Paper presented at the 78th Annual Meeting of the Society for American Archaeology, Honolulu, HI, April 3–7.

Gorenstein, S. 1973. "Tepexi el Viejo: A Postclassic Fortified Site in the Mixteca-Puebla Region of Mexico." *Transactions of the American Philosophical Society* 1 (63): 1–75.

Gosner, K. 1992. *Soldiers of the Virgin: The Moral Economy of a Colonial Maya Rebellion*. Tucson: University of Arizona Press.

Graeber, D. 2001. *Toward an Anthropological Theory of Value*. New York: Palgrave.

Graeber, D. 2014. *Debt—the First 5,000 Years*. London: Melville House.

Graham, E. 1987a. "Resource Diversity in Belize and Its Implications for Models of Lowland Trade." *American Antiquity* 52: 753–767.

Graham, E. 1987b. "Terminal Classic to Early Historic–Period Vessel Forms from Belize." In *Maya Ceramics*, ed. P. Rice and R. Sharer, 78–98. BAR International Series 345. Oxford, England: British Archaeological Reports.

Graham, E. 2004. "Lamanai Reloaded: Alive and Well in the Early Postclassic." *Research Reports in Belizean Archaeology* 1: 223–243.

Graham, E. 2006. "An Ethnicity to Know." In *Maya Ethnicity: The Construction of Ethnic Identity from Preclassic to Modern Times*, ed. F. Sachse, 111–124. Cologne, Germany: Verlag Anton Saurwein.

Graham, E. 2008. "Socially Sanctioned Killing in America, Then and Now." Paper presented at the 73rd Annual Meeting of the Society for American Archaeology, Vancouver, Canada, March 26–30.

Graham, E. 2009. "Close Encounters." In *Maya Worldviews at Conquest*, ed. L. G. Cecil and T. W. Pugh, 17–38. Boulder: University Press of Colorado.

Graham, E. 2011. *Maya Christians and Their Churches in Sixteenth-Century Belize*. Gainesville: University Press of Florida.

Graham, E. 2012. "Control without Controlling." In *Politics, History, and Economy at the Classic Maya Site of Motul de San José, Guatemala*, ed. A. E. Foias and K. F. Emery, 419–430. Gainesville: University Press of Florida.

Graham, E. 2014. "Taxes and Tribute." *Mexicon* 36 (3): 76.

Graham, E., and N. Golson. 2006. "The Faces of Tribute." Paper presented at the 71st Annual Meeting of the Society for American Archaeology, San Juan, Puerto Rico, April 26–30.

Graham, E., D. M. Pendergast, and G. D. Jones. 1989. "On the Fringes of Conquest: Maya-Spanish Contact in Early Belize." *Science* 246: 1254–1259.

Graham, E., S. E. Simmons, and C. D. White. 2013. "The Spanish Conquest and the Maya Collapse: How 'Religious' Is Change?" *World Archaeology* 45 (1): 1–25.

Graham, I. 1975. *Corpus of Maya Hieroglyphic Inscriptions 2 (1): Naranjo*. Cambridge, MA: Peabody Museum of Archaeology and Ethnology, Harvard University.

Graham, I. 1978. *Corpus of Maya Hieroglyphic Inscriptions 2 (2): Naranjo, Chunhuitz, Xunantunich*. Cambridge, MA: Peabody Museum of Archaeology and Ethnology, Harvard University.

Gregor, T., ed. 1996. *A Natural History of Peace*. Nashville, TN: Vanderbilt University Press.

Grube, N. 2000. "Monumentos Esculpidos e Inscripciones Jeroglíficas en el Triángulo Yaxhá-Nakum-Naranjo." In *El Sitio Maya de Topoxté: Investigaciones en una Isla del Lago Yaxhá, Petén, Guatemala*, ed. W. W. Wurster, 249–267. Mainz am Rhein, Germany: Verlag Philipp von Zabern.

Grube, N. 2004a. "El Origen de la Dinastía Kaan." In *Los Cautivos de Dzibanché*, ed. E. Nalda, 117–131. México, DF: Instituto Nacional de Antropología e Historia.

Grube, N. 2004b. "La Historia Dinastica de Naranjo, Peten." *Beiträge zur Allgemeinen und Vergleichenden Archäologie* 24: 197–213.

Grube, N., and S. Martin. 2004. "Patronage, Betrayal, and Revenge: Diplomacy and Politics in the Eastern Maya Lowlands." In *Notebook for the XXVIII Maya Meetings at Texas, March 13–14, 2004*, II-1–II-91. Austin: Department of Art and Art History, University of Texas.

Grube, N., C. Pallán Gayol, and A. Benavides Castillo. 2011. "The Hieroglyphic Stairway of Sabana Piletas, Campeche." In *The Long Silence: Sabana Piletas and Its Neighbours: An Architectural Survey of Maya Puuc Ruins in Northeastern Campeche, Mexico*, ed. S. Merk and A. Benavides Castillo, 251–261. Markt Schwaben, Germany: Verlag Anton Saurwein.

Grube, N., and L. Schele. 1994. "Kuy, the Owl of Omen and War." *Mexicon* 16 (1): 10–17.

Guenter, S. 2007. *The Tomb of K'inich Janaab Pakal: The Temple of the Inscriptions at Palenque*. Mesoweb. http://www.Mesoweb.com/articles/guenter/TI.pdf. Accessed October 21, 2014.

Guilaine, J., and J. Zammit. 2001. *The Origins of War*. Oxford, England: Blackwell.

Guiteras Holmes, C. 1961. *Perils of the Soul*. Glencoe, IL: Free Press.

Gutiérrez, G. 2014. "Aztec Battlefields of Eastern Guerrero: An Archaeological and Ethnohistorical Analysis of the Operational Theater of the Tlapanec War." In *Embattled Bodies, Embattled Places: War in Pre-Columbian Mesoamerica and the Andes*, ed. A.K. Scherer and J. W. Verano, 143–170. Washington, DC: Dumbarton Oaks Research Library and Collection.

Haines, H. R. 2008a. "Causeway Terminus, Minor Centre, Elite Refuge, or Ritual Capital? Ka'Kabish, a New Puzzle on the Ancient Maya Landscape of North-Central Belize." *Research Reports in Belizean Archaeology* 5: 269–280.

Haines, H. R., ed. 2008b. "The 2007 Spring Mapping Project of the Ka'Kabish Archaeological Research Project (KARP)." Report submitted to the Institute of Archaeology, Belmopan, Belize.

Haines, H. R., ed. 2010. "The 2009 Spring Mapping Project of the Ka'Kabish Archaeological Research Project (KARP)." Report submitted to the Institute of Archaeology, Belmopan, Belize.

Haines, H. R. 2011a. "How the Other-Half Lived: Continuing Discussions of the Enigma That Is Ka'Kabish, Belize." *Research Reports in Belizean Archaeology* 8: 137–150.

Haines, H. R. 2011b. "Curiouser and Curiouser: A Glimpse into the Early History of Ka'Kabish." Paper presented at the 76th Annual Meeting of the Society for American Archaeology, Sacramento, CA, March 30–April 3.

Haines, H. R., ed. 2011c. "The 2010 Archaeological Report of the Ka'Kabish Archaeological Research Project (KARP)." Report submitted to the Institute of Archaeology, Belmopan, Belize.

Haines, H. R., ed. 2012. "The 2011 Archaeological Report of the Ka'Kabish Archaeological Research Project (KARP)." Report submitted to the Institute of Archaeology, Belmopan, Belize.

Hamblin, R. L., and B. L. Pitcher. 1980. "The Classic Maya Collapse: Testing Class Conflict Theories." *American Antiquity* 45 (2): 46–67.

Hammond, N. 1973. *Corozal Project, 1973 Interim Report*. Cambridge, England: Centre of Latin American Studies, University of Cambridge.

Hammond, N. 1981. "Settlement Patterns in Belize." In *Lowland Maya Settlement Patterns*, ed. W. Ashmore, 157–186. Albuquerque: School of American Research, University of New Mexico Press.

Hammond, N. 1985. *Nohmul: A Prehistoric Maya Community in Belize, Excavations 1973–1983*. BAR International Series 25. Oxford, England: British Archaeological Reports.

Hammond, N. 1991. *Cuello: An Early Maya Community in Belize*. Cambridge, England: Cambridge University Press.

Hammond, N., A. Clark, and S. Donaghey. 1995. "The Long Goodbye: Middle Preclassic Maya Archaeology at Cuello, Belize." *Latin American Antiquity* 6: 120–128.

Hammond, N., S. Donaghey, C. Gleason, J. C. Staneko, D. Van Tuerenhout, and L. J. Kosakowsky. 1987. "Excavations at Nohmul, Belize, 1985." *Journal of Field Archaeology* 14: 257–281.

Hanks, B. 2008. "Reconsidering Warfare, Status, and Gender in the Eurasian Steppe Iron Age." In *Are All Warriors Male? Gender Roles on the Ancient Eurasian Steppe*, ed. K. M. Linduff and K. S. Rubinson, 15–34. Walnut Creek, CA: Altamira.

Hanson, V. D. 2000. *The Western Way of War: Infantry Battle in Classical Greece*. Berkeley: University of California Press.

Harris, M. 1979. *Cultural Materialism: The Struggle for a Science of Culture*. New York: Random House.

Harrison, P. D. 1999. *The Lords of Tikal: Rulers of an Ancient Maya City*. London: Thames and Hudson.

Hartmann-Mahmud, L. 2002. "War as Metaphor." *Peace Review* 14 (4): 427–432.

Hassig, R. 1988. *Aztec Warfare: Imperial Expansion and Political Control*. Norman: University of Oklahoma Press.

Hassig, R. 1992. *War and Society in Ancient Mesoamerica*. Oakland: University of California Press.

Hassig, R. 1995. *Aztec Warfare: Imperial Expansion and Political Control*. 2nd ed. Norman: University of Oklahoma Press.

Headrick, A. 2003. "Butterfly War at Teotihuacan." In *Ancient Mesoamerican Warfare*, ed. M. K. Brown and T. W. Stanton, 149–170. Walnut Creek, CA: Altamira.

Headrick, A. 2007. *The Teotihuacan Trinity: The Sociopolitical Structure of an Ancient Mesoamerican City*. William and Bettye Nowlin Series in Art, History, and Culture of the Western Hemisphere. Austin: University of Texas Press.

Hegmon, M. 2003. "Setting Theoretical Egos Aside: Issues and Theory in North American Archaeology." *American Antiquity* 68 (2): 213–243.

Heinl, R. D. 1981. *Dictionary of Military and Naval Quotations*. Annapolis, MD: United States Naval Institute.

Helbig, H. 1980. *Der wettinische Ständestaat: Untersuchungen zur Geschichte des Ständewesens und der landständischen Verfassung in Mitteldeutschland bis 1485*. Köln, Germany: Böhlau 2, Unveränderte Auflage.

Helle, H. J. 2008. "Sociology of Competition by Georg Simmel." *Canadian Journal of Sociology* 33 (4): 945–956.

Hellmuth, N. 1975. "The Escuintla Hoards: Teotihuacan Art in Guatemala." *Foundation for Latin American Anthropological Research, Progress Reports* 1 (2): 5–58.

Hellmuth, N. 1987. *The Surface of the Underworld: Iconography of the Gods of Early Classic Maya Art in Petén, Guatemala*. Providence, RI: Foundation for Latin American Anthropological Research.

Helmke, C. 2010. "Comments on the Glyphic Text of Tomb 1, Structure FA-6, Ka'Kabish Belize." In "The 2010 Spring Mapping Project of the Ka'Kabish Archaeological Research Project (KARP)," ed. H. R. Haines, 77–80. Report submitted to the Institute of Archaeology, Belmopan, Belize.

Helmke, C., and J. E. Brady. 2014. "Epigraphic and Archaeological Evidence for Cave Desecration in Ancient Maya Warfare." In *A Celebration of the Life and Work of Pierre Robert Colas*, ed. C. Helmke and F. Sachs, 195–227. Acta Mesoamericana 27. Munich, Germany: Verlag Anton Saurwein.

Helmke, C., S. G. Morton, and M. Peuramaki-Brown. 2012. "Raiding among the Classic Maya?" Paper presented at the 45th Annual Chacmool Archaeological Conference, Calgary, Canada, November 8–11.

Helmke, C., and J. Nielsen. 2011. *The Writing System of Cacaxtla, Tlaxcala, Mexico*. Special Publication 2. Barnardsville, NC: Boundary End Archaeology Research Center.

Helmke, C., and J. Nielsen. 2013. "The Writing on the Wall: A Paleographic Analysis of the Maya Texts of Tetitla, Teotihuacan." In *The Maya in a Mesoamerican Context: Comparative Approaches to Maya Studies*, ed. J. Nielsen and C. Helmke, 123–166. Acta Mesoamericana 26. Markt Schwaben, Germany: Verlag Anton Saurwein.

Helmke, C., and J. Nielsen. 2014. "If Mountains Could Speak: Ancient Toponyms Recorded at Teotihuacan, Mexico." *Contributions in New World Archaeology* 7: 73–112.

Henderson, J. S., and K. M. Hudson. 2015. "The Myth of Maya: Archaeology and the Construction of Mesoamerican Histories." In *On Methods: How We Know What We Think We Know about the Maya*, ed. H. Kettunen and C. Helmke, 7–24. Acta Mesoamericana 28. Markt Schwaben, Germany: Verlag Anton Saurwein.

Hermitte, E. 1964. "Supernatural Power and Social Control in a Modern Maya Village." PhD dissertation, University of Chicago, IL.

Hers, M.-A. 2013. "Un Nuevo Lenguaje Visual en Tiempos de Rupturas (600–900 d. C.)." In *Miradas Renovadas al Occidente Indígena de México*, ed. M.-A. Hers, 215–252. México, DF: Universidad Nacional Autónoma de México / Instituto Nacional de Antropología e Historia.

Hester, T. R. 1983. *A Preliminary Report on the 1983 Investigations at Colha*. San Antonio: Center for Archaeological Research, University of Texas.

Hester, T. R., J. D. Eaton, and H. J. Shafer. 1980. *The Colha Project, Second Season, 1980 Interim Report*. San Antonio: Center for Archaeological Research, University of Texas.

Hester, T. R., G. Ligabue, H. J. Shafer, J. D. Eaton, R. F. Heizer, and S. Salvatori. 1979. "Colha, Belize: A Preliminary Statement on the 1979 Season." *Belizean Studies* 7 (6): 1–7.

Hester, T. R., H. J. Shafer, and J. D. Eaton, eds. 1982. *Archaeology at Colha, Belize: The 1981 Interim Report*. San Antonio: Center for Archaeological Research, University of Texas.

Hester, T. R., H. J. Shafer, and J. D. Eaton, eds. 1994. *Continuing Archeology at Colha, Belize*. Studies in Archeology, vol. 16. Austin: Texas Archeological Research Laboratory, University of Texas.

Hill, R. E., and M. Galvan. 2009. "Terminal Classic Decline and Reorganization in the Bolonchén District of the Puuc Region, Yucatan." Paper presented at the 74th Annual Meeting of the Society for American Archaeology, Atlanta, GA, April 22–26.

Hingley, R. 2008. "Hadrian's Wall in Theory: Pursuing New Agendas?" In *Understanding Hadrian's Wall*, ed. P. Bidwell, 25–28. South Shields, England: Arbeia Society.

Hirth, K. G. 1978. "Teotihuacan Regional Population Administration in Eastern Morelos." *World Archaeology* 9: 320–333.

Hirth, K. G. 1995. "Urbanism, Militarism, and Architectural Design: An Analysis of Epiclassic Sociopolitical Structure at Xochicalco." *Ancient Mesoamerica* 6: 237–250.

Hirth, K. G., and J. A. Villaseñor. 1981. "Early State Expansion in Central Mexico: Teotihuacan in Morelos." *Journal of Field Archaeology* 8 (2): 135–150.

Hoffmann, C. C. 1918. "Las Mariposas Entre los Antiguos Méxicanos." *Cosmos* 1 (18): 1–4.

Hofling, C. A. 2011. *Mopan Maya-Spanish-English Dictionary/Diccionario Maya Mopan-Español-Ingles*. Salt Lake City: University of Utah Press.

Hoggarth, J. A., S.F.M. Brieitenbach, B. J. Culleton, C. E. Ebert, M. A. Masson, and D. J. Kennett. 2016. "The Political Collapse of Chichén Itzá in Climatic and Cultural Context." *Global and Planetary Change* 138: 25–42.

Hogue, C. L. 1993. *Latin American Insects and Entomology*. Berkeley: University of California Press.

Hopkins, N. A. 1996. "Metonym and Metaphor in Chol (Mayan) Ritual Language." Paper presented at the 95th Annual Meeting of the American Anthropological Association, San Francisco, CA, November 20–24.

Hopkins, N. A., J. K. Josserand, and A. Cruz Guzmán. 2011. *A Historical Dictionary of Chol (Mayan): The Lexical Sources from 1789 to 1935*. Foundation for the Advancement of Mesoamerican Studies, Inc. http://www.famsi.org/mayawriting/dictionary/hopkins/CholDictionary2010.pdf. Accessed January 30, 2018.

Houston, S. 1983. "A Reading for the 'Flint-Shield' Glyph." In *Contributions to Maya Hieroglyphic Decipherment* 1, ed. S. Houston, 13–25. New Haven, CT: HRAFLEX Books.

Houston, S. 2014. "Pehk and 'Parliaments.'" *Maya Decipherment*. https://decipherment.wordpress.com/2014/2010/2007/pehk-and-parliaments/. Accessed January 21, 2015.

Houston, S., J. Robertson, and D. Stuart. 2001. "Quality and Quantity in Glyphic Nouns and Adjectives." *Research Reports on Ancient Maya Writing* 47: 1–56.

Houston, S., and D. Stuart. 1996. "Of Gods, Glyphs, and Kings: Divinity and Rulership among the Classic Maya." *Antiquity* 70: 289–312.

Houston, S., and D. Stuart. 1998. "The Ancient Maya Self: Personhood and Portraiture in the Classic Period." *RES: Anthropology and Aesthetics* 33: 73–101.

Houston, S., D. Stuart, and K. Taube. 2006. *The Memory of Bones: Body, Being, and Experience among the Classic Maya*. Austin: University of Texas Press.

Houston, S., and K. Taube. 2000. "An Archaeology of the Senses: Perception and Cultural Expression in Ancient Mesoamerica." *Cambridge Archaeological Journal* 10 (2): 261–294.

Howie, L. A. 2005. "Ceramic Production and Consumption in the Maya Lowlands during the Classic to Postclassic Transition: A Technological Study of Ceramics at Lamanai, Belize." PhD dissertation, University of Sheffield, Sheffield, England.

Howie, L. A. 2012. *Ceramic Change and the Maya Collapse: A Study of Pottery Technology, Manufacture, and Consumption at Lamanai, Belize*. BAR International Series 2373. Oxford, England: British Archaeological Reports.

Howie, L. A., C. D. White, and F. J. Longstaffe. 2010. "Photographies and Biographies: The Role of Food in Ritual and Identity as Seen through Life Histories of Selected Maya Pots and People." In *Pre-Columbian Foodways: Interdisciplinary Approaches to Foods, Cultures, and Markets in Ancient Mesoamerica*, ed. J. E. Staller and M. D. Carrasco, 369–398. New York: Springer.

Hsiang, S. M., M. Burke, and E. Miguel. 2013. "Quantifying the Influence of Climate on Human Conflict." *Science* 341 (6151): 1235367.1–14.

Huizinga, J. 2014 [1950]. *Homo Ludens: A Study of the Play-Element in Culture*. Manfield Center, CT: Martino.

Ikegami, E. 1995. *The Taming of the Samurai*. Cambridge, MA: Harvard University Press.

Inomata, T. 1997. "The Last Day of a Fortified Classic Maya Center." *Ancient Mesoamerica* 8 (2): 337–351.

Inomata, T. 2006. "Politics and Theatricality of Mayan Society." In *Archaeology of Performance: Theaters of Power, Community, and Politics*, ed. T. Inomata and L. S. Coben, 187–221. Walnut Creek, CA: Altamira.

Inomata, T. 2014. "War, Violence, and Society in the Maya Lowlands." In *Embattled Bodies, Embattled Places: War in Pre-Columbian Mesoamerica and the Andes*, ed. A. K. Scherer and J. M. Verano, 25–56. Washington, DC: Dumbarton Oaks Research Library and Collection.

Inomata, T., and D. Triadan. 2009. "Culture and Practice of War in Maya Society." In *Warfare in Cultural Context: Practice, Agency, and the Archaeology of Violence*, ed. A. E. Nielsen and W. H. Walker, 56–83. Tucson: University of Arizona Press.

Inomata, T., and D. Triadan, eds. 2010. *Burned Palaces and Elite Residences of Aguateca: Excavations and Ceramics*. Salt Lake City: University of Utah Press.

Jansen, M., and G. A. Pérez Jiménez. 2005. *Codex Bodley: A Painted Chronicle from the Mixtec Highlands, Mexico*. Oxford, England: Bodleian Library, University of Oxford.

Jansen, M., and G. A. Pérez Jiménez. 2007. *Encounter with the Plumed Serpent: Drama and Power in the Heart of Mesoamerica*. Boulder: University Press of Colorado.

Johnson, W. C. 1983. "The Physical Setting: Northern Belize and Pulltrouser Swamp." In *Pulltrouser Swamp: Ancient Maya Habitat Agriculture, and Settlement in Northern Belize*, ed. B. L. Turner and P. D. Harrison, 8–20. Austin: University of Texas Press.

Johnston, H. 1995. "A Methodology for Frame Analysis: From Discourse to Cognitive Schemata." *Social Movements and Culture* 4: 217–246.

Johnston, K. J. 2001. "Broken Fingers: Classic Maya Scribe Capture and Polity Consolidation." *Antiquity* 75 (288): 373–381.

Jones, C., and L. Satterthwaite. 1982. *The Monuments and Inscriptions of Tikal: The Carved Monuments*. Monograph 44. Philadelphia: University Museum, University of Pennsylvania.

Jones, G. D. 1973. "Ethnology: Tres Siglos de la Dominación Española en Yucatán o sea Historia de Esta Provincia I and II: FRAY DIEGO LOPEZ DE COGOLLUDO." *American Anthropologist* 75 (6): 1806–1808.

Jones, G. D. 1998. *The Conquest of the Last Maya Kingdom*. Stanford, CA: Stanford University Press.

Jones, G. D. 2009. "The Kowoj in Ethnohistorical Perspective." In *The Kowoj: Identity, Migration, and Geopolitics in Late Postclassic Petén, Guatemala*, ed. P. M. Rice and D. S. Rice, 55–69. Boulder: University Press of Colorado.

Joralemon, D. 1974. "Ritual Blood-Sacrifice among the Ancient Maya." In *Primera Mesa Redonda, part 2*, ed. M. Greene Robertson, 59–76. Pebble Beach, CA: Precolumbian Art Research Institute, Robert Louis Stevenson School.

Joyce, R. A., L. M. Meskell, and B. S. Turner, eds. 2003. *Embodied Lives: Figuring Ancient Maya and Egyptian Experience*. London: Routledge.

Kampen, M. E. 1972. *The Sculptures of El Tajín, Veracruz, Mexico*. Gainesville: University of Florida Press.

Kaufman, T. 1972. *El Proto-Tzeltal-Tzotzil: Fonología Comparada y Diccionario Reconstruido. Versión Española e índice Español*. Centro de Estudios Mayas, Cuaderno 5. México, DF: Universidad Nacional Autónoma de México, Coordinacíon de Humanidades.

Kaufman, T., with the assistance of J. Justeson. 2003. *A Preliminary Mayan Etymological Dictionary*. Foundation for the Advancement of Mesoamerican Studies, Inc. http://www.famsi.org/reports/01051/pmed.pdf. Accessed January 30, 2018.

Kaufman, T., and W. Norman. 1984. "An Outline of Proto-Cholan Phonology, Morphology, and Vocabulary." In *Phoneticism in Mayan Hieroglyphic Writing*, ed. J. S. Justeson and L. Campbell, 77–166. Publication 9. Albany: Institute for Mesoamerican Studies, State University of New York.

Keeley, L. H. 1996. *War before Civilization: The Myth of the Peaceful Savage*. Oxford, England: Oxford University Press.

Kelly, R. C. 2000. *Warless Societies and the Origin of War*. Ann Arbor: University of Michigan Press.

Kettunen, H. 2005. "An Old Euphemism in New Clothes: Observations on a Possible Death Difrasismo in Maya Hieroglyphic Writing." *Wayeb Notes* 16: 1–42.

Kettunen, H. 2011. "La Guerra: Técnicas, Tácticas y Estrategias Militares." In *Los Mayas: Voces de Piedra*, ed. A. Martínez de Velasco and M. E. Vega, 403–415. México, DF: Ámbar Diseño, S.C.

Kettunen, H. 2012. "Struggle for Supremacy: Armed Conflicts in the Eastern Peten during the Late Classic Period." *Contributions in New World Archaeology* 3: 127–134.

Kettunen, H. 2014. "Ancient Maya Warfare: An Interdisciplinary Approach." In *Socio-Political Strategies among the Maya from the Classic Period to the Present*, ed. V. A. Vázquez López, R. V. Rivera, and E. G. González, 95–107. BAR International Series 2619. Oxford, England: British Archaeological Reports.

Kettunen, H. 2015. "Corpus Epigraphy: Implications and Applications." Paper presented at the 20th European Maya Conference, Bonn, Germany, December 8–13.

Kidder, A. V., J. D. Jennings, and E. M. Shook. 1946. *Excavations at Kaminaljuyu, Guatemala*. Publication 561. Washington, DC: Carnegie Institution of Washington.

King, M. B. 1988. "Mixtec Political Ideology: Historical Metaphors and the Poetics of Political Symbolism." PhD dissertation, University of Michigan, Ann Arbor.

Kjellström, A. 2014. "Interpreting Violence: A Bioarchaeological Perspective of Violence from Medieval Central Sweden." In *The Routledge Handbook of the Bioarchaeology of Human Conflict*, ed. C. Knüsel and M. J. Smith, 237–250. London: Routledge.

Knowlton, T. 2012. "Some Historical Continuities in Lowland Maya Magical Speech Genres: Keying Shamanic Performance." In *Parallel Worlds: Genre, Discourse, and Poetics in Contemporary, Colonial, and Classic Maya Literature*, ed. K. M. Hull and M. D. Carrasco, 195–220. Boulder: University Press of Colorado.

Knüsel, C., and M. J. Smith. 2014a. "The Osteology of Conflict: What Does It All Mean?" In *The Routledge Handbook of the Bioarchaeology of Human Conflict*, ed. C. Knüsel and M. J. Smith, 656–694. London: Routledge.

Knüsel, C., and M. J. Smith. 2014b. "Introduction: The Bioarchaeology of Conflict." In *The Routledge Handbook of the Bioarchaeology of Human Conflict*, ed. C. Knüsel and M. J. Smith, 3–24. London: Routledge.

Köhler, U. 1989. "Comets and Falling Stars in the Perception of Mesoamerican Indians." In *World Archaeoastronomy: Selected Papers from the Second Oxford International Conference on Archaeoastronomy*, ed. A. F. Aveni, 289–299. Cambridge, England: Cambridge University Press.

Koontz, R. 2009. *Lightning Gods and Feathered Serpents: The Public Sculpture of El Tajín*. Austin: University of Texas Press.

Kosakowsky, L. J. 1987. *Preclassic Maya Pottery at Cuello, Belize*. Anthropological Papers of the University of Arizona 47. Tucson: University of Arizona Press.

Kosakowsky, L. J., and D. C. Pring. 1998. "The Ceramics of Cuello, Belize." *Ancient Mesoamerica* 9: 55–66.

Kovacevich, B. 2011. "The Organization of Jade Production at Cancuen, Guatemala." In *The Technology of Maya Civilizations: Political Economy and Beyond in Lithic Studies*, ed. Z. X. Hruby, G. E. Braswell, and O. Chinchilla Mazariegos, 149–161. San Diego, CA: Equinox.

Kowalski, J. K. 1985. "A Historical Interpretation of the Inscriptions of Uxmal." In *Fourth Palenque Round Table, 1980*, vol. 6, ed. E. P. Benson, 235–247. San Francisco: Pre-Columbian Art Research Institute.

Kowalski, J. K. 2003. "Collaboration and Conflict: An Interpretation of the Relationship between Uxmal and Chichen Itza during the Terminal Classic/Early Postclassic Periods." In *Escondido en la Selva Arqueologia en el Norte de Yucatan*, ed. H. J. Prem, 235–272. México, DF, and Bonn, Germany: Instituto Nacional de Antropología e Historia and Universidad de Bonn.

Kowalski, J. K. 2006. "¿Destrucción? Una Interpretación de Uxmal, Chichén Itzá y el Abandono de las Ciudades del Puuc." In *Los Mayas de Ayer y Hoy: Memorias del Primer Congreso Internacional de Cultura Maya*, vol. 1, ed. A. Barrera Rubio and R. Gubler, 305–339. Mérida, Mexico: Yucatán-Cultura, Consejo Nacional Para la Cultura y las Artes/Instituto Nacional de Antropología e Historia, and Universidad Autónoma de Yucatán.

Kowalski, J. K. 2007. "What's 'Toltec' at Uxmal and Chichén Itzá? Merging Maya and Mesoamerican Worldview and World Systems in Terminal Classic to Early Postclassic Yucatán." In *Twin Tollans: Chichen Itza, Tula, and the Epiclassic to Early Postclassic Mesoamerican World*, ed. J. K. Kowalski and C. Kristan-Graham, 205–250. Washington, DC: Dumbarton Oaks Research Library and Collection.

Kristan-Graham, C., and J. K. Kowalski. 2007. "Chichen Itza, Tula, and Tollan: Changing Perspectives on a Recurring Problem in Mesoamerican Archaeology and Art History." In *Twin Tollans: Chichen Itza, Tula, and the Epiclassic to Early Postclassic Mesoamerican World*, ed. J. K. Kowalski and C. Kristan-Graham, 13–84. Washington, DC: Dumbarton Oaks Research Library and Collection.

Kubler, G. A. 1973. "Iconographic Aspects of Architectural Profiles at Teotihuacan and in Mesoamerica." In *The Iconography of Middle American Sculpture*, 24–39. New York: Metropolitan Museum of Art.

Kurjack, E. B., and S. Garza Tarazona. 1981. "Pre-Columbian Community Form and Distribution in the Northern Maya Area." In *Lowland Maya Settlement Patterns*, ed. W. Ashmore, 287–309. Albuquerque: University of New Mexico Press.

Lacadena, A. 2004. "On the Reading of Two Glyphic Appellatives of the Rain God." In *Continuity and Change: Maya Religious Practices in Temporal Perspective*, ed. D. Graña Behrens, N. Grube, C. M. Prager, F. Sachse, S. Teufel, and E. Wagner, 87–98. Markt Schwaben, Germany: Verlag Anton Saurwein.

Ladrón de Guevara, S. 2005. *Imagen y Pensamiento en El Tajín*. 2nd ed. Xalapa, Mexico: Universidad Veracruzana.

Ladrón de Guevara, S. 2006. *Hombres y Dioses de El Tajín/Sara Ladrón de Guevara*. Colección Ensayos. Veracruz, Mexico: Gobierno del Estado de Veracruz.

Lakoff, G. 1991. "Metaphor and War: The Metaphor System Used to Justify War in the Gulf, Part 1 of 2." *Viet Nam Generation Journal and Newsletter* 3 (3). http://www2.iath .virginia.edu/sixties/HTML_docs/Texts/Scholarly/Lakoff_Gulf_Metaphor_1.html. Accessed March 22, 2018.

Lakoff, G., and M. Johnson. 1980. *Metaphors We Live By*. Chicago: University of Chicago Press.

Lambert, J.D.H., and T. Arnason. 1978. "Distribution of Vegetation on Maya Ruins and Its Relationship to Ancient Land-Use at Lamanai, Belize." *Turrialba* 28 (1): 33–41.

Lane, K. 2010. "Inca." In *The Oxford Handbook of the Archaeology of Ritual and Religion*, ed. T. Insoll, 571–584. Oxford, England: Oxford University Press.

Langley, J. C. 1986. *Symbolic Notation at Teotihuacan: Elements of Writing in a Mesoamerican Culture of the Classic Period.* BAR International Series 313. Oxford, England: British Archaeological Reports.

Laporte, J. P. 2001. "Dispersión y Estructura de las Ciudades del Sureste de Petén, Guatemala." In *Reconstruyendo la Ciudad Maya: El Urbanismo en las Sociedades Antiguas,* ed. A. Ciudad Ruiz, 137–161. Madrid, Spain: Sociedad Española de Estudios Mayas.

Latsanopoulos, N. 2005. "Standing Stones, Knives-Holders, and Flying Felines: An Overview of Ritual Paraphernalia and Actors of Cardiectomy at Teotihuacan, Mexico." In *De l'Altiplano Mexicain à la Patagonie—Travaux et Researches à l'Université de Paris 1,* ed. C. Giorgi, 175–188. BAR International Series 1389. Oxford, England: British Archaeological Reports.

Laughlin, R. M. 1975. *The Great Tzotzil Dictionary of San Lorenzo Zinacantán.* Smithsonian Contributions to Anthropology, vol. 19. Washington, DC: Smithsonian Institution Press.

Laughlin, R. M. 1977. *Of Cabbages and Kings.* Smithsonian Contributions to Anthropology, vol. 23. Washington, DC: Smithsonian Institution Press.

LeBlanc, S. A. 2003. "Warfare in the American Southwest and Mesoamerica: Parallels and Contrasts." In *Ancient Mesoamerican Warfare,* ed. M. K. Brown, and T. W. Stanton, 265–286. Walnut Creek, CA: Altamira.

Leighton, A. C. 1972. *Transport and Communication in Early Medieval Europe, ad 500–1100.* Newton Abbot, England: David and Charles.

Lenkersdorf, G. 1979. *Diccionario Tojolabal-Español.* México, DF: Editorial Nuestro Tiempo.

Leverentz, A. 2010. "People, Places, and Things: How Female Ex-Prisoners Negotiate Their Neighborhood Context." *Journal of Contemporary Ethnography* 39 (6): 646–681.

Levi, L. J. 1993. "Prehispanic Residence and Community at San Estevan, Belize." PhD dissertation, University of Arizona, Tucson.

Levi, L. J. 2002. "An Institutional Perspective on Prehispanic Maya Residential Variation: Settlement and Community at San Estevan, Belize." *Journal of Anthropological Archaeology* 21: 120–141.

Levine, M. N. 2007. *The Tututepec Archaeological Project (TAP): Residential Excavations at Yucu Dzaa, a Late Postclassic Mixtec Capital on the Coast of Oaxaca, Mexico.* Foundation for the Advancement of Mesoamerican Studies, Inc. http://www.famsi.org/reports/05031/05031Levine01.pdf. Accessed April 11, 2013.

Lind, M. 1979. *Postclassic and Early Colonial Mixtec Houses in the Nochixtlan Valley, Oaxaca.* Publications in Anthropology 23. Nashville, TN: Vanderbilt University.

Linné, S. 1934. *Archaeological Researches at Teotihuacan, Mexico.* Publication 1. Stockholm, Sweden: Ethnographic Museum of Sweden.

Livingstone-Smith, D. 2007. *The Most Dangerous Animal: Human Nature and the Origins of War.* New York: St. Martin's Griffen.

Lohse, J. C. 2004. "Intra-Site Settlement Signatures and Implications for Late Classic Maya Commoner Organization at Dos Hombres, Belize." In *Ancient Maya Commoners*, ed. J. C. Lohse and F. Valdez Jr., 117–145. Austin: University of Texas Press.

Looper, M. 2003. *Lightning Warrior: Maya Art and Kingship at Quirigua*. Linda Schele Series in Maya and Pre-Columbian Studies. Austin: University of Texas Press.

Lopes, L. 2005. *A Reading for the "STINGER" Glyph*. Mesoweb. http://www.dcc.fc.up.pt/~lblopes/epigraphy/papers/stinger05.pdf. Accessed January 21, 2015.

Lopez Bravo, R. 2000. "La Veneración de los Ancestros en Palenque." *Arqueología Mexicana* 8 (45): 38–43.

Lopez de Cogolludo, D. 1688. *Historia de Yucatan*. Madrid, Spain: Juan Garcia Infanzón.

Loten, H. S. 2006. "A Distinctive Maya Architectural Format: The Lamanai Temple." In *Reconstructing the Past: Studies in Mesoamerican and Central American Prehistory*, ed. D. M. Pendergast and A. P. Andrews, 89–106. BAR International Series 1529. Oxford, England: British Archaeological Reports.

Loten, H. S., and D. M. Pendergast. 1984. *A Lexicon for Maya Architecture*. Toronto, Canada: Royal Ontario Museum.

Lothrop, S. K. 1924. *Tulum: An Archaeological Study of the East Coast of Yucatan*. Washington, DC: Carnegie Institution of Washington.

Lowe, G. W., and P. Agrinier. 1960. *Mound 1, Chiapa de Corzo, Chiapas, Mexico*. Provo, UT: New World Archaeological Foundation, Brigham Young University.

Lucht, B. 2007. "Introduction." In *The Lost Massey Lectures: Recovered Classics from Five Great Thinkers—John Kenneth Galbraith, Paul Goodman, Jane Jacobs, Eric W. Kierans, and Martin Luther King Jr.*, vii–xvi. Toronto, Canada: Anansi.

Lyall, V. I. 2011. "Between Two Worlds: Northern Maya Mural Painting and the Development of a Regional Identity." PhD dissertation, University of California, Los Angeles.

Maass, P. 2011. *The Toppling: How the Media Inflated a Minor Moment in a Long War*. http://www.newyorker.com/reporting/2011/01/10/110110fa_fact_maass. Accessed February 6, 2013.

Macleod, B. 1990. "The God N/Step Set in the Primary Standard Sequence." In *The Maya Vase Book: A Corpus of Roll-Out Photographs*, vol. 2, ed. J. Kerr, 331–347. New York: Kerr Associates.

MacNeish, R. S. 1964. "Ancient Mesoamerican Civilization." *Science* 143: 531–537.

MacNeish, R. S., A. Nelken-Terner, and I. W. de Johnson. 1967. *The Prehistory of the Tehuacan Valley: The Non-Ceramic Artifacts*. Austin: University of Texas Press.

Mann, M. 1986. *The Sources of Social Power*, vol. 1: *A History of Power from the Beginning to ad 1760*. Cambridge, England: Cambridge University Press.

Manzanilla, L. 2011. "Sistemas de Control de Mano de Obra y del Intercambio de Bienes Suntuarios en el Corredor Teotihuacano hacia la Costa del Golfo en el Clásico." *Anales de Antropología* 45: 9–32.

Manzanilla López, R. 2008. *La Región Arqueológica de la Costa Grande de Guerrero*. México, DF: Colección Científica, Instituto Nacional de Antropología e Historia.

Marcus, J. 1992a. *Mesoamerican Writing Systems: Propaganda, Myth, and History in Four Ancient Civilizations*. Princeton, NJ: Princeton University Press.

Marcus, J. 1992b. "Political Fluctuations in Mesoamerica." *National Geographic Research and Exploration* 8 (4): 392–411.

Marcus, J., and K. V. Flannery. 1996. *Zapotec Civilization: How Urban Society Evolved in Mexico's Oaxaca Valley*. London: Thames and Hudson.

Marshall, J. M., III. 2007. *The Day the World Ended at Little Bighorn: A Lakota History*. New York: Penguin Books.

Martin, S. 1996. "Tikal's 'Star War' against Naranjo." In *Eighth Palenque Round Table, 1993*, ed. M. Greene Robertson, 223–236. San Francisco: Pre-Columbian Art Research Institute.

Martin, S. 1997a. "Painted King List: A Commentary on Codex-Style Dynastic Vases." In *Maya Vase Book: A Corpus of Rollout Photographs of Maya Vases*, vol. 5, ed. J. Kerr, 847–867. New York: Kerr Associates.

Martin, S. 1997b. "Supernatural Patrons and Mythic Paradigms." Paper presented at the Maya Religion Conference, Brigham Young University, Provo, UT, April 4.

Martin, S. 2000a. "At the Periphery: The Movement, Modification and Re-Use of Early Monuments in the Environs of Tikal." *Acta Mesoamericana* 10: 51–61.

Martin, S. 2000b. "Nuevos Datos Epigraficos sobre la Guerra Maya del Clasico." In *La Guerra Entre los Antiguos Mayas: Memorias de la Primera Mesa Redondo de Palenque*, ed. S. Trejo, 105–124. México, DF: Instituto Nacional de Antropología e Historia.

Martin, S. 2002. "The Baby Jaguar: An Explanation of Its Identity and Origins in Maya Art and Writing." In *La Organización Social Entre los Mayas: Memoria de la Tercera Mesa Redonda de Palenque*, vol. 1, ed. V. Tiesler Blos, R. Cobos, and M. Greene Robertson, 49–78. México, DF: Instituto Nacional de Antropología e Historia.

Martin, S. 2003. "In Line of the Founder: A View of Dynastic Politics at Tikal." In *Tikal: Dynasties, Foreigners, and Affairs of State*, ed. J. A. Sabloff, 3–46. Santa Fe, NM: School of American Research Press.

Martin, S. 2004. "Preguntas Epigráficas Acerca de los Escalones de Dzibanché." In *Los Cautivos de Dzibanché*, ed. E. Nalda, 105–115. México, DF: Instituto Nacional de Antropología e Historia.

Martin, S. 2005a. "Caracol Altar 21 Revisited: More Data on Double Bird and Tikal's Wars of the Mid-Sixth Century." *PARI Journal* 6 (1): 1–9.

Martin, S. 2005b. "Of Snakes and Bats: Shifting Identities at Calakmul." *PARI Journal* 6 (2): 5–15.

Martin, S. 2006. "Cacao in Ancient Maya Religion: First Fruits of the Maize Tree and Other Tales from the Underworld." In *Theobroma Cacao in Pre-Columbian and Modern*

Mesoamerican Communities, ed. C. McNeil, 154–183. Gainesville: University of Florida Press.

Martin, S. 2009. "A Time for War: A Return to Statistical Approaches in Studying Classic Maya Conflict." Paper presented at the 14th European Maya Conference, Jagiellonian University and the Polish Academy of Arts and Sciences, Cracow, Poland, November 13–14.

Martin, S. 2014. "The Classic Maya Polity: An Epigraphic Approach to Reconstructing a Pre-Hispanic Political System." PhD dissertation, University College London, England.

Martin, S. 2016. "Stela Temple N10–27." In *Lamanai Guidebook: The Lamanai Archaeological Project*, ed. L. Belanger and C. Belanger. London: Louise Belanger Art and Archaeology.

Martin, S., and N. Grube. 2008. *Chronicle of the Maya Kings and Queens*. 2nd ed. London: Thames and Hudson.

Maschner, H.D.G. 1997. "The Evolution of Northwest Coast Warfare." In *War and Society*, vol. 3: *Troubled Times: Violence and Warfare in the Past*, ed. D. L. Martin and D. W. Frayer, 267–302. Amsterdam, Netherlands: Gordon and Breach.

Masson, M. A., and D. A. Freidel, eds. 2002. *Ancient Maya Political Economies*. Walnut Creek, CA: Altamira.

Mathews, J. P., and J. F. Garber. 2004. "Models of Cosmic Order: Physical Expression of Sacred Space among the Ancient Maya." *Ancient Mesoamerica* 15 (1): 49–59.

Mathews, P. 1991. "Classic Maya Emblem Glyphs." In *Classic Maya Political History: Hieroglyphic and Archaeological Evidence*, ed. T. P. Culbert, 19–29. School of American Research Advanced Seminar Series. Cambridge, England: Cambridge University Press.

Mathews, P. 2000. "Guerra en las Tierras Bajas Occidentales Mayas." In *La Guerra entre los Antiguos Mayas: Memorias de la Primera Mesa Redondo de Palenque*, ed. S. Trejo, 125–155. México, DF: Instituto Nacional de Antropología e Historia.

Matos Moctezuma, E., and I. Kelly. 1974. "Una Vasija que Sugiere Relaciones entre Teotihuacan y Colima." In *The Archaeology of West Mexico*, ed. B. Bell, 202–205. Jalisco, Mexico: Sociedad de estudios avanzados del Occidente de México.

Matthew, L. E., and M. R. Oudijk, eds. 2007. *Indian Conquistadors: Indigenous Allies in the Conquest of Mesoamerica*. Norman: University of Oklahoma Press.

Maxwell, J. M., and R. M. Hill II. 2006. *Kaqchikel Chronicles*. Austin: University of Texas Press.

McAnany, P. A. 2004. *K'axob: Ritual, Work, and Family in an Ancient Maya Village*. Monumenta Archaeologica 22. Los Angeles: Cotsen Institute of Archaeology, University of California.

McAnany, P. A. 2010. *Ancient Maya Economies in Archaeological Perspective*. Cambridge, England: Cambridge University Press.

McLellan, A. 2012. "Settlement Patterns at Ka'Kabish, Belize." MA thesis, Trent University, Peterborough, Canada.

Melchor Cruz Hernández, L., and O. L. Landa Alarcón. 2013. "Tingambato: Un Sitio del Occidente de México y una Tumba Real." *Arqueología Mexicana* 21 (123): 43–46.

Miller, A. 1973. *The Mural Painting of Teotihuacan.* Washington, DC: Dumbarton Oaks Research Library and Collection.

Miller, A. 1974. "West and East in Maya Thought: Death and Rebirth at Palenque and Tulum." In *Primera Mesa Redonda de Palenque Part II, a Conference on the Art, Iconography, and Dynastic History of Palenque: December 14–22, 1973, Palenque, Chiapas, Mexico*, ed. M. Greene Robertson, 45–49. Pebble Beach, CA: Pre-Columbian Art Research, Robertson Louis Stevenson School.

Miller, M. E. 1986. *The Murals of Bonampak.* Princeton, NJ: Princeton University Press.

Miller, M. E. 1998. "A Design for Meaning in Maya Architecture." In *Function and Meaning in Classic Maya Architecture*, ed. S. D. Houston, 187–222. Washington, DC: Dumbarton Oaks Research Library and Collection.

Miller, M. E., and S. Martin. 2004. *Courtly Art of the Ancient Maya.* London: Thames and Hudson.

Millon, C. 1988. "A Reexamination of the Teotihuacan Tassel Headdress Insignia." In *Feathered Serpents and Flowering Trees: Reconstructing the Murals of Teotihuacan*, ed. K. Berrin, 114–134. San Francisco: Fine Arts Museum of San Francisco.

Millon, R. 1973. *Urbanization at Teotihuacán, Mexico*, vol. I, part I: *The Teotihuacan Map: Text.* Austin: University of Texas Press.

Millon, R. 1992. "Teotihuacan Studies: From 1950 to 1990 and Beyond." In *Art, Ideology, and the City of Teotihuacan*, ed. J. C. Berlo, 339–419. Washington, DC: Dumbarton Oaks Research Library and Collection.

Mitani, J. C., D. P. Watts, and S. J. Amsler. 2010. "Lethal Intergroup Aggression Leads to Territorial Expansion in Wild Chimpanzees." *Current Biology* 20 (12): R507–R508.

Mock, S. B. 1998. "The Northern River Lagoon Site (NRL): Late to Terminal Classic Maya Settlement, Salt Making, and Survival on the Northern Belize Coast." PhD dissertation, University of Texas, Austin.

Monaghan, J. 1995. *The Covenants with Earth and Rain: Exchange, Sacrifice, and Revelation in Mixtec Sociality.* Norman: University of Oklahoma Press.

Monks, S., and R. Osgood. 2000. "Introduction." In *Bronze Age Warfare*, ed. R. Osgood, S. Monks, and J. Toms, 1–8. Gloucestershire, England: Sutton.

Montejo, V. 2001. *El Q'anil: Man of Lightning.* Tucson: University of Arizona Press.

Morante López, R. 2005. *Las Pinturas Mural de Las Higueras, Veracruz.* Xalapa, México: Universidad Veracruzana.

Morley, S. G. 1946. *The Ancient Maya.* Palo Alto, CA: Stanford University Press.

Nahm, W. 1994. "Maya Warfare and the Venus Year." *Mexicon* 16 (1): 6–10.

Nash, J. 1970. *In the Eyes of the Ancestors.* New Haven, CT: Yale University Press.

Nations, J. D., and J. E. Clark. 1983. "The Bows and Arrows of the Lacandon Maya." *Archaeology* 36 (1): 36–43.

Navarrete, C. 1986. "The Sculptural Complex at Cerro Bernal on the Coast of Chiapas." *Notes of the New World Archaeological Foundation* 1: 3–28.

Neivens, M., and D. Libbey. 1976. "An Obsidian Workshop at El Pozito, Northern Belize." In *Maya Lithic Studies*, ed. N. Hammond and T. R. Hester, 137–149. San Antonio: Center for Archaeological Research, University of Texas.

Nielsen, A. E., and W. H. Walker. 2009. "The Archaeology of War in Practice." In *Warfare in Cultural Context: Practice, Agency, and the Archaeology of Violence*, ed. A. E. Nielsen and W. H. Walker, 1–14. Tucson: University of Arizona Press.

Nielsen, J. 2003. "Art of the Empire: Teotihuacan Iconography and Style in Early Classic Maya Society (AD 380–500)." Vols. 1 and 2. PhD dissertation, University of Copenhagen, Copenhagen, Denmark.

Nielsen, J. 2004. "The Coyote and the Tasseled Shield: A Possible Titular Glyph on a Late Xolalpan Teotihuacan Tripod." *Mexicon* 26 (3): 61–64.

Nielsen, J. 2006a. "The Coming of the Torch: Observations on Teotihuacan Iconography in Early Classic Tikal." In *Maya Ethnicity: The Construction of Ethnic Identity from the Preclassic to Modern Times*, ed. F. Sachse, 19–30. Acta Mesoamericana 11. Markt Schwaben, Germany: Verlag Anton Saurwein.

Nielsen, J. 2006b. "The Queen's Mirrors: Interpreting the Iconography of Two Teotihuacan Style Mirrors from the Early Classic Margarita Tomb at Copan." *PARI Journal* 6 (4): 1–8.

Nielsen, J. 2014. "'To Sing Arrows': Observations on the Representation of Sound in the Writing and Iconography of Teotihuacan." In *A Celebration of the Life and Work of Pierre Robert Colas*, ed. C. Helmke and F. Sachse, 175–191. Acta Mesoamericana 27. Munich, Germany: Verlag Anton Saurwein.

Nielsen, J., and C. Helmke. 2008. "Spearthrower Owl Hill: A Toponym at Atetelco, Teotihuacan." *Latin American Antiquity* 19 (4): 459–474.

Nielsen, J., and C. Helmke. 2011. "Reinterpreting the Plaza de los Glifos, La Ventilla, Teotihuacan." *Ancient Mesoamerica* 22 (2): 345–370.

Nielsen, J., and C. Helmke. 2014. "House of the Serpent Mat, House of Fire: The Names of Buildings in Teotihuacan Writing." *Contributions in New World Archaeology* 7: 113–140.

Nielsen, J., and C. Helmke. 2015. "Estudio Preliminar de la Iconografía de los Murales de El Rosario, Querétaro, México." In *El Valle de San Juan del Río: Un Palimpsesto Arqueológico*, ed. J. C. Saint-Charles Zetina, 75–83. Santiago de Querétaro, Mexico: Archivo Histórico Municipal.

Nielsen, J. and C. Helmke. 2018. "'Where the sun came into being': Rites of Pyrolatry, Transition, and Transformation in Early Classic Teotihuacan." In *Smoke, Flames, and the Human Body in Mesoamerican Ritual Practice*, ed. V. Tiesler and A.K. Scherer, 77–107. Washington, DC: Dumbarton Oaks Research Library and Collection.

Nielsen, J., E. Jiménez García and I. Rivera. 2019a. "Across the Hills, toward the Ocean: Teotihuacan-style Monuments in Guerrero, Mexico." In *Interregional Interaction in Ancient Mesoamerica*, ed. J.D. Englehardt and M.D. Carrasco, 176–209. Louisville: University Press of Colorado.

Nielsen, J., C. Helmke, F. Fenoglio Limón, C. Viramontes Anzures, and J. C. Saint-Charles Zetina. 2019b. *Early Classic Murals of El Rosario, Querétaro, Mexico: Description and Iconographic Analysis*. Ancient America Monograph 14. Barnardsville, NC: Boundary End Center.

Novak, S. A. 2014. "How to Say Things with Bodies: Meaningful Violence on an American Frontier." In *The Routledge Handbook of the Bioarchaeology of Human Conflict*, ed. C. Knüsel and M. J. Smith, 542–559. London: Routledge.

Núñez de la Vega, F. 1988. *Constituciones Diocesanas del Obispado de Chiapas*. México, DF: Universidad Nacional Autónoma de México.

Nuttall, Z. 1891. *The Atlatl or Spear-Thrower of the Ancient Mexicans*. Cambridge, MA: Peabody Museum of American Archaeology and Ethnology, Harvard University.

Nuttall, Z. 1975. *The Codex Nuttall: A Picture Manuscript from Ancient Mexico: The Peabody Museum Facsimile*. Dover, England: Courier Dover Publications.

Oland, M., S. M. Hart, and L. Frink, eds. 2012. *Decolonizing Indigenous Histories: Exploring Prehistoric/Colonial Transitions in Archaeology*. Tucson: University of Arizona Press.

Oliveros, J. A. 1975. "Arqueología del Estado de Michoacán." In *Los Pueblos y Señoríos Teocráticos: El Periodo de las Ciudades Urbanas, Primera Parte*, ed. E. Matos Moctezuma, 207–214. México, DF: Secretaría de Educación Pública/Instituto Nacional de Antropología e Historia.

Olmos Curiel, A. 2006. *Ruta Arqueológica de Michoacán*. Morelia, Mexico: Consejo Nacional Para la Cultura y las Artes/Secretaría de Cultura, Morelia.

O'Mansky, M., and A. A. Demarest. 2007. "Status Rivalry and Warfare in the Development and Collapse of Classic Maya Civilization." In *Latin American Indigenous Warfare and Ritual Violence*, ed. R. J. Chacon and R. G. Mendoz, 11–33. Tucson: University of Arizona Press.

O'Manksy, M., and N. P. Dunning. 2004. "Settlement and Late Classic Political Disintegration in the Petexbatun Region, Guatemala." In *The Terminal Classic in the Maya Lowlands*, ed. A. A. Demarest, P. M. Rice, and D. S. Rice, 83–101. Boulder: University Press of Colorado.

Orejel, J. 1990. *The "Axe/Comb" Glyph (T333) as Ch'ak*. Research Reports on Ancient Maya Writing, vol. 31. Washington, DC: Center for Maya Research.

Orellana, S. L. 1984. *The Tzutujil Mayas: Continuity and Change, 1250–1630*. Norman: University of Oklahoma Press.

Orr, H., and R. Koontz, eds. 2009. *Blood and Beauty: Organized Violence in the Art and Architecture of Mesoamerica and Central America*. Los Angeles: Cotsen Institute of Archaeology, University of California.

Ortíz Ceballos, P., and M. del Carmen Rodríguez. 1999. "Olmec Ritual Behavior at El Manati: A Sacred Space." In *Social Patterns in Pre-Classic Mesoamerica*, ed. D. C. Grove and R. A. Joyce, 225–254. Washington, DC: Dumbarton Oaks Research Library and Collection.

Otterbein, K. F. 1968. "Internal War: A Cross-Cultural Study." *American Anthropologist* 70: 277–289.

Otterbein, K. F., ed. 1994. *Feuding and Warfare: Selected Works of Keith F. Otterbein*. Langhorn, PA: Gordon and Breach.

Otterbein, K. F. 2000a. "A History of Research on Warfare in Anthropology." *American Anthropologist* 101 (4): 794–805.

Otterbein, K. F. 2000b. "The Killing of Captured Enemies: A Cross-Cultural Study." *Current Anthropology* 41: 439–443.

Otterbein, K. F. 2004. *How War Began*. College Station: Texas A&M University Press.

Oudijk, M. 2002. "La Toma de Posesión: Una Tema Mesoamericano Para la Legitimación del Poder." *Relaciones* 23: 97–131.

Paddock, J., ed. 1966. *Ancient Oaxaca: Discoveries in Mexican Archeology and History*. Stanford, CA: Stanford University Press.

Pagliaro, J. B., J. F. Garber, and T. W. Stanton. 2003. "Evaluating the Archaeological Signature of Maya Ritual and Conflict." In *Ancient Mesoamerican Warfare*, ed. M. K. Brown and T. W. Stanton, 75–89. Walnut Creek, CA: Altamira.

Palacios, E. J. 1928. *En los Confines de la Selva Lacandona: Exploraciones en el Estado de Chiapas, 1926*. México, DF: Talleres Gráficos de la Nación.

Palka, J. W. 2014. *Maya Pilgrimage to Ritual Landscapes: Insights from Archaeology, History, and Ethnography*. Albuquerque: University of New Mexico Press.

Parsons, J. R. 1971. *Prehistoric Settlement Patterns in the Texcoco Region, Mexico*. Memoirs of the Museum of Anthropology 3. Ann Arbor: University of Michigan.

Pasztory, E. 1974. *The Iconography of the Teotihuacan Tlaloc*. Washington, DC: Dumbarton Oaks Research Library and Collection.

Patel, S. 2005. "Pilgrimage and Caves on Cozumel." In *Stone Houses and Earth Lords: Maya Religion in the Cave Context*, ed. K. M. Prufer and J. E. Brady, 91–114. Boulder: University Press of Colorado.

Pendergast, D. M. 1977. "Royal Ontario Museum Excavation: Finds at Lamanai, Belize." *Archaeology* 30: 129–131.

Pendergast, D. M. 1979. *Excavations at Altun Ha, Belize, 1964–1970, Volume 1*. Toronto, Canada: Royal Ontario Museum.

Pendergast, D. M. 1981. "Lamanai, Belize: A Summary of Excavation Results." *Journal of Field Archaeology* 8: 29–53.

Pendergast, D. M. 1982. *Excavations at Altun Ha, Belize, 1964–1970, Volume 2*. Toronto, Canada: Royal Ontario Museum.

Pendergast, D. M. 1983. "Lamanai, 1983: A Real Glyph-Hanger." *ROM Archaeological Newsletter, New Series* 215: 1–3.

Pendergast, D. M. 1984. "Excavations at Lamanai, Belize, 1983." *Mexicon* 6 (1): 5–10.

Pendergast, D. M. 1985. "Lamanai, Belize: An Updated View." In *The Lowland Maya Post-classic*, ed. A. F. Chase and P. M. Rice, 91–103. Austin: University of Texas Press.

Pendergast, D. M. 1986. "Stability through Change: Lamanai, Belize, from the Ninth to the Seventeenth Century." In *Late Lowland Maya Civilization: Classic to Postclassic*, ed. J. A. Sabloff and E. W. Andrews V, 223–249. Albuquerque: School of American Research, University of New Mexico Press.

Pendergast, D. M. 1988. *Lamanai Stela 9: The Archaeological Context*. Research Reports on Ancient Maya Writing, vol. 20. Washington, DC: Center for Maya Research.

Pendergast, D. M. 1990. *Excavations at Altun Ha, Belize, 1964–1970, Volume 3*. Toronto, Canada: Royal Ontario Museum.

Pendergast, D. M. 1992. "Noblesse Oblige: The Elites at Lamanai and Altun Ha, Belize." In *Mesoamerican Elites: An Archaeological Perspective*, ed. D. Z. Chase and A. F. Chase, 61–79. Norman: University of Oklahoma Press.

Pendergast, D. M. 1993. "The Centre of the Edge: Archaeology in Belize, 1809–1992." *Journal of World Prehistory* 7 (1): 1–33.

Pendergast, D. M. 1998. "Intercessions with the Gods: Caches and Their Significance at Altun Ha and Lamanai, Belize." In *The Sowing and the Dawning: Terminations, Dedications, and Transformations in the Archaeological and Ethnographic Record of Mesoamerica*, ed. S. Boteler Mock, 55–63. Albuquerque: University of New Mexico Press.

Pharo, L. K. 2007. "The Concept of 'Religion' in Mesoamerican Languages." *Numen* 54 (1): 28–70.

Pijoan Aguadé, C. M., and J. Mansilla Lory. 1997. "Evidence for Human Sacrifice, Bone Modification, and Cannibalism in Ancient Mexico." In *Troubled Times: Violence and Warfare in the Past*, ed. D. L. Martin and D. W. Frayer, 217–239. Amsterdam, Netherlands: Gordon and Breach.

Pijoan Aguadé, C. M., and A. Pastrana. 1989. "Evidencias de Actividades Rituales en Restos Óseos Humanos en Tlatelcomila, D.F." *El Preclásico o Formativo, Avances y Perspectivas* 1: 287–307.

Piña Chan, R. 1964. "Algunas Consideraciones sobre las Pinturas de Mul-Chic, Yucatán." *Estudios de Cultura Maya* 4: 63–78.

Pinker, S. 2011. *The Better Angels of Our Nature: The Decline of Violence in History and Its Causes*. London: Penguin UK.

Pitarch, P. 2010. *The Jaguar and the Priest: An Ethnography of Tzetzal Souls*. Austin: University of Texas Press.

Pohl, J.M.D. 1991. *Aztec, Mixtec, and Zapotec Armies*. London: Osprey.

Pohl, J.M.D. 2002. *The Legend of Lord Eight Deer: An Epic of Ancient Mexico*. Oxford, England: Oxford University Press.

Pohl, J.M.D. 2003. *Ancient Books: Mixtec Group Codices, John Pohl's Mesoamerica*. Foundation for the Advancement of Mesoamerican Studies, Inc. http://www.famsi.org/research/pohl/jpcodices/pohlmixtec1.html. Accessed April 11, 2013.

Pohl, J.M.D., and C. M. Robinson. 2005. *Aztecs and Conquistadores: The Spanish Invasion and the Collapse of the Aztec Empire*. Oxford, England: Osprey.

Pohl, M., and J.M.D. Pohl. 1994. "Cycles of Conflict: Political Factionalism in the Maya Lowlands." In *Factional Competition and Political Development in the New World*, ed. E. Brumfiel and J. Fox, 138–157. Cambridge, England: Cambridge University Press.

Pollard, H. P. 2000. "Tarascans and Their Ancestors: Prehistory of Michoacán." In *Greater Mesoamerica: The Archaeology of West and Northwest Mexico*, ed. M. S. Foster and S. Gorenstein, 59–70. Salt Lake City: University of Utah Press.

Pollard, H. P., and L. Cahue. 1999. "Mortuary Patterns of Regional Elites in the Lake Patzcuaro Basin of Western Mexico." *Latin American Antiquity* 10 (3): 259–280.

Pollock, H.E.D. 1980. *The Puuc: An Architectural Survey of the Hill Country of Yucatan and Northern Campeche, Mexico*. Memoirs of the Peabody Museum, vol. 19. Cambridge, MA: Harvard University.

Polyukhovych, Y. 2012. "Political and Dynastic History of the Maya State of Baakal According to the Sources of the Epigraphic Corpus of Palenque (Lakamha')." PhD dissertation, Taras Shevchenko National University of Kyiv, Kyiv, Ukraine.

Pool, C. A., and G. J. Bey III, eds. 2007. *Pottery Economics in Mesoamerica*. Tucson: University of Arizona Press.

Poulter, J. 2008. "The Direction and Planning of the Eastern Sector of Hadrian's Wall: Some Further Thoughts." In *Understanding Hadrian's Wall*, ed. P. Bidwell, 99–104. South Shields, England: Arbeia Society.

Powis, T. G. 2001. *The Preclassic Whole Vessels of Lamanai, Belize: A Final Report*. Foundation for the Advancement of Mesoamerican Studies, Inc. http://www.famsi.org/reports/99057/99057Powis01.pdf. Accessed October 2, 2012.

Powis, T. G. 2002. "An Integrative Approach to the Analysis of the Late Preclassic Ceramics at Lamanai, Belize." PhD dissertation, University of Texas, Austin.

Prager, C., E. Wagner, S. Matteo, and G. Krempel. 2010. "A Reading for the Xultun Toponymic Title as B'aax (Tuun) Witz Ajaw 'Lord of the B'aax-(Stone) Hill.'" *Mexicon* 32 (4): 74–77.

Pratchett, T., and N. Gaiman. 1990. *Good Omens. The Nice and Accurate Prophesies of Agnes Nutter, Witch*. London: Corgi Books.

Proskouriakoff, T. 1950. *A Study of Classic Maya Sculpture*. Publication 593. Washington, DC: Carnegie Institution of Washington.

Proskouriakoff, T. 1993. *Maya History*. Austin: University of Texas Press.

Pugh, T. W. 2003. "The Exemplary Center of the Late Postclassic Kowoj Maya." *Latin American Antiquity* 14 (4): 408–430.

Pugh, T. W., and P. M. Rice. 2009a. "Kowoj Ritual Performance and Societal Representations." In *The Kowoj: Identity, Migration, and Geopolitics in the Late Postclassic Petén, Guatemala*, ed. P. M. Rice and D. S. Rice, 141–172. Boulder: University Press of Colorado.

Pugh, T. W., and P. M. Rice. 2009b. "Zacpetén and the Kowoj: Field Methods and Chronologies." In *The Kowoj: Identity, Migration, and Geopolitics in the Late Postclassic Petén, Guatemala*, ed. P. M. Rice and D. S. Rice, 85–115. Boulder: University Press of Colorado.

Pyburn, A. 1990. "Settlement Patterns at Nohmul: Preliminary Results of Four Excavation Seasons." In *Precolumbian Population History in the Maya Lowlands*, ed. T. P. Culbert and D. S. Rice, 183–198. Albuquerque: University of New Mexico Press.

Pyburn, A. 1991. "Chau Hiix: A New Archaeological Site in Northern Belize." *Mexicon* 13 (5): 84–86.

Raaflaub, K. 1999. "Archaic and Classical Greece." In *War and Society in the Ancient and Medieval Worlds*, ed. K. Raaflaub and N. Rosenstein, 129–141. Cambridge, MA: Harvard University Press.

Rashid, A. 2001. "After 1,700 Years, Buddhas Fall to Taliban Dynamite." *The Telegraph*, March 12.

Recinos, A. 1957. *Crónicas Indígenas de Guatemala*. Guatemala City: Editorial Universitaria.

Recinos, A., and D. Goetz. 1953. *The Annals of the Cakchiquels*. Norman: University of Oklahoma Press.

Redmond, E. M., and C. S. Spencer. 2006. "From Raiding to Conquest: Warfare Strategies and Early State Development in Oaxaca, Mexico." In *The Archaeology of Warfare: Prehistories of Raiding and Conquest*, ed. M. W. Allen and E. N. Arkush, 336–393. Gainesville: University Press of Florida.

Reed, N. A. 1964. *The Caste War of Yucatan*. Stanford, CA: Stanford University Press.

Reents-Budet, D. 1988. *The Iconography of Lamanai Stela 9*. Research Reports on Ancient Maya Writing 22. Washington, DC: Center for Maya Research.

Reilly, F. K., III, and J. F. Garber. 2003. "The Symbolic Representation of Warfare in Formative Period Mesoamerica." In *Ancient Mesoamerican Warfare*, ed. M. K. Brown and T. W. Stanton, 127–148. Walnut Creek, CA: Altamira.

Restall, M. 1997. *The Maya World: Yucatec Culture and Society 1550–1850*. Stanford, CA: Stanford University Press.

Reyna, S. P. 1994. "A Mode of Domination Approach to Organized Violence." In *Studying War, Anthropological Perspectives: War and Society*, vol. 2, ed. S. P. Reyna and R. E. Davis, 29–65. Langhorne, PA: Gordon and Breach Science Publishers.

Reyna, S. P., and R. E. Downs, eds. 1994. *Studying War, Anthropological Perspectives: War and Society*, vol. 2. Langhorne, PA: Gordon and Breach Science Publishers.

Reyna Robles, R. M. 2002. "Esculturas, Estelas y Lápidas de la Región del Balsas: Acercamiento a su Cronología e Interpretación." In *El Pasado Arqueológico de Guerrero*, ed. C. Niederberger and R. M. Reyna Robles, 359–386. México, DF: Consejo Nacional Para la Cultura y las Artes/Instituto Nacional de Antropología e Historia.

Rice, P. M. 2009. "The Kowoj in Geopolitical Perspective." In *The Kowoj: Identity, Migration, and Geopolitics in the Late Postclassic Petén, Guatemala*, ed. P. M. Rice and D. S. Rice, 21–51. Boulder: University Press of Colorado.

Rice, P. M., D. S. Rice, T. W. Pugh, and R. S. Polo. 2009. "Defensive Architecture and the Context of Warfare at Zacpetén." In *The Kowoj: Identity, Migration, and Geopolitics in Late Postclassic Petén, Guatemala*, ed. P. M. Rice and D. S. Rice, 123–140. Boulder: University Press of Colorado.

Rincón Mautner, C. 2005. "Sacred Caves and Rituals from the Northern Mixteca of Oaxaca, Mexico: New Revelations." In *In the Maw of the Earth Monster: Mesoamerican Ritual Cave Use*, ed. J. E. Brady and K. M. Prufer, 117–152. Austin: University of Texas Press.

Ringle, W. M. 2009. "The Art of War: Imagery of the Upper Temple of the Jaguars, Chichen Itza." *Ancient Mesoamerica* 20 (1): 15–44.

Ringle, W. M. 2012. "The Nunnery Quadrangle of Uxmal." In *The Ancient Maya of Mexico: Reinterpreting the Past of the Northern Maya Lowlands*, ed. G. E. Braswell, 191–228. Sheffield, England: Equinox.

Ringle, W. M., and G. J. Bey III. 1992. "The Center and Segmentary State Dynamics." Paper presented at the Wenner-Gren Conference on the Segmentary State and the Classic Maya Lowlands, Cleveland State University, Cleveland, OH.

Ringle, W. M., G. J. Bey III, and T. Gallareta Negrón. 2006. "The Urban Process in Northern Yucatan: Puuc to Plains." Paper presented at the 71st Meeting of the Society for American Archaeology, San Juan, Puerto Rico, April 26–30.

Ringle, W. M., G. J. Bey III, and T. Gallareta Negrón. 2009. *A New Monument from Huntichmul, Yucatan, Mexico*. Research Reports on Ancient Maya Writing 57. Barnardsville, NC: Boundary End Archaeological Research Center.

Ringle, W. M., G. J. Bey III, and T. Gallareta Negrón. In press. "A Forest Unmasked: Alternative Pathways to Complexity in the Puuc Hills of Yucatan." In *The Coming of Kings*, ed. M. K. Brown and T. W. Stanton. Boulder: University Press of Colorado.

Ringle, W. M., T. Gallareta Negrón, and G. J. Bey III. 1998. "The Return of Quetzalcoatl: Evidence for the Spread of a World Religion during the Epiclassic Period." *Ancient Mesoamerica* 9: 183–232.

Ringle, W. M., and G. Tun Ayora. 2013. "The Yaxhom Valley Survey: Pioneers of the Puuc Hills, Yucatan." Report submitted to the Waitt Foundation–National Geographic Society in fulfillment of Grant W218–12. National Geographic Society, Washington, DC.

Rivera Guzmán, Á. I. 2011. "Cerro de la Tortuga: Un Sitio Arqueológico con Icono-grafía Teotihuacana en la Región Chatina, Costa de Oaxaca." In *Monte Albán en la Encrucijada Regional y Disciplinaria: Memoria de la Quinta Mesa Redonda de Monte Albán*, ed. N. M. R. García and Á. I. Rivera Guzmán, 429–443. México, DF: Instituto Nacional de Antropología e Historia.

Robertson, M. G. 1991. *The Sculpture of Palenque 4*. Princeton, NJ: Princeton University Press.

Robertson, R. A., and D. A. Friedel. 1986. *Archaeology at Cerros, Belize, Central America*, vol. 1: *An Interim Report*. Dallas, TX: Southern Methodist University Press.

Robicsek, F., and D. M. Hales. 1981. *The Maya Book of the Dead: The Ceramic Codex, the Corpus of Codex Style Ceramics of the Late Classic Period*. Charlottesville: University of Virginia Art Museum.

Robicsek, F., and D. M. Hales. 1988. "A Ceramic Codex Fragment: The Sacrifice of Xbalanque." In *Maya Iconography*, ed. E. P. Benson and G. G. Griffin, 260–276. Princeton, NJ: Princeton University Press.

Robin, C. 1989. *Preclassic Maya Burials at Cuello, Belize*. BAR International Series 480. Oxford, England: British Archaeological Reports.

Robins, N. 2012. *The Corporation That Changed the World*. 2nd ed. London: Pluto.

Rochette, E. 2009. "The Late Classic Organization of Jade Artifact Production in the Middle Motagua Valley, Zacapa, Guatemala." PhD dissertation, Pennsylvania State University, State College.

Romero, G. B. 2015. "Glifos Enigmáticos de la Escritura Maya: El Logograma T514, YEJ, 'filo.'" *Arqueología Mexicana* 23 (135): 78–85.

Roscoe, P. 2011. "Dead Birds: The 'Theater' of War among the Dugum Dani." *American Anthropologist* 113 (1): 56–70.

Rosenswig, R. M. 2008. "Recent Excavations at San Estevan, Northern Belize." *Research Reports in Belizean Archaeology* 5: 261–268.

Rosenswig, R. M. 2009. "The Emergence of Complexity at San Estevan." *Research Reports in Belizean Archaeology* 6: 101–108.

Rosenswig, R. M., and D. J. Kennett. 2008. "Reassessing San Estevan's Role in the Late Formative Political Landscape of Northern Belize." *Latin American Antiquity* 19: 124–146.

Roys, R. L., F. V. Scholes, and E. Burnham Adams. 1940. *Report and Census of the Indians of Cozumel, 1570*. Publication 523. Washington, DC: Carnegie Institution of Washington.

Ruskin, J. 1909. *War (Lecture III) in the Crown of Wild Olive*, 85–120. London: Cassell.

Sagebiel, K. L. 2005a. "Shifting Allegiances at La Milpa, Belize: A Typological, Chrono-logical, and Formal Analysis of the Ceramics." PhD dissertation, University of Arizona, Tucson.

Sagebiel, K. L. 2005b. "Blue Creek Regional Political Ecology Ceramic Report, 2004 Season." In "2004 Season Summaries of the Blue Creek Regional Political Ecology Project, Upper Northwestern Belize," ed. J. C. Lohse and K. L. Sagebiel, 16–40. Report submitted to the Institute of Archaeology, Belmopan, Belize.

Sagebiel, K. L. 2006. "Blue Creek Regional Political Ecology Ceramic Report, 2005 Season." In "Final Season Summaries of the Blue Creek Regional Political Ecology Project, 2005 Investigations in Upper Northwestern Belize," ed. J. C. Lohse, 76–95. Report submitted to the Institute of Archaeology, Belmopan, Belize.

Sahagún, B. de. 1981. *General History of the Things of New Spain: Florentine Codex, Book 2—The Ceremonies*, trans. A.J.O. Anderson and C. E. Dibble. Monographs of the School of American Research 14, part 3. Santa Fe, NM: School of American Research and University of Utah Press.

Saint-Charles Zetina, J. C., C. Viramontes Anzures, and F. Fenoglio Limón. 2010. *El Rosario, Querétaro: Un Enclave Teotihuacano en el Centro Norte, Tiempo y Región*. Estudios Históricos y Sociales, vol. 4. México, DF: Municipio de Querétaro, Instituto Nacional de Antropología e Historia, and Universidad Autónoma de Querétaro.

Sanders, W. T., J. R. Parsons, and R. S. Santley. 1979. *The Basin of Mexico: Ecological Processes in the Evolution of a Civilization*. New York: Academic.

Sanders, W. T., and D. Webster. 1988. "The Mesoamerican Urban Tradition." *American Anthropologist* 90: 521–566.

Santley, R. S. 1989. "Obsidian Working, Long-Distance Exchange, and the Teotihuacan Presence on the South Gulf Coast." In *Mesoamerica after the Decline of Teotihuacan AD 700–900*, ed. R. A. Diehl and J. C. Berlo, 131–151. Washington, DC: Dumbarton Oaks Research Library and Collection.

Saturno, W. 2000. "In the Shadow of the Acropolis: Rio Amarillo and Its Role in the Copan Polity." PhD dissertation, Harvard University, Cambridge, MA.

Saunders, N. J. 2004. "Material Culture and Conflict: The Great War, 1914–2003." In *Matters of Conflict: Material Culture, Memory, and the First World War*, ed. N. J. Saunders, 5–20. London: Routledge.

Schaffer, A. 1987. "Reassembling a Lost Maya Masterpiece." *Bulletin: The Museum of Fine Arts, Texas* 10 (2): 10–13.

Schele, L., and D. Freidel. 1990. *A Forest of Kings: Untold Stories of the Ancient Maya*. New York: William Morrow.

Schele, L., and P. Mathews. 1998. *The Code of Kings: The Language of Seven Sacred Maya Temples and Tombs*. New York: Scribner.

Schele, L., and M. E. Miller. 1986. *The Blood of Kings: Dynasty and Ritual in Maya Art*. Fort Worth, TX: Kimbell Art Museum.

Scherer, A. K., and C. Golden. 2014. "War in the West: History, Landscape, and Classic Maya Conflict." In *Embattled Bodies, Embattled Places: War in Pre-Columbian*

Mesoamerica and the Andes, ed. A. K. Scherer and J. W. Verano, 57–92. Washington, DC: Dumbarton Oaks Research Library and Collection.

Scherer, A. K., and J. M. Verano. 2014. "Introducing War in Pre-Columbian Mesoamerica and the Andes." In *Embattled Bodies, Embattled Places: War in Pre-Columbian Mesoamerica and the Andes*, ed. A. K. Scherer and J. M. Verano, 1–23. Washington, DC: Dumbarton Oaks Research Library and Collection.

Schmidt, B. E. 2001. "The Interpretation of Violent Worldviews: Cannibalism and Other Violent Images of the Caribbean." In *Anthropology of Violence and Conflict*, ed. I. W. Schröder and B. E. Schmidt, 76–96. London: Routledge.

Schmidt, S. M., and T. A. Kochan. 1972. "Conflict: Toward Conceptual Clarity." *Administrative Science Quarterly* 17 (3): 359–370.

Schröder, I. W., and B. E. Schmidt. 2001. "Introduction: Violent Imaginaries and Violent Practices." In *Anthropology of Violence and Conflict*, ed. I. W. Schröder and B. E. Schmidt, 1–24. London: Routledge.

Séjourné, L. 1976 [1956]. *Burning Water: Thought and Religion in Ancient Mexico*. Berkeley, CA: Shambala.

Serafin, S., C. Peraza Lope, and E. Uc González. 2014. "Bioarchaeological Investigation of Ancient Maya Violence and Warfare in Inland Northwest Yucatan, Mexico." *American Journal of Physical Anthropology* 154: 140–151.

Serafin, S., E. Uc González, and C. Peraza Lope. 2014. "Practicas Funerarias y Rituales en el Cenote San José de Mayapán." In *The Archaeology of Yucatán: New Directions and Data*, ed. T. W. Stanton, 81–92. Oxford, England: Archaeopress.

Service, E. R. 1962. *Primitive Social Organization: An Evolutionary Perspective.* New York: Random House.

Service, E. R. 1966. *The Hunters.* Foundations of Modern Anthropology Series. Englewood Cliffs, NJ: Prentice-Hall.

Shankari, P. 2005. "Pilgrimage and Caves on Cozumel." In *Stone Houses and Earth Lords: Maya Religion in the Cave Context*, ed. K. M. Prufer and J. E. Brady, 91–112. Boulder: University Press of Colorado.

Sharer, R. 1994. *The Ancient Maya.* 5th ed. Stanford, CA: Stanford University Press.

Sharer, R. J., D. W. Sedat, L. P. Traxler, J. C. Miller, and E. E. Bell. 2005. "Early Classic Royal Power in Copán: The Origins and Development of the Acropolis (ca. AD 250–600)." In *Copán: The History of a Kingdom*, ed. E. W. Andrews and W. L. Fash, 139–199. Santa Fe, NM, and Oxford, England: School of American Research Press and James Currey.

Sheets, P. D. 2003. "Warfare in Ancient Mesoamerica: A Summary View." In *Ancient Mesoamerican Warfare*, ed. M. K. Brown and T. W. Stanton, 287–302. Walnut Creek, CA: Altamira.

Shiv, B., and A. Fedorikhin. 1999. "Heart and Mind in Conflict: The Interplay of Affect and Cognition in Consumer Decision Making." *Journal of Consumer Research* 26 (3): 278–292.

Silverstein, J. 2001. "Aztec Imperialism at Oztuma, Guerrero: Aztec-Chontal Relations during the Late Postclassic and Early Colonial Periods." *Ancient Mesoamerica* 12: 31–48.

Simmons, S. E. 1995. "Maya Resistance, Maya Resolve: The Tools of Autonomy from Tipu, Belize." *Ancient Mesoamerica* 6: 135–146.

Simmons, S. E. 2005. *Preliminary Report of the 2005 Field Season at Lamanai, Belize: The Maya Archaeometallurgy Project*. UNCW Anthropological Papers 5. Wilmington: University of Northern Carolina.

Simmons, S. E. 2006. *Preliminary Report of the 2006 Field Season at Lamanai, Belize: The Maya Archaeometallurgy Project*. UNCW Anthropological Papers 7. Wilmington: University of Northern Carolina.

Simmons, S. E., D. M. Pendergast, and E. Graham. 2009. "The Context and Significance of Copper Artifacts in Postclassic and Early Historic Lamanai, Belize." *Journal of Field Archaeology* 34 (1): 57–75.

Simms, S. R., E. Parker, G. Bey III, and T. Gallareta Negrón. 2012. "Evidence from Escalera al Cielo: Abandonment of a Terminal Classic Puuc Maya Hill Complex in Yucatán, Mexico." *Journal of Field Archaeology* 37: 270–288.

Simons, A. 1999. "WAR: Back to the Future." *Annual Review of Anthropology* 28: 73–108.

Skoglund, T., B. L. Stark, H. Neff, and M. D. Glascock. 2006. "Compositional and Stylistic Analysis of Aztec-Era Ceramics: Provincial Strategies at the Edge of Empire, South-Central Veracruz, Mexico." *Latin American Antiquity* 17: 541–559.

Slater, D. A. 2011. "Power Materialized: The Dart-Thrower as a Pan-Mesoamerican Status Marker." *Ancient Mesoamerica* 22: 371–388.

Slocum, M., and F. L. Gerdel. 1965. *Vocabulario Tzeltal de Bachajon: Castellano-Tzeltal, Tzeltal-Castellano*. México, DF: Instituto Lingüístico de Verano.

Smailus, O. 1975. *El Maya-Chontal de Acalán: Análisis Lingüístico de un Documento de los Años 1610–12*. Centro de Estudios Mayas, Cuaderno 9. México, DF: Universidad Nacional Autónoma de México Coordinación de Humanidades.

Smith, M. E. 1986. "The Role of Social Stratification in the Aztec Empire: A View from the Provinces." *American Anthropologist* 88 (1): 70–91.

Smith, M. E. 2011. *The Aztecs*. 3rd ed. West Sussex, England: Wiley and Blackwell.

Smith, M. E. 2014. "The Aztecs Paid Taxes, Not Tribute." *Mexicon* 36 (1): 19–22.

Smith, M. E., and L. Montiel. 2001. "The Archaeological Study of Empires and Imperialism in Pre-Hispanic Central Mexico." *Journal of Anthropological Archaeology* 20: 245–284.

Smith, M. J. 2014. "The War to Begin All Wars? Contextualizing Violence in Neolithic Britain." In *The Routledge Handbook of the Bioarchaeology of Human Conflict*, ed. C. Knüsel and M. J. Smith, 109–126. London: Routledge.

Smyth, M. P., and D. Ortegon Zapata. 2008. "A Preclassics Center in the Puuc Region: A Report on Xcoch, Yucatan, Mexico." *Mexicon* 30 (3): 63–68.

Spero, J. 1987. "Lightning Men and Water Serpents: A Comparison of Mayan and Mixe-Zoquean Beliefs." MA thesis, University of Texas, Austin.

Spero, J. 1991. "Beyond Rainstorms: The Kawak as an Ancestor, Warrior, and Patron of Witchcraft." In *Sixth Palenque Round Table 1986*, ed. V. Fields, 184–193. Norman: University of Oklahoma Press.

Spores, R. 1967. *The Mixtec Kings and Their People.* Norman: University of Oklahoma Press.

Spores, R. 1974. "Marital Alliance in the Political Integration of Mixtec Kingdoms." *American Anthropologist* 76 (2): 297–311.

Staines Cicero, L. 1995. "Los Murales Mayas del Posclásico." *Arqueología Mexicana* 3 (16): 56–61.

Stanton, T. W., and G. J. Bey III. n.d. "The Rise and Fall of the New Empire: Reassessing the Classic to Postclassic Transition in Yucatan." Manuscript in possession of the authors.

Stanton, T. W., and M. K. Brown. 2003. "Studying Warfare in Ancient Mesoamerica." In *Ancient Mesoamerican Warfare*, ed. M. K. Brown and T. W. Stanton, 1–16. Walnut Creek, CA: Altamira.

Stanton, T. W., M. K. Brown, and J. B. Pagliaro. 2008. "Garbage of the Gods? Squatters, Refuse Disposal, and Termination Rituals among the Ancient Maya." *Latin American Antiquity* 19: 227–247.

Stanton, T. W., D. A. Freidel, C. K. Suhler, T. Ardren, J. N. Ambrosino, J. M. Shaw, and S. Bennett. 2010. *Excavations at Yaxuná, 1986–1996: Results of the Selz Foundation Yaxuná Project.* BAR International Series 2056. Oxford, England: British Archaeological Reports.

Stanton, T. W., and A. Magnoni. 2013. "Informe Global: Proyecto de Interacción Política del Centro de Yucatán: Temporadas 2007, 2008, 2009 y 2011." Report submitted to the Consejo de Arqueología del Instituto Nacional de Antropología e Historia, México, DF.

Stone, A., and M. Zender. 2011. *Reading Maya Art: A Hieroglyphic Guide to Ancient Maya Painting and Sculpture.* London: Thames and Hudson.

Stuart, D. 1987. *Ten Phonetic Syllables.* Research Reports on Ancient Maya Writing, vol. 14. Washington, DC: Center for Maya Research.

Stuart, D. 1995. "A Study of Maya Inscriptions." PhD. dissertation, Vanderbilt University, Nashville, TN.

Stuart, D. 1996. "Kings of Stone: A Consideration of Stelae in Ancient Maya Ritual and Representation." *RES: Anthropology and Aesthetics* 29–30: 148–180.

Stuart, D. 1998. "'The Fire Enters This House': Architecture and Ritual in Classic Maya Texts." In *Function and Meaning in Classic Maya Architecture*, ed. S. Houston, 373–425. Washington, DC: Dumbarton Oaks Research Library and Collection.

Stuart, D. 2000. "Arrival of Strangers." In *Mesoamerica's Classic Heritage: From Teotihuacan to the Aztecs*, ed. D. Carrasco, L. Jones, and S. Sessions, 465–514. Boulder: University Press of Colorado.

Stuart, D. 2004a. "The Beginnings of the Copan Dynasty: A Review of the Hieroglyphic and Historical Evidence." In *Understanding Early Classic Copan*, ed. E. E. Bell, M. A. Canuto, and R. J. Sharer, 215–248. Philadelphia: University of Pennsylvania Museum of Archaeology and Anthropology.

Stuart, D. 2004b. "New Year Records in Classic Maya Inscriptions." *PARI Journal* 5 (2): 1–6.

Stuart, D. 2005a. "A Foreign Past: The Writing and Representation of History on a Royal Ancestral Shrine at Copan." In *Copan: History of a Maya Kingdom*, ed. E. W. Andrews and W. L. Fash, 373–394. Santa Fe, NM: School for Advanced Research.

Stuart, D. 2005b. *The Inscriptions from Temple 19 at Palenque.* San Francisco: Pre-Columbian Art Research Institute.

Stuart, D. 2006. "Jade and Chocolate: Bundles of Wealth in Classic Maya Economics and Ritual." In *Sacred Bundles: Ritual Acts of Wrapping and Binding in Mesoamerica*, ed. J. Guernsey and F. K. Reilly, 127–144. Ancient America Special Publication 1. Barnardsville, NC: Boundary End Archaeology Research Center.

Stuart, D. 2010. "Shining Stones: Observations on the Ritual Meaning of Early Maya Stelae." In *The Place of Stone Monuments*, ed. J. Guernsey, J. E. Clark, and B. Arroyo, 283–298. Washington, DC: Dumbarton Oaks.

Stuart, D., and I. Graham. 2003. *Corpus of Maya Hieroglyphic Inscriptions*, vol. 9, part 1: *Piedras Negras.* Cambridge, MA: Peabody Museum of Archaeology and Ethnology, Harvard University.

Stuart, D., and S. Houston. 1994. *Classic Maya Place Names.* Studies in Pre-Columbian Art and Archaeology 33. Washington, DC: Dumbarton Oaks Research Library and Collection.

Stuart, D., and M. Rubenstein. 2014. "The Reading of Two Dates from the Codz Pop at Kabah, Yucatan." In *Maya Decipherment: Ideas on Ancient Maya Writing and Iconography.* https://decipherment.wordpress.com/2014/10/30/. Accessed January 30, 2018.

Stuart, D., and G. E. Stuart. 2008. *Palenque, Eternal City of the Maya: New Aspects of Antiquity.* London: Thames and Hudson.

Subrahmanyam, S. 2012. *Courtly Encounters: Translating Courtliness and Violence in Early Modern Eurasia.* Cambridge, MA: Harvard University Press.

Sugiyama, S. 1989. "Iconographic Interpretation of the Temple of Quetzalcoatl at Teotihuacan." *Mexicon* 11: 68–74.

Sugiyama, S. 2005. *Human Sacrifice, Militarism, and Rulership: Materialization of State Ideology at the Feathered Serpent Pyramid, Teotihuacan.* Cambridge, England: Cambridge University Press.

Sullivan, L. A., and K. L. Sagebiel. 2003. "Changing Political Alliances in the Three River Region." In *Heterarchy, Political Economy, and the Ancient Maya: The Three Rivers Region of the East-Central Yucatan Peninsula*, ed. V. L. Scarborough, N. Dunning, and F. Valdez Jr., 25–36. Tucson: University of Arizona Press.

Sullivan, L. A., and F. Valdez Jr. 2004. "NW Belize: A Regional Perspective on Culture History." *Research Reports in Belizean Archaeology* 1: 185–196.

Sullivan, P. 2014. "Anthropology and Ethnohistory of the Maya." *Reviews in Anthropology* 43 (4): 260–281.

Tate, C. 1992. *Yaxchilan: The Design of a Maya Ceremonial City*. Austin: University of Texas Press.

Taube, K. 1991. "Obsidian Polyhedral Cores and Prismatic Blades in the Writing and Art of Ancient Mexico." *Ancient Mesoamerica* 2: 61–70.

Taube, K. 1992a. *The Major Gods of Ancient Yucatan*. Washington, DC: Dumbarton Oaks Research Library and Collection.

Taube, K. 1992b. "The Temple of Quetzalcoatl and the Cult of Sacred War at Teotihuacan." *RES: Anthropology and Aesthetics* 21: 53–87.

Taube, K. 1992c. "The Iconography of Mirrors at Teotihuacan." In *Art, Ideology, and the City of Teotihuacan*, ed. J. C. Berlo, 169–204. Washington, DC: Dumbarton Oaks Research Library and Collection.

Taube, K. 2000a. "The Writing System of Ancient Teotihuacan." *Ancient America* 1: 1–56.

Taube, K. 2000b. "The Turquoise Hearth: Fire, Self-Sacrifice, and the Central Mexican Cult of War." In *Mesoamerica's Classic Heritage: From Teotihuacan to the Aztecs*, ed. D. Carrasco, L. Jones, and S. Sessions, 269–340. Boulder: University Press of Colorado.

Taube, K. 2004a. "Flower Mountain: Concepts of Life, Beauty, and Paradise among the Classic Maya." *RES: Anthropology and Aesthetics* 45: 69–98.

Taube, K. 2004b. "Structure 10L-16 and Its Early Classic Antecedents: Fire and the Evocation and Resurrection of K'inich Yax K'uk' Mo'." In *Understanding Early Classic Copan*, ed. E. E. Bell, M. A. Canuto, and R. J. Sharer, 265–296. Philadelphia: University of Pennsylvania Museum of Archaeology and Anthropology.

Taube, K. 2011. "Teotihuacan and the Development of Writing in Early Classic Central Mexico." In *Their Way of Writing: Scripts, Signs, and Notational Systems in Pre-Columbian America*, ed. E. H. Boone and G. Urton, 77–109. Washington, DC: Dumbarton Oaks Research Library and Collection.

Taube, K., and S. Houston. 2015. "The Temple Stuccos." In *Temple of the Night Sun*, ed. S. Houston, S. Newman, E. Román, and T. Garrison, 208–229. San Francisco: Precolumbian Mesoweb Press.

Taube, K., W. A. Saturno, D. Stuart, and H. Hurst. 2010. *Ancient America*, vol. 10: *The Murals of San Bartolo, El Péten, Guatemala*, part 2: *The West Wall*. Barnardsville, NC: Boundary End Archaeology Research Center.

Taube, K., and M. Zender. 2009. "American Gladiators: Ritual Boxing in Ancient Mesoamerica." In *Blood and Beauty: Organized Violence in the Art and Archaeology of Mesoamerica and Central America*, ed. H. Orr and R. Koontz, 161–220. Los Angeles: Cotsen Institute of Archaeology Press.

Tedlock, B. 1992. *Time and the Highland Maya*. Albuquerque: University of New Mexico Press.

Tedlock, D. 1996. *Popol Vuh: The Definitive Edition of the Maya Book of the Dawn of Life and the Glories of the Gods and Kings*. New York: Simon and Schuster.

Tejeda Monroy, E. A. 2014. "Los Murales de Chichén Itzá, Chacmultún, Ichmac y Mulchic: Implicaciones sobre la Beligerancia Maya en el Clásico Tardío-Terminal (600–1000 d. C.)." *Arqueología* 47: 271–295.

Thompson, J.E.S. 1950. *Maya Hieroglyphic Writing: An Introduction*. Norman: University of Oklahoma Press.

Thompson, J.E.S. 1951. "The Itza of Tayasal, Peten." In *Homenajé al Doctor Alfonso Caso*, 389–399. México, DF: Impr. Nuevo Mundo.

Thompson, J.E.S. 1970. *Maya History and Religion*. Norman: University of Oklahoma Press.

Thompson, J.E.S. 1976. *A Catalog of Maya Hieroglyphs*. Norman: University of Oklahoma Press.

Thomson, P.A.B. 2004. *Belize: A Concise History*. Oxford, England: Macmillan.

Thorpe, I.J.N. 2003. "Anthropology, Archaeology, and the Origin of Warfare." *World Archaeology* 35 (1): 145–165.

Thorpe, I.J.N. 2005. "The Ancient Origins of Warfare and Violence." In *Warfare, Violence, and Slavery in Prehistory*, ed. M. Parker Pearson and I.J.N. Thorpe, 1–18. BAR International Series 1374. Oxford, England: British Archaeological Reports.

Tiesler, V., and A. Cucina. 2006. "Procedures in Human Heart Extraction and Ritual Meaning: A Taphonomic Assessment of Anthropogenic Marks in Classic Maya Skeletons." *Latin American Antiquity* 17: 493–510.

Tiesler, V., and A. Cucina. 2012. "Where Are the Warriors? Cranial Trauma Patterns and Conflict among the Ancient Maya." In *The Bioarchaeology of Violence*, ed. D. L. Martin, R. P. Harrod, and V. R. Pérez, 160–179. Gainesville: University Press of Florida.

Tiesler, V., A. Cucina, T. W. Stanton, and D. A. Freidel. 2017. *Before Kukulkán: Maya Life, Death, and Identity at Classic Period Yaxuná*. Tucson: University of Arizona Press.

Tokovinine, A. 2007. *Classic Maya Place Name Database Project*. Foundation for the Advancement of Mesoamerican Studies, Inc. http://www.famsi.org/reports/06054/06054Tokovinine06001.pdf. Accessed October 21, 2014.

Tokovinine, A. 2008. "The Power of Place: Political Landscape and Identity in Classic Maya Inscriptions, Imagery, and Architecture." PhD dissertation, Harvard University, Cambridge, MA.

Tokovinine, A. 2011. "People from a Place: Re-Interpreting Classic Maya Emblem Glyphs." In *Ecology, Power, and Religion in Maya Landscapes*, ed. C. Isendahl and B. Liljefors-Persson, 96–106. Möckmuhl, Germany: Verlag Saurwein.

Tokovinine, A. 2013a. *3D Imaging Report, 2013*. Peabody Museum of Archaeology and Ethnology. https://www.peabody.harvard.edu/files/x3d/Scan_report_2013_high.pdf. Accessed October 21, 2014.

Tokovinine, A. 2013b. *Place and Identity in Classic Maya Narratives*. Studies in Pre-Columbian Art and Archaeology 37. Washington, DC: Dumbarton Oaks Research Library and Collection.

Tokovinine, A., and D. Beliaev. 2013. "People of the Road: Traders and Travelers in Ancient Maya Words and Images." In *Merchants, Markets, and Exchange in the Pre-Columbian World*, ed. K. G. Hirth and J. Pillsbury, 169–200. Washington, DC: Dumbarton Oaks Research Library and Collection.

Tokovinine, A., and V. Fialko. 2007. "Stela 45 of Naranjo and the Early Classic Lords of Sa'aal." *PARI Journal* 7 (4): 1–14.

Tokovinine, A., and M. Zender. 2012. "Lords of Windy Water: The Royal Court of Motul de San José in Classic Maya Inscriptions." In *Politics, History, and Economy at the Classic Maya Center of Motul de San José, Guatemala*, ed. A. Foias and K. Emery, 30–66. Gainesville: University Press of Florida.

Tozzer, A. M. 1907. *A Comparative Study of the Mayas and the Lacandones*. New York: Archaeological Institute of America.

Tozzer, A. M. 1941. *Landa's Relación de las Cosas de Yucatan*. Papers of the Peabody Museum of American Archaeology and Ethnology, vol. 18. Cambridge, MA: Peabody Museum of American Archaeology and Ethnology.

Tozzer, A. M., and G. Allen. 1910. *Animal Figures in the Maya Codices*. Papers of the Peabody Museum of American Archaeology and Ethnology, vol. 4, no. 3. Cambridge, MA: Harvard University.

Tremain, C. G. 2011. "Investigations in Looters' Trenches at Ka'Kabish, Northern Belize: An Analysis of Ancient Maya Architecture and Construction Practices." MA thesis, Trent University, Peterborough, Canada.

Tremain, C. G., and H. R. Haines, eds. 2013. "The 2012 Archaeological Report of the Ka'Kabish Archaeological Research Project (KARP)." Report submitted to the Institute of Archaeology, Belmopan, Belize.

Trigger, B. G. 2003. *Understanding Early Civilizations: A Comparative Study*. Cambridge, England: Cambridge University Press.

Trigger, B. G. 2006. *A History of Archaeological Thought*. 2nd ed. Cambridge, England: Cambridge University Press.

Tung, T. A. 2012. "Violence against Women: Differential Treatment of Local and Foreign Females in the Heartland of the Wari Empire, Peru." In *The Bioarchaeology of*

Violence, ed. D. L. Martin, R. P. Harrod, and V. R. Pérez, 180–198. Gainesville: University Press of Florida.

Tung, T. A. 2014. "Gender-Based Violence in the Wari and Post-Wari Era of the Andes." In *The Routledge Handbook of the Bioarchaeology of Human Conflict*, ed. C. Knüsel and M. J. Smith, 333–354. London: Routledge.

Turner, J. H. 1975. "Marx and Simmel Revisited: Reassessing the Foundations of Conflict Theory." *Social Forces* 53 (4): 618–627.

Turney-High, H. H. 1949. *Primitive War: Its Practice and Concepts*. Columbia: University of South Carolina Press.

Umberger, E. 1987. "Antiques, Revivals, and References to the Past in Aztec Art." *RES: Anthropology and Aesthetics* 13: 62–105.

Umberger, E. 1996. "Art and Imperial Strategy in Tenochtitlan." In *Aztec Imperial Strategies*, ed. F. F. Berdan, 85–106. Washington, DC: Dumbarton Oaks Research Library and Collection.

Vail, G. 1988. *The Archaeology of Coastal Belize*. BAR International Series 463. Oxford, England: British Archaeological Reports.

Valckx Gutiérrez, A., T. W. Stanton, and T. Ardren. 2011. "Mujeres en la Guerra: Una Vista Desde la Arqueología." *Anales de Antropología* 45: 123–152.

Valdés, J. A., and F. Fahsen. 2004. "Disaster in Sight: The Terminal Classic at Tikal and Uaxactun." In *The Terminal Classic in the Maya Lowlands*, ed. A. A. Demarest, P. M. Rice, and D. S. Rice, 140–161. Boulder: University Press of Colorado.

Vallejo, D. 2011. "Un Estudio de Abandono de dos Estructuras Domésticas del Clásico Tardío-Terminal en el Sitio Maya de Xuenkal, Yucatán." Licenciatura thesis, Universidad de las Américas Puebla, Cholula, Mexico.

Vandkilde, H. 2003. "Commemorative Tales: Archaeological Responses to Modern Myth, Politics, and War." *World Archaeology* 35: 126–144.

Vásquez de Espinosa, Fr. A. 1944. *Descripción de la Nueva España en el Siglo XVII*. México, DF: Editorial Patria.

Vázquez López, V., R. Valencia Rivera, and E. Gutiérrez González. 2014. "Ancient Maya Warfare: An Interdisciplinary Approach." In *Socio-Political Strategies among the Maya from the Classic Period to the Present*, ed. V. Vázquez López, R. Valencia Rivera, and E. Gutiérrez González, 95–107. BAR International Series 2619. Oxford, England: British Archaeological Reports.

Velásquez García, E. 2004. "Los Escalones Jeroglíficos de Dzibanché." In *Los Cautivos de Dzibanché*, ed. E. Nalda, 78–103. México, DF: Instituto Nacional de Antropología e Historia.

Velásquez García, E. 2005. "The Captives of Dzibanche." *PARI Journal* 6 (2): 1–4.

Vencl, S. 1984. "War and Warfare in Archaeology." *Journal of Anthropological Archaeology* 3: 116–132.

Ventura, C. 2003. "The Jakaltek Maya Blowgun in Mythological and Historical Context." *Ancient Mesoamerica* 14 (2): 257–268.

Verano, J. W. 2014. "Many Faces of Death: Warfare, Human Sacrifice, and Mortuary Practices of the Elite in Late Pre-Hispanic Northern Peru." In *The Routledge Handbook of the Bioarchaeology of Human Conflict*, ed. C. Knüsel and M. J. Smith, 355–370. London: Routledge.

Villa Rojas, A. 1945. *The Maya of East Central Quintana Roo*. Publication 559. Washington, DC: Carnegie Institute of Washington.

Villagutierre Soto-Mayor, J. de. 1983 [1701]. *History of the Conquest of the Province of the Itza: Subjugation and Events of the Lacandon and Other Nations of Uncivilized Indians in the Lands from the Kingdom of Guatemala to the Provinces of Yucatan in North America*, trans. R. D. Wood, ed. F. E. Comparato. Culver City, CA: Labyrinthos.

Vogt, E. 1969. *Zinacantán*. Cambridge, MA: Harvard University Press.

Von Winning, H. 1979. "The 'Binding of Years' and the 'New Fire' in Teotihuacan." *Indiana* 5: 15–32.

Von Winning, H. 1987. *La Iconografía de Teotihuacan: Los Dioses y los Signos*, vols. 1 and 2. México, DF: Universidad Nacional Autónoma de México.

Vos, J. de. 1980. *La Paz de Dios y del Rey: La Conquista de la Selva Lacandona (1525–1821)*. México, DF: Fondo de Cultura Económica.

Walker, D. 1990. "Cerros Revisited: Ceramic Indicators of Terminal Classic and Postclassic Settlement and Pilgrimage in Northern Belize." PhD dissertation, Southern Methodist University, Dallas, TX.

Walker, P. L. 2001. "A Bioarchaeological Perspective on the History of Violence." *Annual Review of Anthropology* 30: 573–596.

Watts, J., O. Sheehan, Q. D. Atkinson, J. Bulbulia, and R. D. Gray. 2016. "Ritual Human Sacrifice Promoted and Sustained the Evolution of Stratified Societies." *Nature* 532: 228.

Webster, D. L. 1975. "Warfare and the Evolution of the State: A Reconsideration." *American Antiquity* 40 (4): 464–470.

Webster, D. L. 1976. *Defensive Earthworks at Becan, Campeche, Mexico: Implications for Maya Warfare*. Middle American Research Institute 41. New Orleans, LA: Tulane University.

Webster, D. L. 1993. "The Study of Maya Warfare: What It Tells Us about the Maya and about Maya Archaeology." In *Lowland Maya Civilization in the Eighth Century ad*, ed. J. Sabloff and J. Henderson, 415–444. Washington, DC: Dumbarton Oaks Research Library and Collection.

Webster, D. L. 1998. "Warfare and Status Rivalry: Lowland Maya and Polynesian Comparisons." In *Archaic States*, ed. G. Feinman and J. Marcus, 311–352. Santa Fe, NM: School of American Research.

Webster, D. L. 1999. "Ancient Maya Warfare." In *War and Society in the Ancient and Medieval Worlds*, ed. K. Raaflaub and N. Rosenstein, 333–360. Cambridge, MA: Harvard University Press.

Webster, D. L. 2000. "The Not So Peaceful Civilization: A Review of Maya War." *Journal of World Prehistory* 14 (1): 65–119.

Webster, D. L. 2001. "Copán (Copán, Honduras)." In *Archaeology of Ancient Mexico and Central America: An Encyclopedia*, ed. S. T. Evans and D. L. Webster, 169–176. New York: Garlandrk.

Webster, D. L. 2002. *The Fall of the Ancient Maya: Solving the Mystery of the Maya Collapse.* London: Thames and Hudson.

Weiss-Krecji, E., and T. P. Culbert. 1994. "Preclassic and Classic Burials and Caches in the Maya Lowlands." In *The Emergence of Lowland Maya Civilization: The Transition from the Preclassic to the Early Classic*, ed. N. Grube, 103–116. Cologne, Germany: Verlag Anton Saurwein.

Western, A. G., and J. D. Hurst. 2014. "'Soft Heads': Evidence for Sexualized Warfare during the Later Iron Age from Kemerton Camp, Bredon Hill." In *The Routledge Handbook of the Bioarchaeology of Human Conflict*, ed. C. Knüsel and M. J. Smith, 161–184. London: Routledge.

White, C. D., T. D. Price, and F. J. Longstaffe. 2007. "Residential Histories of the Human Sacrifices at the Moon Pyramid, Teotihuacan." *Ancient Mesoamerica* 18 (1): 159–172.

White, C. D., M. W. Spence, F. J. Longstaffe, and K. R. Law. 2000. "Testing the Nature of Teotihuacan Imperialism at Kaminaljuyu Using Oxygen-Isotope Ratios." *Journal of Anthropological Research* 56 (4): 535–558.

White, C. D., M. W. Spence, F. J. Longstaffe, H. Stuart-Williams, and K. R. Law. 2002. "Geographic Identities of the Sacrificial Victims from the Feathered Serpent Pyramid, Teotihuacan: Implications for the Nature of State Power." *Latin American Antiquity* 13 (2): 217–236.

Whitehead, N. L. 2005. "War and Violence as Cultural Expression." *Anthropology News* 46: 23–26.

Wilk, R. R. 1985. "The Ancient Maya and the Political Present." *Journal of Anthropological Research* 41 (3): 307–326.

Wilkerson, S.J.K. 1970. "Un Yugo In Situ de La Región de Tajín." *Boletín Del Instituto Nacional de Antropología E Historia* 41: 41–44.

Wilkerson, S.J.K. 1991. "And Then They Were Sacrificed: The Ritual Ballgame of Northeastern Mesoamerica through Time and Space." In *The Mesoamerican Ballgame*, ed. V. Scarborough and D. A. Wilcox, 45–71. Tucson: University of Arizona Press.

Williams, E. 2009. *Prehispanic West Mexico: A Mesoamerican Culture Area.* Foundation for the Advancement of Mesoamerican Studies, Inc. www.famsi.org/research /williams/. Accessed November 17, 2014.

Wilson, E. M. 1980. "Physical Geography of the Yucatan Peninsula." In *Yucatan: A World Apart*, ed. E. H. Mosely and E. D. Terry, 5–39. Tuscaloosa: University of Alabama Press.

Winston, R. 2005. "Philip Roth Was Wrong." *The Guardian*, December 16.

Winter, M. 1998. "Monte Albán and Teotihuacan." In *Rutas de Intercambio en Mesoamérica*, ed. E. C. Rattray, 153–184. México, DF: Universidad Nacional Autónoma de México.

Winter, M. 2010. "Teotihuacan et Oaxaca." In *Teotihuacan: Cité des Dieux*, 180–185. Paris: Museé de Quai Branly, SOMOGY Editions d'Art.

Winter, M. 2011. "Social Memory and the Origins of Monte Alban." *Ancient Mesoamerica* 22 (2): 393–409.

Winter, M., C. Martínez López, and A. Herrera Muzgo Torres. 1999. "Monte Albán y Teotihuacan: Política e Ideología." In *Ideologá y Política a Través de Materiales, Imágenes y Símbolos: Memoria de la Primera Mesa Redonda de Teotihuacan*, ed. M.E.R. Gallut, 627–644. México, DF: Consejo Nacional Para la Cultura y las Artes / Instituto Nacional de Antropología e Historia.

Wolff, K. H. 1950. *The Sociology of Georg Simmel*. Glencoe, IL: Free Press.

Workinger, A., and A. Joyce. 2009. "Reconsidering Warfare in Formative Period Oaxaca." In *Blood and Beauty: Organized Violence in the Art and Archaeology of Mesoamerica and Central America*, ed. H. Orr and R. Koontz, 3–38. Los Angeles: Cotsen Institute of Archaeology Press.

Wrangham, R. W. 1999. "Evolution of Coalitionary Killing." *Yearbook of Physical Anthropology* 42: 1–30.

Wrangham, R. W., and D. Peterson. 1996. *Demonic Males: Apes and the Origins of Human Violence*. New York: Houghton Mifflin.

Wren, L., and T. Nygard. 2005. "Images and Text of Rulers in a Watery Realm." In *Quintana Roo Archaeology*, ed. J. M. Shaw and J. P. Mathews, 166–183. Tucson: University of Arizona Press.

Wright, A.C.S., D. H. Romney, R. H. Arbuckle, and V. E. Vial. 1959. *Land in British Honduras: Report of the British Land Use Survey Team*. London: Her Majesty's Stationery Office.

Wright, L. E. 1997. "Ecology or Society? Paleodiet and the Collapse of the Pasion Maya Lowlands." In *Bones of the Maya: Studies of Ancient Skeletons*, ed. S. L. Whittington and D. M. Reed, 181–195. Washington, DC: Smithsonian Institution Press.

Wright, L. E. 2004. "Osteological Investigations of Ancient Maya Lives." In *Continuities and Changes in Maya Archaeology: Perspectives at the Millenium*, ed. C. W. Golden and G. Borgstede, 179–192. New York: Routledge.

Wright, L. E. 2005. "In Search of Yax Nuun Ayiin I: Revisiting the Tikal Project's Burial 10." *Ancient Mesoamerica* 16 (1): 89–100.

Wrobel, G. D., C. Helmke, and C. Freiwald. 2014. "A Case Study of Funerary Cave Use from Je'reftheel, Central Belize." In *The Bioarchaeology of Space and Place: Ideology, Power, and Meaning in Maya Mortuary Contexts*, ed. G. D. Wrobel, 77–106. New York: Springer.

Ximenéz, F. 1929. *Historia de la Provincia de San Vicente de Chiapa y Guatemala de la Orden de Predicadores, Compuesta por el r. P. Pred. Gen. Fray Francisco Ximénez, Hijo de la Misma Provincia de Orden de n. Rmo. p. m. g. fr. Antonio Cloché (1720)*. Prólogo del lic. J. Antonio Villacorta Calderón. Guatemala City: Tipografía Nacional.

Yarborough, C. McJ. 1992. "Teotihuacan and the Gulf Coast: Ceramic Evidence for Contact and Interactional Relationships." PhD dissertation, University of Arizona, Tucson.

Yates, R.D.S. 1999. "Making War and Making Peace in Early China." In *War and Society in the Ancient and Medieval Worlds*, ed. K. Raaflaub and N. Rosenstein, 34–51. Cambridge, MA: Harvard University Press.

Yoffee, N. 2005. *Myths of the Archaic State: Evolution of the Earliest Cities, States, and Civilizations*. Cambridge, England: Cambridge University Press.

Zender, M. 2002. "Toponyms of El Cayo, Piedras Negras, and La Mar." In *Heart of Creation: The Mesoamerican World and the Legacy of Linda Schele*, ed. A. Stone, 166–184. Tuscaloosa: University of Alabama Press.

Zender, M. 2004a. "The Glyphs for 'Handspan' and 'Strike' in Classic Maya Ballgame Texts." *PARI Journal* 4 (4): 1–9.

Zender, M. 2004b. "A Study of Classic Maya Priesthood." PhD dissertation, University of Calgary, Calgary, Canada.

Zender, M. 2005. "The Raccoon Glyph in Classic Maya Writing." *PARI Journal* 5 (4): 6–16.

Zender, M. 2010. "Baj 'Hammer' and Related Affective Verbs in Classic Mayan." *PARI Journal* 11 (2): 1–16.

Zucchino, D. 2004. "Army Stage-Managed Fall of Hussein Statue." *Los Angeles Times*. http://articles.latimes.com/2004/jul/03/nation/na-statue3. Accessed February 6, 2013.

Contributors

Matthew Abtosway is an MA student in the Department of Anthropology and Archaeology at the University of Calgary. His diverse research interests range from Central American prehistory through the East African Paleolithic, with current research focusing on non-destructive lithic raw material sourcing at Olduvai Gorge, Tanzania. Through participation in a number of international projects in Belize and Nicaragua, including those operated by the University of Texas at Tyler, the University of Calgary, and Leiden University, Matthew has developed an appreciation for interregional interaction and exchange, both past and present. Outside his studies, Matthew coordinates the Public Archaeology Program at Cluny Fortified Village and enjoys engaging excited members of the public in an active excavation in Alberta, Canada.

Karen Bassie-Sweet has been a research associate and adjunct lecturer in the Department of Anthropology and Archaeology at the University of Calgary since 2000. She has published five books on Maya culture: *From the Mouth of the Dark Cave: Commemorative Sculpture of the Late Classic* (1991), *At the Edge of the World: Caves and Late Classic Maya World View* (1996), *Maya Sacred Geography and the Creator Deities* (2008), *The Ch'ol Maya of Chiapas* (2015), and *Maya Narrative Arts* (2018). She is preparing a volume on Maya gods of warfare.

George J. Bey III holds a PhD from Tulane University. He is professor of anthropology at Millsaps College, associate dean of international education, and Chisholm Foundation Chair in Arts and Sciences. His research has focused on the early Maya in the northern Maya lowlands. He has studied the ceramics of both Central Mexico and the northern Maya lowlands and co-directed a long-term project at Ek Balam. He is one of the co-directors of the Bolonchen Regional Archaeological Project, where he has focused on studying the Maya site of Kiuic.

M. Kathryn Brown is the Lutcher Brown Endowed Associate Professor in Anthropology at the University of Texas at San Antonio. She received her PhD in anthropology at Southern Methodist University in 2003. Her research focuses on the rise of complexity in the Maya lowlands and the role of ritual and ceremonial architecture in the Formative period. Much of her research examines questions related to the development of divine kingship during the Formative and how this institution was continually maintained and legitimized during the Classic period through religion, economy, and warfare. She is director of the Mopan Valley Preclassic Project and co-director of the Mopan Valley Archaeological Project. She is coeditor of *Ancient Mesoamerican Warfare* (with Travis Stanton, 2003) and *Pathways to Complexity: A View from the Maya Lowlands* (with George J. Bey III, 2018).

Allen J. Christenson is professor of Precolumbian studies at Brigham Young University. His MA and PhD are in Precolumbian art history and literature from the University of Texas, Austin. He has worked in the highland Maya region of Guatemala as a linguist, ethnographer, and art historian since 1976. His research focuses on the art, literature, and ceremonial practices of the highland Maya of Guatemala. His publications include *Art and Society in a Highland Maya Community* (2001), a two-volume critical edition of the *Popol Vuh* (2003, 2007), and *Bearing the Burden of the Ancients: Maya Ceremonies of World-Renewal* (2016).

Tomás Gallareta Negrón completed his PhD at Tulane University and is a senior archaeologist for Mexico's National Institute of Anthropology and History (INAH). Recognized as an expert in settlement archaeology, he has also directed excavations at a number of major Maya centers. He is senior director of the Bolonchen Regional Archaeological Project (BRAP).

Elizabeth Graham is Professor of Mesoamerican Archaeology at the Institute of Archaeology, University College London. She has been carrying out archaeological excavation in Belize since 1973. At the time of publication, her research focuses on the site of Lamanai on the New River Lagoon in northern Belize and on the site of Marco Gonzalez at the southern tip of Ambergris Caye. Her research interests include the Maya collapse and the transition to the Postclassic period, coastal dynamics and commerce, warfare, the impact of Spanish and British colonial activities, and the role of the remains of human activities in soils genesis.

Helen R. Haines is senior lecturer with the Department of Anthropology at Trent University. Her primary research interest focuses on the sociopolitical and economic development of early complex societies in Mesoamerica, and she has worked in Belize since 1990. She is director of the Ka'Kabish Archaeological Research Project (KARP) in north-central Belize (www.kakabish.org), which has been supported by funding from both the National Geographic Society Research and Exploration Grant in 2014 and the Social Science and Humanities Research Council of Canada. In addition to her work in Belize, she has also worked at Tiwanaku, Bolivia, and ShaanXi, China, and on numerous historic and prehistoric sites in south-central Ontario. She is a graduate of the University of Toronto (BA) and the University of London, England (PhD), and held a three-year post-doctoral research appointment at the Field Museum of Natural History, Chicago, IL. She lives in Canada with a mischievous Tibetan terrier named Tashi.

Christopher L. Hernandez received his PhD in anthropology from Northwestern University in 2017 and is a National Science Foundation Social, Behavioral, and Economic Sciences (SBE) postdoctoral fellow at the University of Illinois–Chicago. His primary research interests include warfare, power relations, landscape, and community archaeology. In collaboration with the contemporary Maya community of Mensabak, Chiapas, Mexico, his current research integrates documentary and iconographic analysis with LiDAR mapping and the excavation of fortified settlements to assess trends in Maya war making.

Harri Kettunen has carried out interdisciplinary research projects on Mesoamerican-related topics, combining archaeology, anthropology, iconography, epigraphy, and linguistics. His publications include textbooks on Maya hieroglyphs, methodological studies on Maya iconography, and interdisciplinary articles on Mesoamerican-related topics.

Rex Koontz's research focuses on the public sculpture of ancient Mesoamerica and includes the books *Lightning Gods and Feathered Serpents* (University of Texas Press, 2009) and *Organized Violence in the Art and Architecture of Mesoamerica* (with Heather Orr, UCLA, 2009). Other books include *Landscape and Power in Ancient Mesoamerica*, edited with Kathryn Reese-Taylor and Annabeth Headrick, and *Mexico* (editions in 2002, 2008, and 2013) with Michael Coe. Koontz teaches courses in Pre-Columbian art at the University of Houston.

Geoffrey McCafferty is professor of anthropology and archaeology at the University of Calgary where, among other things, he teaches classes on Mesoamerican writing systems. He first became interested in Mixtec codices while convalescing from a construction accident before entering graduate school. His archaeological research includes work in Cholula, Oaxaca, and, most recently, Pacific Nicaragua.

Shawn G. Morton is instructor of anthropology at Grande Prairie Regional College. He also holds research affiliations with the University of Calgary, Michigan State University, and Northern Arizona University. He is the associate investigator of the Stann

Creek Regional Archaeology Project (SCRAP, www.scraparchaeology.com) and has worked at several sites in Belize, Mexico, Guatemala, Nicaragua, and Canada.

Jesper Nielsen, PhD, is associate professor at the University of Copenhagen. His research focuses on Mesoamerican iconography, epigraphy, and religion, in particular in Maya, Teotihuacan, and Epiclassic cultures. He also has a strong interest in early Colonial studies in Central Mexico and the Maya region, as well as research history. Nielsen is a member of the Proyecto La Pintura Mural Prehispánica en México at the Universidad Nacional Autónoma de México. He has published numerous books, articles in international peer-reviewed journals (including *Ancient Mesoamerica, Antiquity, Latin American Antiquity, PARI Journal*, and *Ancient America*), and edited volumes. Recent publications include "The Fall of the Great Celestial Bird: A Master Myth in Early Classic Central Mexico" (coauthored with Christophe Helmke, *Ancient America*, vol. 13, 2015) and *Restless Blood: Frans Blom, Explorer and Maya Archaeologist* (coauthored with Tore Leifer and Toke S. Reunert, Precolumbia Mesoweb Press and Middle American Research Institute, San Francisco and New Orleans, 2017).

Joel W. Palka is professor of anthropology and Latin American and Latino studies at the University of Illinois–Chicago. His research specialties include historical archaeology, the archaeology of religion, Mesoamerican art and writing, and Maya culture change following the Spanish Conquest. Palka has published the books *Unconquered Lacandon Maya* and *Maya Pilgrimage to Ritual Landscapes*, along with numerous articles and book chapters. He is director of the Mensabak Archaeological Project, where he collaborates with the Lacandon Maya in Chiapas, Mexico.

Meaghan M. Peuramaki-Brown is associate professor of archaeology at Athabasca University and adjunct professor at the University of Calgary, both in Alberta, Canada. Her research focuses primarily on ancient settlement development and household activity patterns. She is principal investigator of the Stann Creek Regional Archaeology Project (SCRAP, www.scraparchaeology.com) and has worked at several sites in Belize, Mexico, Guatemala, Honduras, and Nicaragua. Her university teaching takes place entirely online, and as a result she has a particular interest in technology-enabled learning in archaeological pedagogy, education, and outreach.

Kerry L. Sagebiel is instructor of anthropology at Northern Illinois University, DeKalb, and co-director of the Ka'kabish Archaeological Research Project in Belize. She is a specialist in Maya ceramics and has been involved in numerous archaeological research projects in Belize, Guatemala, and the American Southwest.

Travis W. Stanton is associate professor in and chair of the Department of Anthropology at the University of California, Riverside. Stanton has conducted field research in the northern Maya lowlands since 1995 and received his doctorate from Southern Methodist University in 2000. He co-directs the Proyecto de Interacción Política del Centro de Yucatán in the area of Yaxuna and Chichen Itza and conducts collaborative work at the sites of Coba and San Gervasio in Quintana Roo. His publications include *Ancient Mesoamerican Warfare* (co-edited with M. Kathryn Brown), *Ruins of the Past* (co-edited with Aline Magnoni), and *Before Kukulkán* (coauthored with Vera Tiesler, Andrea Cucina, and David Freidel).

Alexandre Tokovinine is a Maya epigrapher and archaeologist. He has participated in several projects in Guatemala, including the Holmul Archaeological Project and Proyecto Arqueológico de Investigación y Rescate Naranjo. Tokovinine received his PhD in anthropology from Harvard University in 2008. His doctoral research centered on Classic Maya place names and was supported by the Junior Fellowship at Dumbarton Oaks. Its results were published in a monograph, *Place and Identity in Classic Maya Narratives*. Tokovinine's other research projects include 3D documentation of Classic Maya sculpture and contributions to *Ancient Maya Art at Dumbarton Oaks*. He is assistant professor in the Department of Anthropology at the University of Alabama. His previous academic appointments include research associate of the Corpus of Maya Hieroglyphic Inscriptions, Peabody Museum; lecturer in the Department of Anthropology, Harvard University; and research associate at the Dumbarton Oaks Research Library and Collection.

Index

Kabah, 126, 128, 130, 134, 135, 140

Ka'kabish, 15, 102, *103*, 104, 105, 111–120, 213, 234, 235

kaloomte. See titles

Kaminaljuyu, 146, 161, 163, 242

Kaqchikel(s), 19, 20, 22, 23, 24, 26

K'awiil. *See* glyphs/icons/symbols; gods/deities/supernatural figures

K'iche'(s), 13, 14, 19–22, 24, 26, 57, 63, 73

k'iche. See linguistics

king. *See* titles

K'inich Lakam Tuun, 98, 99

Kiuic, 131, *133*, 133, *134*, 134, 137, 138, 141

k'uhul ajaw. See titles

Labna, 133, 134, *135*, 135, 137, 138, 140

Lamanai, 15, 102–108, *107*, *110*, 110, 111, 113, 117–120, 213, 214, 234, 235

landscape(s), 13, 14, 31–35, 38–45, 79, 80, 86–92, 100, 101–105, 120, 121, 123, 129, 132, 134, 135, 140, 141, 210, 211, 213–214, 218, 225–229, 235, 239

linguistics: *ch'ol*, 7; *ch'olti*, 7; *k'iche*, 7; *mopan*, 7

lintel: Tikal, 97, 98; Xcalumkin, 137; Yaxchilan, 58, 61, 62, 67, 70, 90

mace. *See* weapons

Maize God. *See* gods/deities/supernatural figures

marriage alliance, 125, 138, 160, 226, 240–244

Mayapan, 42, 43

militarism. *See* conflict

Mixtec/Mexica, 15, *32*, 32, 148, 152, 153, 157, 166–187, *170*, 189–191, 195, 199, 200, 208, 212, 214–217, 224, 226, 228, 233

Monte Alban, 44, 147, *149*, 149, 168, 185, 242

monuments: banners/banner stone(s)/standards, 13, 16, 21, 25, 128, 183, 194, *195*, 195–203, *199*, 211, 245; hieroglyphic stairway(s), *78*, 78, 81, 82, *84*, 85, 95, 96, 214; lintel(s), 58, 61, *62*, 67, 70, *84*, 90, 96, 97, 98, 128, 137; mural(s), xv, *44*, 64, 67, 76, 83, 128, 129, 135, 137, 139, 140, 149, 150, 151, 152, 155, *156*, 156, 158, *161*, 161, *162*, 163, 164, 191, 192, 195, 202, 215, 219; panel(s), 55, 67, 74, *82*, 82, 83, 92, 94, *194*, 194, 196, *197*, *198*, 198–203, 245; stela(e), 15, 38, *39*, 49, 59, 60, 61, 64, 67–72, *82*, 82, 83, 84, 85, 86, 89, 93–99, 102, 106, 108–111, *110*, 117–120, 126–130, *127*, 135, 137, 138, 147, *148*, 153, *154*, 154, 157, 158, 160, *162*, 162, 163, 202, *203*, 214, 224, 229, 230, 234, 245; tablet(s), 50, *51*, 55, *56*, 56, 95

mopan. See linguistics

moth. *See* glyphs/icons/symbols

Motul de San Jose, 83, *84*, 85, 92, *93*, 97

mountain. *See* glyphs/icons/symbols

murals: Bonampak, xv, 44, 191, 219; Cacaxtla, 83; Chacmultun, 128; Chichen Itza, 191; Las Higueras, 195, 202; Ichmac, 128; Mulchic, 128, 135, 137, 191; El Rosario, 149–152, 156, 158, 163, 164, 215; San Bartolo, 76; Teotihuacan, 67, 155, *156*; Tetitla Portico, 64, *162*; Xelha, *161*, 161

Naranjo, 6, 54, 67, 68, 72, 78–86, *82*, 84, 90, 92, 95–100, 217, 230

Olmec, *133*, 211

operational approaches: definition of, 11, 12

owl(s). *See* gods/deities/supernatural figures

Palenque, 50, 52, 54, 55, *56*, 67, 74, *78*, 78, *82*, 82, 95, 96, 97, 212, 214, 238

panel(s): Brussels, 92, 94; Denver, 83, 92, 94; Palenque, 55, 67, 74, *82*, 82; El Tajín, *194*, 194, 196, 197, 198, 198–203, 245

Piedras Negras, 59, 60, 61, 64, 67, 68, 69, 71, 85, 90, 93, 94, 224

popol nah, 130, *133*, 133, 134

Popol Vuh, 14, 52, 57, 65, 73

Puuc, 15, *123*, 123–141, *132*, *134*, 135, *136*, 137, 210, 213, 233, 243

queen. *See* titles

Quirigua, 69, 81, 230

raid/raiding. *See* conflict

ritual: desecratory termination rituals, 40, 41, 43, 209

El Rosario, 149–164, *150*, *151*, *157*, *158*, 215, 240

royal/royalty. *See* titles

rules of engagement. *See* conflict

sacrifice, 33, 34, 36, 48, 58, 59, 65, 74, 128, 133, 155, 157, 160, 163, 167, 190, 194, 209, 210, 212, 216, 218, 223, 244, 246

sajal. See titles

Santa Rita, 103

Santiago. *See* gods/deities/supernatural figures

Santiago Atitlan, 19, 25, 26, *27*, 28, 29

segmentary states, 202

settlement patterns, 184

shield. *See* weapons

Soyoltepec, 147, 153, *154*, 154